Big Basic Cookbook

Completely Revised,
Updated and
Edited with Commentary by

Kimberly Beeman

Mud Puddle Books
NEW YORK

Big Basic Cookbook
Completely Revised, Updated and
Edited with Commentary by
Kimberly Beeman

© 2007 by
Mud Puddle Books, Inc.
54 W. 21st Street
Suite 601
New York, NY 10010
info@mudpuddlebooks.com

ISBN: 978-1-60311-043-3

Book design and layout by Mulberry Tree Press, Inc.

Printed in China

CONTENTS

INTRODUCTION

This cookbook was originally published in 1941 under the name *The Lily Wallace New American Cookbook*. Lily Wallace was a lecturer in the home economics department at the Ballard School in New York. Her cookbook was given away as a promotional item at grocery stores across the country throughout the 1940s and 50s. It aimed to be a comprehensive guide to cooking and the kitchen. It had thousands of recipes, all of which were carefully cross-referenced, and sections on everything from setting the table to cooking game.

This edition maintains many of the classic dishes from the original. The instructions and ingredients have been updated, and new recipes have been added as well. The new recipes include ingredients and equipment, like mangoes and stand mixers, which weren't widely available when the cookbook was first published.

All of the recipes, new and old, maintain the same simple, straightforward style. Lily Wallace's book was meant to be an everyday cooking guide, full of beloved standards along with a wealth of other information and dishes. This edition aims to be the same kind of useful cooking companion.

APPETIZERS
AND
BEVERAGES

Appetizers should add to a cocktail or dinner party, rather than distracting from it. The best appetizers are simple but delicious. They should be ready to be set on the table or popped in the oven the moment guests start arriving. They should not keep the host or hostess chained to the kitchen all night long, fussing with this detail or that.

Almost all of the work for the following appetizers can be done in advance. The canapés can be carefully covered and refrigerated; the same is true for the various shrimp and crab cocktails. Even those appetizers that require an oven can be put together ahead of time and left on a baking sheet in the refrigerator.

To supplement the appetizers suggested here, try putting together a selection of cheeses, olives, and seasonal fruits. This will expand the offerings with minimal additional work. Simply set the cheeses and olives out an hour or so before the beginning of the party (most cheeses are more flavorful at room temperature). Add pears, apples, grapes, fresh figs, or any other favorite fruits or nuts to accompany the cheese. Some crackers or a baguette are all that are needed to finish out this platter.

When choosing appetizers for a party, be conservative rather than overly ambitious. A few well done dishes, and a host or hostess who is relaxed and mingling, will make for happier guests than an extravaganza with a harried and flour-covered host or hostess.

APPETIZERS

CANAPÉS

Slice bread thin. Cut into small rounds, triangles, or other dainty shapes. Toast or sauté on one side. Mix any of the combinations listed below, spread in layers or use as garnishes.

SPREADS FOR CANAPÉS

- Chopped chicken, almonds, mayonnaise (p. 70).
- Chopped shrimp (boiled, p. 342), celery, mayonnaise (p. 70).
- Chopped celery, Roquefort cheese.
- Chopped bacon (broiled or fried, p. 401) and hard-boiled egg (p. 272), mayonnaise (p. 70).
- Cottage cheese, chopped chives.
- Crabmeat, seasoned, chopped olives, hard-boiled eggs (p. 272).
- Orange marmalade, cream cheese.
- Tuna fish (flaked), capers, chopped celery, mayonnaise (p. 70).
- Chopped shrimp (boiled, p. 342), celery, chili sauce.
- Chopped ripe olives, chopped onion, chopped celery, cream cheese, chopped pimento.
- Shredded crabmeat, butter, lemon juice, paprika, salt.
- Chopped hard-boiled eggs (p. 272), mayonnaise (p. 70), minced boiled shrimp (p. 342), lemon juice.
- Chopped mild cheese, minced onion, mustard.

TOMATO CUPS

Cut off stem ends of small tomatoes. Scoop out centers. Turn upside down and drain thoroughly. Stuff with any canapé spread (p. 8).

CAVIAR CANAPÉ

24 pieces cocktail bread, or 6 slices regular bread,
    cut into fourths
4 ounces caviar
¼ cup onion, finely diced (optional)
3 egg yolks of hard-boiled eggs (p. 272)

Toast bread on one side and spread other side with caviar and a little finely chopped onion. Around the edge put a ¼" border of egg yolks, which have been pressed through a sieve. Either black or red American as well as imported caviar may be used.

CAVIAR CANAPÉ VARIATIONS

Sauté rounds of bread until delicately brown on one side only. Spread plain side with watercress and butter. With a pastry bag, create a border of butter around circumference. Fill centers with caviar and finely chopped yolks of hard-boiled egg (p. 272) used in equal proportions.

Cut hard-boiled eggs lengthwise and replace yolks of half of them with caviar. Arrange eggs on platter with lettuce, alternating light and dark halves. Mash remaining yolks, mix with a little anchovy paste, chopped capers, vinegar, and olive oil. Serve as sauce to eggs.

Add a sprinkle of lemon juice to the caviar. Mix chopped onions and dash of olive oil. Sauté small rounds of bread in olive oil. Cover ½ of each round with caviar, other half with onion. Separate with a little strip of green pepper or red pimento.

Spread crackers with caviar mixed with lemon juice. Cover with whipped cream seasoned with white pepper. Garnish with a line of capers and serve immediately.

Spread small rounds of toast with caviar, mixed with finely chopped onion. Place small raw oyster on each.

Spread small rounds of toast with grated onion mixed with butter. Make a circle around the rim of each toast with the onion-butter mixture. Fill centers with caviar.

MINTY FRUIT SYRUP

½ cup sugar
½ cup water
2 tablespoons fresh mint (more to taste)
1 tablespoon freshly squeezed lemon or lime juice

Heat sugar and water in a small saucepan over medium heat. Remove from heat as soon as the sugar dissolves and the mixture becomes clear. Allow to cool for 5 to 10 minutes. In a blender, mix sugar syrup, mint, and lemon or lime juice. Add more mint if desired, and blend again. Chill. May be used with any fruit salad or fruit cup. Makes 1 cup syrup.

PROSCIUTTO WRAPPED MELON

1 large, ripe cantaloupe
¼ pound prosciutto, thinly sliced

Slice melon in half, removing the seeds. Cut into thin slices, and remove the rind. Wrap each slice in prosciutto. Serve chilled.

SHRIMP COCKTAIL

Serve boiled shrimp (p. 342) on bed of lettuce in cocktail glass with cocktail sauce (p. 424). Allow 1 pound shrimp for 6 servings.

CRABMEAT COCKTAIL

Serve boiled crabmeat (p. 335) on nest of lettuce in cocktail glass with cocktail sauce.

STUFFED CELERY

Thoroughly wash celery. Remove all tough strings. Chill. After filling with mixture, cut in 2" lengths and chill again. Some suggested fillings for celery are:

- Equal parts of Roquefort and cream cheese, beaten together, with enough mayonnaise dressing (p. 70) to moisten.
- 2 parts chopped anchovies, mixed with 1 part mayonnaise (p. 70).
- Cottage cheese and chopped stuffed olives, moistened with mayonnaise dressing (p. 70).

- Cream cheese, minced parsley, paprika, chopped olives, chopped celery, French dressing (p. 71).
- Chopped hard-boiled egg (p. 272), mayonnaise (p. 70).
- Chopped hard-boiled egg (p. 272), chopped olives, chopped pimento, chopped celery, mayonnaise (p. 70).
- Cream cheese, finely chopped walnuts or pistachios.

BACON-WRAPPED SCALLOPS

24 medium scallops
12 slices of bacon, cut in half

Wrap scallops in thin slices of bacon. Broil in high heat until bacon is crisp. Fasten with toothpicks. Serve hot.

CHEESE IN BACON

½ pound Cheddar cheese, cubed
12 slices bacon, cut in half

Wrap slices of bacon around 1" cubes of Cheddar cheese. Broil at high heat until bacon is crisp, turning frequently to prevent cheese from melting. Fasten with toothpicks. Serve hot.

DATES IN BACON

24 dates, pitted
12 slices of bacon, cut in half

Wrap a slice of bacon around each date. Place dates on a cookie sheet, and broil at a moderate temperature until the bacon is crisp. Fasten with a toothpick and serve hot.

OLIVES IN BACON

24 olives, pitted
12 slices bacon, cut in half

Wrap slice of bacon around each olive. Broil at moderate temperature until bacon is crisp. Fasten with toothpicks. Serve hot.

CHEESE STUFFED OLIVES

24 large olives, pitted
⅓ cup cream cheese or other soft, mild cheese
12 slices bacon, cut in half lengthwise

Preheat oven to 400°F. Fill olives with cheese. Wrap a slice of bacon around each olive. Bake until bacon is crisp, about 10 minutes. Skewer with a toothpick. Serve on crackers or toast rounds if desired.

STUFFED CUCUMBER

1 cucumber
⅛ teaspoon salt
½ cup cream cheese
¼ cup green pepper, finely diced
2 tablespoon onion, finely diced
Pepper
Paprika
Worcestershire sauce
¼ cup French dressing (p. 71)

Peel cucumber. Cut in half, lengthwise. Dig out seeds and some of pulp. Sprinkle with salt. Mix cream cheese, green pepper and onion. Season with pepper, paprika, and Worcestershire sauce. Pack mixture in cucumber. Cover with French dressing. Chill. Cut in ¼" slices. Serve garnished with a sprinkling of paprika.

CHEESE BALLS

¼ cup butter
½ cup flour
1 cup milk
¼ teaspoon salt
⅛ teaspoon paprika
2 tablespoon chopped green pepper
1½ cups grated mild cheese, such as Cheddar
2 well-beaten eggs
½ cup breadcrumbs
Oil for frying
Tomatoes, sliced for serving (optional)
Watercress, for serving (optional)

Melt butter in a saucepan over medium heat. Stir in flour. Add milk gradually, stirring constantly. Add salt, paprika, and green pepper. Beat cheese into 1 well-beaten egg. Add cheese and egg mixture to sauce. Stir constantly, cooking until cheese is melted. Chill. Mold into little balls slightly larger than a grape. Roll in crumbs. Dip in slightly beaten egg. Roll again crumbs. Fry in deep hot fat (375°F) for 1½ minutes. Drain on a paper towel. Serve hot on tomato slices or in nests of watercress.

CHEESE FONDUE

¾ pound of Gruyère
¾ pound of Emmental
½ pound of Brie (rind removed)
1 cup dry white wine
1 tablespoon cornstarch
1 tablespoon kirsch
Salt
Pepper
Nutmeg
Loaf of French bread

Grate the Gruyère and Emmental. Scoop Brie out of the rind. Bring cheeses, wine, and cornstarch to a boil over medium heat, stirring constantly. When the fondue is smooth and thick, remove from heat. Add kirsch and season to taste with salt, pepper, and nutmeg. Pour into a fondue pot and keep warm over a low flame. Serve with French bread which has been cut into cubes.

CHEESE BALLS OR CROQUETTES

½ pound grated Cheddar cheese
2 cups soft breadcrumbs
3 eggs, plus 1 egg
1 teaspoon Worcestershire sauce
⅛ teaspoon salt
Dash cayenne
2 tablespoons water
½ cup dry breadcrumbs
Oil for frying

Mix cheese, soft crumbs, 3 beaten eggs, Worcestershire sauce, salt, and cayenne. Form into balls. Dip in slightly beaten egg, diluted with water, and roll in dry crumbs. Fry in deep hot oil (375°F) until a delicate brown. Drain on paper. Serve hot with tomato sauce (p. 424). Serves 6.

CHEESE LOAF

½ pound Cheddar cheese
4 hard-boiled eggs (p. 272)
6 small sweet pickles, chopped
1 small onion, chopped
Dash cayenne

Allow cheese to stand at room temperature until softened. Grate finely. Mash yolks of eggs with fork. Chop whites. Add eggs, pickles, onion, and cayenne to cheese and blend thoroughly. Press in buttered mold. Chill thoroughly. Remove to small platter and slice. Serve with crackers and slices of apple. Serves 6.

CHEESE STRAWS

Basic pastry (p. 445)
Salt
Cayenne
1 cup grated cheese

Preheat oven to 400°F. Roll out pastry to ⅛" thickness. Sprinkle with salt, cayenne, and grated cheese. Fold in 3 layers. Roll out again. Cut in strips ½" wide and 4" or 5" long. Bake for 5 or 6 minutes.

CHEESE FINGERS

1 cup flour
½ teaspoon baking powder
⅛ teaspoon cayenne
½ teaspoon salt
2 tablespoons butter
4 tablespoons grated cheese
Up to 1 tablespoon cold water

Preheat oven to 400°F. Mix and sift flour, baking powder, cayenne, and salt. Cut in butter with a knife or pulse in a food processor. Add cheese and enough cold water to hold mixture together. Chill for at least an hour. Roll out on floured board to ¼" thickness. Cut in very thin strips with a knife. Bake for 20 minutes. Yield: 50 fingers.

CHEESE FRITTERS

1 cup cooked rice
1 egg, slightly beaten
1 tablespoon milk
½ cup grated Cheddar cheese
¼ teaspoon paprika
2 teaspoons prepared mustard
¼ teaspoon salt
Buttered cracker crumbs
Oil for frying

Mix the rice thoroughly with the beaten egg, milk, grated cheese, and seasonings. Shape into balls, roll in buttered cracker crumbs, and fry in deep oil (375°F) until brown. Serves 6.

CHEESE ON TOAST POINTS

½ cup grated Cheddar cheese
1½ tablespoons melted butter
¼ teaspoon salt
¼ teaspoon paprika
3 eggs
2 teaspoons prepared mustard
Toast points

Mix grated cheese, butter, salt, and paprika. Beat eggs until light, add mustard, and pour into the cheese mixture. Cook in double boiler over low heat, stirring constantly until the mixture is smooth and creamy. Serve on hot toast points and garnish with paprika. Serves 6.

ROASTED CAULIFLOWER

1 head of cauliflower
2 tablespoons olive oil
Salt
Pepper

Preheat oven to 450°F. Remove the stem from the cauliflower and break into flowerets. Rinse flowerets. Drain. Remove imperfections. Toss flowerets with olive oil, and sprinkle with salt and pepper. Place on a cookie sheet. Roast in the oven on a high rack until the flowerets have begun to brown, about 15 minutes. Shake or turn the cauliflower a few times while cooking to prevent sticking. Serve immediately.

TOMATO MOZZARELLA SKEWERS

½ pound fresh mozzarella
1 pint grape tomatoes
2 tablespoons olive oil
Salt
Pepper
1 small bunch fresh basil
Bamboo skewers

Cut mozzarella into 1" cubes. Toss cheese and tomatoes with olive oil, salt, and pepper. Alternate with fresh basil leaves on bamboo skewers. Serve at room temperature.

MINIATURE BAKED POTATOES

2 pounds small red potatoes
2 tablespoons olive oil
Salt
Pepper
4 slices of bacon
1 cup sour cream
½ cup grated Cheddar
2 tablespoons chopped fresh chives

Preheat oven to 425°F. Scrub the potatoes clean, and cut them in half. Toss with olive oil, salt, and pepper. Roast potatoes on a cookie sheet for 45 minutes, until the potatoes are cooked through and have begun to brown. Meanwhile, cook the bacon over medium heat until crisp. Remove from the heat, and drain on a paper towel. When the bacon has cooled, cut it into small pieces or crumble by hand. When the potatoes have finished cooking, remove them to a platter, cut side up. Top each with a dollop of sour cream, a sprinkling of cheese, bacon pieces, and chives. Serve immediately.

BEVERAGES

SIMPLE SYRUP FOR BEVERAGES

  2 cups sugar
  2 cups water

Boil sugar and water for 5 minutes. Store in cool place and use to sweeten fruit drinks.

LEMONADE

  2 cups sugar
  4 cups water
  ⅔ cup lemon juice

Heat sugar and water over medium heat just until sugar dissolves. Remove from the heat. Add lemon juice. Chill and serve. Serves 4. Crushed or chopped fresh fruits or berries make a great addition to lemonade.

GLORIFIED LEMONADE

  2 cups sugar
  3 cups water
  Juice of 3 lemons
  Juice of 2 limes
  2 cups orange or lemon soda, or ginger ale

Heat sugar and water over medium heat just until sugar dissolves. Chill. Add lemon juice, lime juice, and soda of choice. Serves 6.

SUPERB LEMONADE

8 cups water
2 cups sugar
1 cup lemon juice
1 orange, halved and sliced
1 cup pineapple cubes

Boil water and immediately remove from heat. Add all ingredients and stir thoroughly. Chill. Serve over cracked ice or ice cubes. Serves 8.

ORANGEADE

½ cup sugar
4 cups water
5 oranges
1 lemon

Dissolve sugar in water. Juice 4 oranges and the lemon. Add juice to sugar mixture. Halve and thinly slice the remaining orange. Serve over cracked ice or ice cubes. Garnish with orange slices. Serves 4.

LIMEADE

½ cup lime juice
½ cup simple syrup for beverages (p. 21)
2 cups water
1 lime, sliced thinly (optional)

Mix lime juice, simple syrup, and water. Garnish with slices of lime, if desired. Chill. Serves 4.

GINGER ALE COCKTAIL

1 grapefruit, segments halved
1 cup crushed pineapple (fresh or canned)
3 tablespoons powdered sugar
1 cup ginger ale
Mint leaves, to garnish

Put a layer of grapefruit and one of pineapple in sherbet or highball glasses. Sprinkle with powdered sugar and chill. When ready to serve, fill glasses with chilled ginger ale and crushed ice. Garnish with mint leaves. Serves 6.

PINEAPPLE-BANANA SMOOTHIE

1 ripe banana
1 cup unsweetened pineapple juice
1 cup milk

Peel banana. Mash well with a fork and put in a blender. Add pineapple juice. Blend. Pour in milk and continue to blend for a few seconds or until ingredients are blended. Serves 2.

PINEAPPLE AND STRAWBERRY COCKTAIL

¼ cup lemon juice
1 cup orange juice
Sugar to taste
1 cup strawberries, hulled and halved, plus more for
    serving
1 cup pineapple chunks

Mix juices and sweeten with sugar. Combine fruits lightly and
put in cocktail glasses. Add juice and sugar to taste. Top each
serving with a whole strawberry. Serves 6.

FRUIT PUNCH

4 cups water
Juice of 3 lemons
2 cups sugar
Juice of 4 oranges
1 small can chopped pineapple
4 cups club soda

Prepare syrup using the water and sugar by boiling together
over medium heat for 5 minutes. Cool. Add fruit, juices, and
club soda. Serve ice-cold. Serves 12.

BLENDED FRUIT PUNCH

3½ cups apricot nectar
1 cup orange juice
3½ cups pineapple juice
3½ cups pear nectar
1 cup ginger ale

Mix first 4 ingredients. Chill. Serve over crushed ice or ice cubes. Add ginger ale just before serving. Serves 25.

CHERRY PUNCH

1 package cherry-flavored gelatin
2 cups hot water
4 tablespoons sugar
⅛ teaspoon salt
3 cups cold water
6 tablespoons lemon juice
2 cups ginger ale

Dissolve gelatin in hot water. Add sugar and salt and stir until dissolved. Add water, lemon juice, and ginger ale. Chill. Serve over cracked ice. Serves 6.

WHOLE FRUIT PUNCH

1 cup sugar
2 cups water
1 small can crushed pineapple
1 small jar maraschino cherries, drained
3 oranges, cut into pieces
2 cups grape soda
2 cups lime soda
1 cup strawberry soda

Make a syrup of the sugar and water by boiling for 5 minutes over medium heat. Cool. Add the fruits. Thoroughly chill. When ready to serve add the sodas; ice cubes may be made of lemon soda or fruit juices.

ORANGE DELIGHT

4 cups orange juice
Juice of 6 limes
1 cup powdered sugar
½ cup chopped mint leaves, plus more for serving
2 cups club soda
1 orange, thinly sliced

Combine the fruit juices, sugar, and chopped mint leaves. Chill 1 hour and strain. Pour over crushed ice in tall glasses. Fill with club soda and stir gently. Garnish with mint and orange slices. Serves 4.

SPICED PINEAPPLE PUNCH

3 cups sugar
3 cinnamon sticks, broken
1 teaspoon whole cloves
2 cups water
8 cups pineapple juice

Boil sugar, cinnamon, and cloves in water for 10 minutes over medium heat. Strain and mix with pineapple juice. Chill and serve over crushed ice or ice cubes. Serves 25.

SPICED FRUIT PUNCH

2½ cups orange juice
1 cup pineapple juice
2 cups water
½ cup sugar
Grated zest of 1 lemon
1 tablespoon honey
6 whole cloves
½ teaspoon grated nutmeg
½ teaspoon cinnamon
6 cups ginger ale

Combine orange juice, pineapple juice, water, and sugar. Add grated zest of lemon, honey, cloves, nutmeg, and cinnamon. Mix and let stand 3 hours. Strain and add the ginger ale. Stir briskly and serve in glasses containing ice cubes. The cubes may be made of sodas or fruit juices. Serves 8.

RUBY FRUIT PUNCH

1½ cups sugar
2 cups boiling water
3 cups cranberry juice
⅓ cup lemon juice
2 cups orange juice
4 cups ginger ale
Orange and lemon slices
Mint sprigs

Dissolve sugar in hot water. Add cranberry juice, lemon juice, and orange juice. Chill. Just before serving pour into punch bowl, and add ginger ale, orange slices, and lemon slices. Serve decorated with mint sprigs. Serves 10.

CIDER PUNCH

3 cups water
1 cup sugar
½ teaspoon grated nutmeg
1 cup grapefruit juice
2 cups cider
4 cups ginger ale
2 cups grape juice
3 sliced lemons

Boil water, sugar, and nutmeg together 5 minutes. Cool. Add other ingredients. Put in punch bowl with cracked ice or ice cubes. Serves 12.

MULLED CIDER

   1 gallon apple cider
   6 sticks cinnamon, broken in 1" pieces
   2 pieces whole mace
   1 tablespoon whole cloves
   1 tablespoon whole allspice
   3 cups brown sugar

Put cider in stockpot. Add cinnamon. Tie the other spices in cheesecloth bag and drop in cider. Stir in sugar. Heat slowly and simmer 20 minutes. Remove spice bag before serving. Serve hot.

GINGER MINT PUNCH

   1½ cups sugar
   ½ cup water
   Juice of 6 lemons
   ½ cup fresh mint leaves, crushed
   4 cups ginger ale

Boil sugar and water for 3 minutes over medium heat. Pour over lemon juice and crushed mint leaves. Let stand till cold. Add ice-cold ginger ale and serve immediately with a sprig of mint in each tall glass. Serves 6.

COFFEE CREAM PUNCH

4 cups freshly brewed coffee
4 cups chocolate ice cream (p. 518)
¼ teaspoon almond flavoring
1 cup heavy cream
Nutmeg

Chill the coffee and pour into punch bowl. Add ½ the chocolate ice cream and stir until it is partially melted. Add almond
flavoring to the cream and whip until stiff. Place whipped
cream and remaining ice cream alternately on top of first mixture. Sprinkle the cream lightly with nutmeg. Serves 12 to 15.

SOUPS

The simplest trick for making a wonderful soup is to use good stock. This chapter starts out with recipes for several simple stocks. Stocks don't need to be an elaborate production. They can and should be made with leftovers. The bones from a roast chicken, the tops from a leek that didn't get used, those carrots in the vegetable drawer that are starting to look a little less than ideal—these are perfect ingredients for a stock. They don't all need to be ready at the same time, either. Save odds and ends of vegetables in the freezer. That way, the next time a chicken carcass presents itself, there's no need to go out and get vegetables to make a stock. There is nothing wrong with using fresh vegetables as well, but stocks are an excellent way to use up things that would otherwise go to waste. Once a stock is made, it can be frozen indefinitely for later use. Having several containers on hand is a great idea for anyone who does a lot of cooking.

When it's not possible to use homemade stock, try to find a good substitute. Many grocery stores make stock, and all grocery stores should carry a variety of canned and powdered options. A good stock adds depth and richness to a soup. It's worth taking a little time to find a suitable one.

BASIC CHICKEN STOCK

5 pounds chicken bones
1 large onion, roughly chopped
2 carrots, roughly chopped
2 celery stalks, roughly chopped
2 bay leaves
4 sprigs of parsley
2 cloves garlic
6 peppercorns
2 teaspoons salt
10 cups water

Put all of the ingredients in a stockpot and cover with water. Bring to a boil over medium heat. Immediately reduce heat, keeping the stock covered and at a low simmer. Allow stock to simmer for 3 to 4 hours. Skim fat, as it rises to the surface. Remove stock from heat and strain. Discard bones, seasonings, and vegetables. Stock may be used immediately, or frozen for later use. Makes about 8 cups.

Making stock is an excellent way to use up old bones and vegetables. In addition to the vegetables listed above, tomatoes, potatoes, parsnips, turnips, and leeks would be good additions to a stock.

BASIC BEEF STOCK

3 pounds beef soup bones
1 large onion
2 large carrots
1 stalk celery
6 cups water, plus ½ cup
½ cup diced turnip or parsnip
½ cup potato peels, well scrubbed
6 peppercorns
1 teaspoon fresh thyme
2 sprigs parsley
1 bay leaf
2 cloves garlic
2 teaspoons salt

Preheat oven to 450°F. Roughly chop onion, carrots, and celery into 1" chunks. Place bones, onions, and carrots in oven in a roasting pan or on a cookie sheet. Cook for 30 minutes, until bones are nicely browned. Turn occasionally to prevent burning or sticking.

Drain off fat. Put bones and roasted vegetables in a stockpot. Rinse the pan from the oven with ½ cup water. Add this water to the bones.

Add remaining vegetables and seasonings to the pot. Add water and bring to a boil. Immediately reduce heat, cover, and simmer for 3 to 4 hours, occasionally skimming froth that rises to the surface.

When stock has cooked for long enough, remove from heat. Strain the stock and discard the bones, vegetables, and seasonings. Adjust the flavor by adding salt and pepper. Stock may be frozen or used immediately. Makes 4 cups.

BASIC VEGETABLE STOCK

1 tablespoon olive oil
1 large onion or 2 medium onions, roughly chopped
2 stalks celery, roughly chopped
2 medium carrots, roughly chopped
Other vegetables, as desired
8 cups water
6 cloves garlic, minced
6 sprigs fresh parsley
6 sprigs fresh thyme
3 bay leaves
8 peppercorns
1 teaspoon salt

In a large stockpot, sauté onions, celery, and carrots in olive oil over medium heat for about 10 minutes, until the onions and celery begin to soften. Other vegetables may be added at this point as well. Potato peelings, mushrooms, green onions, asparagus butts, leek tops, and corn cobs are just a few of the possibilities. Cover vegetables with water and add the rest of the ingredients. Simmer on low heat for 2 to 3 hours, occasionally skimming any foam that rises to the surface. Strain. Discard vegetables and seasonings. Season with salt and pepper to taste. This stock may be substituted for chicken or beef stock in any recipe. May be frozen or used immediately. Makes approximately 6 cups stock.

FISH STOCK

2 tablespoons butter
1 small onion, roughly chopped
1 carrot, roughly chopped
Bones, head and trimmings from 2 fish (excluding
    innards and gills)*
1 stalk celery, roughly chopped
1 bay leaf
1 tomato, quartered
1 ½ teaspoons salt
6 peppercorns
6 cups water

Melt 1 tablespoon butter in a stockpot. Add onion and carrot. Fry, but do not brown. Add bones, head, and trimmings from fish; celery; bay leaf; tomato; salt; and peppercorns. Cover with cold water. Cover and simmer 2 hours. Strain, discarding vegetables, bones, and spices. Stock may be frozen or used immediately. Makes 3 cups stock.

* The type of fish used in the stock depends upon the type of fish used in the dish you're making. Neutral, white fish can be used in almost any recipe, but you should only use salmon or other strong fish in recipes that call for them.

BEET LEAF NOODLE SOUP

4 well-beaten eggs
10 chopped beet leaves and stems, well cleaned
½ cup cottage cheese
½ cup grated Parmesan cheese, plus more for sprinkling
½ cup breadcrumbs
4 cups basic chicken stock (p. 32)
Salt
Pepper
Nutmeg

Thoroughly mix eggs, beet leaves and stems, cottage cheese, Parmesan cheese, and crumbs, either by hand or in a food processor. The dough should form into a ball. Roll ¼" thick on floured board. Cut in narrow 2" lengths. Bring stock to boil over medium heat. Season to taste with salt, pepper, and nutmeg. Drop in noodles. Simmer until they float. Serve hot with grated Parmesan cheese. Serves 4.

RUSSIAN BORSCHT

This is a vegetable soup (e.g., p. 65), usually made from beef stock (p. 33) with varying diced vegetables and sometimes chopped beef or poultry or both. When cooking is finished, stir in some heavy sour cream or whipped sour cream and use for topping on soup.

CHICKEN NOODLE SOUP

1 large onion, sliced
2 medium carrots
2 celery stalks
2 tablespoons olive oil
3 pounds chicken breasts, legs, and thighs
    (or some combination)
½ cup canned tomatoes or fresh, ripe tomatoes, diced
1 bay leaf
2 to 3 small dried red peppers (optional)
1⅛ teaspoons salt
½ teaspoon pepper
6 cups basic chicken stock (p. 32)
2 cups uncooked egg noodles

Dice onions, carrots, and celery. Heat olive oil in a large saucepan or stockpot. Add chicken pieces, turning once or twice, until the skin is lightly browned. Add onions, carrots, celery, tomato, and spices. Stir a few times to coat all of the ingredients in oil. Cover with chicken stock. Bring to a boil and reduce heat to a simmer. Cook over low heat for 1 hour, until chicken is thoroughly cooked. Adjust seasoning.

If desired, remove chicken from the soup. Discard skin and remove meat from bones. Roughly chop meat and return it to the soup.

Raise heat to medium and bring soup to a boil. Drop in noodles and cook until they are tender. Serves 4 to 6.

VELVET SOUP

4 cups basic chicken stock (p. 32)
1 onion, roughly chopped
2 stalks celery, roughly chopped
2 whole cloves
2 sprigs parsley
1 teaspoon salt
⅓ teaspoon pepper
1 cup chopped, cooked chicken
1 cup breadcrumbs
2 tablespoons butter
4 cups milk and cream

Bring stock to a simmer. Add onion, celery, and seasonings. Heat until well blended. Strain. Discard vegetables and return stock to pot. Add chicken. Meanwhile, sauté crumbs in butter over medium heat until browned. Add to stock. Add milk or cream. Bring to boil, stirring constantly. Serves 6.

CHICKEN SOUP WITH OKRA

1 disjointed 3½-pound chicken,
    or 3½ pounds chicken pieces
2 tablespoons chopped onion
2 tablespoons flour
2 tablespoons olive oil
4 cups basic chicken stock (p. 32)
4 cups fresh okra, sliced and chopped
Salt
Pepper
8 cups peeled and seeded tomatoes (optional)

Sauté chicken, onion, and flour in olive oil over medium heat until well browned. Add okra and stock. Bring to boil. Reduce heat. Cover and simmer until okra is dissolved, about 2½ hours, adding water to keep quantity the same. Remove chicken. Strip meat from bones. Return meat to soup. Season to taste. Serves 6. If desired, diced tomatoes may be added with okra, in which case reduce water by half.

MULLIGATAWNY

¼ cup butter
1 medium onion, sliced
1 medium carrot, sliced
1 stalk of celery, sliced
1 green pepper, diced
1 apple, peeled, cored, and sliced
1 cup chopped raw chicken
⅓ cup flour
1 teaspoon curry powder
1 blade mace
4 whole cloves
1 tablespoon chopped parsley
1 cup canned tomatoes
5 cups basic chicken stock (p. 32)
Salt
Pepper
1 cup boiled rice

Melt butter in saucepan. Add onion, carrot, celery, green pepper, apple, and chicken. Cook until chicken has browned. Add flour, curry powder, mace, cloves, parsley, tomatoes, and stock. Cover and simmer 1½ hours. Strain, reserving chicken. Add chicken to soup. Press other ingredients through sieve into soup. Season to taste with salt and pepper. Add rice. Serves 6.

TURKEY SOUP

Remains of 1 roast turkey (p. 311)
1 tablespoon flour
1 cup cream or milk
Salt
Pepper

Place the remains of a roast turkey, meat, bones, stuffing, gravy, etc., in a stockpot. Cover with cold water. Cover and simmer 4 hours. Skim off fat. Remove bones. Bring to boil. Add flour, well blended in cream. Add meat from bones. Season to taste with salt and pepper. Bring to boil. Serve hot. Serves 6.

POT AU FEU

4 pounds chuck roast or beef brisket, tied
1½ pound beef bones
2 stalks of celery, cut into 2" lengths
1 small onion
7 carrots, peeled and cut into 2" lengths
2 bay leaves
2 cloves
12 sprigs of parsley
12 sprigs of thyme
6 peppercorns
1 teaspoon salt
6 small potatoes, peeled
2 leeks, cleaned and diced
Serve with prepared mustard, cornichons, and
    horseradish

Place meat, bones, celery, onion, one carrot, bay leaves, and other seasonings in a large stockpot. Pour in just enough cold water to cover the ingredients. Bring to a boil over medium heat and immediately reduce heat, keeping it at a low simmer. Allow the mixture to cook for 3 hours, occasionally skimming any of the foam that rises to the surface. Heat the oven to 200°F. Remove the meat and keep it warm in the oven. Strain the remaining broth, discarding vegetables and any fat that rises to the surface. Salt and pepper to taste.

Bring a large saucepan of water to a boil over medium heat. Add a dash of salt and the peeled potatoes. Let boil for 10 minutes. Add remaining carrots and leeks. Allow mixture to boil for another 10 minutes. Remove vegetables to a skillet and add 1 cup of the beef broth. Cook over medium heat until broth has reduced by half.

To serve: arrange the meat on a platter with the boiled vegetables. Pour some of the broth over them to moisten. Have the rest of the broth on the side, to add as desired. Serve the meat thinly sliced, with horseradish, mustard (stone ground would be excellent), and cornichons or other small pickles.

FRENCH BEEF SOUP

3 pounds beef shanks
2 tablespoons butter
2 teaspoons salt
1 chopped onion
1 cup shredded cabbage
2 diced potatoes
1 sliced carrot
2 cups canned tomatoes
1 stalk celery, diced
½ teaspoon pepper

Wipe shanks with cold, damp cloth. Place in a large stockpot. Brown in butter, then cover with water. Add 1 teaspoon salt and the onion. Bring to boiling point. Reduce heat. Cover and simmer 1 hour. Add 1 teaspoon salt and simmer until meat is tender, about 1 more hour. Remove shanks and leave 8 cups stock in stockpot. Remove the meat from the bone and return it to the pot. Add the other ingredients. Bring to a boil and simmer, covered, 30 minutes. Serve hot. Serves 6.

PORK AND SPINACH SOUP

1 pork bone
¼ pound pork meat
½ teaspoon salt
Dash of pepper
4 cups water
2 or 3 small dried red peppers (optional)
¼ pound fresh spinach

Simmer pork bone, meat, salt, pepper, and water in a covered pan about 1 hour. Remove pork bone and discard. Cut the pork meat into tiny strips. Bring the broth to a rapid boil, add meat strips and spinach, and cook until spinach is tender but has not lost its green color, about 2 minutes. Adjust seasonings and serve. Serves 6.

CREAM OF ASPARAGUS SOUP

1 pound medium asparagus
3 tablespoons butter
1 medium chopped onion
4 tablespoons flour
2 bay leaves
1 teaspoon fresh thyme
½ teaspoon salt
½ cup cream or half-and-half

Bring 4 cups of water to a boil in a small stockpot. Add asparagus and boil for 4 minutes. Drain. Chop into 1" pieces and set aside in a bowl of ice water. Reserve cooking liquid. Melt butter in a medium saucepan. Add onion, cooking until onion is translucent, about 10 minutes. Add flour, stirring with a wooden spoon to prevent lumps. Pour in reserved cooking liquid, whisking constantly until the flour is incorporated. Add bay leaves, thyme, and salt. Bring to a boil. Simmer for 10 minutes, and then add the reserved asparagus. Bring to a boil and immediately remove from the heat. Remove bay leaves and either run soup through a food mill or use an immersion blender to purée. Whisk in cream and adjust the seasonings. Serves 4.

RED KIDNEY BEAN SOUP

4 cups basic chicken stock (p. 32)
1 large can red kidney beans
1 stalk celery, diced
1 small onion, diced
1 carrot, diced
1 slice bacon, optional
Salt
Pepper
Paprika

Bring stock to a boil in a medium saucepan. Add beans, celery, onion, carrot, and bacon (if desired). Simmer until vegetables are tender, about 20 minutes. Season with salt, pepper, and paprika to taste. Serves 4.

BEAN SOUP

1 tablespoon butter
1 medium carrot, diced
1 small onion, diced
4 cups basic chicken stock (p. 32)
1 ham bone, optional
1 can navy beans or white beans, drained
½ teaspoon salt
2 tablespoons chopped parsley
2 pieces cooked bacon, crumbled

Melt butter in a small stockpot. Add carrot, onion, and ¼ cup stock. Simmer until stock is gone, stirring frequently. Add 2 cups of stock and the optional ham bone. Let simmer, covered, until carrots and onion are tender, about 20 minutes. Add the beans. Bring to boil. Add salt and adjust seasonings. Serve hot, garnished with parsley or crumbled bacon. Serves 6.

BLACK BEAN SOUP

3 tablespoons butter
1 onion, sliced
2 cans of black beans, drained
6 cups basic chicken stock (p. 32)
1 carrot, sliced
2 stalks celery, sliced
2 sprigs parsley
1 teaspoon salt
⅛ teaspoon pepper
⅛ teaspoon cayenne
Sour cream
½ cup grated Cheddar cheese (or to taste)
1 lemon

Melt butter in a medium stockpot. Add sliced onion and sauté 5 minutes. Add beans, stock, sliced carrot, celery, parsley, salt, pepper, and cayenne. For a spicier soup, double or triple the amount of cayenne. Cover and simmer 30 minutes. Press through a food mill, or blend using an immersion blender. Add seasonings if needed. Garnish with sour cream and grated cheese or a slice of lemon, if desired. Serves 6.

CREAM OF CAULIFLOWER SOUP

1 small head cauliflower
1 stalk celery, sliced
1 medium onion, chopped
½ teaspoon fresh thyme
½ teaspoon salt
6 cups basic chicken stock (p. 32)
½ cup cream or half and half

Break cauliflower into small pieces. Soak in cold, slightly salted water 20 minutes. Drain. Put in saucepan with celery, onion, thyme, and salt. Cover with stock. Simmer until cauliflower is tender, about 20 minutes. Strain, reserving 1 ½ cups stock. Press cauliflower through a food mill into stock, or put soup in blender in batches to purée. Add cream. Mix well and adjust seasonings. Serves 4.

CREAM OF CELERY SOUP

1 small bunch celery
½ teaspoon salt
1 slice onion
6 cups basic chicken stock (p. 32)
½ cup heavy cream or half-and-half

Cut tops and stalks of celery into small pieces. Put in saucepan. Add salt, onion, and stock. Bring to boiling point. Reduce heat and let simmer until celery is very tender, about 20 to 30 minutes. Strain, reserving 2 cups stock. Press celery through sieve into stock. Add cream. Mix well. Serves 4.

CORN SOUP

9 ears corn
12 ripe tomatoes
8 cups basic chicken stock (p. 32)
2 tablespoons butter
2 cups milk
1 teaspoon salt
¼ teaspoon pepper
2 tablespoons chopped parsley
½ cup grated Cheddar cheese (optional)

Rinse corn in cold water. Cut corn from cob. Plunge tomatoes in boiling water, then in cold water. Peel. Add to corn. Put in large saucepan. Cover with stock and simmer slowly for 1 hour. Add other ingredients. Simmer 10 minutes longer. To serve, garnish with chopped parsley or grated cheese. Serves 6.

CREAM OF CORN SOUP

2 cups corn (canned, fresh, or frozen)
2 tablespoons onion, diced
1 teaspoon sugar (optional)
¼ teaspoon salt
4 cups basic chicken stock (p. 32)
½ cup heavy cream
Pepper
1½ tablespoons chopped parsley

Simmer corn, onion, sugar, and salt in stock for 20 minutes. Press through a sieve or food mill. Add cream and mix well. Add pepper and parsley. Serves 4.

CORN CHOWDER

4 tablespoons chopped onion
3 tablespoons butter
4 cups milk
3 cups boiled potatoes, cut in ½" cubes
2 cups canned or frozen corn
1½ teaspoons salt
⅛ teaspoon pepper
Few grains cayenne
Crackers (optional)
½ cup grated Cheddar cheese (optional)

Fry onion in butter until a delicate brown. Strain butter into a saucepan. Add milk, potatoes, corn, salt, pepper, and cayenne. Bring to the boiling point. Serve a cracker or grated cheese in each portion of soup. Serves 6.

CREAM OF ZUCCHINI SOUP

3 small zucchini or 2 large
2 tablespoons butter
3 cups milk
2 tablespoons onion, diced
2 well-beaten egg yolks
2 cups cream
Salt
Pepper

Peel and slice zucchini. Sauté in butter 10 minutes, until zucchini begins to soften. Add milk and onion. Bring to boil. Cover and simmer 5 minutes. Whisk in egg yolks. Rub through sieve or food mill. Add cream and heat through. Season with salt and pepper. Serves 6.

CRÈME VICHYSOISSE (LEEK AND POTATO SOUP)

6 leeks
2 medium onions
1 cup butter, divided
8 cups basic chicken stock (p. 32)
¾ pound diced potatoes
Salt
Pepper
1 cup cream
¼ cup chopped chives

Clean leeks thoroughly. Chop leeks and onions and simmer slowly in half of butter over low heat, taking care that they do not brown. As soon as vegetables are soft, add chicken broth and potatoes. Season to taste with salt and pepper and cook gently until potatoes are soft. Press through a sieve or food mill. Add remaining butter and cream and heat through. Serve warm or chilled, with a sprinkling of finely chopped chives. Serves 6.

CREAM OF MUSHROOM SOUP

¾ pound mushrooms
1 medium onion, chopped
½ teaspoon salt
4 tablespoons butter, divided
¼ cup flour
3 cups basic chicken stock (p. 32)
1 cup cream
Pepper

Wash and peel mushrooms. Slice caps and stems. Sauté in a saucepan with onions, salt, and 2 tablespoons butter. Cook for 10 minutes, until mushrooms have shrunk and onions are softened. Add remaining butter and flour, stirring with a wooden spoon to prevent lumps. Whisk in stock, and simmer for 20 minutes. Add cream. Season to taste with salt and pepper.

ONION SOUP

1 pound onions
2 tablespoons butter
1 tablespoon flour
6 cups basic chicken stock (p. 32)
Salt
Pepper
6 pieces French bread
Parmesan cheese or Fontina

Slice and sauté onions in butter over medium heat until brown. Sprinkle with flour and stir. Add stock slowly, stirring until smooth. Heat through. Season with salt and pepper. If made in the morning and allowed to stand several hours before serving, the flavor improves. Serve with a piece of French bread sprinkled with Parmesan cheese. Toast in the oven at the last moment. Serve extra cheese to be sprinkled over soup at the table. Serves 6.

CARROT GINGER SOUP

  2 tablespoons sesame, peanut, or olive oil
  1 medium onion, roughly chopped
  2" piece of fresh ginger, peeled and minced
  5 pounds carrots, peeled and roughly chopped
  6 cups basic chicken stock (p. 32)
  Salt
  Pepper

In a medium stockpot, heat oil. Add onion and ginger. Sauté for 5 minutes over medium heat. Add carrots and sauté for 5 more minutes, adding a bit more oil if the vegetables begin to stick. Cover vegetables with stock and simmer over low heat until carrots have softened, about 30 minutes. Force through a strainer or food mill. Season with salt and pepper to taste. Serves 6.

BUTTERNUT SQUASH SOUP

2 tablespoons butter
1 teaspoons ground turmeric
½ teaspoon mustard seeds
½ teaspoon cumin seeds
½ teaspoon coriander seeds
1 large butternut squash, peeled, seeded,
    and chopped into 1" chunks
1 to 2 apples, peeled, cored, and chopped
    into 1" chunks
6 to 8 cups basic chicken stock (p. 32)
Salt
Pepper
½ cup heavy cream (optional)

In a medium stockpot, melt butter over medium heat and add spices. Spices may be ground in a coffee grinder or used whole, as desired. Sauté the spices for about 1 minute, until the mustard seeds begin to make a popping noise. Add squash and apples. Sauté for 5 more minutes, adding more butter if needed to prevent sticking. Cover with stock and simmer over low heat for 30 minutes, or until the squash is tender. Mix in a blender, or force through a strainer or food mill. Season with salt and pepper to taste. Add cream if desired. Serves 6.

PEA SOUP

1¼ cups fresh or frozen peas
1 cup chopped celery
1 cup onion, diced
4 cups basic chicken stock (p. 32)
2 sausages (uncooked)
2 teaspoons salt
½ teaspoon pepper

Simmer peas, celery, and onion in stock until soft. Rub through sieve. In another pan cover sausages with boiling water and boil 10 minutes. Drain. Slice into soup. Add salt and pepper. Serves 6.

SPLIT PEA SOUP

1½ cups dried split peas
12 cups basic chicken stock (p. 32)
Ham bone
1 onion, sliced
1 medium carrot, sliced
2 cups milk
2 tablespoons butter
Salt
Pepper

Wash and pick over peas and soak overnight. Drain. Add stock, ham bone, onion, and carrot. Cover and cook slowly 3 hours or until peas are soft. Press through a sieve or food mill. Add milk and butter. Season to taste with salt and pepper. Heat thoroughly. Serves 6.

CREAM OF POTATO SOUP

3 medium-size potatoes
1 medium onion, diced
1 sliced stalk celery
½ teaspoon salt
4 cups basic chicken stock (p. 32)
1 cup cream
3 tablespoons chopped parsley

Wash and cut potatoes in half. Put in saucepan with onion, celery, salt, and stock. Simmer until potatoes are tender, about 30 minutes. Strain, reserving 2 cups stock. Press potatoes through a sieve or food mill into reserved stock. Add cream and heat through. Mix well. Sprinkle with parsley. Serves 4.

BAKED POTATO SOUP

4 medium potatoes, baked
4 cups basic chicken stock (p. 32)
1 egg yolk
½ cup heavy cream
1 tablespoon chopped parsley
Salt
Pepper
Paprika

Bake 3 or 4 medium-sized potatoes. Once they are out of the oven, bring stock to a low boil in a medium stock pan. Force the potatoes through a sieve or food mill into the stock. Thicken with the yolk of an egg, whisking vigorously to make sure it gets incorporated. When serving, place cream and chopped parsley in the bottom of a warmed soup tureen and pour soup over it. Adjust seasoning with salt and pepper. Sprinkle paprika on top and serve at once. Serves 6.

CREAM OF TOMATO SOUP

    2 cups canned tomatoes, or fresh, ripe tomatoes,
        peeled and chopped
    2 teaspoons sugar (optional)
    ½ teaspoon thyme
    ½ teaspoon salt
    2 tablespoons chopped onion
    2 cups basic chicken stock (p. 32)
    1 cup cream, milk, or cream cheese
    ½ cup grated Cheddar cheese (optional)

Simmer tomatoes, sugar, thyme, salt, onion, and stock for 20 minutes over medium-low heat. Strain. Add cream, milk, or cream cheese. Mix well. If using cream cheese, whisk vigorously to incorporate. Garnish with grated cheese, if desired. Serves 4.

CLEAR TOMATO SOUP

3½ cups canned or fresh, ripe tomatoes
2 tablespoons onion, diced
1 cup celery, chopped
2 cups basic chicken stock (p. 32)
1 teaspoon tapioca
½ teaspoon salt
¼ teaspoon pepper
¼ teaspoon paprika
1 teaspoon Worcestershire sauce
1 teaspoon sugar
Croutons (p. 443)

Simmer tomatoes, onion, and celery for 20 minutes. Rub through a sieve or food mill. Pour stock through sieve into mixture. Soak tapioca in cold water 10 minutes. Discard water and add tapioca to soup. Simmer until tapioca is clear. Add salt, pepper, paprika, Worcestershire sauce, and sugar. Combine thoroughly. Garnish with croutons. Serves 6.

TOMATO SOUP WITH OKRA

¼ cup rice, uncooked
3½ tablespoons butter
5 cups basic chicken stock (p. 32)
2 stalks chopped celery
1 diced bell pepper
¼ cup diced onion
3 cups canned or fresh tomatoes
1½ teaspoons salt
2 cups sliced okra pods
3 tablespoons chopped parsley

Brown rice to a light golden color with 2 tablespoons melted butter in saucepan. Add stock. Bring to boil. Sauté celery, bell pepper, and onion in another pan with remaining butter for 6 minutes. Add tomatoes and sautéed vegetables to stock. Bring to boil. Pour into rice. Add salt. Simmer, covered, until rice is tender. Add okra pods and simmer 15 minutes more. Serve hot, sprinkled with parsley. Serves 6.

SPICY TOMATO SOUP WITH PASTA

    2 tablespoons butter
    ¼ chopped green pepper
    1 small chopped onion
    2 tablespoons flour
    1½ cups canned or fresh tomatoes
    2 cups basic chicken stock (p. 32)
    Salt
    Pepper
    ¼ teaspoon cayenne
    ½ cup cooked macaroni, or other small pasta
    1 tablespoon grated horseradish

Melt butter in saucepan. Add green pepper and onion. Sauté 5 minutes. Add flour, blending well. Add tomatoes slowly, stirring constantly. Cover and simmer slowly for 15 minutes. Add stock, and salt, pepper, and cayenne to taste. Strain or force through food mill. At time of serving add macaroni and horseradish if desired. Serves 4.

WHITE BEAN SOUP

1 cup dried white beans
½ cup dried peas
2 tablespoons barley
8 cups cold water
½ cup celery cut in pieces
2 potatoes, peeled and sliced
2 onions, diced
1 cup canned or fresh tomatoes
1 ham bone or ¼ pound bacon
2 cloves garlic, minced
1 teaspoon salt
¼ teaspoon pepper
2 tablespoons fresh chives, diced

Wash beans, peas, and barley. Soak overnight in cold water. Bring to boiling point in a large stockpot. Add celery, potatoes, onions, tomatoes, ham bone or bacon, garlic, salt, and pepper. Simmer slowly 2 hours. Add water as it cooks away. Adjust seasoning if necessary. Remove bone before serving. Garnish with chives. This soup should be quite thick and is a meal in itself. Serves 6.

SOUP JULIENNE

2 small carrots
2 small turnips
¼ head of cabbage
1 stalk celery
½ teaspoon salt
1 onion, diced
1 tablespoon butter
4 cups beef stock (p. 33)

Wash the carrots, turnips, cabbage, and celery and cut into narrow strips. Cover with cold water. Add salt. Bring to a boil in a saucepan over medium heat. Reduce heat. Cover and simmer until vegetables are tender. Drain the water. Sauté onion in butter in another pan until soft but not browned. Add stock and boiled vegetables, bring to a boil, and serve hot. Serves 4.

CLAM BROTH

8 pounds large clams (48 cherrystone clams)
3 to 4 cups water (enough to cover clams completely)
Salt
Pepper

Discard any clams with broken shells or clams that stay open. Scrub clams well. Bring water to a boil over high heat. Add clams and cover. Allow clams to boil for about 10 minutes (until most, but not all, of the clams have opened). Smaller clams will need less time. Remove clams and pour broth through a fine sieve or cheesecloth. Allow broth to settle and repeat straining process. Adjust seasoning. Makes approximately 6 cups of broth and 2 cups of cooked clams.

CLAM CHOWDER

4 tablespoons chopped onion
2 tablespoons butter
6 cups clam broth and steamed clams,
      removed from their shells and diced (p. 333)
3 cups boiled potatoes, cut in cubes
1½ teaspoons salt
⅛ teaspoon pepper
2 cups milk or cream
2 tablespoons flour
2 tablespoons finely chopped fresh parsley
2 tablespoons finely chopped fresh chives

Fry onion in butter until a delicate brown. Add onions and butter to the clams. Heat clams and clam broth in a stockpot over medium heat. Add potatoes, salt, pepper, and milk. Bring to the boiling point. Mix flour with a little cold water to make a smooth paste and add to the chowder. Stir gently until it thickens. Adjust seasonings, garnish with parsley and chives, and serve at once. Serves 6.

CLAM BISQUE

6 cups clam broth and steamed clams,
   removed from the shell and chopped fine (p. 333)
½ cup celery, cut in pieces
2 tablespoons parsley, chopped
2 tablespoons butter
5 tablespoons flour
1 teaspoon salt
⅛ teaspoon pepper
1 cup thin cream
2 cups milk or half and half

Simmer clams, celery, parsley, and broth together 10 minutes. Press through a sieve and keep hot. In another pan, melt butter over medium heat. Add flour, salt, and pepper. Mix to a smooth paste. Add cream and milk. Bring to boiling point, stirring constantly. Add the strained clam liquid. Serve immediately. Serves 6.

LOBSTER BISQUE

2 tablespoons butter
1 medium onion, diced
1 stalk celery, diced
4 tablespoons flour
2 cups cream or milk
2 pounds boiled lobster (p. 338)
2½ cups stock

In a medium saucepan, melt butter. Add onions and celery. Sauté for 10 minutes, until onions and celery have softened. Add flour, stirring until it is incorporated. Slowly add cream, whisking constantly to prevent lumps. Add lobster and stock. Season with salt and pepper to taste. Serves 4.

SHRIMP BISQUE

Follow recipe for lobster bisque (p. 61), substituting canned or boiled shrimp (p. 342) for lobster.

CRAB BISQUE

Follow recipe for lobster bisque (p. 61), substituting boiled crab meat (p. 335) for lobster.

FISH CHOWDER

2 tablespoons butter
1 onion, sliced
6 potatoes, peeled and chopped
2 cups chopped fresh white fish, such as halibut or cod
4 cups milk
1 tablespoon salt
⅛ teaspoon pepper

Melt butter and sauté onion in a saucepan over medium heat, until onion is slightly browned. Add potatoes and 2 cups boiling water. Simmer 10 minutes. Add fish and simmer 20 minutes. Add milk, salt, and pepper. Heat to boiling point. Remove from heat and serve immediately. Serves 6.

CONEY ISLAND CHOWDER

Fish chowder (p. 62)
2 cups canned tomatoes
⅓ cup chopped green peppers
¼ cup chopped celery

To fish chowder, add tomatoes, green peppers, and celery, adding them with the milk. Adjust seasonings to taste. Serves 6.

OLD-FASHIONED SOUTHERN CRAB SOUP

1 dozen "she" crabs
1 tablespoon butter
1 medium onion, diced
⅛ teaspoon pepper
2 cups milk
1 teaspoon flour
½ cup heavy cream
½ teaspoon Worcestershire sauce
1 tablespoon sherry
Salt

Simmer crabs until tender in boiling salted water. This will take about 20 minutes. Pick the meat from the shells and put the crab flakes and the crab eggs in a double boiler. Add butter, onion, and pepper. Simmer gently for 5 minutes. Heat milk almost to boiling and add to the mixture. Thicken with 1 teaspoon flour, blended with a little milk. Add cream, Worcestershire sauce, sherry, and salt to taste. Reheat. Serve immediately. Serves 4.

PEACH SOUP

2 cups water
⅛ teaspoon cinnamon
2 cloves
2 cups peaches
2 cups white wine
Sugar to taste

Heat water and spices to boiling in a medium saucepan. Add peaches. Cook until tender, about 15 minutes. Press through colander. Put back with the juice and boil for a few minutes. Stir in the wine and add sugar to taste. Heat just until boiling point and serve in hot plates or with vanilla ice cream. Cider or grape juice may be used in place of wine. Serves 6.

CHEESE SOUP

½ cup butter
6 tablespoons flour
4 cups whole milk
2 cups grated Cheddar cheese
½ cup chopped onion
2 cups basic chicken stock (p. 32)
Salt
Pepper

Melt 6 tablespoons butter. Add flour, blending well. Pour in milk gradually, stirring constantly. Bring to boil. Add cheese. Remove from heat but keep warm. Melt remaining butter in another pan. Add onion. Sauté to a light brown. Add stock. Mix well and season with salt and pepper to taste. Combine two mixtures. Reheat. Serves 6.

VEGETABLE SOUP (VENETIAN)

1 chopped onion
2 tablespoons olive oil
2 cups canned crushed tomatoes
1 cup steamed rice
1 cup basic chicken stock (p. 32)
½ cup canned garbanzo beans
½ cup boiled carrots (p. 222), chopped
½ cup cooked cabbage (p. 220), chopped
Salt
Pepper
Grated Parmesan cheese

Sauté onion in oil over medium heat until slightly brown. Add tomatoes, rice, and stock. Heat slowly and let simmer, covered, 25 minutes. Add beans, carrots, and cabbage. Season to taste with salt and pepper. Heat 5 minutes longer. Serve with parmesan cheese on the side. Serves 6.

BEEF STEW WITH PASTA

4 cups canned crushed tomatoes
3 chopped onions
1 teaspoon salt
¼ teaspoon red pepper
1 pound chopped beef
1 cup boiled spaghetti or other pasta
2 tablespoons butter, melted

Put tomatoes in saucepan. Add onions, salt, and pepper. Mix well. Let stand 1 hour. Add meat. Bring to boil. Reduce heat. Let simmer 30 minutes. Stir in spaghetti and melted butter. Serve hot. Serves 6.

DANISH GOULASH

2 pounds top round steak, ¼" thick
¼ cup butter or fat
⅛ teaspoon pepper
2½ teaspoons salt
4 medium-sized onions
2 cups boiling water
1 tablespoon brown sugar
6 small bay leaves
4 tablespoons flour
6 tablespoons cold water

Wipe meat with cold, damp cloth. Cut in ¼" cubes. Melt butter in frying pan over medium heat. Add pepper and 2 teaspoons salt. Add meat and brown on all sides over high heat about 10 minutes. Peel onions. Cut in half, lengthwise. Shave paper-thin and add to browning meat cubes. Continue searing for 5 minutes, stirring constantly. Transfer to stockpot. Add boiling water, brown sugar, remaining salt, and bay leaves. Thicken stew with flour, mixed to a smooth paste with cold water. Cook until thickened, stirring well. Serve over hot, mashed potatoes (p. 244) on hot platter. Serves 6.

HUNGARIAN GOULASH

2 pounds beef or veal in any proportion
¼ cup butter
2 sliced onions
1 teaspoon salt
½ teaspoon pepper
½ teaspoon paprika
1 cup canned crushed tomatoes
4 medium-sized potatoes, diced

Wipe meat with cold, damp cloth. Cut in 1" cubes. Melt butter in saucepan. Add meat and onions. Sauté until brown. Add salt, pepper, paprika, and tomatoes. Simmer 30 minutes. Add potatoes and more tomatoes or water if necessary. Cook 30 minutes longer. If desired, 1 cup of cream and ½ cup of water can be substituted for tomatoes.

MINESTRONE

> 1 cup dried white beans
> 1½ tablespoons chopped onion
> 1 stalk celery, chopped
> 1 clove garlic, chopped
> 2 tablespoons chopped parsley
> ¼ cup olive oil
> 1 cup tomato pulp
> 1 cup cabbage, chopped
> Salt
> Pepper
> 1 cup cooked macaroni
> Grated Parmesan cheese

Soak beans in cold water 10 hours. Drain, rinse, and cover with water in a large stockpot. Simmer until tender, adding more water if necessary. Sauté onion, celery, garlic, and parsley in olive oil until brown. Add tomato and cabbage. Season to taste with salt and pepper. Bring to a boil. Add mixture to beans. Add macaroni or rice. Simmer 30 minutes. Serve with grated parmesan cheese. Serves 6.

CHILI CON CARNE

4 pounds ground beef
1 onion, diced
1 teaspoon salt
2 tablespoons chili powder
1 large (28 ounce) can crushed tomatoes
1 can tomato paste
1 large can kidney beans, drained
Sour cream, to garnish
Grated Cheddar cheese, to garnish

Brown beef with onion, salt, and chili powder in a large saucepan or stockpot. Add tomatoes, tomato paste, and kidney beans. Bring to a boil over medium heat. Reduce heat and simmer for 30 minutes, adding more liquid if necessary. Serve with sour cream and grated cheese on the side.

SALADS
AND
SALAD DRESSINGS

With salads, as with most foods, the best results will come from the best ingredients. Lettuce, carrots, and many other salad fixings may be in season year round, but there are many fruits and vegetables for which the season is still very important. Anyone who has had a grainy, tasteless hot house tomato in January and a sweet, juicy tomato in August can attest to this. When fruits and vegetables are in season, they are not only more delicious, but often much cheaper. So it pays to know a little bit about the ingredients. Farmers' markets and farm stands are an excellent source of this kind of seasonal produce. Remember— a ripe, flavorful tomato or some perfectly sweet corn can turn an otherwise a run-of-the-mill salad into something memorable.

Homemade salad dressings are another way to easily improve upon a basic salad. Most of the dressings take just a few moments to make and can be endlessly varied to suit individual tastes. This is a good alternative to buying bottled dressings, which can be filled with sugar and preservatives.

A few word about mayonnaise—the first dressing listed in this chapter. Every good cook should make mayonnaise at least once, because the results are so rewarding. Homemade mayonnaise is richer, creamier, and more complex than any of the commercial alternatives. It is simple to make and hard to forget. Good mayonnaise can be quite habit forming.

MAYONNAISE

1 egg yolk
2 tablespoons vinegar
¼ teaspoon prepared mustard
¾ teaspoon salt
⅛ teaspoon pepper
1 cup salad oil

Combine egg yolk and 1 tablespoon vinegar in a blender. Mix on medium speed. Add mustard, salt, and pepper and blend well. Drop oil a teaspoonful at a time into the egg mixture, blending constantly until ¼ cup oil is added. Then add it in larger quantities, beating thoroughly after each addition. As the mixture thickens, add the remaining vinegar a little at a time. (Half lemon juice and half vinegar may be used.) Refrigerate.

FRUIT SALAD MAYONNAISE

Fold ⅓ cup whipped cream lightly into mayonnaise (above).

RUSSIAN MAYONNAISE

Add ⅓ cup chili sauce and 2 tablespoons chopped green pepper to mayonnaise (above).

HORSERADISH MAYONNAISE

Add 2 tablespoons grated horseradish to recipe for mayonnaise (above).

FRUIT SALAD DRESSING

¼ cup freshly squeezed lime juice
2 tablespoons honey
1 tablespoon fresh mint, finely chopped

Whisk lime juice and honey together. Add mint.

FRENCH DRESSING

1 cup olive oil
3 tablespoons vinegar
1 teaspoon salt
1 teaspoon sugar
⅛ teaspoon pepper
⅛ teaspoon paprika

Mix ingredients and beat or shake until thoroughly mixed.

THOUSAND ISLAND FRENCH DRESSING

Add ¼ cup chopped green pepper, 2 tablespoons chopped, stuffed olives, 1 tablespoon chopped parsley, and 2 tablespoons chopped onion to French dressing (above).

CHILI DRESSING

Add 12 drops Tabasco sauce, 4 tablespoons chili sauce, and 1 tablespoon chopped onion to recipe for French dressing (above).

CREAM CHEESE DRESSING

Add ¼ cup cream cheese to recipe for French dressing (p. 71), beating it in thoroughly.

ALL-PURPOSE FRENCH DRESSING

1 teaspoon salt
2 tablespoons tomato ketchup
2½ teaspoons powdered sugar
⅔ cup orange juice
¼ cup lemon juice
½ cup oil
2 tablespoons olive oil

Combine the salt, ketchup, and sugar. Add alternately the remaining ingredients, beating well after each addition.

ROQUEFORT FRENCH DRESSING

2 teaspoons salt
½ teaspoon black pepper
1 teaspoon paprika
½ teaspoon dry mustard
½ teaspoon powdered sugar
½ cup vinegar
Dash red pepper sauce
1 cup salad or olive oil
1 clove garlic cut in half
2 ounces Roquefort cheese or blue cheese

Combine all ingredients except the cheese and let stand overnight. Then remove garlic from dressing and add the cheese. Mash until fairly smooth.

HONEY FRENCH DRESSING

⅓ cup olive oil
3 tablespoons lemon juice
½ teaspoon salt
⅓ cup honey

Beat together the oil, lemon juice, and salt. Add honey slowly while beating. Serve with fruit salad.

COOKED SALAD DRESSING

½ teaspoon mustard
1½ teaspoons salt
1½ teaspoons sugar
1½ tablespoons flour
⅛ teaspoon paprika
Few grains cayenne
1 beaten egg
1 cup milk
4 tablespoons cider vinegar
1½ tablespoons butter, cold

Mix mustard, salt, sugar, flour, paprika, and cayenne. Add egg and mix thoroughly. Add milk and vinegar. Cook over a double boiler, stirring frequently, until thick. Add butter. Cook and stir until melted.

SOUR CREAM DRESSING

½ cup sour cream
½ teaspoon salt
1 tablespoon tarragon vinegar
1 tablespoon chopped chives or onions
Pepper
Paprika

Mix and beat ingredients together with an eggbeater, beating until light.

VINAIGRETTE DRESSING

1 teaspoon salt
⅛ teaspoon paprika
⅛ teaspoon pepper
⅓ cup oil
2 tablespoons cider vinegar or balsamic vinegar
1 tablespoon chopped parsley (optional)

Mix all ingredients. Chill.

PINEAPPLE DRESSING

2 cups crushed pineapple
2 tablespoons freshly squeezed lime juice
1 tablespoon honey
¼ cup cilantro, finely diced
1 jalapeño, seeded and diced (optional)
Salt
Pepper
Cayenne

Mix pineapple, lime juice, honey, cilanto, and jalapeño. Allow to sit for at least 20 minutes, so the flavors can mix. Add salt, pepper, and cayenne. Serve cold or at room temperature.

GRAPEFRUIT VINAIGRETTE

½ cup olive oil
⅓ cup grapefruit juice
1 tablespoon honey
1 teaspoon fresh tarragon
Salt
Pepper

Mix olive oil, grapefruit juice, honey, and tarragon in a blender. Add salt and pepper to taste.

SLAW DRESSING

3 egg yolks
½ cup sugar
2 tablespoons butter
1 tablespoon salt
1 cup cream or milk
1 cup vinegar
⅛ teaspoon cayenne
3 egg whites

Mix egg yolks, sugar, butter, salt, cream or milk, vinegar, and cayenne. Beat well. Beat egg whites until stiff and fold in. Cook in double boiler until thickened.

GERMAN SALAD DRESSING

2 cups milk
2 tablespoons flour
2 tablespoons cold water
2 tablespoons sugar
1 teaspoon butter
½ teaspoon celery salt
1 well-beaten egg
Salt
Pepper
3 tablespoons mustard
2 tablespoons vinegar

Bring milk to a boil in double boiler. Mix flour to a smooth paste with water and add to milk, blending well. Add sugar, butter, celery salt, and egg. Stir vigorously to combine. Season to taste with salt and pepper. Cool. Add mustard and vinegar. Beat thoroughly.

BACON SALAD DRESSING

⅔ cup cider vinegar
⅓ cup bacon fat
3 slices bacon, cooked and crumbled
1 tablespoon maple syrup
Pepper

Mix vinegar with bacon fat. Add chopped bacon, maple syrup, and pepper to taste.

LETTUCE AND TOMATO SALAD

Chill lettuce leaves and tomatoes. Arrange lettuce on platter or individual dishes. Top with tomato slices or quarters. Serve with French dressing (p. 71) or vinaigrette (p. 74).

MIXED GREEN SALAD

> 6 lettuce leaves
> 1 cup thinly sliced Chinese cabbage
> 6 romaine leaves
> 1 tablespoon minced onion
> 6 escarole leaves
> French dressing (p. 71) or vinaigrette (p. 74)

Rub bowl with garlic. Arrange the greens in layers and sprinkle with minced onion. Add dressing and toss. Serves 6.

Other suitable combinations for mixed greens are:

- Chicory, sliced green pepper, lettuce, romaine, watercress.
- Cucumber slices, garlic slices, green pepper slices, lettuce, sliced radishes, chopped scallions.
- Cucumber slices, radish slices, romaine.
- Curly endive, lettuce, spinach.
- Green pepper, green olives, diced pimento, romaine.

ENDIVE SALAD

Wash endives. Drain. Separate leaves or slice into halves or quarters. Rinse in cold water and either spin dry or drain dry. Serve with French dressing (p. 71).

SPINACH AND BLUE CHEESE SALAD

Wash the tender inside leaves of spinach. Rinse in ice-cold water. Spin leaves or allow them to drain dry. Crumble blue cheese generously over the spinach. Serve with bacon salad dressing (p. 76). Diced hard-boiled eggs (p. 272) would make an excellent addition to the salad.

SLICED CUCUMBERS

Chill cucumbers. Wash, dry, peel, and slice thin. Sprinkle with French dressing (p. 71) a few minutes before serving. Or, season to taste at the table with lemon juice, salt, and pepper.

CARROT SALAD

  2 cups chopped carrots
  1 cup chopped celery
  1 cup chopped walnuts
  1 tablespoon chopped onion
  1 tablespoon chopped parsley
  ⅓ cup mayonnaise (p. 70)

Mix thoroughly. Chill. Serves 6.

STUFFED TOMATO SALAD

6 medium-sized tomatoes
2 cups boiled shrimp (p. 342)
1 cup celery, cut in pieces
1 teaspoon chopped parsley
½ teaspoon salt
⅛ teaspoon pepper
Mayonnaise (p. 70)

Put tomatoes in boiling water for a moment to loosen skins. Peel and chill. Cut slices from the stem end and scoop out some of the pulp. Cut shrimp in pieces and add celery, parsley, salt, and pepper. Moisten with mayonnaise. Fill the tomatoes with the shrimp mixture. Garnish with a spoonful of mayonnaise and a whole shrimp. Serve on crisp lettuce leaves. Crab meat may be used in place of shrimp. Serves 6. Other suggestions for stuffing tomato are:

- Mixture of chopped celery, diced cucumber, tomato pulp, chopped parsley, mayonnaise (p. 70).
- Mixture of chopped celery, chopped walnuts, tomato pulp, chopped parsley, mayonnaise (p. 70).
- Boiled asparagus tips (p. 210) and mayonnaise (p. 70).

TOMATO WITH CHEESE BALL

Cut slice from stem end of tomato. Scoop out some of pulp. Drop in a small ball of cottage cheese. Sprinkle with salt and pepper. Allow 1 tomato per serving.

DEVILED EGG SALAD IN TOMATO CUPS

8 medium tomatoes
2 teaspoons salt
Dash of cayenne
16 hard-boiled eggs (p. 272)
1 cup minced celery
2 tablespoons minced onion
½ cup freshly squeezed lemon juice
4 teaspoons prepared mustard
½ cup mayonnaise (p. 70)

Wash tomatoes and remove the stem end. Then cut each tomato into fourths without cutting all the way through. Press back the petals and sprinkle on the inside with salt and cayenne. Chill. Meanwhile chop the shelled hard-cooked eggs and add the remaining ingredients. Mix well and spoon some of this mixture in the center of the tomatoes that have been arranged on individual beds of lettuce. Serves 8.

POTATO SALAD

5 diced, cold, boiled potatoes
½ cup French dressing (p. 71)
1 ½ cups sliced celery
½ teaspoon onion, chopped
2 tablespoons parsley, chopped
1 teaspoon salt
⅛ teaspoon paprika
½ cup mayonnaise (p. 70)
2 hard-boiled eggs (p. 272), chopped (for garnish)
Olives (for garnish)

Marinate potatoes in French dressing. Chill. Mix all ingredients. Garnish with hard-boiled egg slices and olives. Serves 6.

HOT GERMAN POTATO SALAD

3 pounds hot, boiled, sliced potatoes
1 onion, chopped
1 tablespoon chopped parsley
2 tablespoons olive oil
1 tablespoon flour
1 tablespoon sugar
⅓ cup white wine vinegar
4 slices bacon, cooked and diced (optional)
½ cup green onions, chopped
Salt
Pepper

Mix potatoes with half of the onion and all of the parsley. Sauté remaining onion in oil until soft. Add flour and blend well. Add sugar, vinegar, and ⅓ cup water. Bring to boil, stirring constantly. Add potatoes, bacon, and green onions piece by piece, mixing well. Season with salt and pepper. Serve hot or cold. Serves 6.

SWEET POTATO SALAD

2 cups diced, cold, boiled sweet potatoes (p. 259)
1 cup chopped celery
1 tablespoon chopped bell pepper
1 tablespoon chopped onion
1 tablespoon chopped parsley
½ cup mayonnaise (p. 70)
Salt
Pepper

Mix thoroughly. Season with salt and pepper to taste. Chill for at least 1 hour. Serves 6.

COLE SLAW

½ cup cream
½ cup sugar
½ cup vinegar
1 teaspoon salt
½ teaspoon pepper
1 young cabbage
1 medium carrot, grated

Beat cream, sugar, vinegar, salt, and pepper together thoroughly until the dressing is thick like whipped cream. Discard outer leaves of cabbage. Shred finely and combine with carrots and dressing just before it is ready to serve. Serves 6.

CARROT AND BELL PEPPER SALAD

1 chopped bell pepper
1 cup chopped carrots
3 cups chopped cabbage
¼ cup chopped onion
2 tablespoons chopped parsley
2 tablespoons mayonnaise (p. 70)
1 tablespoon squeezed lemon juice
Salt
Pepper

Mix thoroughly. Season to taste with salt and pepper. Chill for at least 1 hour. Serves 6.

PEA SALAD

2½ cups frozen green peas
1 chopped onion
¼ cup chopped celery
¼ cup chopped nuts
¼ cup French dressing (p. 71)
Head of lettuce, for serving

Cook peas according to directions on container. Drain. Mix with onion, celery, nuts, and French dressing. Arrange on lettuce leaves. Serves 6.

SPINACH SALAD

4 cups fresh spinach
½ cup vinaigrette (p. 74)
1 sliced, hard-boiled egg (p. 272)
4 ounces parmesan or other hard cheese, shaved

Cut off spinach stems. Rinse thoroughly and either spin or drip dry. Mix with salad dressing. Top with eggs and cheese. Serves 6.

CHEESE, NUT, AND AVOCADO SALAD

1 head lettuce, preferably butter or Romaine
2 teaspoons lemon juice
2 tablespoons (or to taste) grapefruit vinaigrette (p. 75)
⅛ teaspoon salt
⅛ teaspoon paprika
4 ounces Cheddar, grated or cut into small cubes
¼ cup toasted salted almonds or sunflower seeds
2 tomatoes, thinly sliced
1 avocado, peeled and cut into small pieces

Break lettuce into leaves, discarding the tough stems and any imperfections. Gently clean and either spin or drip dry. Toss lettuce with lemon juice, vinaigrette, salt, and paprika in a serving bowl. Top with cheese, almonds, tomatoes, and avocado. Serve immediately.

PASTA SALAD

1 cup boiled macaroni
½ cup diced celery
½ cup diced carrots
½ cup boiled green peas
1 tablespoon chopped onion
½ cup mayonnaise (p. 70)
Salt
Pepper

Mix thoroughly. Season with salt and pepper to taste. Chill for at least an hour. Serves 6.

COTTAGE CHEESE SALAD

1 cup cottage cheese
¼ cup cream
1 green pepper, sliced into rings
½ cup alfalfa sprouts
2 tablespoons chopped nuts
½ teaspoon paprika
Salt
Pepper

Blend cheese and cream. Put mounds of cheese in center of pepper rings. Toss with some sprouts. Sprinkle with nuts, paprika, salt, and pepper. Serves 6.

CORN SALAD

2½ cups canned corn
8 tomatoes
1 chopped jalapeño or pimento
1 chopped onion
1 chopped green pepper
1 cup diced cucumber
2 tablespoons chopped cilantro
Cayenne
Paprika
Salt
Pepper
2 tablespoons freshly squeezed lime juice
2 tablespoons honey

Drain the corn. Scoop out the center of the tomatoes, making shells. Mix the tomato centers with the corn, jalapeño or pimento, onion, green pepper, cucumber, and seasonings. Blend lime juice and honey. Pour over the corn mixture. Fill tomato cups with the mixture. Chill, if desired. Serves 8.

MARBLED LETTUCE

1 head lettuce, preferably butter or Boston
3 ounces cream cheese
1 tablespoon minced green pepper
2 tablespoons diced tomatoes
2 tablespoons carrots, grated
¼ teaspoon salt
⅛ teaspoon Worcestershire sauce
⅛ teaspoon pepper
⅛ teaspoon minced onion
¼ tablespoon salt

Remove loose outer leaves from head of lettuce. With a sharp knife core it as you would an apple and remove the entire heart. Add vegetables and seasonings to the cream cheese and pack tightly in center of lettuce. Wrap in damp cloth and saran wrap and chill in refrigerator until ready to use. Slice head in quarters. Serves 4.

FRUIT SALAD

1 grapefruit
3 oranges
1 banana
3 slices pineapple
½ pound seedless red grapes

Peel grapefruit and oranges. Separate segments, discarding white membrane. Cut banana and pineapple in small cubes. Skin and seed grapes. Mix all ingredients. Drain. Serve with fruit salad dressing (p. 71). Serves 6.

WALDORF SALAD

3 cups diced apples
1 cup celery cut in pieces
½ cup walnuts cut in pieces
¾ cup mayonnaise (p. 70)
Lettuce leaves (for serving)

Mix apple, nuts, and celery. Moisten with mayonnaise. Arrange on crisp leaves of lettuce and garnish with whole walnuts. Serves 6.

TROPICAL FRUIT SALAD

1 pineapple, peeled, cored, and cut into chunks
1 mango, peeled and diced
1 banana, peeled and sliced
1 star fruit, sliced
1 guava, seeded and diced
1 tablespoon lime juice
Sugar to taste
Fresh mint leaves, for garnish

Combine fruit. Drizzle lime juice over the salad, and sprinkle a little sugar. Chill. Garnish with mint leaves, if desired.

FRUIT AND NUT SALAD

1 cup diced pineapple
1 cup sliced bananas
1 cup diced oranges
Fruit salad dressing (p. 71)
¼ cup chopped walnuts
Whipped cream (optional)

Mix fruits in a salad bowl. Pour fruit salad dressing (p. 71) over the mixture. Sprinkle with nuts. Garnish with whipped cream, if desired. Serves 6.

GRAPEFRUIT AND PEAR SALAD

3 ripe pears
2 grapefruits
Arugula
Grapefruit vinaigrette (p. 75)
2 ounces blue cheese, crumbled
¼ cup toasted walnuts

Cut pears in half, then peel and remove their cores. Cut into thin slices. Peel grapefruit, and remove the segments, discarding the white membrane. In a salad bowl, toss arugula, pears, and grapefruit with vinaigrette. Sprinkle with blue cheese and walnuts.

AVOCADO SALAD

1 large avocado
2 cups finely chopped fresh tomatoes
1 small onion, chopped
⅓ cup cottage cheese
1 tablespoon olive oil
1 tablespoon lemon juice or vinegar
1 teaspoon salt
Pepper

Peel avocado, remove pit and chop into small pieces. Toss with remaining ingredients in a salad bowl until thoroughly combined with oil and seasonings. Serves 6.

QUICK HUMMUS

2 cups canned chickpeas, drained
⅓ cup tahini (sesame paste)
Juice of 2 lemons
1 teaspoon salt, or to taste
3 cloves garlic
1 tablespoon olive oil
Pinch paprika
1 teaspoon fresh parsley, finely diced

Combine all of the ingredients, except parsley, in a blender. Blend on high until the hummus has reached a smooth, creamy consistency. Additional lemon juice or olive oil may be added if the mixture is too thick to blend. Season to taste and garnish with parsley. Makes 2 cups.

MOLDED FRUIT SALAD

   2 tablespoons lemon or orange gelatin
   ⅓ cup cold water
   2 tablespoons sugar
   1 cup orange soda
   1 cup cherry soda
   ½ cup pineapple, cubed
   ½ cup maraschino cherries, halved
   ½ cup white grapes, halved

Soak gelatin in cold water. Dissolve over boiling water. Add sugar. Cool. Add sodas. Chill. When slightly stiffened, after about 30 minutes, add fruits. Pour into gelatin mold, if desired. Chill again, until gelatin is set. Serves 8.

GINGER ALE FRUIT SALAD

   2 tablespoons unflavored gelatin
   ¼ cup cold water
   ½ cup boiling water
   ¼ cup lemon juice
   2 tablespoons sugar
   1 cup ginger ale
   1 cup seedless grapes
   1 banana
   1 apple
   2 oranges

Soak gelatin in cold water for 5 minutes and then dissolve in boiling water. Add lemon juice, sugar and ginger ale. Chill. Cut grapes in half. Slice banana. Peel and chop apple. Separate oranges into sections and remove membranes. When ginger ale mixture begins to thicken, after about 30 minutes, fold in fruit. Turn into gelatin molds and chill. Serve with fruit salad dressing (p. 71). Serves 6.

CRANBERRY SALAD

    1 package unflavored gelatin
    1⅓ cups sugar
    1 cup strained, unsweetened cranberry sauce,
        heated (p. 429)*
    2 tablespoons lemon juice
    1 cup ginger ale
    1 cup crushed drained pineapple

Dissolve gelatin and sugar in hot cranberry sauce. When cool add lemon juice, ginger ale, and pineapple. When slightly congealed, turn into gelatin mold, if desired. When firm, unmold. Serves 6.

* This recipe already contains sugar. Remember that the cranberry sauce recipe should be unsweetened.

PEACH AND PECAN SALAD

    8 peach halves
    2 cups cottage cheese
    2 tablespoons sugar
    1 teaspoon cinnamon
    1 tablespoon melted butter
    1 cup pecans, chopped

Place the peach halves, hollow side up on a plate. Place a spoonful of cottage cheese in each half. Combine sugar, cinnamon, melted butter, and pecans. Sprinkle the mixture over the peaches. Serves 8.

FROZEN FRUIT SALAD

6 ounces cream cheese
½ cup heavy cream
2 tablespoons sugar
2 peaches, peeled and diced
1 pear, peeled and diced
1 banana, peeled and sliced
10 cherries, pitted and diced
½ cup chopped nuts
Fresh mint, for garnish

Mash cream cheese with a spoon until softened. Whip cream with sugar. Fold into cream cheese. Fold fruit and nuts into first mixture. Pack into a 10" baking pan. Freeze until firm, but not quite solid, about an hour. Serve in small bowls and garnish with a sprig of mint. Serves 8.

FROZEN PINEAPPLE SALAD

½ cup cream cheese
1½ cups cream, whipped
½ pound marshmallows cut fine
1 small can crushed pineapple
1 cup ginger ale
Maraschino cherries for garnish

Mash the cream cheese with a spoon until softened. Add whipped cream, marshmallows, pineapple, and ginger ale. Blend well. Freeze until firm, but not solid. Cut into squares and serve with cherries as garnish. Serves 6.

CRABMEAT SALAD

1 head lettuce
1 pound lump crabmeat
Juice of 1 lemon
Mayonnaise (p. 70)
Salt
Pepper

Clean the lettuce and arrange into 6 nests about 4" across. Mix crabmeat, lemon juice, and enough mayonnaise to hold the crabmeat together when pressed into a small cup. Season to taste with salt and pepper. Invert the contents of the cup into a lettuce nest and repeat. Put a spoonful of mayonnaise over each. Not over 1 cup (total) of chopped celery, apple, hard-boiled egg (p. 272), olives, etc., may be mixed with the crabmeat if desired. Serves 6.

SHRIMP SALAD

1 pound boiled shrimp (p. 342)
2 cups finely minced celery
Juice of 1 lemon
Mayonnaise (p. 70)
Salt
Paprika
1 head lettuce

Dice the shrimp and mix with celery, lemon juice, mayonnaise, and seasoning. Clean the lettuce and arrange into 6 nests about 4" across. Use a small cup as a mold, fill with the shrimp mixture and press firm; invert the molded contents into each lettuce nest. Top with a teaspoon of mayonnaise and a sprinkle of paprika. Serves 6.

SHRIMP AND GREEN PEA SALAD
IN GREEN PEPPER CUPS

1 cup boiled shrimp (p. 342)
1 cup boiled green peas (p. 240)
½ cup mayonnaise (p. 70)
Salt
Pepper
6 green peppers
Lettuce

Remove veins from shrimp. Mix shrimp and peas. Moisten with mayonnaise. Season to taste with salt and pepper. Wash green peppers. Slice off top. Remove seeds. Fill with shrimp-pea mixture. Chill. Serve on lettuce, garnished with mayonnaise if desired. Serves 6.

CHICKEN SALAD

3 diced cold chicken
2¼ cups chopped celery
⅔ cup mayonnaise
2 tablespoons freshly squeezed lemon juice
Salt
Pepper

Mix chicken and chopped celery. Add mayonnaise and lemon juice, stirring to combine. Use more mayonnaise if desired. Season with salt and pepper to taste.

CHICKEN SALAD SUPREME

1 cup cold chopped cooked chicken
1 cup diced celery
¼ cup chopped walnuts
½ cup mayonnaise (p. 70)
Salt
Pepper
Lettuce
6 stuffed olives

Mix chicken, celery, walnuts, and mayonnaise. Season to taste with salt and pepper. Form into mounds on beds of lettuce in 6 salad plates. Top each mound with an olive. Serves 6. Boiled asparagus tips (p. 210), chopped green pepper, shredded or chopped cooked cabbage (p. 220), diced cooked ham, chopped celery, diced cucumbers, capers, sautéed mushrooms (p. 235), ripe olives, diced pineapple, diced crisp bacon, cubed tomatoes, and hard-boiled eggs (p. 272) are also excellent additions to chicken salad, whether in combination or alone.

CURRIED CHICKEN SALAD

2 cups cooked, diced chicken
½ cup celery, diced
½ cup carrot, grated
½ cup raisins
⅔ cup mayonnaise
1 tablespoon curry powder
Salt
Pepper

Combine chicken, celery, carrot, and raisins. Stir mayonnaise and curry powder together and add to chicken mixture. Season to taste with salt and pepper.

HAM SALAD

2 cups diced cold ham
1 teaspoon chopped onion
1 tablespoon chopped parsley
1 tablespoon chopped pickle
2 chopped hard-boiled eggs (p. 272)
½ cup French dressing (p. 71) or mayonnaise (p. 70)
Salt
Pepper

Mix ingredients. Allow mixture to marinate in the refrigerator for 30 minutes before serving. If desired, 1 cup shredded cabbage may be added to this. Other appropriate dressings are Russian dressing (p. 70), horseradish dressing (p. 70), chili dressing (p. 71), cooked salad dressing (p. 73), or bacon salad dressing (p. 76).

MACARONI AND OLIVE SALAD

1 cup boiled macaroni or other small pasta
1 cup chopped celery
¾ cup olives, pitted and diced
1 tablespoon chopped onion
1 tablespoon chopped parsley
½ cup mayonnaise (p. 70)
Salt
Pepper

Mix thoroughly and season to taste. Chill before serving. Serves 6.

COTTAGE CHEESE AND STRAWBERRY SALAD

2 cups cottage cheese
2 cups strawberries, hulled and sliced
3 tablespoons honey
Lettuce
Fresh mint (for garnish)

Mix cottage cheese, strawberries, and honey. Scoop about ⅔ cup of the mixture onto a lettuce leaf. Repeat for each serving. Garnish with sprigs of mint. Serves 6.

WINTER VEGETABLE SALAD BOWL

½ head lettuce
1 cup boiled cauliflower (p. 224)
1 cup string beans (p. 213)
1 cup boiled beets (p. 217)
6 boiled carrots (p. 222), cut into fourths, lengthwise
½ cup vinaigrette (p. 74)

Arrange lettuce in a salad bowl. Arrange the cauliflower, string beans, and beets in separate piles. Then place long pieces of carrot between each pile of vegetables. Pour salad dressing over the vegetables and chill ½ hour in the refrigerator. Serves 6.

RASPBERRY RING WITH PINEAPPLE

1 package raspberry-flavored gelatin
Syrup drained from pineapple and water to make 2 cups
1 cup evaporated milk, chilled
1 tablespoon lemon juice
1 14-ounce can pineapple chunks, drained
1 pint red raspberries
8 sprigs of mint
Powdered sugar

Dissolve gelatin in hot syrup and water. When it begins to set, whip evaporated milk until very stiff. Add lemon juice and fold into gelatin. Pour into a ring mold that has been rinsed in cold water. Refrigerate until set. When ready to serve, unmold on a cold platter. Fill center with pineapple chunks that have been thoroughly chilled and well drained. Top with red raspberries. Garnish with sprigs of mint dipped in powdered sugar to make edges frosty. Serves 8.

WREATH SALAD

1 14-ounce can unsweetened sliced pineapple, chilled
1 3-ounce package cream cheese
Small seedless white grapes
Watercress
2 tablespoons fresh mint
½ cup orange juice

Drain pineapple slices that have been well chilled in can. Spread one side of each slice with cream cheese that has been softened with a fork. Top cream cheese with a double row of grapes that have been cut in half lengthwise, placing cut side next to cheese. Chill in refrigerator ½ hour. Serve each slice on salad plate. Garnish with watercress. Serve with orange mint dressing which has been made by blending mint with orange juice. Serves 4.

HAWAIIAN CHICKEN SALAD

2½ cups cooked chicken, cut into ½" chunks
1 14 ounce can pineapple chunks, drained
1 cup celery, diced
3 tablespoons olive oil
2 tablespoons lemon juice
¼ teaspoon salt
5 tablespoons mayonnaise (p. 70)
Greens (lettuce or fresh spinach)
¼ cup slivered almonds

Combine chicken, pineapple chunks, and celery. Mix salad oil, lemon juice, and salt. Marinate salad for 1 hour. Then add mayonnaise and mix well. Serve on a bed of greens and sprinkle almonds over the top. Serves 6.

PINEAPPLE BANANA CRISSCROSS

3 ripe bananas
6 slices canned pineapple
2 cups raspberries or cherries
Fresh mint, for garnishing
Fruit salad dressing (p. 71)

Peel and cut bananas lengthwise into quarters. Place 2 quarters on salad plate, crossing one over the other. Cut through one side of pineapple slice and twist into S-shape so that it will stand upright where the banana pieces cross. Place a mound of berries beside the banana. Garnish with mint. Serve immediately with fruit salad dressing (p. 71). Serves 6.

RUSSIAN COLESLAW

Coleslaw (p. 82)
½ cup white wine vinegar
2 cups sour cream
Salt
Paprika
2 tablespoons chopped onion

Serve coleslaw with a sauce made by beating together vinegar with sour cream. Season to taste with salt, paprika, and chopped onion.

SANDWICHES

Sandwich-making possibilities are only limited by the imagination of the maker. This chapter has a number of suggested combinations, but they should be viewed as a jumping-off point. Remember that almost anything can go in a sandwich!

From tortillas to cornbread to pitas and beyond, the possibilities begin with the bread. Some sandwiches are more suited to certain types of bread than others. Tortillas and pitas are great for spreads, for example, while cornbread and ham are a natural combination. Don't be afraid to try a new version of a favorite sandwich. Peanut butter and jelly, spread thinly on a tortilla and rolled up, makes for a nice variation on a lunchtime classic.

The options for fillings are even more varied. Tired of peanut butter? Try almond or hazelnut butter. Tired of tuna? Try canned salmon. Tired of grocery store mayonnaise? Try making it (p. 70). It tastes wonderful, and it only takes a few minutes to make.

Cheeses are another excellent way to bring new life to sandwiches. Cheddar, for example, comes in dozens of varieties, and it's only one of the hundreds of types of cheese out there. Most grocery stores now carry a wide selection of cheeses. Try making a toasted cheese sandwich (p. 107) with Brie, or making a hot ham and cheese (p. 106) with Gruyère. A nice cheese can really improve an otherwise ordinary sandwich.

THREE-DECKER TURKEY CLUB SANDWICHES

12 slices toasted sandwich bread
Butter, for toast
4 large lettuce leaves
Mayonnaise (p. 70)
8 slices of roast turkey (or other roast meat)
8 slices crisp bacon
4 thin slices of a sweet onion (e.g. Vidalia)
4 slices of tomato

Take toasted bread. Butter 1 side of 4 slices and place, butter side up, on dish. Cover each with a lettuce leaf. Brush with mayonnaise. Add 2 slices of turkey to each. Spread with more mayonnaise. Butter 4 more slices of toast on both sides. Put on sandwich. Add 2 slices of crisp bacon and onion or tomato slices to each sandwich. Spread with more mayonnaise. Butter third slice of toast and place, butter side down, on sandwich. Cut diagonally. Makes 4 sandwiches.

CHILLED CUCUMBER CHECKERBOARDS

3 slices white sandwich bread
3 slices whole wheat sandwich bread
Cream cheese, softened to a spreadable consistency
½ cucumber, peeled and very thinly sliced

Remove crusts from the bread. Spread a slice of white bread with cream cheese and cucumber slices, and place a slice of whole wheat bread on top. Spread this bread with a thin layer of cream cheese and cucumber. Place on it a slice of white bread, making whole wheat bread the middle layer. Set aside. Repeat this process with remaining slices, beginning with whole wheat this time so that a slice of white bread is the middle layer. Trim each pile evenly, and cut each pile in 3 slices, each 1" thick. Spread these slices with cream cheese and cucumbers as well. Put together in such a way that a white block will alternate with a whole wheat one, forming a checkerboard at ends. There will be 2 "checkered" loaves. Wrap each loaf in waxed paper or saran wrap, and place in refrigerator to chill. When ready to serve, slice about ¼" thick. Serves 4.

CHILLED PINWHEELS

>   1 loaf Pullman bread,* unsliced
>   Butter or cream cheese, softened
>   1 bunch watercress or 1 green pepper, seeded and cut
>   into thin strips
>   Salt
>   Pepper

Remove the crust from top and sides of a fresh loaf of bread. With a sharp knife, cut bread lengthwise in slices ⅛" to ¼" thick. Discard bottom crust. Spread the long slices of bread with butter, cream cheese or any very smooth spread. Lay alternating strips of green pepper or watercress, crosswise, 1" apart, over entire strip of bread. Sprinkle with salt and pepper. Beginning at one end, roll the bread as for jelly roll. Spread a little soft butter on the last lap of bread to make it stick, wrap the small rolls in waxed paper or saran wrap and place in refrigerator to chill. When ready to serve, slice about ¼" thick. Serves 4.

* Pullman bread is a large, white rectangular loaf which may have originated in the early 1930s as the bread served on Pullman railway cars.

CLUB SANDWICH

8 slices of sandwich bread
Butter, at room temperature
4 large lettuce leaves
Mayonnaise (p. 70)
Sliced cooked chicken, as desired
1 tomato, thinly sliced
8 slices crisp bacon
Salt
Pepper

Toast bread. Spread one side with butter. Lay a crisp lettuce leaf on the 4 slices of bread, and spread with mayonnaise. On top of lettuce put layers of sliced chicken, sliced tomatoes, and crisp bacon. Season well with salt and pepper and cover with top piece of toast. Cut in halves diagonally. Makes 4 sandwiches.

THANKSGIVING TURKEY SANDWICH

8 slices of sandwich bread
Butter, at room temperature
8 slices of roast turkey
Salt
Pepper
4 slices of cooked ham
¼ cup cranberry sauce (p. 429)
Mayonnaise (p. 70)

Spread softened butter on bread. Place slices of turkey meat on 4 pieces bread, using more turkey if desired. Season to taste with salt and pepper. Add a slice of ham and 1 tablespoon of cranberry sauce. Dot generously with mayonnaise. Top each with another of slice bread. Cut diagonally. Makes 4 sandwiches.

OPEN-FACED BACON, CHEESE
AND TOMATO SANDWICH

4 slices of sandwich bread
Butter, at room temperature
4 large slices Cheddar cheese, more as needed
4 slices of tomato
Salt
Pepper
Mayonnaise (p. 70)
8 strips of uncooked bacon

Turn on broiler. Spread slices of bread lightly with butter. Cover each with thin slices of Cheddar, enough to nearly cover the bread. Then put slices of tomato on the cheese and sprinkle with salt and pepper. Lay 2 strips of bacon over the top. Put in broiler and broil until cheese melts and bacon is crisp. Makes 4 sandwiches.

STEAK SANDWICH

4 thin slices of steak, uncooked
8 slices of sandwich bread, toasted and buttered
Salt
Pepper
8 slices of crisp bacon
1 tomato, thinly sliced
Fried onions (p. 238)

Broil the slices of steak rare (in the same manner as the thicker steak on p. 350). Place steak on 4 slices of toast. Add 2 slices bacon to each. Season to taste with salt, pepper, and mayonnaise (p. 70) or any favorite meat sauce. Top with slice of tomato, fried onions, and another slice of buttered toast. Cut diagonally. Makes 4 sandwiches.

CHICKEN SALAD SANDWICH

2 cups cold cooked chicken
1 cup celery, finely diced
Salt
Pepper
½ cup mayonnaise (p. 70), or to taste
8 slices of sandwich bread

Mix chicken, cut in small cubes, with celery. Season to taste with salt and pepper. Moisten with mayonnaise. Spread about ½ cup of the mixture between 2 slices of bread. Cut in halves diagonally. Makes 4 sandwiches.

HOT HAM AND CHEESE SANDWICH

8 slices of sandwich bread
2 tablespoons butter, plus more for spreading
4 thin slices of cooked ham
4 slices of Cheddar cheese
¾ cup milk
1 well-beaten egg
¼ teaspoon salt

Spread bread lightly with butter. On 4 slices, arrange a slice of ham and a thin slice of cheese. Put another slice of bread on top. In a separate bowl, mix milk, egg, and salt together. Melt 2 tablespoons butter in a skillet over medium-high heat. Dip each sandwich in the milk mixture and immediately sauté in butter until brown on both sides. Drain on paper towels. Add more butter to the skillet between sandwiches, if necessary. Serve hot. This sandwich is also excellent with a fried egg (p. 272). Makes 4 sandwiches.

TOASTED CHEESE SANDWICHES

½ pound of Cheddar or Monterey Jack, thinly sliced
8 slices of sandwich bread
2 tablespoons butter

Place slices of cheese between 2 slices buttered bread. Brown sandwiches on both sides by broiling, grilling or toasting. Thinly sliced apples or tomatoes make an excellent addition. Serve hot. Makes 4 sandwiches.

OPEN-FACED CHEESE SANDWICH

1 pound Cheddar cheese
1 teaspoon Worcestershire sauce
1 teaspoon mustard
1 egg
½ teaspoon baking powder
2 tablespoons milk
Dash of cayenne
8 slices sandwich bread

Preheat oven to 500°F. Finely grate cheese. Rub in other ingredients and mix to a creamy consistency. Spread on slices of bread. Bake to a light brown, about 5 minutes. Check the sandwiches frequently, to make sure they don't burn. The bread should be crispy on the edges and the cheese mixture should be puffy. Serve at once. Makes 8 sandwiches.

CHEESE DREAMS

8 slices sandwich bread
½ pound Cheddar, thinly sliced
Salt
Paprika
Dash of cayenne
1 beaten egg
½ cup milk
2 tablespoons butter

Place slices of cheese on 4 slices of bread. Sprinkle cheese with salt, paprika, and cayenne. Top with other slices of bread. In a shallow bowl, mix egg, milk, and ¼ teaspoon salt. Cut sandwiches in halves and dip in egg mixture. Fry in butter over medium-high heat until brown on both sides. Drain on paper towels and serve hot. Add butter to skillet between sandwiches if necessary. Makes 4 sandwiches.

TUNA CLUB SANDWICH

1 tomato, thinly sliced
8 slices sandwich bread, toasted
4 large lettuce leaves
1 can of tuna
2 tablespoons mayonnaise (p. 70), more to taste
1 teaspoon prepared mustard
1 teaspoon lemon juice
2 tablespoons finely diced celery
Salt
Pepper

Arrange slices of tomato on 4 slices of toast. Cover with lettuce leaves. Mix tuna, mayonnaise, mustard, lemon juice, and celery in a separate bowl. Season to taste with salt and pepper. Spread this mixture on the lettuce. Top with remaining slices of bread. Cut diagonally. Makes 4 sandwiches.

SPICY SHRIMP SALAD

1¼ cups boiled shrimp (p. 342)
¼ cup finely chopped sweet pickle
¼ cup chopped celery
1 teaspoon lemon juice
1 teaspoon grated onion
Salt
Pepper
2 teaspoons horseradish
¼ cup mayonnaise (p. 70)

Chop shrimp into small pieces. Add pickle, celery, lemon juice, and grated onion. Mix thoroughly. Add salt and pepper to taste. Combine horseradish and mayonnaise with shrimp mixture. Spread on buttered slices of bread or use for making canapés. Yield: 2 cups spread.

BANANA AND PEANUT BUTTER SANDWICH

8 slices bread
Peanut butter
2 bananas, sliced
2 tablespoons honey

Spread 4 slices bread with peanut butter. Place banana slices on peanut butter. Drizzle honey over remaining slices of bread and use to top sandwiches. Makes 4 sandwiches.

HUMMUS AND AVOCADO PITA

1 avocado
1 teaspoon lemon juice (optional)
1 tomato
4 pitas or other small flat bread
Hummus (p. 89)
Salt
Pepper
Sprouts (optional)

Cut avocado in half and remove the pit. Cut thin slices of avocado. Sprinkle with lemon juice to prevent browning, if desired. Thinly slice the tomato. Cut open pitas and spread a thin layer of hummus all around the inside. Add ¼ of the avocado and tomato slices to each pita. Season to taste with salt and pepper. Add sprouts, if desired. Makes 4 pitas.

WELSH RAREBIT

2 tablespoons butter
2 tablespoons flour
¼ teaspoon dry mustard
½ teaspoon salt
Dash cayenne
1 cup half-and-half
1½ cups grated mild cheese
1 egg
Toast

Melt butter in a medium saucepan. Add flour, mustard, salt, and cayenne and mix well. Add half-and-half slowly and bring to boiling point over medium heat, stirring constantly. Add cheese and stir until melted. Remove from heat. Beat the egg well and mix into the hot cheese sauce. Blend. Serve hot on buttered pieces of toast. Serves 4.

RAREBIT SUPREME

2 tablespoons butter
1½ tablespoons chopped onion
2 tablespoons chopped green pepper
2 tablespoons flour
1 teaspoon salt
⅛ teaspoon cayenne
1 teaspoon prepared mustard
1 cup tomato juice
1¼ cups grated mild cheese
1 well-beaten egg
½ cup cream, heated
1 cup cooked flaked crabmeat

Melt butter in a medium saucepan. Add onion and pepper and sauté until lightly browned. Mix flour, salt, and cayenne. Add to the mixture. Add mustard and tomato juice. Simmer slowly over low heat, stirring constantly, until smooth and thickened. Add cheese and stir thoroughly. Stir in egg. Simmer 3 minutes, stirring constantly. Remove from heat. Add hot cream and crabmeat. Mix well. Serve on buttered toast. Serves 6.

CORN AND CHEESE TOASTS

2 tablespoons butter
2 tablespoons chopped green pepper
2 tablespoons flour
1 teaspoon salt
¼ teaspoon dry mustard
Few grains cayenne
1 cup strained tomato juice
1 cup stewed (p. 228) or canned corn
1½ cup grated Cheddar cheese
1 egg

Melt butter in a medium saucepan, add green pepper, and cook until soft. Add flour, salt, mustard and cayenne and mix well. Add tomato juice slowly and cook until thick, stirring constantly. Add corn and cheese and cook until cheese is melted. Remove from heat. Beat the egg well and pour the hot cheese sauce over it. Mix well. Serve hot on buttered toast. Serves 6.

TRÈS BIENS

4 slices of bread
2 tomatoes cut into slices
Salt
Pepper
4 slices of Cheddar or American cheese
1 medium onion, cut into rings
1 green pepper, cut into rings
8 slices of bacon

Preheat oven to 400°F. Cover a slice of bread with tomato slices. Sprinkle with salt and pepper. Then add a slice of cheese, a slice of onion, a ring of green pepper, and 2 strips of bacon over the top. Bake for about 20 minutes or until bacon is crispy. Do not put under broiler. Serve with sauce of your choice.

MISCELLANEOUS MEAT SANDWICHES

- Chopped cooked chicken, diced celery, chopped pimento, chopped olives, grated onion, salt, pepper, and mayonnaise (p. 70).
- Minced cooked ham with mayonnaise (p. 70), chopped hard-boiled eggs (p. 272), chopped parsley, and chopped celery.
- Minced cooked ham with chopped pickles and mayonnaise (p. 70).
- Sliced ham with cream cheese and shredded lettuce, chopped watercress, or thin slices of crisp cucumber.
- Chopped cooked ham mixed with chopped cooked turkey or chicken, salt, pepper, and mayonnaise (p. 70).
- Minced cooked meat (any kind), mixed with chopped celery, salt, pepper, and mayonnaise (p. 70).
- Minced, cooked poultry, mixed with chopped nuts, chopped green pepper, salt, paprika, and mayonnaise (p. 70).

MISCELLANEOUS FISH SANDWICHES

- Tuna fish, plain or mixed with salad dressing and lettuce.
- Anchovy paste, mixed with cream cheese or sprinkled with lemon juice.
- Boiled shrimp (p. 342), chopped celery, and chili sauce.
- Tuna fish or salmon, diced celery, chopped pimento, chopped ripe olives, grated onion, salt, pepper, and mayonnaise (p. 70).
- Minced boiled shrimp (p. 342), mixed with chopped cucumber, salt, paprika, and mayonnaise (p. 70).

- Flaked tuna mixed with any combination of chopped green peppers, onion, pimento, tomatoes, and chives and moistened with mayonnaise (p. 70).

MISCELLEANOUS CHEESE SANDWICHES

- Cream cheese with chopped nuts, olives or peppers, or a combination of these.
- India relish with well-seasoned fresh cottage cheese.
- Chopped English walnuts with cottage cheese.
- Grated cheese with chopped sweet pickle and mayonnaise (p. 70).
- Cottage cheese mixed with almost any jam or jelly.
- Roquefort cheese, cream, chopped ripe olives, chopped celery, and lettuce leaf.
- Grated cheese mixed with chopped pimento, and mayonnaise (p. 70).
- Cream cheese mixed with butter, pepper, salt, paprika, and Worcestershire sauce.
- Grated cheese mixed with chopped green pepper, mustard, and Worcestershire sauce.
- Cream cheese mixed with crushed pineapple.

MISCELLANEOUS EGG SANDWICHES

- Scrambled eggs (p. 279), plain or in milk, or with bits of diced crisp bacon (p. 401).
- Scrambled eggs (p. 279) mixed with stewed tomatoes (p. 264) and a little grated onion, if desired.
- Chopped hard-boiled egg (p. 272) mixed with chopped dill pickle and mayonnaise (p. 70).

- Chopped hard-boiled egg (p. 272) mixed with chopped olives and French dressing (p. 71).
- Chopped hard-boiled egg (p. 272) mixed with diced broiled bacon (p. 401) or minced ham, and mayonnaise (p. 70).
- Chopped hard-boiled egg (p. 272) mixed with chopped celery, chopped pimento, and mayonnaise (p. 70).
- Fried egg (p. 272), cooked on both sides and sprinkled with chopped onion.

MISCELLANEOUS FRUIT SANDWICHES

- Chopped dates, mixed with an equal amount of peanut butter or cream cheese, seasoned with salt and sprinkled with lemon juice.
- Mashed ripe bananas, mixed with chopped peanuts or peanut butter.
- Chopped dried figs, fresh ricotta, and honey.
- A mixture of chopped dates, figs and raisins with fresh ricotta.
- Crushed pineapple and chopped pecans, with or without cream cheese.

MISCELLANEOUS VEGETABLE SANDWICHES

- Diced pickled cucumber, mixed with cottage cheese.
- Mixed pickles, sour or sweet, with chopped hard-boiled eggs (p. 272).
- Cucumber slices, sprinkled with grated onion, lettuce leaf and mayonnaise (p. 70).

- A mixture of chopped onion, chopped parsley, chopped green pepper, chopped cucumber, chopped celery, tomato pulp and mayonnaise (p. 70) on lettuce leaf.

PASTA

Pasta dishes are quick and versatile, making them an ideal dinner dish. Following a few simple rules when cooking pasta will result in perfect pasta every time:

- Make sure to use enough water, and a large enough pot for the pasta. This gives the pasta room to move without sticking, and makes it less likely that the pasta will boil over.
- Always salt the pasta water, and add a splash of oil. The salt enhances the flavor of the pasta, and the oil prevents it from sticking.
- Make sure that the water is boiling before adding the pasta. Pasta should boil for as little time as possible, just long enough to cook it properly. Adding pasta too early can leave it waterlogged, and keeping it in too long can leave it gummy and limp. Pasta should be firm, but not crunchy, and definitely not limp.
- Cook the pasta according to the directions on its package, but begin checking it a minute or two early. The cooking times listed on pasta boxes are often a little longer than ideal.
- Once the pasta has finished cooking, drain the liquid off, either by putting the pasta in a strainer or pulling it out of the pot with tongs. Do not, unless making a pasta salad, rinse the pasta. Unrinsed pasta will be a little sticky, which allows sauces to adhere to it a bit better.
- If making a sauce, reserve some of the liquid in which the pasta was cooked. Pasta water can be used to stretch or thicken a sauce.

NOODLE DOUGH

1 cup flour
¼ teaspoon salt
1 slightly beaten egg

Mix and sift flour and salt. Add gradually to egg until a stiff dough is formed. Knead for a few minutes on floured board. Roll out to ¹⁄₁₆" thickness. Let stand ½ hour. Cut in long ¼" wide strips. Dry thoroughly. Noodles may be cut into any size strips or any tiny fancy shapes. This makes 1½ cups raw noodles.

BAKED MACARONI

4 cups boiled macaroni
2 cups medium white sauce (p. 416)
½ cup buttered breadcrumbs

Preheat oven to 400°F. Combine macaroni and sauce. Turn into greased baking dish. Top with crumbs. Bake until brown. Serves 6.

MACARONI AND CHEESE

¾ pound Cheddar or Gruyère
2 cups whole milk
1 cup cottage cheese
½ teaspoon salt
½ teaspoon pepper
¼ teaspoon nutmeg
½ pound macaroni, uncooked
Buttered crumbs (optional)

Preheat oven to 375°F. Grate the cheese and set aside. In a blender, blend the milk, cottage cheese, and spices. In a large bowl, combine pasta, cheese, and milk mixture. Pour into a large buttered baking dish and top with buttered crumbs if desired. Bake for 30 minutes covered. Remove the cover and bake for another 30 minutes, or until the cheese is brown and the pasta tastes cooked.

BAKED NOODLES, CHEESE AND HAM

4 cups boiled noodles
1 cup ham, cut fine
⅔ cup grated cheese
2 cups thin white sauce (p. 416)

Preheat oven to 400°F. Put a layer of noodles in a greased baking dish. Sprinkle with ham and cheese, then cover with a layer of white sauce. Repeat until all ingredients are used. Sprinkle top with cheese. Bake for 20 to 25 minutes. Serves 6.

HAM WITH NOODLES

2 cups boiled noodles
3 cups ground cooked ham
3 cups thin white sauce (p. 416)
1 cup buttered breadcrumbs

Preheat oven to 375°F. Make alternate layers of noodles and ham in a shallow baking dish. Pour on the white sauce. Sprinkle buttered crumbs over the top. Bake for about 20 minutes. Serves 6. As a variation, tomato sauce (p. 424) may be substituted for white sauce.

NOODLES WITH NUTS

8 ounces wide egg noodles
¼ cup butter
½ cup chopped almonds or Brazil nuts
2 teaspoons poppy seeds

Cook wide egg noodles and drain. Melt 1 tablespoon butter in a skillet over low heat. Add chopped nuts and stir until light brown. Add remaining butter, the egg noodles and poppy seeds and stir lightly until heated thoroughly. Serves 6.

BAKED SPAGHETTI

8 ounces spaghetti
2 tablespoons butter
1½ tablespoons onion, chopped
1½ tablespoons green pepper, chopped
2 cups canned tomatoes
1 teaspoon salt
¼ teaspoon pepper
⅛ teaspoon paprika
1 tablespoon sugar
1 cup grated cheese

Boil spaghetti in salted water until tender. Drain. Preheat oven to 400°F. Melt butter in pan and sauté onion and green pepper until soft. Add tomatoes, salt, pepper, paprika, and sugar. Simmer 10 minutes. Add spaghetti and mix well. Add ½ cup cheese. Turn into greased baking dish. Sprinkle with remaining cheese. Bake until cheese is brown, 20 to 25 minutes. As a variation, this dish can also be made by adding ground sausage meat with the tomatoes. Serves 6.

SPAGHETTI AND TOMATOES

Preheat oven to 400°F. Put a layer of boiled spaghetti in the bottom of a greased baking dish. Add layer of tomato sauce (p. 424). Dot with ¼" cubes of bacon and onion. Continue alternating layers to fill dish. Cover with buttered crumbs and grated cheese, if desired. Bake for 20 to 25 minutes. 4 cups boiled spaghetti serves 6.

SPAGHETTI WITH MEAT SAUCE

½ pound ground veal
½ pound ground pork
½ pound ground beef
½ pound sausage
½ cup butter
1¼ pounds onions, chopped
¼ clove garlic, cut fine
1 green pepper, chopped
2 sprigs parsley, chopped
½ pound button mushrooms, sliced
2½ cups tomato puree
1 cup tomato paste
12 cups water
2 teaspoons lemon juice
2 teaspoons salt
¼ teaspoon pepper
8 ounces spaghetti
Grated Parmesan cheese, to taste

Brown meats in butter in iron skillet. Add onions, garlic, pepper, and parsley. Cook until slightly brown. Add mushrooms, tomato puree, tomato paste, water, lemon juice, salt, and pepper. Simmer, covered, 1½ hours. Boil spaghetti in salted water until tender. Pour sauce over spaghetti and serve on platter. Sprinkle top generously with grated Parmesan cheese. Serves 8.

SPAGHETTI WITH BACON-TOMATO SAUCE

4 slices bacon, diced
1 onion, sliced
¾ cup canned tomatoes
½ teaspoon salt
⅛ teaspoon pepper
⅛ teaspoon allspice
Dash cayenne
8 ounces spaghetti
Grated Parmesan cheese (optional)

Heat bacon in frying pan. Add onion, tomatoes, salt, pepper, allspice, and cayenne. Bring to boiling point. Cover and let simmer 30 minutes. Boil spaghetti in salted water until tender. Drain. Pour sauce over hot spaghetti. Sprinkle with grated Parmesan cheese if desired. Serves 6.

RAVIOLI (ITALIAN)

Roll out noodle dough (p. 118) thin. Cut into rounds with a large cookie cutter. Place 1½ tablespoons chopped meat on ½ of each round. Moisten edges of dough with water. Fold over in half circle and press tightly together. Fry in deep hot fat, and drain on unglazed paper. Or, drop in boiling salted water or stock and cook until they rise to surface. Serve with a strongly seasoned tomato sauce (p. 424) and sprinkle with chopped parsley.

SPICY BAKED SPAGHETTI

¼ cup olive oil
1 chopped onion
1 tablespoon chili powder
½ teaspoon salt
⅛ teaspoon pepper
2½ cups canned crushed tomatoes
3 cups boiled, drained spaghetti
1½ cups grated Cheddar cheese
¼ cup chopped olives

Preheat oven to 350°F. Heat oil in saucepan. Add onion and sauté until lightly browned. Add chili powder, salt, and pepper. Mix well. Add tomatoes and simmer 20 minutes, stirring frequently. Put alternate layers of spaghetti and cheese in a greased baking dish, seasoning each layer with salt and pepper. Top with olives and then the sauce, mixing well. Top with a layer of cheese. Bake until cheese is melted and slightly browned, about 20 minutes. Serves 6.

PASTA WITH TOMATOES AND BASIL

1 pound fettuccine
3 large, ripe tomatoes
3 tablespoons fresh basil, plus a few leaves for
     garnishing
¼ pound fresh mozzarella, diced (optional)
3 tablespoons good olive oil
Salt
Pepper

Bring a large pot of salted water to a boil. Add fettuccine, and cook according to the instructions on the package. While the pasta cooks, cut the tomatoes into chunks or slices, as preferred. (This dish is best for ripe tomatoes in the peak of summer. A mealy winter tomato will produce a disappointing result.) Dice the basil. When the pasta is done, drain it and return it to the pot or put it in a serving bowl. Toss with olive oil and season to taste with salt and pepper. Add tomatoes, basil, and mozzarella, if desired. Garnish with basil leaves and serve immediately. Serves 4 to 6.

BACON PASTA

    1 pound fettuccine
    8 slices uncooked bacon
    4 to 6 ounces Parmesan cheese
    2 well-beaten eggs
    Salt
    Pepper
    1 tablespoon parsley, finely diced (optional)

Bring a large pot of salted water to a boil. Add pasta and cook according to the instructions on package. While the pasta boils, cook the bacon in a skillet over medium-high heat. When the bacon is done, remove from heat and drain on paper towels. Reserve some of the bacon fat. Finely grate the cheese. When the bacon has cooled a bit, chop it into small pieces. When the pasta is ready, drain it and return it to the pot. Pour a tablespoon or so of the reserved bacon grease over the pasta to lubricate it. Then add the eggs, cheese, and bacon. Mix well. Season to taste with salt and pepper. Garnish with parsley, if desired. Serves 4.

PASTA WITH CRAB

1 pound spaghetti or fettuccine
¼ cup olive oil
6 cloves garlic, crushed
½ pound fresh lump crab meat
Salt
Pepper
2 tablespoons parsley, finely diced

Bring a large pot of salted water to a boil. Add pasta and cook according to the instructions on package. While the pasta boils, heat the olive oil in a large skillet over medium heat. Add the crushed garlic and cook for a minute or so, until garlic turns golden. Add the crab, cooking just long enough to heat through. When the pasta is ready, drain it, and add it to the skillet. Mix well and season to taste with salt and pepper. Toss with parsley and serve immediately. Serves 4.

GRAINS

Grains are a staple food for much of the world's population, because they are inexpensive and readily available. They are also healthful and fun to use in cooking.

Whole grains, such as oatmeal and barley, are an excellent source of dietary fiber and protein. Dietary fiber has been shown to reduce the risk of heart disease and cancer. Refined grains, like white flour and white rice, do not offer the same health benefits, though they are fine to eat in moderation. The larger the percentage of whole grains (as opposed to refined grains) in a diet, the larger the health benefit.

Whole grains can often be easily substituted for refined grains. Wild rice and brown rice, for instance, can be used in many recipes that call for white rice.

Grains, whether whole or refined, are versatile. They can be used as side dishes, breakfast cereals, and additions to soups and casseroles.

GENERAL DIRECTIONS FOR COOKING GRAINS

Use a large saucepan. Mix water, grain, and salt. Cook over medium heat. If using the grain in a sweet dish, cut the amount of salt in half. Once the mixture comes to a boil, immediately reduce heat, and continue simmering for the amount of time indicated. Stir frequently to prevent grains from sticking or boiling over.

TIMETABLE AND DIRECTIONS
FOR COOKING 1 CUP OF GRAIN

	WATER	SALT (TSPS)
SIMMERING TIME *(after bringing to a boil)*		
Barley, pearled *45 minutes*	3 cups	1
Cornmeal *25 to 30 minutes*	4 cups	1
Couscous *5 minutes*	1 cups	1
Oats, rolled *10 minutes*	2½ cups	1
Oats, steel cut *20 to 30 minutes*	4 cups	1
Quinoa *20 minutes*	2 cups	1
Rice, brown *30 to 40 minutes*	2½ cups	1
Rice, white *25 to 30 minutes*	2 cups	1
Rice, wild *50 to 60 minutes*	3 cups	1
Wheat, berries *Soak overnight, then 45 to 60 minutes*	4 cups	1
Wheat, cracked *20 to 25 minutes*	2 cups	1

Any of the above grains may be cooked with milk instead of water. In that case put in ⅓ the amount of water required at start of cooking. Boil 10 minutes. Add milk to make up the required amount of liquid.

SPANISH RICE

½ cup raw rice
3½ tablespoons butter
1½ cups water
3 tablespoons chopped onion
2 tablespoons chopped green peppers
⅛ teaspoon sage
Salt
Pepper
1½ tablespoon flour
1½ cups tomato pulp

Sauté rice to a light brown in 1 tablespoon butter over medium heat. Add hot water. Bring to a boil. Cover and steam slowly 10 minutes. Put remaining butter, onion, green peppers, sage, salt, and pepper to taste in another pan and brown lightly. Add flour and ½ cup tomato pulp. Blend well. Add remaining pulp and boil 5 minutes. Pour over rice. Let steam until sauce has desired consistency. Serves 6.

RICE AU GRATIN

3 cups cooked rice
1 cup mild grated cheese, such as Fontina or Swiss
1½ cups thin white sauce (p. 416)

Preheat oven to 425°F. Put a layer of rice in greased baking dish. Sprinkle with cheese. Cover with layer of sauce. Keep alternating ingredients until all are used, saving a layer of cheese for the top. Bake for 20 minutes. Serves 6.

BAKED RICE AND CHEESE

3 cups cooked rice
2 tablespoons butter
1½ cups mild grated cheese
½ teaspoon salt
1 cup milk
¼ cup breadcrumbs

Preheat oven to 350°F. Line bottom of greased baking dish with rice. Dot with butter. Alternate layers of rice and cheese, dotting each layer with butter, until rice and cheese are all used. Sprinkle with salt. Add milk. Spread top with crumbs. Bake until cheese has melted and crumbs are brown, about 20 minutes. Serves 6.

RICE WITH SLICED ALMONDS

3 cups cooked rice
½ cup blanched almonds, sliced thin
Paprika
2 tablespoons chopped parsley

Combine hot cooked rice with the sliced almonds. Place on serving dish and sprinkle with paprika; garnish with parsley. Serves 6.

CREAMY RICE EN CASSEROLE

3 cups hot cooked rice
½ lb. fresh shrimp, boiled (p. 342)
2 cups medium white sauce (p. 416)
1 cup peas, fresh or frozen
½ cup grated cheese

Preheat oven to 400°F. Combine ingredients lightly. Turn into greased 9" x 9" casserole, sprinkle with cheese, and bake until cheese is melted and slightly browned. Serves 4.

ITALIAN BAKED RICE

1 cup raw rice
3 tablespoons olive oil
1½ teaspoons salt
½ cup macaroni or other small pasta
2 tablespoon chopped green pepper
2 tablespoons chopped onion
2 cloves of garlic
¼ teaspoon powdered thyme
1½ cups tomato pulp
1 tablespoon butter

Preheat oven to 350°. Sauté the rice with 1 tablespoon oil until lightly browned. Add ½ teaspoon salt and 2½ cups water. Bring to a boil and reduce heat. Cover and simmer over low heat until cooked, about 20 minutes. In another pot, bring water to a boil. Add ½ teaspoon salt and the macaroni. Boil according to the directions on the package. Strain in a colander. Sauté pepper, onion, garlic, and thyme in the remaining oil until brown, stirring constantly. Add tomato and remaining salt. Heat thoroughly and pour over rice. Put half of rice mixture in a greased baking dish. Add the macaroni and put remaining rice on top. Dot with butter. Bake for 30 to 40 minutes. Serves 6.

RICE AND PEAS

2 tablespoons butter
2 tablespoons diced onion
2 cups cooked short-grain rice, such as Arborio
3 cups chicken stock, more if necessary
2 cups boiled peas (p. 240)
¼ cup grated Parmesan cheese (optional)

Melt butter in a medium saucepan over medium-low heat. Add onions. Cook until onions have become translucent. Add rice, stirring to coat each grain. Begin adding stock, ½ cup at a time. As the rice absorbs the stock, add more while constantly stirring. Check the rice after 2½ cups have been added—the rice should be creamy, but not mushy or hard. Keep adding stock a bit at a time until rice seems done. Add peas and stir well. Add a bit more stock—the consistency should be thicker than a soup, but still somewhat liquid. Add cheese if desired. Serves 6.

RICE AND BACON

1 slice bacon, chopped
3 cups canned tomatoes
1 cup cooked rice
1 onion, sliced
1 teaspoon salt

Fry bacon until crisp. Add tomatoes, onion, and rice. Cook to desired consistency. Add salt. Serve hot. Serves 6.

GRAIN RAREBIT

1 cup milk
¼ cup butter (½ stick)
3 cups any cooked grain (See General Directions for
    Cooking Grains, p. 127)
1 teaspoon prepared mustard
3 cups mild, grated cheese, such as Cheddar
2 well-beaten eggs
½ teaspoon pepper
1 tablespoon Worcestershire sauce
6 slices of bread

Bring milk to a boil over medium heat. Add butter. Add grain and beat well with a wooden spoon. Add mustard, cheese, eggs, and pepper. Heat thoroughly. Stir in Worcestershire sauce and serve, piping hot, on toast. Serves 6.

BAKED HOMINY

2 cups canned hominy, drained
2 well-beaten eggs
½ teaspoon salt

Preheat oven to 350°. Mix ingredients. Put in a 9" x 9" baking dish. Bake for 40 minutes. Serves 6.

BAKED HOMINY AND CHEESE

2 cups canned or strained tomatoes
2 tablespoons chopped onion
2 cloves
½ teaspoon salt
1 tablespoon sugar (optional)
⅛ teaspoon cayenne
3 tablespoons butter or fat
2 tablespoons flour
2½ cups canned hominy, drained
½ cup mild grated cheese, such as Cheddar
½ cup breadcrumbs

Preheat oven to 425°F. Simmer tomatoes, onion, cloves, salt, sugar, and cayenne over low heat in a saucepan for 20 minutes. Strain. Melt 2 tablespoons butter or fat and blend with flour. Add strained tomato juice and bring slowly to a boil, stirring constantly. Put layer of hominy in greased 10" x 12" baking dish. Add layer of cheese. Add layer of the tomato sauce. Repeat until all are used. Spread top with crumbs. Dot with butter or fat. Bake for 20 minutes or until crumbs are brown. Serves 6.

COUSCOUS

2 cups chicken, beef or vegetable broth
2 tablespoons butter
½ teaspoon salt (optional)
2 cups instant couscous

Bring stock, butter, and salt to a boil in a saucepan over medium heat. Add couscous, cover, and remove from heat. Let stand for 5 minutes. Fluff with a fork before serving. Serves 4.

POLENTA

4 cups water, milk, or buttermilk
½ teaspoon salt
2 cups cornmeal
Pepper
2 tablespoons butter

Bring water or milk and salt to a boil in a medium saucepan. Reduce heat to simmer and slowly add cornmeal, stirring constantly, until mixture begins to thicken. Add pepper to taste, and finish with the butter. May be used as a side dish. Serves 6.

FRIED POLENTA

2 cups milk
½ cup cornmeal
1 tablespoon butter
½ teaspoon salt
¼ cup flour
1 beaten egg
½ cup breadcrumbs

Preheat oven to 350°F. Bring milk to a boil. Sift in cornmeal slowly, stirring constantly. Add butter and salt. Cover and let simmer over low heat for 20 minutes. Pour into greased 9" x 9" pan. Cool. Cut into small squares or diamonds. Dip in flour. Dip in egg, diluted with a little water. Dip in breadcrumbs. Put in greased baking pan and bake until brown. Serves 6.

POLENTA WITH CHEESE

4 cups water or milk
½ teaspoon salt
2 cups cornmeal
pepper
2 tablespoons butter
¼ cup breadcrumbs
1 cup grated hard cheese, such as Parmesan or Cheddar

Make as for polenta (p. 135). Just after adding the butter, stir in cheese. Mix until cheese melts. Serves 6.

BAKED CORN TAMALE

1 cup milk
1 teaspoon salt
¼ cup cornmeal
1½ cups corn
10 ripe olives, stoned and sliced
1 slightly beaten egg
2 tablespoons butter
2 tablespoons chopped onion
½ cup chopped green pepper
2 cups canned tomatoes

Preheat oven to 325°F. Bring milk to a boil. Add salt and sift in cornmeal slowly. Stir until smooth and thickened. Add corn, olives, and egg. Mix thoroughly. Melt butter in frying pan over medium heat. Add onion and pepper. Sauté until lightly browned. Add tomatoes and bring to a boil. Mix both mixtures. Pour into greased 10" x 10" baking pan. Bake until firm and nicely browned, about 20 minutes. Serves 6.

POPCORN

2 tablespoons butter, plus more for serving
½ cup popcorn kernels
Salt

Making popcorn over the stove is fun, and the end result is more flavorful than microwave popcorn. Melt butter in pan or stockpot over medium heat and turn to coat entire inside with grease. Add corn. Stir until each kernel is coated with butter. Cover and shake without removing from heat until popping is completed. Turn into a bowl and sprinkle with salt. Pour melted butter over if desired.

BREADS

YEAST BREADS

Yeast breads are a wonderful addition to any cook's repertoire. Though more time-consuming than baking a quick bread or buying a baguette, making these breads can be relaxing and enjoyable. With just a little practice and a few pointers, yeast breads can be conquered in no time.

Make sure to use fresh yeast. Old yeast may keep a dough from rising properly. If in doubt, buy a new yeast cake or packet. Yeast is inexpensive and it may prevent some heartache. When activating the yeast, take care to use a lukewarm liquid (about 120°F is ideal). A cooler liquid may not activate the yeast sufficiently and a warmer one may kill it. The liquid should feel just slightly warm to the touch.

Once the dough is made, find a nice, warm spot for it to rise. In a drafty kitchen, or sub-zero temperatures, try putting the dough in a gas oven with the pilot light (but not the heat) turned on. A heat register or a warm corner of a room will also do. Don't expose the dough to too much heat, though, or it will rise too quickly.

A stand mixer with a dough hook can be a great help when making these breads. The dough hook takes all of the hard work out of kneading and mixing. Kneading by hand, though, can be a pleasure in itself.

QUICK BREADS AND BISCUITS

Quick breads are called "quick" because they are made without yeast and do not need to rise before being baked. Instead, they usually contain some combination of baking powder, baking soda, and eggs. These are all leavening agents, which help the bread to rise in a much shorter period of time.

As with all baking, the temperature of the ingredients and the speed with which they are combined is the key to making an excellent quick bread. The ingredients in most of the bread recipes, for instance, should be as close to room temperature as possible. This is especially true for butter and eggs. They will combine more easily with the other ingredients and lend additional volume to the batter. This will result in a lighter crumb and tastier bread.

For biscuits, on the other hand, the butter should be quite cold. Butter does not need to be fully incorporated into the dough; a few pea-sized pieces here and there will actually make for a better biscuit. The dough should also be made quickly and handled as little as possible. Rolling the dough out with strong, swift strokes and immediately getting the biscuits into a hot oven will produce light, fluffy results.

Whether making bread or biscuits, be careful not to overwork the dough. The more a dough is stirred or mixed after the flour has been added, the tougher the end result will be. Having all of the ingredients measured out and at the right temperature is an excellent way to combat this problem.

YEAST BREADS

BREAD I

    1 cup water, plus ¼ cup
    1 cup milk
    3 tablespoons butter
    2 tablespoons sugar
    2½ teaspoons salt
    1 yeast cake (0.6 ounces) or 1 packet active dry yeast
    6½ cups flour

Add 1 cup water to milk. Heat. Add butter, sugar, and salt. Remove from heat and allow to cool slightly, until the mixture is warm to the touch. Dissolve yeast in ¼ cup lukewarm water and add to mixture. Stir in 3 to 4 cups flour and beat thoroughly. Cover and set in a warm place to rise overnight. In the morning add enough flour to make a firm dough. Knead on floured board or in a stand mixer until smooth and elastic to touch. Cover and set in warm place to rise until it triples in bulk. Knead again. Shape into loaves and put in greased bread pans. Cover and let rise again until double in bulk. Bake at 350°F for 50 to 60 minutes.

BREAD II

    1 cup milk
    2 tablespoons butter
    1½ tablespoons sugar
    1½ teaspoons salt
    1 yeast cake (0.6 ounces) or 1 packet active dry yeast
    ¼ cup lukewarm water
    2½ cups flour, plus more as needed

Heat milk. Add butter, sugar, and salt. Remove from heat and allow to cool slightly, until the mixture is warm to the touch. Dissolve yeast in lukewarm water. Add to mixture. Add flour and beat thoroughly. Cover and set in a warm place to rise until doubled, about 1 hour. Add enough flour to make a firm dough. Knead on a floured board or in a stand mixer until smooth and elastic to touch. Cover and set in warm place to rise until it triples in bulk. Knead again. Shape into a loaf and put in greased bread pans. Cover and set in a warm place to rise until double in bulk. Bake at 350°F for 50 to 60 minutes.

FRENCH BREAD

    2 teaspoons sugar
    2 teaspoons salt
    1 yeast cake (0.6 ounces) or 1 packet active dry yeast
    4 cups lukewarm water
    12 cups sifted flour
    ½ teaspoon cornstarch

Blend sugar, salt, and yeast with a knife or back of a spoon. Add lukewarm water. Put flour in a mixing bowl. Hollow out center and add liquid mixture. Mix and knead on a floured board or in a stand mixer until smooth and elastic. Cover and set in a warm place to rise until double in bulk, about 4 hours. Knead or mix again and cover and set in a warm place to rise again until doubled in bulk. Mold into long loaves. Put on baking sheets. Cover and again set in a warm place to rise until double in bulk. Bake at 350°F for 1¼ to 1½ hours. Fifteen minutes before cooking is finished, blend cornstarch in 2 teaspoons cold water and boil for 5 minutes in ⅓ cup boiling water. Brush this mixture on the bread.

RYE BREAD

6⅓ cups sifted rye flour
4½ cups sifted hard-wheat flour
5½ cups sifted all-purpose flour
3 cups lukewarm water, plus ¼ cup
2 yeast cakes (0.6 ounces each) or 2 packets active dry
    yeasts
3 tablespoons sugar
5 teaspoons salt
2 tablespoons melted butter

Sift the rye flour with the other flours and proceed as for bread I (p. 140) until ready to form the loaves. Mold into long, sharply pointed loaves, place on a greased shallow pan or one on which flour or cornmeal has been sprinkled. Rub butter lightly on the tops of the loaves. Cover and let rise until the bulk has increased 1¾ times. Make about 3 slashes with a sharp knife at an angle across the top of each loaf. Bake loaves for 30 to 35 minutes at 400°F. A pan of hot water should be placed in the oven during baking. Remove loaves from pan and glaze with a mixture of egg white and water or cooked starch paste.

WHOLE WHEAT BREAD

1 cup milk
2 tablespoons butter
¼ cup sugar
1 teaspoon salt
1 yeast cake
2 tablespoons lukewarm water
2 cups flour
1½–2 cups whole wheat flour

Heat milk and add butter, sugar, and salt. Dissolve yeast in lukewarm water. When milk mixture has cooled, add the yeast. Add the white flour and beat until smooth. Cover and set in a warm plate to rise for about 1 hour. Add the whole wheat flour and knead or mix in a stand mixer until it is elastic to touch and does not stick to an un-floured board. Cover and set in warm place to rise until double in bulk. Knead or mix again until free from air bubbles. Put in a greased loaf pan. Cover and set in a warm place to rise until doubled in bulk. Bake at 350°F for 50 to 60 minutes.

RAISIN BREAD

    1 cup milk
    3 tablespoons butter
    4 tablespoons sugar
    1 teaspoon salt
    1 yeast cake (0.6 ounces) or 1 packet active dry yeast
    2 tablespoons lukewarm water
    4½ cups flour
    1 cup raisins

Heat milk. Add butter, sugar, and salt. Dissolve yeast in lukewarm water. Add to mixture once it has cooled. Add 2 cups flour and beat until smooth. Cover and set in a warm place to rise for 1 hour. Add raisins and remaining flour to make a firm dough. Knead or mix in a stand mixer until smooth and elastic to touch. Cover and set in a warm place to rise until double in bulk. Knead or mix again. Form into loaf and put in greased baking pan. Cover and set in warm place to rise until doubled in bulk. Bake at 350°F for 50 to 60 minutes.

CHEESE BREAD

Add ⅔ cup grated cheese to recipe for whole wheat bread (p. 142).

NUT BREAD

Add ⅔ cup chopped nuts to recipe for whole wheat bread (p. 142).

REFRIGERATOR ROLLS

2 yeast cakes (0.6 ounces each) or 2 packets active dry
yeasts
¼ cup sugar
1 cup milk
½ cup butter
1 teaspoon salt
3 beaten eggs
5 cups flour

Crumble yeast and mix with sugar. Let stand 20 minutes. Heat milk. Add butter and salt. Cool to lukewarm. Add yeast-sugar mixture and eggs. Add flour, mixing thoroughly. Turn out on flour board and knead in a stand mixer until satiny. Place in greased bowl. Cover and set in warm place to rise until double in bulk, about 2 hours. Knead or mix again. Form into a smooth ball. Grease surface. Cover and keep in refrigerator, or make immediately. Bake rolls at 425°F for 15 to 20 minutes.

SWEET YEAST DOUGH

2 yeast cakes (0.6 ounces each) or 2 packets active dry
yeasts
¼ cup lukewarm water
1 cup milk
¼ cup butter
½ cup sugar
1 teaspoon salt
5 cups flour
2 eggs, beaten

Soften yeast in lukewarm water. Bring milk to a boil and remove from the heat. Add butter, sugar, and salt. Cool to lukewarm. Add flour to make a thick batter. Add yeast and eggs. Beat well. Add enough flour to make satiny. Place in a greased bowl in a warm place. Cover and let rise until doubled in bulk, about 2 hours. When light, punch down, shape into tea ring, rolls, or coffee cakes. Let rise until doubled in bulk, about 30 to 45 minutes. Bake at 375°F for 25 to 30 minutes for coffee cakes, 20 to 25 minutes for rolls. Yield: 2 12" tea rings.

BOHEMIAN BRAID

Prepare sweet yeast dough (above). Divide into 9 parts. Roll each part into long strip. Braid 4 strips and place on greased baking sheet. Braid 3 parts and place on top. Twist remaining 2 parts and place on top, tucking ends under. Cover and set in a warm place to rise until double in bulk. Bake at 400°F for 45 minutes. When cool, brush with powdered sugar icing (p. 626) and sprinkle with chopped nuts.

CARAMEL ROLLS

Sweet yeast dough (p. 145)
¼ cup melted butter, plus more for greasing
½ cup brown sugar, plus more for muffin tins

Prepare dough. When dough has risen, roll ½" thick. Brush with ¼ cup melted butter. Sprinkle with ½ cup brown sugar. Roll as a jellyroll. Cut in 1" slices. Brush muffin cups with melted butter, allowing ½ teaspoon per cup. Add 1 teaspoon brown sugar to each cup. Put roll slices, cut side down, in cups. Set in warm place to rise until doubled. Bake at 375°F for 20 to 25 minutes.

BRIOCHE

3 cups sifted flour
1 cup hot milk
1 yeast cake (0.6 ounces) or 1 packet active dry yeast
1 cup melted butter
3 tablespoons sugar
4 well-beaten eggs
½ teaspoon salt

Put 2 cups flour in bowl or stand mixer. Cool milk to luke-warm. Add yeast and dissolve. Add mixture to flour. Beat until smooth. Cover and set in a warm place to rise until doubled in volume, about 1 hour. Add butter, sugar, eggs, remaining flour, and salt. Mix well and knead on floured board or in stand mixer until smooth. Cover and set in a warm place to rise until doubled in volume, about 4 hours. Knead again and form into any desired shape. Cover and let rise again in warm place until doubled. Bake at 375°F for 20 minutes. Serves 6.

PARKER HOUSE ROLLS

2 cups milk
3 tablespoons sugar
3 teaspoons salt
¼ cup butter, plus 5 tablespoons
2 yeast cakes (0.6 ounces each) or 2 packets active dry
 yeasts
¼ cup lukewarm water
6½ cups flour

Heat milk. Add sugar, salt, and 5 tablespoons butter. Dissolve yeast in lukewarm water. Add to mixture once milk has cooled. Add 2 cups flour and beat thoroughly. Cover and set in a warm place to rise until doubled, about 1½ hours. Add enough flour to make a firm dough. Knead on a floured board or in a stand mixer with a dough hook until smooth and elastic to touch. Cover and set in a warm place to rise until doubled in bulk. Knead or mix again. Roll the dough to ¼" thickness and cut with a large, round cutter. Brush each piece with melted butter. Mark through the center with the back of a knife and fold over, pressing edges together. Place rolls in a greased, shallow pan 1" apart. Cover and set in a warm place to rise until doubled in bulk. Bake at 400°F for 15 to 20 minutes. Yield: 30 rolls.

CLOVER LEAF ROLLS

Follow recipe for Parker House rolls (above) with following changes: Pull off small bits of dough after the third rising. Shape in small balls. Place 3 balls in each greased muffin pan. Yield: 36 rolls.

DINNER ROLLS

Follow recipe for Parker House rolls (p. 147) with following changes: Roll dough to ½" thickness. Cut with small, round cookie cutter. Yield: 36 rolls.

PLAIN YEAST ROLLS

½ cup milk
2 tablespoons butter
2 tablespoons sugar
2 teaspoons salt
1 yeast cake (0.6 ounces) or 1 packet active dry yeast
½ cup lukewarm water
1 egg or 2 egg yolks
3½ cups flour

Heat milk and add butter, sugar, and salt. Soften yeast in lukewarm water. Cool milk to lukewarm and add yeast and beaten egg. Add flour to make a soft dough. Turn out on lightly floured board and knead until smooth and satiny. Place in lightly greased bowl and cover. Set in a warm place and allow to double in bulk. Punch down and mold into rolls. Cover and set in warm place to rise until double in bulk. Bake at 400°F for 15 to 20 minutes. Yield: 20 rolls.

SOUR CREAM ROLLS

2 cups thick sour cream
1 yeast cake (0.6 ounces) or 1 packet active dry yeast
¼ teaspoon baking soda
2 teaspoons salt
¼ cup sugar
4 cups flour
Melted butter

Bring sour cream to a boil, remove from heat, and cool to lukewarm. Crumble the yeast and stir into ⅓ cup of the lukewarm sour cream. Add baking soda, salt, and sugar to the remaining cream and mix well. Combine the 2 mixtures and add flour gradually, stirring constantly until smooth. Brush with melted butter. Cover and put in a warm place and let rise to about 2½ to 3 times the original volume. Knead lightly for about one minute and cut dough in 2 parts. Roll out one part at a time in rectangular shape about ⅛" thick. Brush with butter and cut in lengthwise strips about 2" wide. Place strips on top of each other and cut off pieces about 1½" wide. Place pieces in small buttered muffin tins with the cut edges up. Let rise in a warm place until double in size. Bake at 425°F for 10 to 15 minutes, or until a golden brown. Brush with butter if desired. Yield: 24 rolls.

PECAN ROLLS

½ yeast cake (0.3 ounces) or ½ packet active dry yeast
2 tablespoons lukewarm water
¼ cup sugar
¾ cup butter, at room temperature,
    plus more for muffin tins
1 beaten egg
1 cup lukewarm milk
¾ teaspoon salt
4 cups sifted flour
1 cup brown sugar
1 cup chopped pecans
4 whole pecans

Soften yeast in lukewarm water. Add ½ teaspoon sugar.
Cream ¼ cup butter. Add sugar, egg, and lukewarm milk.
Add yeast. Mix and sift salt and flour. Stir into first mixture
until dough is firm. Knead 10 to 15 minutes on a floured
board or in a stand mixer, until smooth and elastic to touch.
Put dough in a greased bowl. Cover and set in a warm place
to rise until doubled in bulk. Knead again. Roll out in rectangular shape ¼" thick. Spread with the remaining softened butter. Dredge with brown sugar. Sprinkle with
chopped pecans. Roll like jellyroll. Cut in 1" thick slices.
Place 4 whole pecans, 2 teaspoons brown sugar, and ½ teaspoon butter in each muffin pan. Press 1 roll into each hard
enough to make nuts stick. Cover and set in warm place to
rise until doubled in bulk. Bake at 350°F for about 20 minutes, or until lightly browned. Turn out, bottom side up, so
pecans will be on top. Yield: 12 rolls.

BRAN REFRIGERATOR ROLLS

1 cup boiling water
1 cup butter
¾ cup sugar
1½ cups bran
1½ teaspoons salt
2 eggs
2 yeast cakes (0.6 ounces each) or
    2 packets active dry yeasts
1 cup lukewarm water
7 to 8 cups flour

Pour boiling water over the butter and stir until melted. Add sugar, bran, and salt and mix well. When cool, add beaten eggs and yeast, dissolved in the lukewarm water. Add flour and knead by hand or in a stand mixer until smooth. Put dough into a bowl and spread with a little melted butter and cover with wax paper. Set in the refrigerator until ready to use. Pull off a small amount of the dough and shape in ball and place in greased muffin pan. Cover and let rise in a warm place until double in bulk, about 1 hour. Pre-heat oven to 400°F. Bake rolls for about 20 minutes. Makes 3½ dozen rolls.

COFFEE ROLLS

1 cup milk
¼ cup butter
¼ cup sugar, plus 2 tablespoons
1 teaspoon salt
1 yeast cake (0.6 ounces) or 1 packet active dry yeast
2 tablespoons lukewarm water
4 to 5 cups flour
2 eggs
½ teaspoon cinnamon
2 tablespoons raisins

Heat milk and add butter, ¼ cup sugar, and salt. When luke-warm, add the yeast, dissolved in lukewarm water. Add ½ cup flour and beat well. Cover and set in a warm place to rise. When double in bulk, add the beaten eggs and mix well. Add enough flour to make a firm dough. Knead on a slightly floured board or in a stand mixer until smooth and elastic to touch. Cover and set in a warm place to rise until double in bulk. Knead again. Break off small pieces of dough, shape into balls, and flatten like biscuits. Fit into a greased loaf pan. Cover and set in a warm place to rise until tripled in bulk. Brush tops with melted butter. Sprinkle with remaining sugar, cinnamon, and raisins. Bake at 400°F for 25 to 30 minutes. Yield: 30 rolls.

BUTTERMILK ROLLS

1 yeast cake (0.6 ounces) or 1 packet active dry yeast
¼ cup lukewarm water
2 cups buttermilk
¼ cup sugar
2 teaspoons salt
¼ teaspoon baking soda
¼ cup melted butter
5 cups flour

Soften yeast in lukewarm water. Heat buttermilk in top of double boiler. Add sugar, salt, baking soda, and melted butter. Cool to lukewarm. Add softened yeast and half the flour, beating well. Add enough flour to make a soft dough. Turn out on lightly floured board and knead or mix in a stand mixer until satiny. Shape into small round biscuits and place in greased pan or roll out ½" thick and cut with biscuit cutter. Brush each round with melted butter, fold over like Parker House rolls (p. 147), and place on greased baking sheet or in shallow pan. Brush lightly with melted butter. Cover and let rise until double in bulk about 1½ hours. Bake at 400°F for 15 to 20 minutes. Yield: 6 dozen small rolls.

POTATO ROLLS

1 cup mashed potatoes (p. 244)
7 cups flour
¾ cup butter, at room temperature
½ cup sugar
½ teaspoon salt
2 well-beaten eggs
1 cup scalded milk
1 yeast cake (0.6 ounces) or 1 packet active dry yeast
½ cup lukewarm water

Mix potatoes, 1 cup flour, butter, sugar, and salt. Add eggs and milk, cooled to lukewarm. Dissolve yeast in lukewarm water and add to first mixture. Cover and set in a warm place to rise 2 hours. Add remaining flour. Knead, or mix in a stand mixer with a dough hook, until smooth and elastic to the touch. Cover and set in a warm place to rise again 1½ hours. Knead. Roll ¼" thick. Cut with biscuit cutter. Fold like Parker House rolls (p. 147). Lay with space between, on greased baking pan. Set in warm place and let rise 1½ hours. Bake at 450°F for 20 minutes. Yield: 30 rolls.

WHOLE WHEAT MUFFINS

2 cups scalded milk
1 yeast cake (0.6 ounces) or 1 packet active dry yeast
¼ cup brown sugar
¼ cup melted butter
1 well-beaten egg
2½ cups whole wheat flour
½ teaspoon salt

Cool milk to lukewarm. Add yeast and dissolve. Add sugar, butter, and egg. Sift flour with salt and add it to the mixture. Beat until smooth. Cover and set in a warm place to rise until light. Pour into greased muffin cups, ⅔ full. Cover and set in a warm place to rise until cups are full. Bake at 350°F for 20 to 25 minutes. Yield: 12 muffins.

ENGLISH MUFFINS

¼ cup boiled diced potatoes
1 cup boiling water
1 teaspoon salt
1 yeast cake (0.6 ounces) or 1 packet active dry yeast
2 cups sifted flour

Measure potatoes by packing down well. Place in mixing bowl and stir in hot water. When lukewarm, add salt, crumbled yeast and 2 cups flour and beat thoroughly for about 2 minutes. Cover and let rise in warm place until doubled in bulk. Turn dough out on floured board, dust lightly with flour to facilitate handling and shape small mound of dough in 3" rounds, ¼" thick. Cover again. Let rise until doubled in bulk. Carefully slip spatula under muffins and place on slightly greased hot griddle. Brown muffins on both sides. Care must be taken as dough is very soft and falls easily. Bake at 350°F for 15 minutes. Yield: 9 muffins.

ENGLISH TEA CAKE

1 yeast cake (0.6 ounces) or 1 packet active dry yeast
½ cup hot milk
¼ cup butter, at room temperature
¼ cup sugar, plus 2 tablespoons
1 egg or 2 egg yolks
½ teaspoon salt
½ cup raisins
1½ cups flour
½ teaspoon cinnamon
½ cup chopped nuts

Soften yeast in milk that has been cooled to lukewarm. Add butter, ¼ cup sugar, eggs, salt, raisins, and flour. This makes a rather stiff drop batter. Beat until smooth. Let rise covered, in a warm place, for 2 hours or until doubled in bulk. Stir down and fill oiled, 2" deep pan about ½ to ¾ full. Make a topping of cinnamon, nuts, and remaining sugar. Combine and sprinkle over dough. Let rise until puffy. Bake at 400°F for 25 to 30 minutes.

RAISIN BUNS

2 yeast cakes (0.6 ounces each) or 2 active dry yeast
    packets
¼ cup lukewarm water
1 cup milk
¼ cup butter
½ cup sugar
1 teaspoon salt
5 cups sifted flour
2 well-beaten eggs
1 cup raisins

Soften yeast in lukewarm water. Heat milk in a saucepan over medium heat. Add butter, sugar, and salt and remove from heat. Cool to lukewarm. Add flour to make a thick batter. Add yeast and eggs. Beat well. Add raisins and enough flour to make a soft dough. Turn out on lightly floured board and knead, or mix in a stand mixer with a dough hook, until satiny. Place in greased bowl, cover and set in a warm place to rise. When doubled, punch down and shape into rolls. Let rise again until double in bulk. Bake at 375°F for 20 to 25 minutes. Frost with powdered sugar icing (p. 626). Yield: 4 dozen rolls.

HOT CROSS BUNS

1 cup hot milk
1 yeast cake (0.6 ounces) or 1 packet active dry yeast
6½ tablespoons sugar
3½ cups flour
1 cup butter, at room temperature
2 well-beaten eggs
½ cup raisins
1 teaspoon salt
¼ cup powdered sugar icing (p. 626)

Cool milk to lukewarm. Add yeast and 1½ tablespoons sugar. Dissolve. Add 1½ cups flour. Beat thoroughly. Cover and set aside in a warm place to rise until doubled in volume. Cream butter, remaining sugar, and 1 egg. Add to first mixture, along with the raisins. Sift remaining flour with the salt and add as well. Knead, or mix in a stand mixer with the dough hook, until satiny. Cover and set in a warm place to rise again until double in bulk. Mold into round buns. Put on greased baking sheet. Cover and set in a warm place to rise again until doubled or tripled in volume. Brush tops with remaining egg. Form the design of a cross on tops with back of a knife. Bake at 350°F for 15 to 20 minutes. Top with icing. Yield: 12 buns.

QUICK BREADS
AND BISCUITS

HOMEMADE BISCUIT MIX

8 cups flour
4 teaspoons salt
8 teaspoons baking powder
1½ cups butter, chilled

Sift flour with baking powder and salt. Add the butter, and cut in with knives, or pulse in a food processor, until the mixture has a fine even crumb. Place in closed container and keep in refrigerator, using as desired. This mixture will keep at least a month in the refrigerator. It will yield 5 batches with 2 cups of the mixture to each batch. It may be used for biscuits, dumplings, shortcake, waffles, muffins, quick coffee cake and dozens of other things.

BATTER BREAD

2 cups milk
⅔ cup cornmeal
4 eggs

Preheat oven to 400°F. Grease an 8" baking pan and put it in the oven to heat. Heat milk. Add cornmeal. Mix well. Separate eggs. Beat yolks and add to mixture, mixing thoroughly. Beat egg whites stiff. Fold into mixture. Remove baking pan from the oven and pour the batter into it. Bake until browned, about 40 minutes.

MOLASSES BREAD

1 cup sifted white flour
2 cups graham flour
1 teaspoon salt
½ cup sugar
1 teaspoon baking soda
½ cup milk
½ cup molasses

Preheat the oven to 325°F. Mix the flour, salt, and sugar together. Dissolve the baking soda in the milk and add the molasses. Add liquids to dry ingredients and mix thoroughly. Pour into greased loaf pans and bake for 1½ hours or until a knife inserted in the center comes out clean. Dates or raisins may be added.

SPOON BREAD

1 cup cornmeal
¾ cup boiling water
1 teaspoon salt
1 tablespoon sugar
1 beaten egg
½ teaspoon baking soda
1 cup buttermilk or sour milk
1½ tablespoons butter

Preheat oven to 375°F. Put cornmeal into a bowl. Pour boiling water over cornmeal. Cover and let cool. Add salt, sugar, and egg. Dissolve baking soda in buttermilk and add to first mixture. Mix thoroughly. Add butter. Pour into a deep, greased baking dish. Bake for 30 to 35 minutes, or until a knife inserted in the center comes out clean.

CORNBREAD

1½ cups milk
1 cup cornmeal
1½ tablespoons butter
2 beaten eggs
1½ teaspoons baking powder
½ teaspoon salt
2 teaspoons sugar

Preheat oven to 400°F. Heat milk and pour over cornmeal and butter. Cool. Add eggs, baking powder, salt, and sugar. Mix well. Pour into a greased 8″ baking pan and bake for 25 to 30 minutes, or until a knife inserted in the center comes out clean.

DATE-NUT BREAD

1 egg
¼ cup sugar
½ cup crushed walnuts or pecans
½ cup dates, pitted and chopped
2 cups flour
4 teaspoons baking powder
½ teaspoon salt
1 cup milk

Preheat oven to 350°F. Beat egg and add sugar. Add nuts and dates. Sift dry ingredients together and add alternately with milk to first mixture. Turn into a greased 9″ baking pan. Bake for 45 minutes, or until a knife inserted in the center comes out clean. Either all dates or all nuts may be used.

WALNUT BREAD

3 cups flour
3 tablespoons baking powder
1 cup sugar
1 teaspoon cinnamon
1 teaspoon salt
1 beaten egg
1½ cups milk
1 cup chopped walnuts
1 cup raisins
2 tablespoons melted butter

Sift flour, baking powder, sugar, cinnamon, and salt together. Combine egg and milk, mixing well. Add to first mixture and combine thoroughly. Add nuts, raisins, and butter. Pour into bread pan. Let stand 30 minutes. Bake at 325°F for 50 to 60 minutes, or until a knife inserted in the center comes out clean.

BANANA BREAD

1¾ cups sifted flour
¾ teaspoon baking soda
1¼ teaspoons cream of tartar
½ teaspoon salt
⅓ cup butter
⅔ cup sugar, plus more for sprinkling
2 eggs, beaten
1 cup mashed bananas (about 2 bananas)

Preheat oven to 350°F. Sift flour, baking soda, cream of tartar, and salt together. Rub butter to a creamy consistency with the back of a spoon. Beat in the sugar, a few tablespoons at a time, and continue beating until light and fluffy. Add eggs and beat well. Add flour mixture alternately with banana, a small amount at a time. Beat after each addition until smooth. Pour into a well-greased loaf pan and sprinkle with sugar. Bake for about 1 hour, or until a knife inserted in the center comes out clean.

WAFFLES

2 cups flour
4 teaspoons baking powder
1 teaspoon salt
1 tablespoon sugar
1¼ cups milk
2 eggs
2 tablespoons melted butter

Sift flour, baking powder, salt, and sugar together. Add milk. Separate eggs. Beat yolks and add to mixture. Mix thoroughly. Beat egg whites stiff and fold into mixture. Add butter. Heat waffle iron. Grease well. Put a little batter in center. Close iron. Waffles are done when they are golden brown all over. Serve with honey, maple syrup or marmalade.

PECAN SOUR CREAM WAFFLES

Follow recipe for waffles (p. 162), using 2 cups sour cream in place of milk, adding 1 teaspoon baking soda and ½ cup chopped pecans, and eliminating baking powder.

PINEAPPLE WAFFLES

Follow recipe for waffles (p. 162), adding ½ cup drained, crushed pineapple to batter.

BANANA WAFFLES

Follow recipe for waffles (p. 162), adding ¾ cup mashed banana pulp to batter.

BERRY WAFFLES

Follow recipe for waffles (p. 162), adding ¾ cup washed blueberries or blackberries to batter.

APPLE CINNAMON WAFFLES

Follow recipe for waffles (p. 162), adding 2 cups diced apple, 1½ teaspoons cinnamon and 2 tablespoons sugar.

DATE WAFFLES

Follow recipe for waffles (p. 162), adding 1 cup finely chopped dates to batter.

COCONUT WAFFLES

Follow recipe for waffles (p. 162), sprinkling batter with 1 teaspoon shredded coconut before cooking.

CORNMEAL WAFFLES

Follow recipe for waffles (p. 162), substituting 1 cup cornmeal for 1 of the cups of flour.

NUT WAFFLES

Follow recipe for waffles (p. 162), sprinkling 1 teaspoon chopped nuts on each waffle before cooking.

POPOVERS

    1 cup flour
    ¼ teaspoon salt
    1 cup milk
    2 eggs, beaten
    1 tablespoon melted butter

Preheat oven to 400°F. Grease a popover or muffin tin and put it in the oven to heat. Mix and sift flour and salt. Add milk gradually. Add eggs and butter. Beat batter for 5 minutes. Remove hot pan from oven and pour batter into it. Bake at 400°F for 30 minutes. Reduce heat to 325°F and bake for 15 more minutes. Do not open oven door for the first 15 minutes of baking. This recipe makes 8 to 10 popovers.

FRUIT POPOVERS

After popovers (p. 164) are cooked, open at the side and fill with any desired well-sugared berries or fruit.

DUMPLINGS

> 2 cups flour
> 1 teaspoon salt
> 4 teaspoons baking powder
> 3 tablespoons butter, chilled
> ¾ cup milk

Sift flour, salt, and baking powder together. Rub in butter with fingertips, or pulse in a food processor, until as fine as coarse cornmeal. Add milk to make a soft dough. Drop, a tablespoon at a time, on chicken or meat stew during the last 15 to 20 minutes of cooking. The stockpot must be covered tightly. Do not remove the cover during cooking.

POTATO DUMPLINGS

> 6 finely minced boiled potatoes (p. 244)
> 1 teaspoon salt
> ½ teaspoon pepper
> 2 tablespoons melted butter
> 1 teaspoon ground nutmeg
> 4 beaten eggs
> 2 tablespoons flour
> 2 tablespoons breadcrumbs

Beat all ingredients together thoroughly. Using a tablespoon, drop into boiling, slightly salted water. Cover tightly and boil until light, about 12 minutes. Yield: 20 dumplings.

APPLE DUMPLINGS

Plain pastry (p. 445)
4 tart apples (e.g. Granny Smith)
½ cup sugar
½ teaspoon ground nutmeg
2 tablespoons butter

Preheat oven to 425°F. Roll out pastry to ⅛" thickness on a lightly floured board. Cut in large circles. Cut tart apples in thin slices. Put a small amount in center of each circle of pastry. Sprinkle with sugar and a little nutmeg. Dot with butter. Moisten edge of pastry with water. Bring opposite edges to center and press tightly together. Prick top with a fork to allow steam to escape. Bake at 425°F for 10 minutes. Reduce heat to 350°F and bake for 15 to 20 minutes longer, or until the pastry is nicely browned.

PEACH DUMPLINGS

Follow recipe for apple dumplings (above), using peaches instead of apples and lemon juice instead of nutmeg.

SHORTCAKES

2 cups flour
5 teaspoons baking powder
1 teaspoon salt
2 tablespoons sugar
¼ cup butter, chilled
⅔ cup milk

Preheat oven to 425°F. Mix and sift flour, baking powder, salt, and sugar. Cut in butter with a knife or pulse in a food processor, until mixture is as fine as coarse cornmeal. Add milk gradually and mix to a soft dough. Roll out on slightly floured board to ½" thickness. Cut with large cookie cutter. Bake for 15 minutes, or until nicely browned. Break apart and put sliced and sweetened fruit or crushed berries between and on top of cakes. Serve with whipped cream. Makes 8 shortcakes.

DOUGHNUTS

⅓ cup sugar
1½ tablespoons butter, at room temperature
1 well-beaten egg
⅓ cup milk
2 cups flour
2 teaspoons baking powder
¼ teaspoon cinnamon
¼ teaspoon clove
½ teaspoon mace
½ teaspoon salt
Oil for frying
Powdered sugar for sprinkling

Cream sugar and butter together. Add egg and milk. Mix well. Mix and sift remaining ingredients. Add them to liquid mixture and mix thoroughly. Turn out on slightly floured board and roll to ½" thickness. Cut with a doughnut cutter. Fry in deep, hot oil (375°F) until dark brown. Drain on paper towels. Sprinkle with powdered sugar. Makes 24 doughnuts.

FRENCH CRULLERS

¼ cup sugar
1 teaspoon salt
1 teaspoon grated orange zest
¼ cup butter
1 cup hot water
1 cup flour
3 eggs
Oil for frying
Powdered sugar icing (p. 626)

Put sugar, salt, orange zest, and butter in a saucepan with hot water. Bring to a boil. Add flour. Blend thoroughly. Cook until thick, stirring constantly. Cool slightly. Add 1 egg at a time, beating each one in thoroughly before adding another. Press dough through a pastry tube, using a rose tube, onto waxed paper or a well-greased square of heavy paper, in desired shape. Turn paper upside down and let crullers drop into deep, hot oil (375°F). Fry until well puffed up and a golden brown in color, about 6 to 7 minutes. Drain on paper towels. Ice with powdered frosting. This makes 18 crullers.

CHOCOLATE DOUGHNUTS

Follow recipe for doughnuts (p. 167), adding 1 ounce melted dark chocolate, ½ teaspoon vanilla, and 2 tablespoons sugar.

SWEET MILK PANCAKES

2 cups flour
1 teaspoon salt
1½ teaspoons baking powder
2 tablespoons sugar
2 cups milk
1 egg, beaten
1 tablespoon melted butter

Mix and sift flour, salt, baking powder, and sugar. Add milk, egg, and butter. Mix well. Drop by tablespoons on a hot griddle, greased well. Brown on both sides. Serve hot with marmalade or honey.

BREADCRUMB PANCAKES

1 cup dry breadcrumbs
½ teaspoon salt
1½ cups hot milk
½ cup cold milk
2 eggs, well-beaten

Mix crumbs and salt in bowl. Add hot milk. Add cold milk. Fold eggs into crumb mixture. Drop from tablespoon onto hot griddle and brown both sides. Serves 4.

BLUEBERRY PANCAKES

1 egg
¼ teaspoon salt
1 cup milk
2 teaspoons baking powder
1 cup flour
½ cup blueberries

Beat egg until light. Add salt and milk. Sift baking powder with flour and stir it into first mixture. Beat until smooth. Add blueberries. Drop from spoon onto hot griddle and brown both sides. Serves 4.

CORN PANCAKES

2½ cups flour
4 teaspoons baking powder
½ teaspoon salt
2 cups milk
1 egg, beaten
1 tablespoon melted butter
1 tablespoon sugar
2½ cups canned corn

Mix and sift the dry ingredients. Add milk slowly and then beat in egg. Beat until smooth, about 1 minute. Add melted butter and blend well. Add well-drained corn. Drop by table-spoonfuls on a hot griddle and bake until bubbles form on top, then turn and bake on the other side. These cakes are very tender and should be handled carefully in turning or they will break. This makes about 36 pancakes. They should be served at once and may be used in a meal in the place of potato, or as the main dish of luncheon or supper. Serves 4–6.

JELLY PANCAKES

1 cup sifted flour
1 teaspoon baking powder
½ teaspoon salt
1 teaspoon sugar
2 eggs, separated
1 cup milk
2 tablespoons butter

Sift flour, baking powder, salt, and sugar together. Beat egg yolks and milk together with a fork. Add gradually to flour mixture, beating only until smooth. Add butter. Stiffly beat egg whites, and gently fold them into the batter. Cook on a hot, greased griddle. Spread with jelly and roll, or roll and serve around fried sausages or bacon. Makes six 7" pancakes.

BANANA PANCAKES

Follow recipe for sweet milk pancakes (p. 169), substituting 2 mashed bananas for ½ cup flour and reducing milk content to 1 cup.

CEREAL PANCAKES

Follow recipe for sweet milk pancakes (p. 169), substituting 1 cup any cooked cereal for 1 cup flour, adding 1 well-beaten egg, and reducing milk to 1 cup.

MELBA TOAST

Preheat oven to 250°F. Cut stale bread in very thin slices or ½" strips. Cut off crust. Put in oven and toast thoroughly until a delicate brown.

FRENCH TOAST

¼ teaspoon salt
2 tablespoons sugar
1 cup whole milk
1 egg, slightly beaten
5 slices of bread

Add salt, sugar, and milk to slightly beaten egg. Dip the pieces of bread into egg mixture. Cook soaked slices of bread on well-oiled griddle. Brown on one side. Turn and brown on the other. Serve with maple syrup, butter, jam, or fruit.

CINNAMON TOAST

Spread buttered toast with a mixture of 3 parts sugar and 1 part cinnamon. Place on platter and bake at 350°F until sugar melts.

GOLDEN TOAST STICKS

Preheat oven to 300°F. Cut a loaf of bread into ½" slices. Then cut in sticks ½" wide. Arrange sticks on a baking sheet and bake for 20 minutes or until they are crisp throughout and evenly browned. Turn sticks once during baking. Serve with soup, allowing 3 sticks for each person.

CROUSTADES

Cut stale bread in 2½" slices, and cut the slices in squares, oblongs or circles. Scoop out the centers with a fork leaving cases ¼" thick. Fry in deep hot fat (375°F) until a delicate brown. Drain on paper towels. Fill with creamed vegetables, meat or fish.

JOHNNYCAKE

    1 cup cornmeal
    2 tablespoons whole wheat flour
    ½ teaspoon salt
    1 tablespoon sugar
    1½ tablespoons melted butter
    1 cup boiling milk
    1 egg

Preheat oven to 400°F. Sift cornmeal, flour, salt, and sugar together. Add butter and pour milk in quickly. Separate egg. Beat the white stiff. Beat the yolk and fold into the white. Add cornmeal mixture and stir in with a gentle folding motion. Drop batter from a spoon, in rectangular shape, onto a greased baking sheet, leaving ½" between each biscuit. Bake for 30 minutes. Yield: 12 Johnnycakes.

COFFEE CAKE

    3 cups flour
    2 cups brown sugar
    1 teaspoon salt
    1 teaspoon cinnamon
    ½ cup butter, chilled
    2 teaspoons baking powder
    2 eggs
    ¾ cup milk

Preheat oven to 400°F. Mix and sift flour, sugar, salt, and cinnamon. Cut in butter with a knife or pulse in a food processor, until mixture is as fine as coarse cornmeal. Reserve 1 cup of this mixture to sprinkle on top of cake. To the remainder add the baking powder and mix well. Add the beaten eggs and milk and beat thoroughly. Pour into 2 8" greased cake pans and sprinkle top with crumbs reserved for this purpose. Bake for 20 to 25 minutes, or until a knife inserted in the center comes out clean.

COFFEE RING

    3 cups flour
    ⅓ cup sugar, plus 1 tablespoon
    2 tablespoons baking powder
    1 teaspoon salt
    ¼ cup chilled butter, plus 1 tablespoon melted butter
    1 egg
    ¾ cup milk
    ¾ cup raisins
    ½ cup nuts, chopped
    Powdered sugar icing (p. 626)

Preheat oven to 350°F. Mix and sift flour, ⅓ cup sugar, baking powder, and salt. Cut in ¼ cup butter with a knife or pulse in a food processor, until mixture is as fine as coarse cornmeal. Add beaten egg and milk to make a soft dough. Roll out a rectangular-shaped piece about ¼" thick. Spread lightly with melted butter, sprinkle with raisins, nuts, and remaining sugar. Roll lengthwise like a jellyroll. Bring ends together to make a circle and press together. Put on a large greased pan and cut gashes around outside edges with scissors, 2" apart. Bake for 25 to 30 minutes. Spread top with powdered sugar icing.

BAKING POWDER BISCUITS

2 cups flour
4 teaspoons baking powder
½ teaspoon salt
¼ cup butter, chilled
¾ cup milk

Preheat oven to 450°F. Sift flour, baking powder, and salt together. Rub butter in with fingertips. Add milk slowly and mix to soft dough. Roll out on a slightly floured board to ½" thickness. Cut with biscuit cutter. Bake for 10 to 15 minutes, or until nicely browned. Yield: 12 biscuits.

CREAM OF TARTAR BISCUITS

3 cups flour
1 teaspoon salt
2 teaspoons cream of tartar
1½ tablespoons butter, chilled
1 teaspoon baking soda
1 cup milk

Preheat oven to 425°F. Mix and sift flour, salt, and cream of tartar together. Work in butter with fingertips. Mix baking soda and milk and add to flour mixture. Mix thoroughly and knead on a floured board until satiny. Roll ¾" thick. Cut with biscuit cutter. Bake on greased pan, with space between, for 15 minutes, or until nicely browned. Yield: 12 biscuits.

SOUR MILK BISCUITS

2 cups flour
1 tablespoon baking powder
1 teaspoon salt
2 tablespoons butter, chilled
½ teaspoon baking soda
¾ cup sour milk or buttermilk

Preheat oven to 450°F. Sift flour, baking powder, and salt together. Rub in butter with fingertips. Mix baking soda and sour milk. Add slowly to first mixture and mix to a soft dough. Roll out on slightly floured board to ½" thickness. Cut with a biscuit cutter. Bake for 10 to 15 minutes. Yield: 12 biscuits.

SWEET POTATO BISCUITS

1 cup mashed sweet potatoes (p. 259)
1 tablespoon butter, at room temperature
1 tablespoon sugar
½ teaspoon baking soda
1 cup buttermilk
2 cups flour
1 teaspoon salt

Preheat oven to 400°F. Beat potatoes, butter, and sugar together until well blended. Dissolve baking soda in buttermilk and add to potato mixture. Mix and sift flour and salt and add to first mixture. Mix well. Roll out to ½" thickness on floured board. Cut with small cookie cutter. Put on greased baking sheet. Bake for 15 to 20 minutes, or until nicely browned. Yield: 24 biscuits.

OATMEAL BISCUITS

1½ cups flour
1 tablespoon sugar
4 teaspoons baking powder
1½ teaspoons salt
1½ cups raw rolled oats
¼ cup butter, chilled
¾ cup milk

Preheat oven to 450°F. Sift flour, sugar, baking powder, and salt together. Add rolled oats and mix. Rub butter in with fingertips. Add milk slowly and mix to a soft dough. Roll out on floured board to ¾" thickness. Cut with biscuit cutter. Brush tops with milk and bake for 15 to 20 minutes. Yield: 15 biscuits.

CHEESE BISCUITS

Follow recipe for baking powder biscuits (p. 175), adding ½ cup grated cheese before adding milk.

EMERGENCY BISCUITS

Follow recipe for baking powder biscuits (p. 175), using 1 cup milk. Drop by tablespoons onto a greased pan.

SAUSAGE BISCUITS

    2 cups flour
    5 teaspoons baking powder
    ¾ teaspoon salt
    2 tablespoons butter or shortening, chilled
    ¾ cup milk
    8 pan-fried sausage links, fully cooked

Mixed and sift dry ingredients. Rub in butter with fingertips. Add milk gradually, stirring mixture with a knife. Roll out on floured pastry cloth to ¾" thickness. Cut into 3" round biscuits. Place a sausage in the center of each biscuit and roll up. Place on oiled baking sheet and bake for 15 minutes. Yield: 8 biscuits.

HONEY DATE BISCUITS

2 cups baking powder biscuit dough (p. 175)
¼ cup butter, at room temperature
2 tablespoons honey
¼ cup chopped nuts
½ cup chopped, pitted dates

Preheat oven to 425°F. Roll dough in rectangle to ¼" thickness. Cream the butter. Add honey gradually. Add nuts and dates. Mix well. Spread mixture on dough. Roll as a jellyroll. Cut into 1" slices. Place cut side down, on greased baking sheet. Bake for 25 minutes. Yield: 8 to 12 biscuits. Whole nuts may be pressed into each biscuit before baking.

SCONES

2 cups flour
1 teaspoon salt
5 teaspoons baking powder
2 tablespoons sugar
¼ cup butter, chilled
2 eggs
⅓ cup milk

Preheat oven to 425°F. Mix and sift flour, salt, baking powder, and 1 tablespoon sugar. Cut in butter with a knife or pulse in a food processor, until mixture is as fine as coarse cornmeal. Beat the eggs (reserving 1 egg white for the tops). Add eggs and milk. Mix to a soft dough. Roll out on a slightly floured board to ½" thickness into a round piece and cut into quarters. Brush with white of egg and sprinkle with the remaining tablespoon of sugar. Bake for 10 to 15 minutes, or until nicely browned. This recipe makes 10 to 12 scones. Currants or other dried fruit may be added to the dough before baking, if desired.

179

CREAM SCONES

2 cups flour
½ teaspoon baking soda
¾ teaspoon salt
2 tablespoons sugar
¼ cup butter, chilled
Grated zest of 1 lemon
¾ cup light cream
4 teaspoons vinegar
1 egg, slightly beaten

Preheat oven to 475°F. Sift flour with baking soda, salt, and sugar. Cut in butter, or pulse in a food processor, until as fine as coarse cornmeal. Add lemon zest. Combine cream and vinegar. Add to flour mixture stirring quickly to form a stiff dough. Knead slightly on slightly floured board. Roll out ⅜" thick. Cut in diamond shapes. Brush with egg. Place on ungreased baking sheet. Bake for 10 to 20 minutes, or until nicely browned. Yield: 12 scones.

PARKER HOUSE ROLLS (QUICK)

Follow recipe for baking powder biscuits (p. 175), with following changes: Roll out to ¼" thickness. Cut with large cookie cutter. Spread with melted butter. Fold over double and press edges together lightly.

QUICK CINNAMON ROLLS

Baking powder biscuit batter (p. 175)
2 tablespoons sugar
½ teaspoon cinnamon
¼ cup chopped walnuts or pecans

Preheat oven to 450°F. Roll biscuit batter ½" thick. Spread with mixture of sugar and cinnamon. Roll like a jellyroll. Cut slices ¾" thick. Bake at 450°F for 10 to 15 minutes. Yield: 12 rolls. Chopped nuts may be added to the sugar-cinnamon mixture.

FLUFFY MUFFINS

1 cup milk
1 beaten egg
¼ cup melted butter
2 cups flour
1 tablespoon baking powder
3 tablespoons sugar
½ teaspoon salt

Preheat oven to 425°F. Mix milk, egg, and butter. Sift other ingredients together and mix with first mixture lightly. Do not beat. Pour batter into greased muffins pans, ⅔ full, and bake for 20 to 25 minutes. Yield: 12 muffins.

BRAN MUFFINS

1 cup sifted flour
3½ teaspoons baking powder
½ teaspoon salt
3 tablespoons brown sugar
1 cup bran
1 well-beaten egg
⅔ cup milk
3 tablespoons melted butter
½ cup raisins

Preheat oven to 425°F. Mix and sift dry ingredients. Add bran. Combine egg, milk, and butter. Add to flour mixture. Then add raisins, stirring only until mixed. Grease muffin pans and fill them ⅔ full. Bake for 20 to 30 minutes, according to size of muffin. Yield: 12 muffins.

CORNMEAL MUFFINS

½ cup cornmeal
1 cup flour
1 tablespoon baking powder
1 tablespoon sugar
½ teaspoon salt
¾ cup milk
1 well-beaten egg
1 tablespoon melted butter

Preheat oven to 400°F. Mix and sift dry ingredients. Gradually add milk, egg, and butter. Bake in greased muffin pans for about 25 minutes. Yield: 8 muffins.

BLUEBERRY MUFFINS

¼ cup butter, at room temperature
⅓ cup sugar
2 well-beaten eggs
2 cups flour
5 teaspoons baking powder
1 teaspoon salt
⅔ cup milk
½ cup blueberries

Preheat oven to 400°F. Cream butter and sugar together. Add eggs and mix well. Sift 1½ cups flour, baking powder, and salt together. Add this mixture to first mixture alternately with milk. Sprinkle blueberries with remaining flour and stir in lightly. Bake in greased muffin pans for 25 to 30 minutes. Yield: 12 muffins.

QUICK FRUIT MUFFINS

2 cups homemade biscuit mix (p. 158)
¼ cup sugar
1 well-beaten egg
1 cup milk
½ cup dates, nuts, blueberries, sliced cranberries, or
    chopped fruits

Preheat oven to 400°F. Combine biscuit mix and sugar. Beat egg and milk together with a fork. Add this to dough, combining thoroughly without beating. Add dates, nuts, etc., singly or in combination, as desired. Pour into greased muffin pans. Bake for 20 minutes. Yield: 8 muffins.

CEREAL MUFFINS

Follow recipe for fluffy muffins (p. 181), adding 1 cup cold, cooked or flaked cereal. Increase milk slightly if dry cereal is used and decrease milk if cooked cereal is employed. Add cereal with sifted dry ingredients.

BANANA BRAN MUFFINS

    1 cup flour
    ½ teaspoon salt
    ½ teaspoon baking soda
    1 teaspoon baking powder
    2 tablespoons butter, at room temperature
    ¼ cup sugar
    1 well-beaten egg
    1 cup shredded bran
    2 tablespoons milk
    2 cups bananas, thinly sliced

Preheat oven to 375°F. Sift flour with salt, baking soda, and baking powder. Cream butter. Add sugar and cream gradually. Add egg, bran, and milk. Mix and allow to stand while slicing bananas. Add bananas and mix well. Add sifted dry ingredients, stirring as little as possible. Bake in greased muffin tins for 20 to 30 minutes. Yield: 12 muffins.

SALLY LUNN MUFFINS

Follow recipe for blueberry muffins (p. 183), omitting blueberries and using only 4 teaspoons baking powder.

APPLE GEMS

¼ cup butter, at room temperature
2 tablespoons sugar
⅔ cup yellow cornmeal
1¼ cups warm milk
1 well-beaten egg
1 cup flour
2 teaspoons baking powder
1 teaspoon salt
1½ cups chopped apples

Preheat oven to 350°F. Add butter, sugar, and cornmeal to milk and mix well. Add the egg, blending well. Sift flour, baking powder, and salt. Fold in gently to the cornmeal mixture, stirring as little as possible to combine. Add apples to batter and stir thoroughly. Drop into greased muffin pans and bake for 25 to 30 minutes. Yield: 12 to 14 muffins.

CINNAMON BUNS

Homemade biscuit mix (p. 158)
¼ cup melted butter
3 tablespoons sugar
1 tablespoon cinnamon

Preheat oven to 350°F. Roll out biscuit mix ⅓" thick and 8" wide. Brush with melted butter. Mix sugar and cinnamon. Sprinkle mixture over the dough. Fold over twice, making 3 layers of dough. Slice into 1" strips. Bake in a greased baking pan for 25 to 30 minutes. Allow 2 cups biscuit mix for 8 buns.

WHEAT STICKS

1 cup flour
½ cup whole wheat flour
1 teaspoon salt
½ teaspoon baking soda
1 tablespoon sugar
1½ tablespoons butter, chilled
⅓ cup water

Preheat oven to 350°F. Mix and sift flours, salt, baking soda, and sugar. Work butter in with fingertips or pulse in a food processor, until as fine as coarse cornmeal. Add water gradually, stirring constantly. Mix well and knead for a few moments on a floured board. Roll to ½" thickness. Cut into 3" by ¼" strips. Put on greased baking sheet with space between and bake until golden brown, turning once. Yield: 12 sticks.

CORN STICKS

1 cup sifted flour
1 cup cornmeal
½ teaspoon baking soda
1 teaspoon salt
1 egg, beaten
1 cup sour milk or buttermilk
1 tablespoon melted butter

Preheat oven to 425°F. Mix and sift flour, cornmeal, baking soda, and salt. Combine egg and milk. Add to flour mixture, stirring until well mixed. Stir in butter. Cut into 3" by ¼" strips. Bake on a greased baking sheet for 15 to 20 minutes. To use regular milk instead of sour milk, substitute 1 tablespoon baking powder for soda. For cornbread, bake in greased, shallow pan at 400°F for about 30 minutes. Yield: 12 corn sticks.

FRUIT

Fruit can be used in savory and sweet dishes with equally good results. Just as applesauce and pork chops go together, so do cherries and pie.

When selecting fruit for a cooking project, there are several considerations. Some fruits, like apples, come in dozens of varieties. Tart apples, like Granny Smith, are excellent for baking. Sweeter apples, like Fuji and Gala, might be good in an applesauce. An apple pie with Gala apples would still be delicious, but it might be a little sweeter and softer than a traditional apple pie.

Pears also come in number of varieties. Sheckel pears are excellent for baking, while Asian pears are better for salads, because of their firm flesh. Oranges, too, come in a number of different varieties. Some of the small, thin-skinned oranges aren't so good to eat, but may make wonderful juice. Navel oranges, on the other hand, are good to eat, but don't juice very well.

Try to imagine how a recipe should taste when picking the fruit. Should the fruit be firm or soft? Sweet or tart? Juicy or dry? There isn't necessarily one correct answer. The recipes in this chapter often include a suggestion for a specific variety of apple or pear. If those fruits aren't available, don't despair! Many other varieties should be equally delicious.

Fruits, like most foods, are especially nice in season. This chart outlines some common fruits, their seasons, and the characteristics to look for when selecting them:

A FIELD GUIDE TO FRUIT

NAME	IN SEASON	CHARACTERISTICS
Apples	Sept. to May	Firm to the touch, smooth skin, no bruises
Apricots	June to July	Plump and firm with a sweet smell
Bananas	All year	Bright yellow skin, no bruises
Blueberries	June to Aug.	Plump berries with deep color, no shriveling
Cantaloupes	May to Sept.	Sweet smell, firm, hollow sounding
Cherries	May to June	Bright color, no shriveling or bruising
Coconuts	Sept. to March	Milk inside when shaken
Cranberries	Sept. to Dec.	Plump with good coloring, no shriveling
Figs	July to Sept.	Unbroken flesh, firm but not hard, plump
Grapefruit	Oct. to June	Firm skin, good color, heavy
Grapes	June to Dec.	Soft, plump, no shriveling or molding
Honeydews	Feb. to Oct.	Firm skin, heavy, sweet smell

Kiwi	June to Aug.	Firm and plump, not hard or bruised
Lemons	All year	Heavy for its size, firm skin
Limes	May to Oct.	Heavy for its size, brightly colored skin
Mangoes	April to Aug.	Sweet smell, firm, but not hard, flesh
Nectarines	June to Sept.	Firm, but not hard, flesh, soft skin, plump
Oranges	Nov.to June	Heavy and firm
Peaches	June to Sept.	Firm, plump, sweet smell
Pears	Aug.to May	Tender near stem, sweet smell, smooth skin
Pineapples	Feb. to Aug.	Sweet smell, vibrant tops, firm flesh
Plums	June to Sept.	Plump, firm, not hard, flesh
Watermelons	May to Aug.	Symmetrical, with a dull surface

APPLESAUCE

12 tart cooking apples, e.g. Granny Smith
5 tablespoons sugar (optional)
Cinnamon stick (optional)

Wash, peel, core, and quarter apples. Put them in saucepan with a cinnamon stick. Half cover with cold water. Bring to boil. Cover. Reduce heat and let simmer until tender. Stir in sugar. Remove cinnamon stick, cook 5 minutes more. Mash apples with a spoon or force through a sieve. Chill. If desired, a little lemon juice, cinnamon, or nutmeg may be added after cooking. Serves 6.

BAKED APPLESAUCE

12 tart cooking apples
½ cup sugar
½ teaspoon nutmeg

Preheat oven to 350°F. Wash, peel, core, and divide apples into eighths. Place in greased baking dish. Half cover with water. Sprinkle with seasonings. Cover tightly and bake 2 ½ to 3 hours. Remove and scrape through a sieve or mash. Serves 6.

BAKED APPLES

6 apples
6 tablespoons brown sugar

Preheat oven to 350°F. Select smooth apples of uniform size. Wash and remove cores. Fill the center of each with 1 table-spoon brown sugar. Put in baking dish. Add enough boiling water to cover bottom of dish. Bake, basting frequently with dish liquor, until tender, about 20 to 40 minutes, depending on size and variety of apple. A little lemon juice or cinnamon may be added to the water, if desired. There are several alternates for brown sugar as a filling, such as strips of bananas, marmalade, preserves, honey, and lemon juice, hard cinnamon candy, fresh berries, candied orange peel, chopped pineapple, chopped peach, preserved ginger, or nuts. Baked apples may be served with whipped cream.

APPLE FRITTERS

1 cup flour
1½ teaspoons baking powder
2 tablespoons sugar
½ teaspoon salt
½ cup milk
1 egg
5 or 6 tart apples, such as Granny Smith
Oil, for frying
Powdered sugar

Mix and sift flour, baking powder, sugar, and salt. Add milk and well-beaten egg. Mix well. Peel and core apples. Cut in sections. Dip each piece of apple in the batter and fry in deep hot oil (340° to 375°F) until brown. If you don't have a thermometer for your oil, just heat the oil until a drop of water splatters if dropped in the oil. Drain on paper towels and sprinkle with powdered sugar.

APPLE COMPOTE

3 uniform-size eating apples
3 cups syrup for stewed berries (p. 195)
1–2 whole sticks cinnamon

Wash, peel, core, and quarter apples. Place apples and cinnamon sticks in a medium saucepan. Simmer in syrup over medium heat until tender. Chill and serve. If desired, the apples may be sliced into rings before cooking. Chopped ginger and cloves may be added to the syrup for a different effect.

FRIED APPLES

6 tart apples
4 tablespoons butter (more if needed)

Wash apples. Slice ½-inch thick. Remove cores. Sauté in melted butter until soft, turning occasionally to brown evenly. Or, they may be cored, quartered, and then sautéed.

DEEP-FRIED APPLE RINGS

4–6 tart apples
Oil for frying
Sugar

Wash and core apples. Slice crosswise ¼-inch thick. Fry in approximately 2 inches of hot fat (340° to 390°F) until brown, about 2 to 3 minutes. Drain on a paper towel. Sprinkle with sugar. This is an excellent garnish for pork dishes.

STEWED APPLES

6 tart cooking apples
6 tablespoons sugar
½ teaspoon vanilla extract
½ teaspoon nutmeg

Wash apples. Put in medium saucepan. Half cover with water. Sprinkle with sugar, vanilla, and nutmeg. Bring to a boil and reduce heat, simmering until skins are broken and apples are tender. Season with more sugar if too tart. Serve hot or cold with the syrup from the pan and cream.

APRICOT COMPOTE

2 cups water
1 cup sugar
1 tablespoon freshly squeezed lemon juice
8 almost-ripe apricots

Bring water, sugar, and lemon juice to a boil over medium heat. Let boil for 5 minutes, so that the sugar is completely dissolved, and the syrup is clear. Wash apricots and cut in half, removing the pit. Puncture them in several places. Plunge into boiling syrup. Boil until tender. Chill and serve. Serves 4.

SAUTÉED BANANAS

4 firm, ripe bananas
¼ cup lemon juice
½ cup corn flake crumbs
2 tablespoons butter, more as needed

Peel bananas. Cut in quarters. Dip in lemon juice. Roll in crumbs. Melt butter in pan and sauté bananas until well browned. A well-beaten egg may be substituted for lemon juice. Breadcrumbs or corn meal may be used instead of corn flakes. Serves 4.

FRIED BANANAS

3 bananas
½ teaspoon salt
2 tablespoons lemon juice
½ cup flour
1 egg, slightly beaten
2 tablespoons water
½ cup breadcrumbs
Oil, for frying

Remove skins from 3 bananas. Cut in halves, lengthwise and crosswise. Sprinkle with salt and lemon juice. Dip in flour, then dip in slightly beaten egg, diluted with 2 tablespoons water. Roll in fine crumbs and fry in deep hot oil (340° to 375°F) 3 or 4 minutes or until brown. Drain on paper towels. Serve with ice cream, or alone. Serves 6.

BANANA FRITTERS

1 cup flour
1½ teaspoon baking powder
2 tablespoons sugar
½ teaspoon salt
½ cup milk
1 egg
4 or 5 bananas
Oil, for frying
Powdered sugar

Peel bananas. Cut through lengthwise and again in pieces 1½ to 2 inches long. Follow recipe for apple fritters (p. 191).

STEWED BERRIES

1 quart berries, such as strawberries, raspberries, or
   blackberries
1 cup water
1 tablespoon freshly squeezed lemon juice
1 cup sugar

Wash and drain berries, handling them gently so as not to bruise the fruit. Put in saucepan. Add 1 cup cold water and lemon juice. Bring to boil. Cover. Reduce heat and let simmer 10 minutes. Stir in sugar. Bring to boil. Reduce heat. Let simmer 2 minutes. May be served over pound cake, or with ice cream or whipped cream. Serves 4.

STEWED BLUEBERRIES

1 cup sugar
1 cup water
1 tablespoon freshly squeezed lemon juice
1 quart blueberries

Mix sugar, water, and lemon juice. Bring to boil and boil 3 minutes. Wash and drain berries. Add to syrup. Let simmer 5 minutes. May be served over pound cake, or with ice cream or whipped cream. Serves 4.

CHERRY COMPOTE

2 cups water
1 cup sugar
1 tablespoon freshly squeezed lemon juice
2 cups cherries

Prepare syrup as in Apricot Compote (p. 193). Wash and remove stones from cherries. Boil cherries in syrup 10 minutes. Chill and serve. Serves 4.

STEWED CHERRIES

1½ pounds fresh or frozen cherries

Wash and remove stems from cherries. Put in saucepan. Cover with cold water. Bring to a boil. Reduce heat and let simmer until soft. May be served with ice cream or whipped cream.

CHERRY FRITTERS

1 cup flour
1½ teaspoons baking powder
2 tablespoons sugar
½ teaspoon salt
½ cup milk
1 egg
1½ pounds fresh or frozen cherries
Oil, for frying
Powdered sugar

Remove stones if using fresh cherries. Thaw if frozen cherries are used. Follow recipe for apple fritters (p. 191).

CRANBERRY SAUCE

2 cups water
1 quart fresh or frozen whole cranberries
1¾ cups sugar

Bring water to a boil. Add berries. Cover and cook over medium-low heat until outer skins have burst. Add sugar and let simmer 8 minutes. Pour into mold. Chill. For strained cranberry sauce, cook cranberries as above. Then strain through a sieve, scraping berries to force pulp through. Return strained liquid to stove. Add sugar. Simmer 8 minutes. Pour into mold. Chill.

PEACH OR APRICOT FRITTERS

1 cup flour
1½ teaspoons baking powder
2 tablespoons sugar
½ teaspoon salt
½ cup milk
1 egg
6 large peaches or 10 to 12 apricots
Oil, for frying
Powdered sugar

Cut halves of peach or apricot in quarters. Follow recipe for apple fritters (p. 191).

BAKED PEACHES

3 nearly ripe peaches
½ tablespoon lemon juice
2 tablespoons brown sugar

Preheat oven to 400°F. Bring a medium saucepan filled with water to a boil. Drop the peaches in the water for a minute or so, until the skin bursts and starts to come away from the fruit. Quickly remove the fruit from the boiling water and run them under cold water, removing the skins completely. Let the peaches cool for a few minutes, then cut in half and remove the pit. Put peaches, flat side down, in a baking pan, being careful that they do not touch one another. Sprinkle with sugar and lemon juice. Bake until brown, adding a little syrup if they seem too dry.

PEACH COMPOTE

2 cups water
1 cup sugar
1 tablespoon freshly squeezed lemon juice
4 peaches

Prepare syrup as in Apricot Compote (p. 193). Bring some water to a boil. Add peaches and boil 2 minutes. Remove peaches and plunge them into cold water. Remove skins. Boil peaches in syrup until tender. Chill and serve. Serves 4.

BAKED FRESH PEARS

1 quart Sheldon or Seckel pears
½ cup maple sugar
½ cup brown sugar
¼ teaspoon ginger
½ cup water

Preheat oven to 300°F. Wash pears and put in a casserole or earthen pot, whole and unpeeled. Add other ingredients and ½ cup hot water. Cover and bake for 1½ hours. Add water as needed to prevent burning and to make syrup at bottom of pot. May be served over ice cream or with whipped cream.

FRIED PLANTAINS

3 plantains
½ teaspoon salt
2 tablespoons freshly squeezed lemon juice
½ cup flour
1 egg, slightly beaten
2 tablespoons water
½ cup breadcrumbs
Oil, for frying

Follow recipe for sautéed bananas (p. 194).

BAKED RHUBARB

1 pound rhubarb
1 cup boiling water
¾ cup sugar

Preheat oven to 350°F. Wash rhubarb. Do not peel unless skin is very tough. Cut in 1-inch pieces. Put in baking dish. Add 1 cup boiling water and sugar. Cover and bake until tender, about 2½ hours. If desired, raisins may be added to dish before cooking. Serves 4.

RHUBARB SAUCE

1 pound rhubarb
¼ cup sugar

Wash. Peel if skin is tough. Cut in 1-inch pieces. Put in saucepan. Sprinkle with sugar. Cover bottom of pan with water. Cook slowly until soft. May be served with ice cream or whipped cream. Serves 4.

TAFFY APPLES

1 cup granulated sugar
½ cup boiling water
½ cup cream
1 cup brown sugar
2 tablespoons butter
6 apples
6 wooden skewers

Melt one-half cup of the granulated sugar over a direct flame. Add the boiling water and cook to a smooth syrup. In a separate pan, cook the cream with remaining granulated sugar, brown sugar, and butter to the soft ball stage (236°F). Combine the two syrups and cook until drops of syrup will form a hard ball when dropped into cold water or to a temperature of 250°F. Cool the syrup to lukewarm. Place apples on skewers and twirl them in the caramel syrup. Dip them immediately in ice water to harden the caramel.

APPLE CRISP

3 pounds tart apples, such as Granny Smith
2 tablespoons freshly squeezed lemon juice
½ cup brown sugar
½ teaspoon cinnamon
½ teaspoon nutmeg
⅓ cup flour
⅓ cup rolled oats
4 tablespoons cold butter
½ cup chopped walnuts (optional)

Preheat oven to 375°F. Peel, core, and chop apples. Toss with lemon juice and set aside. In another bowl, combine the sugar, cinnamon, nutmeg, flour, and oats. Cut butter into small pieces and then work it into the sugar and flour mixture by hand, or in a stand mixer, until the mixture looks like crumbs. Add in the nuts, if desired. Butter a 10" x 10" baking dish. Arrange the apples and sprinkle the butter/flour mixture over the top. Bake for 30 to 45 minutes, or until tender. Serve alone or with ice cream.

SPICED APPLES WITH CIDER

6 tart cooking apples, such as Granny Smith
12 whole cloves
4 cups cider
6 whole allspice
2½ cups sugar
¼ teaspoon ginger
1 stick cinnamon
Juice of 1 lemon

Wash, peel, core, and quarter apples. Combine other ingredients in a medium saucepan. Bring to a boil. Boil 10 minutes. Add apples. Simmer slowly until soft. Remove to hot platter.

Boil syrup until thick. Strain and pour over apples. Serve with whipped cream or ice cream. Serves 6.

BROILED GRAPEFRUIT

    2 grapefruits
    2 teaspoons butter
    4 teaspoons brown sugar

Wash grapefruit. Cut in halves. Run a sharp blade, preferably a grapefruit knife, inside the rind, separating it from the pulp. Sprinkle each half with sugar and dot with butter. Broil at moderate heat until heated through and skin is slightly brown. Serve hot. Baked grapefruit is prepared as above but is baked at 450°F until the sugar has melted and the fruit lightly browned. Serves 4.

BAKED GINGER PEACHES

    5 to 6 whole, nearly ripe peaches
    ½ cup brown sugar
    2 teaspoons diced fresh ginger
    2 tablespoons butter
    ½ cup water

Preheat oven to 350°F. Bring water to a boil in a medium saucepan. Add peaches. Let them boil for about one minute, until their skins burst. Remove peaches, plunge into cold water, and peel. Put peaches, cut side up, in shallow baking dish. Sprinkle with sugar and ginger. Dot with butter. Add water to the dish. Bake until brown, 15 to 20 minutes. Serves 6.

BAKED PEACHES ON FRENCH TOAST

2 large peaches
¾ cup sugar
Juice of ½ lemon, about 2 tablespoons
Zest of 1 lemon, chopped
2 tablespoons butter
4 slices bread, ¼-inch thick
1 well-beaten egg
¼ cup milk
1 tablespoon honey
⅛ teaspoon salt

Preheat oven to 425°F. Peel, halve and remove stone from peaches. Dissolve sugar in ¾ cup water in a saucepan over medium-low heat. Add peaches and simmer gently until tender, but not mushy. Remove peaches from syrup to a greased baking dish. To syrup, add lemon juice and lemon zest and boil 5 minutes. Pour syrup over peaches. Dot peaches with butter. Bake for 30 minutes, basting frequently with syrup. Cut bread in halves, diagonally. Mix egg, milk, honey, and salt. Dip bread in mixture. Sauté bread on both sides in greased pan over medium-high heat. Put on hot platter. Put peaches on top of bread. Add pan syrup. Serves 4.

CANDIED ORANGE PEEL

Peel of 3 oranges
1 cup sugar, plus ½ cup
2 tablespoons light corn syrup
½ cup water

Remove peel in quarters from 3 oranges. Cover with water and boil ½ hour. Drain. Cover again with water. Boil ½ hour longer or until tender. Drain. Cut peel in strips. Bring 1 cup sugar, corn syrup, and water to boil. Add the peel and cook gently in syrup to cover until peel is translucent. Cool in syrup several hours or overnight. Reheat. Drain. Roll in granulated sugar.

FRUIT CUPS

When selecting fruit for a fruit cup, keep in mind seasonality (for example, citrus fruits are excellent in winter, while peaches and berries are best in mid-summer), color (bright contrasts can be lovely), and presentation. Below are some ideas for attractive and delicious fruit cups.

- Segments of 1 orange, 2 sliced bananas, ½ cup crushed pineapple, ½ cup sliced grapes, dash of lemon juice, and 2 tablespoons honey. Chill before serving.
- Two sliced bananas, 1 cup grated coconut, 1 cup pineapple cubes, 1 pear, cut in cubes, segments of 1 orange, dash of lemon juice, and 2 tablespoons honey. Chill before serving.
- 1 cup crushed pineapple, 2 cups sliced strawberries, dash of lemon juice.
- 1 pint red raspberries, 1 pint blueberries, 4 sliced peaches or nectarines, tossed with lemon or lime juice, and 2 tablespoons honey.
- 1 cup crushed pineapple, 2 cups cubed watermelon, 2 cups cantaloupe balls.
- 1 pint blackberries, orange segments from 3 oranges.
- Orange segments from 3 oranges, 1 pint halved strawberries, and 1 cup sliced white grapes.
- 12 apricot halves, sliced banana, cranberry sauce (p. 429).
- Seedless grapes, cantaloupe balls, orange sections.
- Diced watermelon, raspberries.
- Strawberries, orange juice, sugar.
- Halved strawberries, pineapple wedges.

- 2 cups diced mango, 2 cups blueberries, 2 cups raspberries.
- 2 cups peeled and sliced kiwis, 1 cup diced pineapple, 1 cup blueberries.

FROZEN FRUIT COCKTAIL

½ cup crushed pineapple
¼ cup powdered sugar
2 cups orange pulp
¾ cup grapefruit pulp
1 cup ginger ale

Add the sugar to the fruits and stir gently until sugar is dissolved. Add ginger ale. Set into freezer. Freeze to slush. Serve as an appetizer. Serves 6.

VEGETABLES
AND
LEGUMES

Vegetables should, whenever possible, be eaten at their peak. Even though many vegetables are available year round, that does not mean that they are in season year round. When vegetables are in season, they are both cheaper and more delicious.

Corn, for instance, is at its peak in the summer. It will be sweeter and plumper than the corn available the rest of the year. The same goes for tomatoes.

Farmers' markets are an excellent source of produce at its peak. A true farmers' market will bring in produce from the surrounding farms as they ripen. There will be asparagus and peas in the spring, tomatoes in the summer, and pumpkins in the fall. The selection will depend on the climate in the area, but all farmers' markets will have a wide variety of seasonal produce.

When good produce isn't available, canned and frozen options are a reasonable alternative. There are many excellent canned tomato options, for instance, and they will often produce a richer flavor than an out-of-season tomato would. The same goes for corn and peas.

For some vegetables, like potatoes and carrots, the season makes little difference. Even then, there are ways to distinguish the delicious from the merely passable. This chart outlines some common vegetables, their seasons, and the characteristics to look for when choosing them.

FIELD GUIDE TO VEGETABLES

NAME	IN SEASON	CHARACTERISTICS
Artichokes	March to May	Plump and heavy with closed scales
Asparagus	March to June	Straight, slender, vivid green stalks with closed tips
Beets	June to Oct.	Fresh tops, smooth (not rough and scaly) skins
Broccoli	Oct. to May	Firm, tender, bright green stalks and florets
Brussels sprouts	Oct. to Nov.	Tight, closed buds with bright green color
Cabbage	All year	Heavy with firm leaves (no bruising)
Carrots	All year	Fresh tops with bright orange flesh
Cauliflower	Sept. to Nov.	Bright green stem, firm and bright florets
Celery	All year	Firm light green to green stalks, no wilting
Corn	May to Sept.	Plum kernels, fresh husks, sweet smell
Cucumbers	May to Aug.	Firm flesh, with no bruising or dimpling
Eggplant	August to Sept.	Firm, smooth flesh, with bright color and no bruises

Lettuce	All year	Bright color, crisp leaves, no bruising or wilting
Mushrooms	Nov. to April	Firm caps and stems, with no puckering or withering
Okra	May to Sept.	Firm, bright green pods
Onions	All year	Firm flesh, papery skins, fresh smell
Parsnips	Oct. to April	Firm and smooth, no dimples or dents
Peas	April to July	Plump and bright green
Peppers	All year	Smooth, brightly colored skin, no wilting
Potatoes	All year	Smooth, no eyes, firm flesh
Spinach	March to May	Vivid green color, fresh stems, no wilting
Sweet potatoes	Sept. to Dec.	Firm, smooth flesh, no soft spots
Tomatoes	May to Aug.	Plump, firm skin, sweet smell

ARTICHOKES

Cut stem and tough outside leaves from artichokes. Soak in salted water for ½ hour. Steam for about 25 minutes in salted water to which 1 tablespoon vinegar has been added. Drain. Serve with hollandaise sauce (p. 418) or with vinaigrette dressing (p. 74). Allow 1 artichoke per serving.

BOILED ASPARAGUS

Tough lower ends should be snapped off or cut off. Cook in deep saucepan over medium heat, with the asparagus standing upright. The steam will cook the tender tips while the hard stalks will be cooked in the boiling water. Or break into 1" pieces, cooking tough parts first and adding the tender tips last. The asparagus is ready when the stems can be pierced with a knife. Allow 6 stalks per serving.

GRILLED ASPARAGUS

2½ cups boiled asparagus (above), cut in pieces
½ cup grated cheese
1½ cups breadcrumbs
1 tablespoon melted butter
Salt
Pepper
Paprika

Drain asparagus. Mix cheese, crumbs, and butter. Add seasonings to taste. Roll asparagus in crumbs. Place on broiler pan and heat through, turning frequently to brown evenly. Serve on hot platter, garnished with parsley and pimento. Serves 6.

ASPARAGUS WITH SOUR CREAM

2½ cups boiled asparagus (p. 210), cut in pieces
1 cup buttered breadcrumbs
¼ cup sour cream

Preheat oven to 350°F. Drain asparagus. Lay in single layer in greased baking dish. Cover with crumbs. Add cream. Bake until crumbs are golden brown, about 15 minutes. Serves 6. If desired, the asparagus may be rolled in crumbs before being placed in dish.

SLOW-BAKED BEANS

2 cups dried kidney or navy beans
½ cup cubed salt pork or bacon
¼ cup molasses
¼ teaspoon mustard
⅛ teaspoon pepper
2 tablespoons butter

Rinse beans in colander with cold water. Cover with cold water and soak 12 hours. Drain. Cover with salted boiling water. Simmer slowly 1½ hours over low heat. Drain. Preheat oven to 350°F. Put in greased baking dish or bean pot with salt pork or bacon scattered in. Mix molasses, mustard, pepper, and 2 cups hot water. Add to beans. Dot with butter. Cover and bake until beans are soft, about 3 hours. Uncover last 30 minutes of cooking to brown beans. Serves 6.

PICNIC BEANS

    1 1-pound 14-ounce can baked beans with molasses and
        pork
    2 tablespoons dark brown sugar
    Dash of salt
    ¼ teaspoon dry mustard
    1 14-ounce can pineapple chunks
    2 tablespoons syrup, drained from pineapple
    4 slices bacon, if desired

Preheat oven to 375°F. Pour beans into an oven casserole or
4 individual casseroles. Add brown sugar, salt, mustard,
drained pineapple, and the reserved pineapple syrup. Mix
well, cover and bake for 25 to 30 minutes or until beans are
very hot. Beans may be topped with bacon slices before placing in the oven, if desired. Serves 4.

BEAN LOAF

    ½ pound slow-baked beans (p. 211)
    ½ cup tomato juice
    ½ onion, diced
    1 cup grated Cheddar, or other mild cheese
    Salt
    Pepper

Preheat oven to 350°F. Mix ingredients, including cheese, if
desired, seasoning to taste with salt and pepper. Mold into a
loaf. Put in greased baking pan. Bake for 30 minutes. Serve
with ketchup or slices of onion. Serves 6.

STRING (GREEN) OR WAX BEANS

Remove strings from beans. Snap or cut off the ends. Cook in a small amount of boiling water (about 1 cup) until tender, adding a little salt during the last few minutes of cooking. Drain and serve at once. They may be covered generously with butter. Allow ¼ pound raw beans per serving.

BEANS WITH BROWN BUTTER

2½ cups cooked string or wax beans (above)
2 tablespoons butter
⅛ teaspoon nutmeg
Dash pepper

Drain the beans. Brown the butter in a saucepan by heating and stirring it constantly until lightly browned. Add the beans, nutmeg, and pepper. Simmer together for a few minutes. Serve immediately.

SPICY STRING BEANS

2½ cups boiled string or wax beans (above)
2 tablespoons butter
¼ teaspoon cayenne or other dried red pepper,
    more to taste
Salt

Drain beans. Melt butter in a skillet over medium-high heat. Add beans, pepper, and a dash of salt. Sauté for about 5 minutes, until beans have browned a little. Adjust seasonings and serve.

STRING BEANS WITH ROSEMARY

2 pounds string beans
Salt
½ cup water
4 tablespoons olive oil
1 clove garlic
½ teaspoon fresh rosemary, finely diced
Pepper

Remove strings from the beans and snap or cut off ends. Put a layer into a saucepan. Salt them, then add another layer and more salt and so on until all are used. Add water, cover tightly, and steam 10 minutes over slow heat. Heat the oil in a frying pan, add garlic, and let it brown. Add beans. Add rosemary. Stir well and add a dash of pepper and more salt if needed. Sauté for 5 minutes. Serve either hot or cold. Serves 6.

SWEET & SOUR BEANS

2 tablespoons cooking oil
2 tablespoons flour
1 tablespoon brown sugar
1½ tablespoons vinegar
⅛ teaspoon cinnamon
¼ teaspoon salt
2½ cups cooked string beans (p. 213)

Heat oil. Add flour and stir until smooth. Add other ingredients. Cover and simmer until liquid is reduced about two-thirds. Serves 6. The amounts of sugar and vinegar may be changed to suit individual taste.

BOILED LIMA BEANS

2 cups dried lima beans
½ teaspoon salt
2 tablespoons butter

Soak dried lima beans in enough water to cover for at least 12 hours. Drain. Cook in boiling salted water until tender. Drain. Add salt and butter. For creamed lima beans serve these in thin white sauce (p. 416). Allow ¼ pound raw, shelled beans per serving.

BOILED DRIED BEANS

2 cups beans (black, kidney, navy, lima, pea,
    or yellow-eye)
½ teaspoon salt

Pick over beans. Soak in water 10 hours. Drain. Cover generously with fresh water. Add salt to water. Boil, covered, in a large saucepan or stockpot until tender, 2 to 3 hours. 1 cup dried beans yields about 2½ cups boiled beans.

BAKED KIDNEY BEANS

2 tablespoons diced onion
2 tablespoons diced pimento
⅓ cup ketchup
2½ cup boiled kidney beans (p. 215, boiled dried beans)
2 strips bacon

Preheat oven to 375°F. Mix together the onion, pimento, ketchup, and beans. Pour into a shallow baking dish. Cut the bacon in 2" pieces and arrange on top of beans. Bake for 1 hour, or until bacon is crisp. Serves 5. Plain baked beans (p. 211) or baked beans with tomato sauce (p. 424) may be used instead of kidney beans.

SPICY KIDNEY BEANS

2 medium-sized onions
1 pound ground beef
¼ cup olive oil
2 teaspoons salt
2 tablespoons chili powder
⅛ teaspoon pepper
2½ cups canned tomatoes
2½ cups boiled red kidney beans (p. 215, boiled
    dried beans)

Chop onions. Cook them and the beef in the oil until lightly browned, stirring often. Add seasonings and tomatoes and simmer gently over low heat for 1 hour. Add the kidney beans and simmer several minutes more to allow the flavors to blend. Serves 6.

KIDNEY BEANS WITH BACON

2½ cups boiled kidney beans (p. 215, boiled
   dried beans)
¼ pound bacon, chopped
1 cup diced tomatoes, canned or fresh
1 onion chopped

Preheat oven to 300°F. Place layer of beans in greased baking dish. Sprinkle with some of bacon, tomatoes, and onion. Repeat until all ingredients are used. Bake until bacon is crisp, about an hour. Serves 4 to 6.

SHELL BEANS

Cook same as string beans (p. 213), using very little water which should be absorbed in cooking.

BOILED BEETS

6 medium beets
Salt
Pepper
3 tablespoons butter (optional)
1 tablespoon balsamic vinegar (optional)

Wash beets. Cut off most of stalks and roots. Cook in a large stock pot in boiling salted water until tender, about an hour. Plunge into cold water. Peel. Slice into warm dish. Season to taste with salt and pepper. Serve hot with vinegar or spread generously with butter. Allow 1 beet per serving.

DICED BEETS AND BACON

4 slices bacon, chopped
2½ cups diced boiled beets (p. 217)
Salt
Pepper
1 teaspoon cider vinegar (optional)

Fry bacon crisp. Add beets and heat through. Season to taste with salt and pepper. Serves 4 to 6. Vinegar may be added if desired.

PICKLED BEETS

12 medium beets
2 cups white wine vinegar
3 teaspoons salt
1 cup sugar
2 cups water

Select beets of uniform size, cut off the tops, but allow at least 1-inch of the stems to remain so that the beets will not bleed and lose color and sweetness. Wash and boil in a large stock-pot with enough water to cover until the beets are tender. For young beets this will require about ½ hour. When tender, plunge into cold water, remove the skins, and when cool, cut in dice or thin slices. Pack into jars. In a saucepan, heat vinegar, salt, sugar, and water until the sugar has dissolved. Pour this mixture over the beets, adding more vinegar to top off if necessary. Refrigerate 1 week before serving.

BEET AND TOMATO EN CASSEROLE

2½ cups diced boiled beets (p. 217)
2½ cups diced tomatoes, canned or fresh
½ cup grated cheese
Salt
Pepper
1 cup breadcrumbs
2 tablespoons butter

Preheat oven to 350°F. Put ½ beets into bottom of greased baking dish. Add half the tomatoes then half the cheese in layers. Season to taste with salt and pepper. Add ½ breadcrumbs. Dot with 1 tablespoon butter. Repeat. Brown for 20 minutes. Serves 6.

BROCCOLI WITH ONION SAUCE

1 bunch broccoli
2 tablespoon minced onion
3 tablespoons butter
Salt
Pepper
2 teaspoons lemon juice

Cut off woody portions of broccoli and the large outer leaves. Break broccoli into flowerets. Wash and soak in salted water a few minutes. Cook, uncovered, in boiling salted water 10 to 15 minutes, or until tender. Sauté onion in butter until lightly browned. Add salt, pepper, and lemon juice. Add broccoli and heat through. Serves 4.

BOILED BRUSSELS SPROUTS

4 cups of Brussels sprouts
1 teaspoon salt
3 tablespoons butter
Pepper

Wash and clean Brussels sprouts and remove any withered leaves. Rinse in cold water. Drain. Cover with boiling salted water and cook 15 minutes in uncovered saucepan. Drain and toss with butter. Season to taste with salt and pepper. Serves 6.

COOKED CABBAGE

Cut a head of cabbage in quarters and rinse in cold water. Shred and discard the hard core. Cook in a small amount of boiling salted water 20 minutes. Drain and season with salt and pepper. Serves 4.

SCALLOPED CABBAGE

3 cups cooked shredded cabbage (above)
2 cups medium white sauce (p. 416)
1 cup soft breadcrumbs
½ cup grated cheese

Preheat oven to 375°F. Mix cabbage and white sauce together. Put a layer of cabbage in a greased baking dish, add a layer of crumbs and repeat process until all the ingredients are used. Sprinkle with cheese. Bake about 20 minutes or until brown. Serves 6.

SAUTÉED BRUSSELS SPROUTS

4 cups Brussels sprouts
2 tablespoons butter
2 tablespoons chicken stock or water
½ teaspoon salt
Pepper

Wash and clean Brussels sprouts. Remove withered leaves. Cut Brussels sprouts in half. Melt butter in a large saucepan over medium heat. Add Brussels sprouts and stir to coat. Add stock, salt, and pepper to taste. Cover and cook for 10 minutes, stirring occasionally and adding more liquid if necessary to prevent sticking. When Brussels sprouts are tender, remove lid and cook for 1 minute longer.

STUFFED CABBAGE

1 medium-sized cabbage
1 pound beef
1 slice bacon or salt pork
1 onion
½ cup breadcrumbs
½ cup milk
1 beaten egg
Salt
Pepper

Select solid cabbage, not too large. Remove outside leaves. Cut out stalk end, leaving a hollow shell. Chop uncooked beef with bacon and onion. Add crumbs soaked in milk, beaten egg, salt, and pepper. Shape mixture in balls or cakes, arrange in cabbage. Tie in cheesecloth, then steam or boil until tender, about an hour. Serve with tomato sauce (p. 424), if desired. Serves 6.

SAUERKRAUT AND POTATOES

¼ pound diced bacon
3½ cups sauerkraut
Salt
Pepper
6 boiled sliced potatoes (p. 244)
½ tablespoon melted bacon fat

Fry bacon until crisp. Add sauerkraut and season to taste with salt and pepper. Cook slowly 10 minutes over low heat. Turn onto hot platter. Arrange potatoes on top. Brush potatoes with fat. Serves 6.

SAUERKRAUT AND APPLES

¼ cup butter or bacon fat
2 tablespoons flour
2½ cups sauerkraut
¼ cup cider vinegar
3 whole cloves
2 tablespoons brown sugar
¾ cup water
1 large apple, peeled and chopped fine

Melt butter of fat in pan. Add flour and stir until smooth. Add sauerkraut, vinegar, cloves, brown sugar, and ¾ cup water. Cover and let simmer 20 minutes. Add apple just before serving. Serves 6.

BOILED CARROTS

Wash and peel carrots. Put in boiling water and boil until tender, adding salt during cooking.

STEAMED CARROTS

2 tablespoons butter
2 cups peeled and sliced carrots
2 tablespoons chopped onion
Salt
Pepper

Melt butter and put with other ingredients in a vegetable steamer. Cover and steam until tender. Serves 6.

CALIFORNIA CARROTS

8 medium-sized carrots
1 teaspoon salt
1 onion, minced
1 clove garlic
¼ cup butter
1 tablespoon flour
½ cup basic chicken stock (p. 32)
½ cup white wine
Salt
Pepper
1 tablespoon parsley, diced

Peel and slice or dice carrots. Simmer for 10 minutes in boiling salted water. Drain. Fry onion and a small clove of garlic in butter. When yellow, lower heat and add flour. Blend well. Stir in stock and white wine. Season to taste. Put in partially cooked carrots and let simmer until tender, adding a little more stock if sauce gets too thick. Garnish with parsley. Serves 6.

BOILED CAULIFLOWER

Prepare and cook same as boiled cabbage (p. 220), breaking cauliflower into small pieces. 1 cauliflower serves 6.

CREAMED CAULIFLOWER

Mix 1 boiled cauliflower (above) with 2 cups medium white sauce (p. 416). Heat through. Serves 6.

FRENCH FRIED CAULIFLOWER

  1 medium-sized head cauliflower
  1 cup breadcrumbs
  1 egg
  2 tablespoons cold water
  Oil for frying
  Salt
  Pepper

Break the cauliflower into flowerets and boil gently for 10 minutes. Drain. Roll in breadcrumbs, then in the mixture of egg and water and again in crumbs. Fry in deep hot fat (375°F) until browned. Drain on paper towels. Sprinkle with salt and pepper and serve very hot. Serves 6.

CAULIFLOWER AU GRATIN

1 boiled cauliflower (p. 224), broken in pieces
1 cup medium white sauce (p. 416)
1 cup grated cheese, such as Gruyère or Emmental

Preheat oven to 400°F. Drain cauliflower. Put in greased baking dish. Pour over sauce. Sprinkle with cheese. Bake for 20 to 25 minutes. Serves 6.

CELERY

Celery should be carefully washed and broken apart. The tender heart should be used in salads. The tough outer stalks can be used for cooking or soup. It can be kept crisp in ice water or in a cold covered container.

BOILED CELERY

Scrub stalks clean. Remove all tough strings. Slice thin in saucepan. Cover with water. Boil gently until tender. Season with salt during cooking.

CREAMED CELERY

1½ tablespoons butter
3 tablespoons flour
1 teaspoon salt
⅛ teaspoon pepper
¾ cup liquid in which celery was boiled
¾ cup whole milk
1 large bunch celery, cut in ½" lengths
    and boiled (p. 225)

Preheat oven to 350°F. Melt butter in pan. Add flour, salt, and pepper. Blend well. Add celery liquid and milk. Bring to a boil, stirring constantly. Add celery. Heat through. Serves 6. This can be turned into a greased baking dish, sprinkled with breadcrumbs and grated cheese, and bake for 20 minutes.

CELERY, CREOLE STYLE

1 cup diced celery
½ cup boiling water
1 tablespoon butter
2 tablespoons finely chopped onion
2 teaspoons finely chopped green pepper
⅓ teaspoon salt
Pepper, to taste
⅓ cup canned tomatoes

Put celery in saucepan with boiling water and boil for 10 minutes or until tender. Melt butter, and add onion, green pepper, salt, and pepper in a skillet over low heat. Cook for 5 minutes and stir in the tomatoes. Add celery and cook the entire mixture 10 to 15 minutes longer. Serves 4.

CHICORY OR ENDIVE

1 pound chicory or endive
1 teaspoon salt
Pepper, to taste
2 tablespoons butter

Wash carefully several times, each time using clean water. Tie each head securely. Put in generous amount of boiling, salted water and cook until tender, about ½ hour. Drain. Sauté in small amount of butter for 8 to 10 minutes, turning occasionally to cook evenly. Season to taste with salt and pepper. Serve hot. Allow 1 pound chicory for 4 servings.

CORN-ON-THE-COB

Remove outer husks from corn. Peel back inner husks. Remove silk. Drop into a generous amount of boiling water and boil 7 to 10 minutes. Provide plenty of butter, salt, and pepper. Allow 1 or 2 ears per serving.

OVEN ROASTED CORN

Preheat oven to 350°F. Place ears of corn (with husks) in the oven and bake for 30 minutes. Remove husks and silk and serve with butter. Allow 1 or 2 ears per serving.

PAN ROASTED CORN-ON-THE-COB

6 ears of corn
½ cup water
6 tablespoons butter
1 teaspoon salt

Remove husks and silks from corn. Rinse in cold water. Arrange ears of corn in a large heavy skillet or a heavy Dutch oven. Add water, cover tightly, and steam over medium heat 5 to 8 minutes. Remove cover and allow water to evaporate. Add butter and salt. Continue cooking for 5 minutes, rolling corn to prevent browning. Allow 1 or 2 ears per serving.

STEWED CORN

4 ears of corn
2 tablespoons butter
¼ cup water
Salt
Pepper

Shave kernels off ears of corn without cutting too close to cob. Put in saucepan. Add butter and water. Cook gently about 15 minutes, seasoning with salt and pepper during cooking.

CREAMED CORN

2½ cups stewed corn (p. 228)
1 cup white sauce (p. 416)
Salt
Pepper
Paprika

Heat corn in double boiler 10 minutes. Mix with hot white sauce. Season to taste with salt, pepper, and paprika.

BUTTERED CORN

Cut kernels from boiled corn-on-the-cob (p. 227). Mix with butter. Sprinkle with salt. Allow 1 ear per serving.

FRIED CORN

2½ cups stewed corn (p. 228)
3 tablespoons butter
Salt
Pepper

Sauté stewed corn in butter in a frying pan until slightly browned. Season to taste with salt and pepper. Serve hot.

CORN LOAF

2½ cups stewed corn (p. 228)
1 cup thick white sauce (p. 416)
1½ cups breadcrumbs
¾ teaspoon salt
½ teaspoon paprika
2 tablespoons butter
1 onion, chopped

Preheat oven to 350°F. Drain corn and use liquid for white sauce, adding milk if necessary. Mix corn, sauce, and 1 cup crumbs. Add salt and paprika. Melt fat and brown onion in it. Add to mixture. Put in greased baking dish. Cover with remaining crumbs. Dot with butter. Bake for 30 to 40 minutes. Serve hot with cheese sauce (p. 417) or tomato sauce (p. 424). Serves 6.

CORN PUDDING

3 eggs
2 cups milk
2 tablespoons sugar
1 teaspoon salt
2 cups stewed corn (p. 228)
1 tablespoon butter
1 tablespoon minced onion
¼ cup minced green pepper
1 minced pimento

Preheat oven to 350°F. Beat eggs slightly, add the milk, sugar, and salt. Combine corn with other ingredients and add to the milk mixture. Mix well. Turn into a buttered casserole and bake for 1 hour. Serves 6.

CORN FRITTERS

2 cups raw corn
1 well-beaten egg
1½ teaspoons sugar
⅓ teaspoon salt
⅛ teaspoon pepper
1 tablespoon melted butter
¼ cup flour
½ teaspoon baking powder
3 tablespoons butter or fat

Combine corn, egg, sugar, salt, pepper, and butter. Mix and sift flour and baking powder. Add to first mixture. Mix thoroughly. Drop batter from spoon into little fat in hot frying pan and brown both sides. Serves 6.

BAKED CORN

2 tablespoons butter or fat
2 tablespoons flour
1¼ cups milk
2 cups canned or stewed corn (p. 228)
1 tablespoon sugar
Salt
Pepper
2 well-beaten eggs

Preheat oven to 350°F. Melt fat in pan. Add flour. Blend well. Add milk slowly. Bring to a boil, stirring constantly. Add corn and sugar. Season to taste with salt and pepper. Add eggs. Mix thoroughly. Turn into greased baking dish. Bake for 25 to 30 minutes. Serves 6.

CORN AND TOMATOES

1¼ cups canned tomatoes
2½ cups stewed corn (p. 228)
1 teaspoon sugar
Salt
Pepper
1 tablespoon butter

Mix tomatoes and corn. Simmer, covered, 15 minutes. Add other ingredients. Heat through. Serves 6.

BAKED CORN AND CARROTS

12 medium-sized carrots, peeled and sliced
1 small onion, sliced
2 tablespoons butter
2½ tablespoons flour
1¼ cups milk
Salt
Pepper
1½ cups stewed corn (p. 228) or canned whole grain
    corn
6 slices cooked bacon

Preheat oven to 350°F. Cook the carrots and onion in boiling salted water until tender. Drain and place in a buttered baking dish. Boil down liquid to ¼ cup. Melt the butter in a double boiler and add the flour and mix well. Add the milk and carrot liquid gradually and cook, stirring constantly, until thickened. Season to taste with salt and pepper. Add corn and pour over the carrots. Bake until heated through, about 10 minutes. Top with the bacon. Serves 6.

FRIED EGGPLANT

2 medium eggplants
¼ cup flour
1 well-beaten egg
2 tablespoons water
½ teaspoon salt
⅛ teaspoon pepper
½ cup breadcrumbs
½ cup oil, for frying

Peel eggplant and cut in thin slices. Sprinkle with salt and let stand under a weight until some of the juices run out. Drain off liquid and sprinkle with flour. Dip in slightly beaten egg, diluted with water and seasoned with salt and pepper. Cover with fine dry breadcrumbs. Fry in little fat 8 to 10 minutes, turning once to brown both sides. Serves 6.

BAKED EGGPLANT

2 eggplants
2 eggs
½ cup milk
Salt
Pepper
1 cup corn flakes
1 tablespoon butter

Preheat oven to 350°F. Boil the eggplant for about 20 minutes. Cool. Remove the skin. Press the pulp through a colander. Beat the eggs and milk together. Add the pulp and seasonings. Put the mixture in a buttered baking dish. Sprinkle the corn flakes over the top. Dot with butter and bake until lightly browned, about 20 minutes. Serves 6.

EGGPLANT AU GRATIN

1 large eggplant
1 cup grated cheese, such as Gruyère or Emmental
1 teaspoon salt
⅛ teaspoon pepper
Few grains cayenne
2 tablespoons butter

Preheat oven to 400°F. Peel eggplant and cut in slices. Cook in boiling salted water until tender. Drain well and mash. Put in a layer in greased baking dish, sprinkle with cheese, salt, pepper and cayenne and dot with butter. Repeat this process until all the ingredients are used, having a layer of cheese on top. Bake for 20 minutes, or until cheese has melted and is browning. Serves 6.

BAKED SLICED EGGPLANT

1 eggplant
⅓ cup melted butter, plus 1 teaspoon
1 teaspoon salt
Pepper, to taste
½ cup breadcrumbs

Preheat oven to 450°F. Cut eggplant, crosswise, into 8½" slices and peel. Brush each slice with melted butter. Add 1 teaspoon melted butter, salt, and pepper to crumbs. Dip slices into buttered crumbs. Bake, uncovered, on a baking sheet for 18 minutes. Serves 4.

STUFFED EGGPLANT

1 large eggplant
½ cup minced ham
2 tablespoons butter
½ onion, chopped
Salt
Pepper

Preheat oven to 350°F. Cut eggplant in half. Scrape out insides and mix with ham. Put in saucepan. Cover with boiling water and boil until tender, about 20 minutes. Drain. Add butter and onion. Season with salt and pepper to taste. Fill each half of hull with mixture. Dot with butter. Bake for 15 minutes. Serves 6. Breadcrumbs, seasoned with chopped onion, also make a delicious stuffing.

SAUTÉED MUSHROOMS

4 cups white mushrooms
2 tablespoons butter
Salt
Pepper
Parsley, if desired

Peel and stem mushrooms. Rinse in water, or gently wipe with a moist paper towel to clean. Sauté 8 to 10 minutes in a little butter turning frequently to brown evenly. Season to taste with salt and pepper. Garnish with diced parsley if desired.

CREAMED MUSHROOMS

18 large mushrooms
¼ cup butter
Flour for dredging
Salt
Pepper
1 cup cream

Wash and remove stems from mushrooms. Peel caps if skin is tough. Melt butter in saucepan. Add mushrooms. Cover closely and cook slowly over low heat for 10 minutes. Dredge with flour. Season to taste with salt and pepper. Cover with cream. Cover and cook slowly 5 minutes longer, or until the sauce begins to thicken. Serve on buttered toast, if desired. Serves 6.

SCALLOPED MUSHROOMS

2½ tablespoons butter
1 tablespoon flour
2 cups basic chicken stock (p. 32)
2 cups mushrooms
Salt
Pepper
1 tablespoon chopped parsley
¼ cup crumbs

Preheat oven to 400°F. Melt 1 tablespoon butter. Stir in flour, blending well. Add hot stock. Clean and stem mushrooms. Chop stalks and add to mixture. Simmer, stirring occasionally, until liquid is reduced by half. Season to taste with salt and pepper. Add parsley. Put mushroom caps in greased baking dish. Add sauce. Sprinkle with crumbs. Dot with remaining butter. Bake for 8 to 10 minutes. Serves 6.

MUSTARD GREENS

Follow recipe for chicory (p. 227) through boiling, cooking about 18 minutes.

STEWED OKRA

50 okra pods
¼ pound ham, chopped
1 cup basic chicken stock (p. 32)
1 cup canned tomatoes
Salt
Pepper
1 tablespoon butter
1 tablespoon flour
2 tablespoons chopped parsley

Wash pods and cut off both ends. Put in saucepan. Add ham, stock, and tomatoes. Season to taste with salt and pepper. Simmer, covered, 30 to 40 minutes. Blend butter and flour and add to mixture. Cook slowly, stirring constantly, until thickened. Put in heated dish. Sprinkle with parsley. Serves 6.

BOILED ONIONS

6 medium onions
Salt
Pepper
3 tablespoons butter, or as desired

Remove outer skins. Cook in boiling salted water until soft. Season to taste with salt and pepper. Add butter generously. Allow 1 or 2 onions per serving.

SAUTÉED ONIONS

2 tablespoons butter or olive oil
2 cups onions, sliced
1 teaspoon salt
¼ teaspoon pepper
⅛ teaspoon paprika

Melt butter in frying pan. Add onions and sprinkle with seasonings. Mix thoroughly. Cover and cook slowly over low heat for 30 minutes, stirring frequently. Serves 6.

FRIED ONIONS

Thinly slice 5 Vidalia onions. Fry in deep hot fat (375°F) until brown. Drain on unglazed paper. Sprinkle with salt. Serves 6.

CREAMED ONIONS

Boil 6 medium-sized onions (p. 237). Mix with 1½ cups hot medium white sauce (p. 416). Heat thoroughly. Serves 6.

BAKED ONIONS

3 tablespoons butter, melted
¾ cup chopped nuts
1 tablespoon sugar
Salt
Pepper
24 small white onions, peeled

Preheat oven to 350°F. Heat butter, nuts, sugar, salt, and pepper in baking dish. Add peeled onions and stir until completely covered with nutmeats. Cover dish tightly and bake for 1 hour. Serves 4.

STUFFED ONIONS

6 large boiled onions (p. 237)
¾ cup chopped cooked meat (chicken, pork,
    lamb, or beef)
2 tablespoons melted butter
2 tablespoons tomato paste
Salt
Pepper
¼ cup breadcrumbs

Preheat oven to 350°F. Slice off top and remove centers from onions. Combine meat, butter, and tomato paste and season to taste with salt and pepper. Stuff mixture in onions. Put in greased baking dish, cover, and bake for 1 hour. Remove cover. Sprinkle with crumbs. Dot with butter. Bake, uncovered, until crumbs are brown. Serves 6. Diced boiled beets (p. 217) may be substituted for meat.

STUFFED VIDALIA ONIONS

6 Vidalia onions (or other large, sweet onions)
2 tablespoons butter
2 tablespoons flour
1 cup milk
½ teaspoon salt
3 hard-boiled egg yolks (p. 272), crumbled
1 tablespoon parsley, chopped
2 tablespoons green pepper, chopped
1 pound canned salmon or tuna
½ cup breadcrumbs

Preheat oven to 350°F. Peel onions and cut off tops. Cook in boiling salted water 20 minutes. Drain and remove center sections, leaving onion cups. Melt butter in skillet and add flour. Blend to smooth paste. Add milk and salt and cook, stirring constantly, until smooth and thickened. Add egg yolks, chopped parsley, green pepper, and flaked salmon or tuna. Fill mixture into onion cups. Sprinkle with breadcrumbs, dot with butter, and bake for 30 minutes. Serves 6.

BOILED PEAS

Remove peas from pods. Rinse in cold water. Drain. Cook in little boiling water until tender. Sprinkle with salt. Spread generously with butter.

PEAS IN THE POD

Leave peas in pod. Wash thoroughly. Cook them in boiling salted water for 20 to 25 minutes, or until tender. Serve in pods with mayonnaise (p. 70) or melted butter.

CREAMED PEAS

2 tablespoons butter
2 tablespoons flour
Salt
Pepper
2 cups milk
2½ cups boiled peas (p. 240)

Melt butter. Add flour and stir until smooth. Season with salt and pepper. Add milk. Heat, stirring constantly, until it bubbles. Add peas. Heat thoroughly. Serves 6. A richer sauce can be made by substituting ½ cup cream for milk and reducing butter to 1 tablespoon and flour to ½ tablespoon.

PEAS AND CHEESE

2½ cups boiled peas (p. 240)
3 tablespoons butter or olive oil
1 cup grated cheese
¼ teaspoon salt
⅛ teaspoon pepper

Mix ingredients and cook in a saucepan over low heat until cheese melts. Serve on buttered toast, if desired. Serves 6.

PEAS ANGLAISE

¼ cup chopped scallions
2 tablespoons butter
½ teaspoon flour
¼ teaspoon sugar
2½ cups boiled peas (p. 240)
Salt
Pepper

Sauté scallions in butter for 3 minutes. Mix flour and sugar and add to scallions. Add peas and a bit of the liquid from cooking. Season to taste with salt and pepper. Cook for 5 minutes longer. Serves 4.

FRIED PEPPER RINGS

3 large red or green peppers
1 egg, well beaten
1 teaspoon cold water
½ cup breadcrumbs
3 tablespoons butter or oil for frying

Wash peppers. Slice thin, crosswise. Remove seeds and hard tissue. Dip slices in beaten egg, diluted with a little cold water. Dip in breadcrumbs. Sauté in little fat until brown on both sides. Or fry in deep, hot fat (375°F) until browned. Drain on unglazed paper. 1 pepper will serve 2.

STUFFED PEPPERS

6 green peppers
1 cup minced cold cooked meat (beef or lamb)
1 cup chopped tomatoes
1 cup boiled rice
2 tablespoons butter or olive oil
½ cup chopped onion
1 teaspoon salt
¼ teaspoon pepper

Preheat oven to 400°F. Wash peppers. Cut a slice from stem end and remove seeds and membranes. Mix other ingredients and stuff in peppers. Put in baking dish. Pour 1 cup of hot water around the peppers. Bake for 35 minutes. Serves 6. Breadcrumbs may be substituted for rice. Almost any combination of cooked meats or vegetables may be used. Chopped nuts are good, added to stuffing.

GREEN PEPPERS IN OLIVE OIL

10 sweet green peppers
1 clove garlic
½ cup olive oil
Salt
Pepper

Bring a large pot of salted water to a boil. Wash and remove seeds from green peppers. Blanche the peppers in water, letting them boil for a minute or two, but no longer. Drain and dry on a cloth. Put garlic in a frying pan with olive oil. When hot, remove the garlic, and add the peppers, quartered. Cook until the peppers begin to brown. Add salt and pepper to taste. Serves 8.

BOILED POTATOES

Wash potatoes and rinse in cold water. Peel and boil them in salted water until soft. Drain and keep hot until ready to serve. Do not cover them.

MASHED POTATOES

    2 pounds medium potatoes
    4 tablespoons butter
    1 teaspoon salt
    ⅛ teaspoon pepper
    4 tablespoons milk or sour cream

Select uniform and medium-sized potatoes. Wash, peel, and rinse in cold water. Boil in salted water until tender. Drain. Mash or force thorough a ricer. To potatoes, add butter, salt, pepper, and milk or sour cream. Beat until creamy. Serve hot.

FRENCH FRIED POTATOES

    6 medium potatoes
    Oil for frying
    Salt
    Pepper
    1 tablespoon parsley, finely chopped

Peel potatoes. Slice in strips 2" long, ¾" wide and ½" thick. Put in ice water. Let stand 1 hour. Drain and dry between towels. Fry in deep fat or oil (325°F) until a golden brown. Drain on paper towels. Allow 1 potato per serving. Season to taste with salt and pepper. Sprinkle with parsley. For Parisienne potatoes scoop out little balls with potato scoop and fry as above.

BAKED POTATOES

Preheat oven to 400°F. Select medium-sized potatoes. Wash with a vegetable brush to remove all particles of dirt. Rinse in cold water. Wrap each potato in aluminum foil. Bake for 40 to 50 minutes or until soft. Rub skins with butter to soften them. Serve at once with sour cream, crumbled bacon, grated Cheddar, and diced chives, if desired.

ROAST POTATOES

2–3 pounds baking potatoes
2 cloves garlic
¼ cup olive oil
Salt
Pepper
1 teaspoon fresh rosemary, finely diced (optional)

Preheat oven to 425°F. Wash potatoes and rinse in cold water. Peel and cut the potatoes into large chunks. Crush the garlic, and add it and the olive oil to the potatoes. Toss or stir to make sure the potatoes are coated. Sprinkle with salt, pepper, and rosemary if desired. Put the potatoes on a cookie sheet and bake them for about an hour, or until the potatoes are browned and tender.

SAUTÉED OR BROILED POTATOES

5 medium-sized potatoes
¼ cup butter or bacon fat
Salt
Pepper

Wash potatoes but do not peel. Cook in boiling salted water until just tender. Drain. Peel and cut into ¼" slices and sauté in hot butter or fat over medium-high heat until nicely browned on both sides or broil over moderate heat, turning to brown both sides. Sprinkle with salt and pepper and serve at once. Serves 6.

SHOESTRING POTATOES

6 medium potatoes
Oil for frying
Salt
Pepper
½ teaspoon parsley, finely diced

Peel potatoes. Cut in strips ¼" by ¼" by 2". Rinse in ice water. Drain and dry between towels. Fry in deep fat (325°F) until golden brown. Drain on paper towels. Season with salt, pepper, and parsley. Allow 1 potato per serving.

GERMAN-FRIED POTATOES

4 medium potatoes
2 tablespoons butter or fat
Salt

Wash and peel potatoes and slice very thin. Soak them in cold water 1 hour. Drain and dry thoroughly. Put butter or fat in a frying pan. Add the potatoes, sprinkle with salt, and cover with a tight fitting lid. Fry slowly until tender and brown, turning occasionally to prevent burning. Serves 4.

HASHED BROWNED POTATOES

2 tablespoons fat or olive oil
2 cups boiled potatoes (p. 244), cold and finely chopped
1 tablespoon chopped parsley
½ teaspoon salt
Pepper

Melt fat in a frying pan over medium heat. Add boiled potatoes, parsley, salt, and pepper. Mix thoroughly, then allow the potatoes to brown on the under side. Fold over like an omelet. Serves 6.

LYONNAISE POTATOES

1 small onion
1 tablespoon butter or fat
2 cups boiled potatoes (p. 244), cold and
    cut in ¼" slices
½ teaspoon salt
Dash cayenne
1 teaspoon chopped parsley

Slice onion thin and fry in fat until a delicate brown. Add boiled potatoes. Sprinkle with salt and cayenne. Let potatoes brown on the under side, fold over and turn out on hot platter. Sprinkle with parsley. Serves 6.

CREAMED POTATOES

1 cup milk
1½ tablespoons flour
1 tablespoon butter
2 cups sliced cold boiled potatoes (p. 244)
1 teaspoon chopped parsley

Heat milk in a saucepan over medium heat. Stir in flour and butter. Heat and stir until smooth and thick. Add potatoes and parsley. Heat, shaking occasionally, until potatoes are heated through. Serves 6. If desired, this can be turned into a greased baking dish, sprinkled with breadcrumbs and grated cheese and baked at 350°F for 20 to 25 minutes.

POTATOES AU GRATIN

2 cups sliced cold boiled potatoes (p. 244)
1 cup grated Gruyère or Emmental
Salt
Pepper
2 tablespoons butter
½ to 1 cup whole milk or cream

Preheat oven to 400°F. Grease a baking dish. Arrange slices of boiled potatoes on bottom. Sprinkle with grated cheese, salt, and pepper. Dot with butter. Repeat process until all materials needed are used. Add enough milk to almost cover top layer. Bake for 20 to 25 minutes. Serves 4.

DUCHESS POTATOES

2 pounds medium potatoes
3 tablespoons butter
1 teaspoon salt
Dash paprika
4 egg yolks, plus 1, beaten

Preheat oven to 350°F. Select potatoes of uniform size. Wash, peel, and rinse in cold water. Boil in salted water until tender. Drain off all the water. Mash the potatoes by forcing through a potato ricer. To potatoes add butter, salt, paprika, and the egg yolks. Force through a pastry bag into different shapes such as pyramids, roses and circles. Brush over with a beaten egg yolk diluted with 1 tablespoon water. Bake for 15 minutes or until a delicate brown. This is an excellent garnish for planked steak or fish.

SCALLOPED POTATOES

Preheat oven to 350°F. Follow recipe for potatoes au gratin (p. 249), eliminating cheese and sprinkling a little flour on each layer. Or, use thin slices of raw potatoes, soaked 1 hour in cold water, and bake for 1¼ hours.

DUTCH POTATOES

    1 small onion, chopped
    1 tablespoon fat or olive oil
    3 medium-sized potatoes, cubed and peeled
    2 tablespoons chopped parsley
    Salt
    Pepper

Brown onion in fat in a medium skillet. Add potato, parsley, and seasonings. Barely cover with water. Cook over low heat until potatoes are tender. Serves 6.

SMASHED POTATOES WITH GARLIC AND ROSEMARY

    2 pounds red or new potatoes
    3 cloves of garlic, crushed
    2 teaspoons fresh rosemary, finely chopped
    ¼ cup butter, at room temperature
    ¼ cup sour cream or milk
    Salt
    Pepper
    1 tablespoon chives, diced (optional)

Bring a large pot of water to a boil. Scrub the potatoes, but do not peel. Add them to the boiling water and cook for about 20 minutes, or until the potatoes can be pierced easily with a fork. Drain potatoes and return them to the pot. Mash them with a potato masher or a fork. Add garlic, rosemary, butter, and sour cream or milk. Beat with a hand mixer to desired consistency. Season to taste with salt and pepper. Serves 4.

GREEN ONION POTATOES

4 large potatoes
¼ cup butter
¼ to ⅓ cup milk (not skim)
1 teaspoon salt
¼ teaspoon pepper
¼ cup green onions

Wash, peel, and quarter potatoes. Cook in boiling salted water to cover for about 20 minutes or until tender. Drain. Mash. Add butter and heated milk gradually, beating continuously until light and fluffy. Season with salt and pepper. Chop onions fine, including about 3" of green stem and fold into potatoes just before serving. Serves 6.

TWICE BAKED POTATOES

6 medium-sized baked potatoes (p. 245)
¼ cup hot milk (not skim)
2 tablespoons butter or fat
1 teaspoon salt
¼ teaspoon pepper
⅛ teaspoon paprika

Preheat oven to 350°F. Cut a cross in the side of each potato. Turn back corners. Scoop out insides without breaking skin. Combine with other ingredients. Mash and beat until light. Fill potato skins with mixture. Dot with butter. Bake until brown, about 15 minutes. Serves 6. Grated cheese may be sprinkled on potatoes before cooking. Chopped onion and chopped cooked ham may be added to stuffing, if desired.

BAKED POTATOES WITH SAUSAGE

6 medium potatoes
2 large sausages, cut into pieces
3 tablespoons melted butter or olive oil
Salt
Pepper

Preheat oven to 350°F. Wash and peel potatoes. Remove centers with an apple corer. Put in each potato a part of a sausage. Place in baking pan and bake until potatoes are brown, about 40 minutes. Baste with butter or oil while baking. Sprinkle with salt and pepper. Allow 1 potato per serving.

POTATO CAKES

Mold cold mashed potatoes (p. 244) into patties. Dredge with flour. Fry in little fat, turning once to brown both sides.

POTATO PANCAKES

  3 medium-sized raw potatoes
  1 tablespoon flour
  1 tablespoon cream
  1 egg
  1 teaspoon salt

Peel and grate potatoes. Add other ingredients. Stir well. Drop by spoonfuls in heavy frying pan in hot fat. Serve with applesauce (p. 190) or sour cream. Serves 6.

POTATO FRITTERS

  3 cups hot mashed potatoes (p. 244)
  2 tablespoons butter, at room temperature
  1 teaspoon salt
  1 teaspoon sugar
  Few grains pepper
  2 tablespoons flour
  1 tablespoon chopped parsley
  2 eggs, separated
  Oil, for frying

To the potatoes add fat, salt, sugar, pepper, flour, and parsley. Beat egg yolks and add to the mixture. Beat the egg whites until stiff and gently fold them in as well. Drop by tablespoons in deep hot fat (375°F) and fry 5 to 8 minutes or until a delicate brown. Drain on paper towels. Serve hot. Serves 6.

POTATO PUFFS

½ cup butter or olive oil
½ cup boiling water
½ cup flour
2 eggs
⅛ teaspoon nutmeg
½ teaspoon salt
¼ teaspoon pepper
3 boiled potatoes, peeled and riced (p. 244)
Oil for frying

Mix butter or oil with ½ cup boiling water. Bring to a boil. Stir in flour and cook until well blended. Cool. Beat in eggs, one at a time. Add other ingredients. Drop from spoon in deep hot fat (350°F) and fry 10 minutes, or until golden brown. Yield: 10 puffs.

STUFFED MASHED POTATO

2 cups mashed potatoes (p. 244)
1 cup boiled peas
½ cup thick white sauce (p. 416)
1 cup breadcrumbs
1 beaten egg
Oil, for frying

Mold potatoes into small balls. Combine peas and sauce. Push finger into center of balls and fill hole with pea mixture. Mold to completely cover peas with potato. Roll balls in crumbs. Dip in egg, diluted with a little cold water. Roll again in crumbs. Fry in deep hot fat (375°F) until well browned. Drain on paper towels. Serves 6.

POTATO CHIPS

6 medium potatoes
Oil for frying
Salt

Peel potatoes. Cut, crosswise, in very thin slices. Let stand, covered with ice water, for 45 minutes. Drain and dry between towels. Fry in deep fat (325°F) until golden brown. Drain on unglazed paper. Sprinkle liberally with salt.

CHEESY POTATO CHIPS

Potato chips (above)
½–¾ cup grated Cheddar cheese

Preheat oven to 400°F. Spread out potato chips in shallow pans. Sprinkle generously with grated cheese. Bake for 10 minutes. Serve hot.

BOILED SPINACH

Cut leaves from roots. Wash several times in water, making certain that all sand is removed. Put in saucepan. Heat gradually over medium heat in a little bit of water and boil until tender, about 5 minutes. Season to taste with salt, pepper and butter. Allow 1 pound uncooked spinach for 3 servings.

CREAMED SPINACH

Heat 4 cups chopped, boiled spinach (above) in 2 cups medium white sauce (p. 416). Serves 6.

SPINACH TIMBALES

2 cups boiled spinach (p. 255)
2 tablespoons butter
2 slightly beaten eggs
1 cup milk
¾ teaspoon salt
⅛ teaspoon pepper
⅛ teaspoon paprika
Dash cayenne
2 teaspoons lemon juice
1 cup crushed tomatoes

Preheat oven to 350°F. Combine all ingredients except crushed tomatoes. Pack in greased timbale molds or muffin tins. Bake in pan of hot water until firm, about 20 minutes. Unmold and serve with heated crushed tomatoes. Serves 6.

CHEESE AND SPINACH LOAF

4 cups boiled spinach (p. 255), chopped
2 cups grated cheese
1 cup boiled rice (p. 128)
1 tablespoon horseradish
2 tablespoons melted butter
1 teaspoon salt
¼ teaspoon pepper
2 hard-boiled eggs (p. 272)

Preheat oven to 350°F. Combine ingredients. Mold into a loaf. Put in greased baking pan. Bake for 15 to 18 minutes. Serve garnished with slices of hard-boiled egg. Tomato sauce (p. 424) goes well with this. Serves 6.

ITALIAN SPINACH

4 cups boiled spinach (p. 255)
½ cup grated Parmesan cheese, or to taste
Salt
Pepper
Tomato sauce (p. 424)

Chop boiled spinach. Mix with grated cheese and season to taste with salt and pepper. Cover with highly seasoned tomato sauce.

BAKED SQUASH

Small Hubbard squash, or acorn squash
3 tablespoons butter
3 tablespoons chopped onion
2 tablespoons chopped green pepper
1 teaspoon salt
⅛ teaspoon pepper
⅛ teaspoon paprika
¼ cup fine breadcrumbs

Cut squash in pieces, peel, and boil in salted water for 30 minutes or until tender. Preheat oven to 400°F. Drain and mash squash. Melt butter. Add onion and pepper and sauté slowly for 5 minutes. Add onion, green pepper, salt, pepper, and paprika to the squash. Mix well and turn into a greased baking dish. Sprinkle with crumbs, salt, and pepper and bake for 25 minutes. Serves 6.

SUMMER SQUASH

Wash and quarter. Cook 30 minutes, or until tender, in a steamer or colander over boiling water. Mash, adding salt to taste and a little cream or butter.

SAUTÉED SQUASH

> 1 large summer squash
> Salt
> Pepper
> 1 to 2 tablespoons flour
> 1 egg, slightly beaten
> 2 tablespoons water
> ½ cup breadcrumbs
> Oil for frying

Peel summer squash and cut in uniform pieces. Sprinkle with salt, pepper, and flour. Dip in egg, diluted with water, then in breadcrumbs. Fry in small quantity of oil 6 to 8 minutes. Brown on both sides. Serves 6.

BAKED SQUASH WITH BACON

> 3 pound Hubbard squash, or acorn squash
> Melted butter
> Salt
> Pepper
> ½ to ⅔ cup milk
> 1 cup diced bacon

Preheat oven to 350°F. Cut squash in 2 pieces and remove seeds and stringy portions. Brush with butter, sprinkle with salt and pepper and bake until tender, about 30 minutes. Scoop out the inside. Mash and add the hot milk and additional salt to taste. Pour into a buttered baking dish. Fry bacon until crisp. Drain and sprinkle over squash. Bake for 25 to 30 minutes. Serves 6.

BOILED SWEET POTATOES

Boil sweet potatoes with skins on, following recipe for boiled potatoes (p. 244).

MASHED SWEET POTATOES

4 boiled sweet potatoes
Salt
2 tablespoons butter
2 tablespoons heavy cream or sour cream

Mashed boiled sweet potatoes (above) and add salt to taste, a little butter, and cream. Beat until light.

CANDIED SWEET POTATOES

4 medium sweet potatoes
⅔ cup sugar
⅓ cup water
1½ tablespoons butter

Preheat oven to 400°F. Select medium-sized potatoes. Scrub with a vegetable brush to remove all particles of dirt. Boil in water until tender, about 20 minutes. Drain off water and remove the skins. Cut in halves, lengthwise, and put them in a greased shallow pan. Make syrup by boiling sugar, water, and butter for 5 minutes. Pour this over the sweet potatoes. Bake for 20 minutes or until a delicate brown, basting occasionally with the syrup. Allow 1 potato for 2 servings.

FRENCH FRIED SWEET POTATOES

3 large sweet potatoes
Oil for frying
Salt

Boil sweet potatoes 10 minutes. Peel and cut in strips, 3" long. Fry in deep hot oil (325°F) until a delicate brown. Drain on paper towels. Sprinkle with salt. Allow ½ potato per serving.

ROAST SWEET POTATOES

Prepare and cook same as roast potatoes (p. 245), omitting the garlic and rosemary.

BAKED STUFFED SWEET POTATOES

6 sweet potatoes
2 tablespoons butter, at room temperature
1 egg yolk
¼ teaspoon grated orange zest
¼ teaspoon salt
⅛ teaspoon white pepper

Preheat oven to 350°F. Wash potatoes. Bake until soft when pressed, about 45 minutes. Cut off the tops and carefully remove and mash the pulp. Reserve the potato cases. Add other ingredients to the pulp. Beat well and roughly refill the cases. Bake for 20 minutes. Serves 6.

SWEET POTATOES AND APPLES

3 cooking apples, such as Granny Smith
3 large boiled sweet potatoes (p. 259)
½ cup brown sugar
2 tablespoons butter

Preheat oven to 325°F. Grease casserole with butter. Peel, core, and cut the apples into thick slices. Place a layer in the dish. Cover with slices of boiled sweet potatoes and top with apples. Sprinkle with ½ cup sugar and dot with butter. Repeat until all ingredients are used. Place casserole in a pan of boiling water and bake for 1 hour. Serves 6.

SPICED SWEET POTATO BALLS

3 large sweet potatoes
1 cup chopped nuts, such as pecans or walnuts
2 tablespoons butter
½ teaspoon salt
⅛ teaspoon nutmeg
⅛ teaspoon allspice
⅛ teaspoon cinnamon
½ cup flour
Oil for frying

Scrub potatoes to remove all dirt. Boil with skins on until tender. Peel and mash. Mix with other ingredients except the flour. Shape into balls. Roll in flour. Fry in deep hot fat (375°F) until well browned. Drain on paper towels. Serves 6.

ORANGE SWEET POTATOES

2½ cups sliced boiled sweet potatoes (p. 259)
3 tablespoons butter
3 tablespoons brown sugar
1 tablespoon grated orange zest
2 tablespoons orange juice

Sauté the sweet potatoes in butter over medium heat until browned on one side. Turn and sprinkle with sugar, zest, and juice. Cover and brown slowly on other side. Serves 5.

SWEET POTATO PUFFS

2 cups mashed sweet potatoes (p. 259)
2 eggs, separated
1 cup cream
½ teaspoon salt

Preheat oven to 350°F. Mix potatoes, yolks, cream, and salt. Heat in saucepan, over medium heat. Meanwhile, beat egg whites until stiff. When very hot, remove from heat and add egg whites. Beat until light. Pile loosely on buttered cookie sheet or baking pan. Brush with egg white. Heat until brown. Serves 6.

FRIED TOMATOES WITH CREAM GRAVY

3 tablespoons butter or olive oil
¼ cup flour
2 tablespoons sugar
1½ teaspoons salt
½ teaspoon pepper
4 large ripe tomatoes
2 cups milk (not skim)

Melt butter in frying pan. In a separate bowl, mix flour, sugar, salt, and pepper. Cut tomatoes in ½" slices. Dip in flour mixture and fry in butter until brown. Remove to a hot platter. Put the milk in the pan and bring to boiling point. Stir constantly until it thickens. Add a little salt, if necessary. Pour over the tomatoes, if desired, and serve hot. Serves 6.

STEWED TOMATOES

Pour boiling water over tomatoes. Plunge into cold water. Drain. Remove skins and hard parts. Quarter. Put in saucepan. Season to taste with salt and pepper. Bring slowly to a boil. Serve hot.

PICKLED GREEN TOMATOES

20 green tomatoes, sliced
6 tablespoons salt
6 onions, sliced
1 teaspoon ground dry mustard
2 tablespoons whole cloves
2 tablespoons mustard seed
2 tablespoons black pepper
2 tablespoons whole allspice
4 cups vinegar
2 cups sugar

Mix tomatoes with 4 tablespoons salt. Mix onions with 2 tablespoons salt. Let stand overnight. Drain. Tie spices in bag and place into a pot with the vinegar and sugar. Heat to the boiling point, add tomatoes and onions, and let simmer over low heat for 20 minutes. Pack into clean, hot jars. Seal immediately. Refrigerate for a week before serving.

BROILED TOMATOES WITH CHICKEN

1 cup chopped cooked chicken
Flour for dredging
¼ cup milk (not skim)
6 tomatoes
2 tablespoons grated cheese
Salt
Pepper

Turn oven to broil. Coat chicken lightly with flour. Put in saucepan. Moisten with milk. Heat over medium heat until thickened. Wash tomatoes. Cut in halves, crosswise. Spread them with chicken mixture. Sprinkle with cheese. Season to taste with salt and pepper. Put into broiler. Broil for just a minute or two, until the tomatoes are delicately browned on top. Serves 6.

BROILED TOMATOES WITH CHEESE

6 slices American or Cheddar cheese
12 slices tomato
12 slices bacon
6 slices stale bread
Salt
Pepper
Parsley for garnishing

Turn oven to broil. Place 1 slice cheese, 2 slices tomato and 2 slices bacon on bread. Cook on rack in broiler until bacon is crisp and cheese well melted. Season to taste with salt and pepper. Serve very hot and garnish with sprigs of parsley, if desired. Serves 6.

CHEESE AND ONION TOMATOES

6 ripe tomatoes
½ cup diced green pepper
½ cup diced onion
Salt
Pepper
2 tablespoons butter

Preheat oven to 450°F. Cut tomatoes in half. Place in a baking pan and cover each tomato with a thick layer of equal parts green pepper and onions. Season with salt, pepper and butter. Bake for 15 minutes. Pour cream sauce (p. 417) over tomatoes, if desired, after placing each on a square of fresh buttered toast. Serves 6.

BAKED STUFFED TOMATOES

2 cups soft breadcrumbs
1 teaspoon salt
⅛ teaspoon pepper
2 tablespoons sugar
3 tablespoons butter
6 tomatoes

Preheat oven to 350°F. Mix breadcrumbs with salt, pepper, 1 tablespoon sugar, and 2 tablespoons melted butter. Cut thin slice from stem end of tomatoes and remove a scoop out of the center. Sprinkle with salt, pepper, and sugar. Fill with the stuffing. Dot with small bits of butter and bake for 1 hour. Serves 6. 2 cups of shredded cabbage, seasoned with 1 chopped onion, salt, and pepper is another good stuffing. Or, tomatoes may be filled with balls of sausage meat. Buttered corn flakes may be sprinkled on tomatoes before cooking. 1 cup cooked, quartered boiled shrimp (p. 342) may be substituted for 1 cup crumbs.

266

TOMATO SCRAPPLE

2½ cups stewed tomatoes (p. 264)
1 onion, chopped
1 carrot, chopped
½ cup corn meal
1 teaspoon sugar
Salt
Pepper
1 cup chopped roasted peanuts (optional)
Oil for frying

Mix tomatoes, onion, carrot, corn meal, and sugar in a large saucepan and season to taste with salt and pepper. Cook slowly over low heat until thick, about 1 hour. Beat in peanuts. Pack into an oiled pan or baking powder tin. Cool. Slice and fry in little oil over medium heat. Serves 8.

BOILED TURNIPS

Peel and slice. Boil in slightly salted water until tender, about 1 to 1¼ hours. Season to taste with butter, salt, and pepper.

TURNIP GREENS

Follow recipe for chicory (p. 227) through boiling, cooking about 25 minutes.

CREAMED VEGETABLES

2½ cups mixed cooked vegetables
½ cup light cream
2 tablespoons butter
1 tablespoon flour
¼ teaspoon dry mustard
Salt
Pepper

Drain vegetables and add ½ cup of liquid to cream. Melt butter in a skillet over medium heat. Add flour and mustard. Season to taste with salt and pepper. Add liquid. Cook until thick, stirring constantly. Add vegetables. Heat thoroughly. Serves 6. If desired, ½ cup grated cheese or sliced hard-boiled eggs (p. 272) may be added with vegetables.

SCALLOPED VEGETABLES

Preheat oven to 350°F. Fill bottom of casserole or baking dish with diced cooked vegetables. Pour over with layer of medium white sauce (p. 416). Continue to alternate with vegetable and white sauce to the top of the dish, making the top layer one of white sauce. Add a small chip of butter occasionally as the dish is being filled. Scatter soft crumbs over the top and bake until browned, about 20 minutes.

VEGETABLES AU GRATIN

Preheat oven to 350°F. Put creamed vegetables (above) in greased baking dish. Sprinkle with breadcrumbs and grated cheese, if desired. Dot with butter. Bake for 15 minutes or until crumbs are browned. Serves 6.

VEGETABLES LYONNAISE

2 medium-sized onions
3 tablespoons butter
2½ cups stewed corn (p. 228)
2½ cups cooked peas
Salt
Pepper
2 tablespoons chopped parsley

Slice onions thin. Separate into rings. Sauté over medium heat until golden brown in butter. Drain corn and add liquid to onions. Simmer until reduced to ½ cup. Add peas and corn. Season to taste with salt and pepper. Heat thoroughly. Sprinkle with parsley just before serving. Serves 6.

VEGETABLE FRITTERS

1¾ cups flour
1 teaspoon salt
Few grains pepper
3½ teaspoons baking powder
2 eggs
½ cup milk
½ cup boiled carrots (p. 222), chopped
¼ cup cooked peas
¼ cup boiled lima beans (p. 215)
1 tablespoon chopped parsley
2 tablespoons melted butter
Oil for frying

Mix and sift flour, salt, pepper, and baking powder. Beat eggs and add milk. Add to the flour mixture and beat thoroughly. Add carrots, peas, lima beans, parsley, and butter and mix well. Drop by tablespoons into deep hot fat (375°F) and fry until a delicate brown. Drain on paper towels. Serve hot with cheese sauce (p. 417), if desired. Serves 6.

VEGETABLE PIE

1 small onion, sliced
3 tablespoons butter
1 tablespoon flour
1½ teaspoons salt
½ teaspoon pepper
2 cups cooked mixed vegetables
1 egg, slightly beaten
1 cup mashed potatoes (p. 244)

Preheat oven to 400°F. Sauté onion in butter over low heat until soft. Add flour, salt, and pepper. Mix well. Add vegetables without draining. Simmer slowly, stirring constantly, until mixture thickens. Turn into greased baking pan. Combine egg and potatoes and beat until fluffy. Spread potatoes over vegetable mixture. Bake until brown, about 15 or 20 minutes. Serves 6.

EGG DISHES

Eggs are the chameleons of the food world. They can be sweet or savory, fluffy or hard, breakfast or dinner. They rise in soufflés and roll up in omelets. Eggs are wonderful. In addition to their versatility, they are a cheap, excellent source of protein. Eaten in moderation, they are a part of a healthy diet.

Most grocery stores only carry chicken eggs, but some specialty stores or farmers' markets may carry duck, goose, and even quail eggs. Duck and goose eggs often have a higher fat content and are excellent for custards, cakes, and other desserts as a result. They can be substituted for chicken eggs in most recipes. They are somewhat larger; recipes calling for several chicken eggs would not need quite as many duck or goose eggs.

Regardless of the type of egg, freshness makes a huge difference. Farm fresh eggs are always going to taste and cook better. When farm fresh eggs are not available, still be sure to use up eggs fairly quickly. The longer an egg sits in a refrigerator, the more the white breaks down. It won't beat as fully, or taste as delicious.

Many recipes call for the eggs to be beaten, either separately or together, before they are added to the rest of the ingredients. In the case of whole eggs and yolks, this is necessary to ensure that the eggs will incorporate fully into the other ingredients. Egg whites are often beaten to soft or stiff peaks to add volume to a batter of some sort. When the beater used to beat the egg whites is removed and the egg whites form little mountains with a top that flops over, they have reached soft peaks. When that top stays upright, they have reached stiff peaks. Eggs will always beat up best if they are at room temperature. Removing them from the refrigerator an hour or so before cooking should do the trick.

SOFT- OR HARD-BOILED EGGS

4 to 6 eggs

Heat enough water to cover the eggs to simmering, but do not let it boil. A rolling boil toughens egg whites. Gently lower the eggs into the water, using a spoon. The temperature of the water should not be allowed to go higher than 185°F. For soft-boiled eggs, remove from heat after 3 minutes. The length of time may vary slightly depending upon the size of the eggs. The number of eggs cooked at a time, the size of the pan and the quantity and temperature of the water also affect the rate at which eggs cook. For hard-boiled eggs, continue the cooking over a low heat for 8 minutes, slightly longer (10 minutes) for a large egg.

FRIED EGGS

1 tablespoon butter
3 eggs

Heat a frying pan over medium heat. Cover bottom of pan generously with butter. Drop eggs into it. Fry slowly until white is set. If a harder yolk is desired, the eggs may be turned and cooked on the other side. Serve hot. Allow 1 or 2 eggs per serving.

CODDLED EGGS

Bring pan of water to a boil. Remove from heat. Gently add eggs one at a time, using a spoon. Cover and let stand 8 to 10 minutes. The eggs will be slightly cooked. The white should be firm. The yolk will be runny.

POACHED EGGS

½ teaspoon salt
1 tablespoon vinegar
4 eggs
Butter
Salt
Pepper

Fill a skillet with 2" to 3" of water. Add ½ teaspoon salt and 1 tablespoon vinegar to the water. Bring to a simmer. Break each egg into a small bowl or ramekin, one at a time. Transfer without breaking yolk to water. Cover skillet with a lid and continue cooking on very low heat for 3 minutes. Do not let water boil after eggs are in it. Cook until white is firm and there is a film over yolk. For firmer yolks, cook eggs longer. Remove eggs from water with a slotted spoon. Dot with butter. Sprinkle with salt and pepper to taste. Poached eggs are good when served on corned beef hash (p. 373), on buttered toast, or on their own with bacon or other breakfast meats.

POACHED EGGS WITH ASPARAGUS

6 poached eggs (above)
6 slices buttered toast
1 cup boiled asparagus tips (p. 210)
⅓ cup grated Parmesan
2 cups béchamel sauce (p. 423)

Serve poached eggs on buttered toast. Add asparagus tips and Parmesan cheese to the hot béchamel sauce. Cover eggs and toast. Serves 6.

POACHED EGGS WITH CHEESE

 6 poached eggs (p. 273)
 6 slices buttered toast
 ½ cup cheese sauce (p. 417)

Place poached eggs on slices of toast. Put 1 tablespoon cheese sauce on each. Serves 6.

EGGS FLORENTINE

 6 poached eggs (p. 273)
 2 cups boiled spinach (p. 255), seasoned
 2 cups béchamel sauce
 ½ cup grated Parmesan cheese

Arrange poached eggs on nests of spinach. Pour béchamel sauce over the eggs and sprinkle with Parmesan. Serves 6.

EGGS BENEDICT

 3 English muffins or 6 slices of toast
 6 slices fried ham (p. 397)
 6 poached eggs (p. 273)
 2 cups hollandaise sauce (p. 418)

Toast slices of bread, or split and toasted English muffins. Place on each piece of toast a thin slice of fried ham, and on top of this a poached egg. Cover with hot hollandaise sauce and serve at once. Serves 6

MEXICAN POACHED EGGS

1½ tablespoons green olives, sliced
1 pimento, diced and seeded
2 tablespoons chopped green pepper
1 cup tomato sauce (p. 424), hot
6 slices buttered toast
6 poached eggs
2 tablespoons chopped parsley

Add olives, pimento, and green pepper to tomato sauce and pour over toast. Put poached eggs on top and garnish with parsley.

OMELETS

2 to 3 eggs
Salt
Pepper
1 tablespoon butter

Crack the eggs into a medium mixing bowl. Add a big pinch of salt and a small pinch of pepper. Mix vigorously with a fork or whisk for 20 to 30 seconds. Heat a medium skillet over high heat. Add the butter, swirling the pan to make sure the butter coats the bottom and sides of the pan. When the pan is fully coated, add the eggs. Gently shake or slide the pan over the heat, while also using a fork or spatula to spread the eggs continuously over the bottom of the pan. The eggs will begin to thicken after 4 or 5 seconds. Tilt the pan to the left or the right, and use a spatula or fork to loosen the top of the omelet from the pan. Using the fork or spatula to guide the eggs, roll it over on itself at the bottom of the pan. Cook for a few seconds longer, allowing the omelet to brown slightly if you like. Remove to a plate, using the spatula to guide it. The center of the omelet will be soft and creamy—for a drier omelet, increase the cooking times. Serves 1 to 2.

OMELET VARIATIONS

Before rolling the omelet up, any number of fillings can be added. Some ideas:

- Sautéed onions or mushrooms
- Crumbled bacon
- ½ cup mild, grated cheese
- Fine chopped fresh herbs.

CHEESE OMELET

Omelet (p. 275)
½ cup grated cheese, such as Swiss or Cheddar

Preheat oven to 475°F. Follow recipe for omelet. Sprinkle cheese on it and put in the oven until cheese melts. Fold and turn out on hot platter. Serves 1 to 2.

SPANISH OMELET

4 thin slices bacon, minced
1 tomato, diced
1 onion, chopped
5 mushrooms, chopped
6 eggs
3 tablespoons milk
Salt
Red pepper
1 tablespoon butter

Heat a skillet over medium heat. Add bacon and cook until it is browned. Add tomato, onion, and mushrooms. Cook slowly 15 minutes, stirring occasionally. Meanwhile, beat eggs with milk. Season to taste with salt and pepper. Melt butter in another pan over medium heat and pour eggs in. Stir constantly with a fork or spatula until eggs are set. Pour sauce from first pan over eggs. Fold omelet and turn onto a plate. Cover with remaining sauce from both pans. If desired, chopped green pepper may be substituted for mushrooms. Serves 2 to 3.

CHICKEN OMELET

    1 cup chopped, cooked chicken
    1 cup milk
    1 tablespoon flour
    1 tablespoon butter
    Salt
    Pepper
    Omelet (p. 275)
    1 tablespoon chopped chives or parsley (optional)

Warm cooked chicken with milk, flour, butter, salt, and pepper. Make omelet. Pour chicken mixture over it just before folding. Fold omelet and turn onto a plate. May be garnished with chives or parsley, if desired. Serves 2 to 3.

CORN OMELET

6 eggs, separated
1 cup corn, fresh or frozen
1 teaspoon salt
Pepper

Preheat oven to 350°F. Beat egg yolks with a mixer until they have begun to thicken, approximately 2 minutes. Add salt and pepper. Fold yolk mixture into egg whites. Fold corn gently into egg mixture. Put in buttered skillet and cook over low heat until browned on bottom. Transfer to oven and bake until dry. Fold and remove to hot platter. Serves 6.

BREAD OMELET

¾ cup breadcrumbs
½ cup milk
3 eggs, separated
½ teaspoon salt
1 tablespoon butter

Put breadcrumbs in a medium mixing bowl. Add milk. Let stand 5 minutes. Lightly beat the egg yolks. Beat the whites with a mixer until they form stiff peaks. Drain excess milk from crumbs. Beat crumbs and yolks together. Add salt. Fold in the whites. Melt butter in a skillet. Put in mixture and cook at high heat for 1 minute. Reduce heat. Cover and let cook slowly 20 minutes. Remove to hot platter and fold. Serves 4.

SCRAMBLED EGGS

6 eggs
½ cup milk, cream, or sour cream
Salt
Pepper
1 tablespoon butter

Beat eggs slightly and combine with milk. Season to taste with salt and pepper. Melt butter in a frying pan over medium-low heat. Pour in egg mixture. Cook slowly, stirring constantly, until creamy. Scrambled eggs may also be cooked over high heat, for a less creamy, more omelet-like consistency. Serves 4 to 6.

MORE IDEAS FOR SCRAMBLED EGGS

- Cook with 1 tablespoon chopped chives or scallions and ½ cup of cheese. Goat cheese, Cheddar, Fontina, or any other mild cheese would be delicious.
- Add diced ham, sausage, or crumbled bacon during cooking.
- Add sautéed mushrooms or onions during cooking.
- Add ½ pound sautéed shrimp, diced scallions, and soy sauce to taste.

SCRAMBLED EGGS WITH TOMATO

2 medium-sized tomatoes
½ teaspoon salt
1 ½ tablespoons butter
4 eggs

Peel tomatoes. Cut in eighths. Put in saucepan and sprinkle with salt. Cook over medium heat. Bring to boil and boil 1 minute. Drain off juice in a colander. Set tomatoes aside and dot with half of the butter. Melt remaining butter in a skillet. Break eggs into a bowl and mix with a fork for 20 to 30 seconds, until combined. Drop eggs into pan. Stir quickly. When partly cooked, add tomatoes. Stir to mix well and serve hot. ½ cup corn, enriched with 1 tablespoon butter, can be substituted for tomatoes. Serves 4.

SCRAMBLED EGGS AND BACON

4 eggs
4 tablespoons cream or milk (not skim)
Salt
Pepper
1 tablespoon butter
3 slices bacon, cooked and crumbled

Beat the eggs slightly with 1 tablespoon of cream or whole milk for each egg. Season with salt and pepper. Pour the mixture into a skillet containing melted butter or other fat. Cook, stirring constantly, until thickened. Just before removing from heat, add crumbled bacon. Serves 2 to 3.

BAKED EGGS

6 slices bread
6 eggs
Salt
Pepper
1 tablespoon butter
½ cup milk

Preheat oven to 350°F. Cut bread in rounds. Cut out piece in center of each. Toast lightly. Place in a greased 10" x 12" baking dish. Break eggs and drop each into center of toast slices. Sprinkle with salt and pepper to taste. Dot with butter. Pour on milk. Bake for 15 to 20 minutes or until whites have set. Serves 6.

SHIRRED EGGS

2 tablespoons butter
½ cup dry breadcrumbs (optional)
6 eggs
Salt
Pepper

Preheat oven to 275°F. Grease 6 individual custard cups with butter. Cover bottom and sides of cup with crumbs, if desired. Break eggs carefully into cups. Sprinkle with salt and pepper. Cover with crumbs, if desired. Bake for 15 to 20 minutes until white is set. Serve plain or with brown butter sauce (p. 419).

STUFFED EGGS

3 tablespoons butter
½ pound mushrooms, washed and sliced
2 teaspoons chopped fresh herbs, such as chives thyme
Salt
Pepper
6 hard-boiled eggs (p. 272)
1 cup Béarnaise sauce (p. 422)
½ cup grated mild cheese, such as Fontina or Swiss

Preheat oven to 350°F. Melt 2 tablespoons butter in a frying pan over medium heat. Add mushrooms, herbs, and salt and pepper to taste. Cook until mushrooms have shrunk and softened, about 5 to 7 minutes. Grease a 9" x 9" baking pan with remaining butter. Arrange mushroom mixture on the bottom of the dish. Set aside. Slice hard-boiled eggs using an egg slicer, or by hand, creating about 8 lengthwise sections per egg. Arrange slices on top of the mushrooms. Cover with Béarnaise sauce and sprinkle with cheese. Bake for 15 to 20 minutes, or until the cheese is browned and the mixture is heated through. Serves 4 to 6.

DEVILED EGGS

6 hard-boiled eggs (p. 272)
2 tablespoons mayonnaise (p. 70)
2 teaspoons prepared mustard
1 tablespoon chopped parsley
Salt
Pepper
Paprika

Remove shells from eggs. Cut eggs in halves, crosswise. Remove yolks. Mash yolks, adding mayonnaise, mustard, and parsley. Season with salt and pepper to taste. Mix well. Fill whites with mixture. Sprinkle with paprika. Serves 6.

SUGGESTED STUFFINGS FOR DEVILED EGGS

- Mashed yolks, 2 tablespoons grated cheese, ¼ teaspoon mustard, 1 teaspoon vinegar, 1 tablespoon mayonnaise, salt and pepper.
- Mashed yolks, 2 tablespoons anchovy paste, 2 tablespoons mayonnaise (p. 70), 2 tablespoons lemon juice, 2 tablespoons chopped olives, salt and cayenne.
- Mashed yolks, 2 tablespoons diced, crisp bacon, ½ tablespoon Worcestershire sauce, ½ teaspoon mustard, salt and pepper.
- Mashed yolks, 2 tablespoons sautéed chopped onion (p. 238), ¼ cup chopped, sautéed mushrooms (p. 235), 2 tablespoons mayonnaise, salt, and cayenne.
- Mashed yolks, 1 teaspoon horseradish, juice of ½ lemon, 1 tablespoon French dressing (p. 71), salt, and pepper.
- Fill eggs with caviar or chopped anchovies. Mash yolks with 2 tablespoons mayonnaise. Top caviar with a little of this mixture. Serve on buttered toasts with a slice of tomato.

FRENCH EGGS

6 hard-boiled eggs, quartered (p. 272)
1 tablespoon freshly squeezed lemon juice
½ cup butter (1 stick)
1 tablespoon flour
2 cups milk
1 tablespoon chopped parsley
Salt
Pepper

Arrange egg quarters on dish. Sprinkle with lemon juice. Melt half of butter in pan. Add flour and cook slowly, stirring constantly, until thickened. Bring milk to a boil and add slowly to butter. Add remaining butter, parsley, and salt and pepper to taste. Heat well. Pour sauce over eggs. Serves 6.

SCOTCH EGGS

½ cup breadcrumbs
½ cup milk
1 cup chopped, cooked ham
½ teaspoon prepared mustard, or more to taste
¼ teaspoon pepper
1 beaten egg
6 hard-boiled eggs (p. 272), shells removed
Oil for frying

Mix crumbs and milk in saucepan. Heat slowly and stir into a smooth paste. Add ham, mustard, pepper, and beaten egg, mixing well. Take hard-boiled eggs and cover each thoroughly with mixture. Fry in deep hot fat at 375°F for 2 minutes. Drain on paper towels. Serve hot. Serves 6.

LYONNAISE EGGS

2 tablespoons butter
2 tablespoons chopped onion
1 tablespoon chopped parsley, or other fresh herbs,
    such as chives
1 tablespoon flour
1 cup hot milk
4 hard-boiled eggs, sliced (p. 272)
6 slices of buttered toast

Melt butter in pan. Sauté onion and parsley to light brown.
Stir in flour. Add milk. Bring to boil, blending thoroughly.
Reduce heat and add eggs. Heat thoroughly. Serve on buttered toast. Serves 6.

EGGS À LA KING

2 cups medium white sauce (p. 416)
1 cup sliced, sautéed mushrooms (p. 235)
2 tablespoon chopped parsley
½ cup peas, fresh or frozen
6 hard-boiled eggs (p. 272)
6 slices of buttered toast

Mix sauce, mushrooms, parsley, and peas. Cut eggs in eighths
and add to sauce. Heat thoroughly and serve on buttered
toast. Serves 6.

EGGS AND MUSHROOMS

½ pound mushrooms
1½ cups water
1 tablespoon butter
4 tablespoons flour
Salt
Pepper
Cayenne
1 cup milk
6 hard-boiled eggs, sliced (p. 272)
½ cup Swiss or Fontina cheese, grated

Preheat oven to 350°F. Wash mushrooms. Drain, peel, and remove stems. Bring water to a boil over medium heat. Cook stems and peels together in the water for 15 minutes. Strain liquid into a cup. Discard stems and peels. Slice mushrooms and cook slowly in the butter until tender. Mix flour, salt, and a dash of pepper and cayenne together. Add milk slowly to make a smooth paste. Add the cup of mushroom stock and cook over low heat, stirring constantly until thickened. Add mushrooms. Put a layer of eggs in a casserole, then a layer of the mushroom mixture. Repeat this process until all the ingredients are used. Sprinkle top with cheese. Bake for 20 minutes or until cheese is browned. Serves 6.

SCALLOPED EGGS

6 hard-boiled eggs (p. 272)
¼ teaspoon salt
1½ cups soft breadcrumbs
2 cups thin white sauce (p. 416)
1 tablespoon butter

Preheat oven to 350°F. Chop eggs and season with salt. Grease a 9" x 9" baking dish with butter and put layer of crumbs in bottom. Add a layer of egg. Add layer of sauce. Repeat until all ingredients are used, having a layer of crumbs on top. Bake for 20 minutes or until crumbs are brown. Layers of chopped ham, other cooked meats, poultry, or grated cheese can be added to this dish. Serves 6.

CURRIED EGGS

4 tablespoons butter
1 tablespoon chopped green pepper
2 tablespoons chopped onion
2 tablespoons chopped celery
1 teaspoon curry powder
3 drops Tabasco sauce
1 teaspoon salt
Pepper, to taste
3 tablespoons flour
2 cups milk
2 cups cooked rice (p. 128)
6 hard-boiled eggs (p. 272)
2 tablespoons finely chopped parsley

Melt the butter in a skillet over medium heat. Add the green pepper, onion, and celery and cook for 2 or 3 minutes, until onion becomes translucent. Stir into this the seasoning and the flour. Mix well and add the cold milk. Cook for 3 or 4 minutes, stirring constantly, until the sauce begins to thicken. Make a bed of the hot cooked rice on a platter. Arrange over it the hard-boiled eggs, cut in quarters, and pour the hot sauce over the eggs and rice. Sprinkle the top with chopped parsley and serve at once. Serves 6.

BAKED EGGS WITH ONION

3 tablespoons butter
2 small onions, sliced
Salt
Pepper
2 tablespoons lemon juice
6 poached eggs (p. 273)
¼ cup mild grated cheese, such as Cheddar or Swiss

Preheat oven to 350°F. Melt butter in a skillet over medium heat. Add onions, and salt and pepper to taste. Cook for 2 to 3 minutes, until onions are translucent, but not browned. Put onion in greased 9" x 9" baking dish. Add lemon juice and butter from pan. Place eggs on top. Sprinkle with cheese. Bake for 10 to 15 minutes, long enough to melt cheese. Serves 6.

PLANKED EGGS

1 cup chopped, cooked ham
1 cup cream
1 cup breadcrumbs
2 cups mashed potatoes (p. 244)
1 tablespoon melted butter
4 poached eggs (p. 273)

Preheat oven to 350°F. Mix ham with cream and breadcrumbs to make a paste. Spread on a heated, buttered wooden plank. Make border with mashed potatoes, using a pastry tube if desired. Brush with butter. Put eggs on top of meat mixture. Brush eggs with butter. Bake for 10 minutes, until potatoes are slightly browned. Serves 4.

POACHED EGGS WITH TOMATOES

    3 tablespoons butter
    1 tablespoon chopped onion
    1 tablespoon chopped pimento
    1 tablespoon chopped parsley
    6 slices buttered toast
    6 slices fried tomatoes (p. 263, without cream gravy)
    6 poached eggs (p. 273)

Melt butter in a skillet over medium heat. Add onion, pimento, and parsley. Cook for 2 to 3 minutes, until onions are translucent. Meanwhile, arrange toast on platter. Put 1 slice tomato on each piece of toast. Put 1 poached egg on each. Top with onion and pimento mixture. Serves 6.

BAKED FRENCH EGGS

    4 tablespoons butter
    6 eggs
    Salt
    Pepper
    1 tablespoon chopped parsley

Preheat oven to 350°F. Butter a 9" x 9" baking dish. Break eggs in dish. Lay slice of butter on each egg. Season with salt and pepper. Bake until whites are set, about 15 to 20 minutes. Remove to hot platter. Sprinkle with parsley. Serves 6.

BAKED EGGS WITH CHEESE SAUCE

3 cups cheese sauce (p. 417)
6 eggs
½ cup grated mild cheese

Preheat oven to 325°F. Put a thin layer of cheese sauce in the bottom of a greased 9" x 9" baking dish or individual ramekins. Break eggs, one at a time, into a cup and drop carefully on the sauce. Cover them with another layer of cheese sauce. Sprinkle top with cheese. Bake for 15 to 20 minutes or until the egg whites are firm and the cheese is brown. Serves 6.

BAKED EGGS WITH MACARONI

2 cups boiled macaroni, or other similar pasta
1 cup cream or milk (not skim)
1 cup mild, grated cheese, such as Cheddar
Salt
Pepper
4 eggs

Preheat oven to 350°F. Heat macaroni and place in greased baking dish. Mix cream, cheese, and salt and pepper to taste. Pour over macaroni. Crack eggs over the top. Bake until eggs are set, about 15 to 20 minutes. Serves 4.

BAKED EGGS WITH CHEESE

6 eggs
3 tablespoons cream
Salt
⅔ cup mild, grated cheese, such as Cheddar or Swiss
Paprika

Preheat oven to 350°F. Break the desired number of eggs in a shallow, greased 9" x 9" baking dish. Add cream and salt enough to season. Sprinkle with grated cheese. Set this dish in a slightly larger pan containing hot water and bake until the eggs are set and the cheese browns, about 15 to 20 minutes. Just before serving add a few dashes of paprika. Serves 6.

EGGS IN BACON RINGS

6 slices of bacon
6 eggs

Preheat oven to 350°F. Cook bacon over medium heat for a few minutes. Remove from heat just before the bacon begins to brown. Slip each slice in custard cups or ramekins, lining the cup. Drop eggs into cups individually. Bake until eggs are set, about 15 to 20 minutes. Serves 6.

EGGS AND SPINACH EN CASSEROLE

1½ cups cold, chopped, boiled spinach (p. 255)
6 eggs
Salt
Pepper
1 cup cheese sauce (p. 417)
Paprika

Preheat oven to 325°F. Put 4 tablespoons well-seasoned spinach in bottom of individual baking dishes or ramekins. Drop a raw egg on top of each. Sprinkle with salt and pepper. Cover with sauce. Cook for 15 to 20 minutes or until eggs are set. Sprinkle with paprika. Serves 6.

ITALIAN STYLE EGGS

3 tablespoons ketchup or tomato paste
1 tablespoon prepared mustard
2 tablespoons butter
1 tablespoon Worcestershire sauce
1 teaspoon salt
1 teaspoon paprika
6 eggs
6 slices buttered toast

Mix all ingredients but eggs and toast in a saucepan. Bring to boil over medium heat. Break and drop in eggs. Cook slowly until set. Serve on buttered toast with sauce. Serves 6.

BAKED EGGS IN TOMATO CUPS

6 large, firm, ripe tomatoes
Salt
3 tablespoons butter
6 eggs
Pepper
1 cup mild, grated cheese

Preheat oven to 350°F. Scoop out the centers of the tomatoes. Sprinkle the tomato cups lightly on the inside with salt and dot with butter. Break an egg into each tomato, sprinkle with salt, pepper, and cheese. Dot with butter. Bake until the tomato skins are slightly wrinkled and the eggs are set, about 20 minutes. Serves 6.

EGG FLUFF

1 slice bread
¾ cup milk
1 tablespoon melted butter
4 eggs
Salt
Pepper

Preheat oven to 350°F. Break bread in pieces and put in a small cup. Fill cup with milk. Pour into a bowl and add butter, beaten eggs, and salt and pepper to taste. Grease 4 custard cups and fill each ¾ full with mixture. Bake for 25 minutes. Serve hot. Serves 4.

CHEESE SOUFFLÉ

3 tablespoons butter
3 tablespoons flour
1 teaspoon dry mustard
¼ teaspoon salt
1⅓ cups hot milk (not skim)
4 eggs, separated, plus 1 egg white
½ pound Cheddar or Swiss cheese
½ teaspoon cream of tartar

Preheat oven to 375 °F. Butter an 8" soufflé dish and set aside. Melt the butter in a saucepan over low heat. Add the flour, mustard, and salt. Stir until combined and free of lumps. Add the milk, stirring constantly. Remove from the heat as soon as it reaches a boil. In a separate bowl, beat the egg yolks until light. Add a small amount of the hot milk mixture to the yolks. Mix thoroughly, and then add the yolks to the milk mixture, whisking constantly. Add the cheese, whisking until the cheese has melted and the mixture is smooth. Meanwhile, beat egg whites until foamy. Add the cream of tartar, and beat until the whites hold stiff peaks. Gently fold the egg whites into the cheese mixture, being careful to deflate the egg whites as little as possible. Pour the mixture into the soufflé dish. Bake for 35 minutes. Serve immediately.

SOUFFLÉ VARIATIONS

- Other cheeses: Parmesan, Cheddar, jack or many other cheeses may be substituted for the Swiss cheese.
- ½ cup to 1 cup cooked meats, such as ham or bacon, may be added to the sauce with the cheese.
- Cooked greens, like spinach, may also be added to the sauce. ½ cup greens would be sufficient.

POULTRY
AND
FISH

POULTRY

A roast chicken, though simple, can be a thing of perfection, with its crisp, golden skin and moist, flavorful flesh. However, poultry, especially chicken, is often quite lean. This means that care must be taken to achieve that delicious combination of moist meat and crispy skin. Chicken and turkey are both quite prone to drying out; this chapter offers several ways to combat that problem.

One solution is to coat, baste, or bard the poultry in fat. Rubbing a chicken with olive oil or melted butter is one approach to coating; getting some of that fat under the skin and closer to the flesh is even better.

Basting refers to the process of collecting the juices and fat which have dripped from a bird during roasting and pouring them right back over the bird. Both coating and basting will produce a golden brown, crispy skin and tender meat.

Barding, or wrapping in fat, is another option. This automatically bastes the skin and keeps the flesh tender. Bacon or fat back can be used for barding. The fat from these meats cooks and seals the skin of the bird, preventing it from drying out. This is an especially good option for game birds, which are the leanest of all.

Slow cooking, or stewing, is another option for producing tender meat. Poultry should be simmered over low heat for a long time in order to achieve the best results. High heat can cause the meat to stay tough.

FISH

Fish are an excellent source of lean protein and good fat. Eating fish regularly has even been shown to increase heart health. Fish are an excellent addition to a well-balanced diet.

The preparations listed in this chapter can be used for many kinds of fish, beyond even what is what is listed here. Nearly any fish, for instance, can be poached, baked, or broiled with great success.

Don't be afraid to ask questions when buying fresh fish. Find out how often the store or fish market gets new deliveries of fish. Never buy fish that is more than a day (or at most, two days) old. Smell the fish. It should smell like the ocean. It should not have a strong "fishy" odor. This can be an early sign of spoilage.

Find out where the fish comes from. Certain fish populations are in danger because of over-fishing. The fish seller should have some basic information about the fish's origins.

If possible, buy fish directly from a fish market or a store that specializes in fish. They are more likely to get daily (or more than daily) deliveries of fish and are more likely to be knowledgeable about where the fish came from and how it can best be enjoyed.

Try to cook fish within a day of buying it, to ensure maximum flavor and freshness. Store the fish in the refrigerator until just before cooking. Fish can spoil very rapidly at room temperature.

POULTRY

TIMETABLE FOR ROASTING YOUNG BIRDS

	WEIGHT OF BIRD (pounds)	OVEN TEMP.	TIME (hours)
Chicken	4–5	375°F	1¾–2
Duck	5–6	375°F	2–2½
Goose	10–12	375°F	2–3
Cornish Hen	1–1½	350°F	1–1 ¼
Turkey	6–9	325°F	2½–3
	10–13	325°F	3–4
	14–17	325°F	4–5
	18–25	325°F	5–6

ROAST CHICKEN WITH HERBS

4–5 pound chicken
1 lemon
½ cup butter, plus 3 tablespoons
1 tablespoon fresh rosemary, finely diced
1 teaspoon salt
½ teaspoon pepper

Preheat oven to 450°F. Remove giblets and neck bone from inside the chicken. Wipe with cold, damp cloth. Pierce the lemon with a knife in several places and insert it in the chicken's cavity. Fasten wings and legs close to body with skewers or by tying. Spread 3 tablespoons butter over breast and legs. Sprinkle with salt and pepper. Combine the rest of the butter with the rosemary and rub under the chicken's skin. Place chicken breast side up in pan. Roast at 450°F for 15 minutes. Reduce heat to 350°F and cook until thigh juices run clear when a cut is made, about 1½ hours. Baste every 10 minutes with butter and juices from the pan. Thyme or other fresh herbs may be used in place of rosemary, if desired.

FRUIT GLAZED ROAST CHICKEN

4–5 pound chicken
2 teaspoons salt
½ teaspoon pepper
½ cup butter, plus 3 tablespoons
1 cup finely cut celery
½ cup sliced onion
⅓ cup minced parsley
8½ cups white bread cubes
½ teaspoon sage
½ cup peach or nectarine nectar

Preheat oven to 375°F. Prepare chicken for roasting. Sprinkle inside and out with salt and pepper. Heat ½ cup butter in large saucepan or stockpot over medium heat. Add bread cubes and cook and stir about 5 minutes. Add vegetables and seasonings. Cook, stirring frequently, until bread cubes are slightly browned and vegetables are wilted. Remove from heat, add ¼ cup nectar and stir to blend. Use to stuff chicken. Sew up opening. Bake, uncovered, at 375°F for about 15 minutes. Baste with remaining nectar and continue baking, basting frequently, for 1½ to 2 hours, or until thigh juices run clear when a cut is made. Cover pan when chicken is sufficiently brown. Any other nectar of the whole fruit variety— apricot, plum, pear or peach— makes an equally delightful glaze and stuffing for roast chicken. Serves 6.

BROILED CHICKEN

3 broilers (young chicken) from 1½ to 2 pounds each
¼ cup melted butter
Salt
Pepper
1 egg, well-beaten
⅓ cup fine breadcrumbs

Have the broilers split down the back. Wash. Dry thoroughly. Rub all over with butter. Season with salt and pepper. Put on a greased broiler pan and sear one side quickly at high heat in the broiler. Turn and sear other side. Move to oven and cook at 350°F until tender, about 15 minutes more. To cook broiled breaded chicken, prepare and clean chicken as above. Brush it with butter. Season with salt and pepper. Sprinkle with chopped parsley and onion. Put in baking pan. Bake at 450°F for 10 minutes, turning once. Reduce heat. Cover and bake at 325°F for 25 to 30 minutes more, turning frequently. Brush with well-beaten egg. Sprinkle with fine breadcrumbs and broil at high heat until nicely browned all over. Allow ¾ pounds of chicken per serving.

SOUTHERN-STYLE FRIED CHICKEN

4–5 pound chicken, disjointed,
 or 4–5 pounds assorted chicken pieces
1 teaspoon salt
½ teaspoon pepper
1 cup flour
¼ cup butter

Dip each piece of chicken in cold water. Sprinkle with salt and pepper and roll in flour. Melt butter in pan and fry chicken until it is well and uniformly browned, turning occasionally. Serve on hot platter with giblet gravy (p. 414), white sauce (p. 416), or brown sauce (p. 418). Serves 6.

CHICKEN À LA MARYLAND

4–5 pound chicken, disjointed,
 or 4–5 pounds assorted chicken pieces
Salt
Pepper
1 cup flour
1 egg
1 teaspoon water
1 cup breadcrumbs
¼ cup butter or 6 slices bacon

Preheat oven to 450°F. Prepare chicken as for southern-style fried chicken (above). Season with salt and pepper. Roll in flour. Dip in well-beaten egg, diluted with a little water. Roll in breadcrumbs. Put in greased baking pan. Dot heavily with butter or cover with slices of bacon. Bake for 30 minutes, basting often. If bacon is used, remove last 10 minutes of cooking. Allow ¾ pound of chicken per serving.

DEEP-FRIED CHICKEN

4–5 pound chicken, disjointed,
 or 4–5 pounds assorted chicken pieces
Fritter batter (p. 447)
Oil for frying

Prepare chicken as for southern-style fried chicken (p. 300). Dip in fritter batter and fry in deep oil, about 380° to 400°F, until brown. Remove to baking dish and bake at 300°F until tender, about 45 minutes.

COVERED FRIED CHICKEN

4–5 pound chicken, disjointed,
 or 4–5 pounds assorted chicken pieces
2 tablespoons butter

Preheat oven to 450°F. Prepare chicken as for southern-style fried chicken (p. 300). Melt 2 tablespoons butter in shallow pan. Put chicken in pan and cover tightly. Cook until well browned on bottom, about 12 minutes. Turn and repeat cooking. Add more grease if necessary. Serves 6.

BAKED CHICKEN

4–5 pound chicken
Salt
Pepper
¼ cup butter
1 cup basic chicken stock (p. 32)
2 medium onions, roughly chopped

Have butcher split the chicken down the back. Preheat oven to 450°F. Wash and dry thoroughly. Sprinkle with salt and pepper. Put in pan, skin side up. Dot with butter. Add stock and onions. Bake at 450°F for 15 minutes, turning once, and again sprinkle with salt and pepper. Baste. Reduce heat to 350°F and bake until tender, about 1½ hours, basting every 15 minutes and turning when bottom side is well browned. Serve with giblet gravy (p. 414). Allow ¾ pound of chicken per serving.

CHICKEN PIE

4–5 pound chicken
6 cups basic chicken stock (p. 32), more as needed
1 sliced carrot
1 stalk celery
1 sprig parsley
1 sliced onion
1 teaspoon salt
½ teaspoon pepper
Basic pastry (p. 445)
4 tablespoons flour
½ pound sliced sautéed mushrooms (p. 235)

Wipe chicken with a cold, damp cloth. Put in saucepan and cover with stock. Add carrot, celery, parsley, and onion. Bring to boiling point. Reduce heat, cover, and let simmer until chicken is tender, allowing about 20 minutes per pound. Season with salt and pepper when half done. Remove chicken from pan. Remove skin and bones, keeping meat in large pieces. Roll out 2 pieces of pastry to ⅛" thickness. Line the sides of a baking dish with one of the pieces. Add chicken. Reduce chicken stock to 3 cups by boiling. Skim off fat and strain. Mix flour to a smooth paste in cold water. Add to stock. Bring stock to boiling point, stirring constantly, until thickened. Add stock and mushrooms to chicken. Cover with remaining piece of dough. Bake at 450°F for 15 minutes or until well browned. Serves 6.

CHICKEN AND DUMPLINGS

4–5 pound roasting chicken
6 medium-sized potatoes
2 carrots, peeled and chopped
1 onion, roughly chopped
1 teaspoon salt
½ teaspoon pepper
Dumplings (p. 165)
2 tablespoons butter
2 tablespoons flour

Wipe chicken with a cold damp cloth. Put in stockpot, cover with hot water, and bring to boiling point. Cover and let simmer until chicken is almost tender, allowing about 20 minutes per pound. Add potatoes, carrots, and onions. Cook 20 minutes longer, or until potatoes are soft. Season to taste with salt and pepper. Place dumplings on top. Cover tightly and cook until dumplings are light, about 10 minutes. Remove chicken, vegetables, and dumplings to a hot platter. Melt butter and mix to a smooth paste with flour. Add to liquid from pan and bring to a boil. Serve as sauce. Serves 6.

CHICKEN DIXIE STYLE

4–5 pound chicken, disjointed,
   or 4–5 pounds assorted chicken pieces
4 cups water
2 teaspoons salt
½ teaspoon black pepper
2 cups fresh or canned corn
2 tablespoons flour
1 cup cream or half-and-half

Preheat oven to 350°F. Wipe chicken with cold, damp cloth. Stew in water over medium heat until tender, about 1½ hours. Season to taste with salt and pepper. Remove chicken from broth and place alternately with corn in casserole. Mix flour with a little cold water, and add it to the stock, stirring until slightly thickened. Pour cream and thickened broth over the chicken and corn. Bake for 40 minutes. Serves 6.

CHICKEN COUNTRY STYLE

4–5 pound chicken
2 teaspoons salt
½ cup flour
6 tablespoons butter
6 medium-size potatoes
6 small onions
6 large carrots
2 large green peppers
1 tablespoon sugar
¼ teaspoon pepper
2½ cups canned crushed tomatoes
3 cups boiling water

Wipe chicken with cold, damp cloth, and remove giblets and neck bone from the cavity. Mix ½ teaspoon of salt with flour and roll chicken in mixture. Melt butter in frying pan and brown the chicken on all sides at high heat for about 10 minutes. Peel potatoes, onions, and carrots. Cut into large chunks. Seed green peppers and slice them in ½" strips. Mix balance of salt, sugar, and pepper with tomatoes. Place ⅔ of vegetables in bottom of a stockpot. Place chicken on top and add remaining vegetables. Pour tomatoes and 3 cups boiling water over all. Cover tightly and bring to a boil. Reduce heat and let simmer until tender, about 1½ hours. Season to taste. Serves 6.

CREAMED CHICKEN

Combine 2 cups cold, cooked chicken, cut in little cubes with 1 cup medium white sauce (p. 416) and heat thoroughly. Serve on toast. Serves 6.

CHICKEN À LA KING

    2 tablespoons butter
    1 cup sliced mushrooms
    2 tablespoons flour
    2 cups milk
    2 cups cooked chicken, diced
    1 pimento, in thin strips
    1 teaspoon salt
    ¼ teaspoon pepper

Melt butter. Add mushrooms. Cover and cook about 5 minutes. Sprinkle with flour. Add all other ingredients. Let cook until sauce thickens. Serve on toast. 1 cup of cream and 1 cup of basic chicken stock (p. 32) may be substituted for the 2 cups milk. Serves 8.

CHICKEN WITH RICE

4–5 pound chicken
8 cups water
2 cups rice
2 teaspoons salt
½ teaspoon pepper
3 tablespoons butter
1 chopped onion
½ cup chopped celery
3 sliced tomatoes

Wash chicken, being careful to remove any giblets or bones from the cavity. Dry thoroughly. Boil water in a stockpot or large saucepan. Add rice and chicken. Cover and simmer until chicken is about tender, about 1½ hours, adding salt and pepper last 30 minutes of cooking. Melt butter in frying pan and brown vegetables. Add to chicken. Cover and simmer 30 minutes more. Serves 6.

CHICKEN STEW WITH DUMPLINGS

4–5 pound chicken, disjointed,
    or 4–5 pounds assorted chicken pieces
1 tablespoon salt
1 teaspoon pepper
¼ cup flour
¼ butter, softened (optional)
Dumplings (p. 165)

Wipe chicken with cold, damp cloth. Put in a stockpot and cover with cold water. Bring to a boil. Let simmer until tender, about 1 hour. Add salt and pepper after 30 minutes of cooking. Thicken stock with flour, mixed to a smooth, thin paste with cold water. If desired, flour can be mixed to a paste with an equal amount of melted butter. Serve with dumplings. Serves 6.

SMOTHERED CHICKEN

Preheat chicken to 350°F. Select and prepare chicken as for southern-style fried chicken (p. 300). Sauté until well browned in a little butter or fat. Cover with cream or with milk and cream in equal proportions. Bring to boil. Put chicken and liquid in greased baking dish. Cover tightly and bake until tender, about 30 to 45 minutes. Allow ¾ pound of chicken per serving.

EAST INDIAN CHICKEN CURRY

    1 onion, chopped
    ¼ cup butter
    3 pounds chicken, cubed
    1½ tablespoons curry powder
    1½ cups basic chicken stock (p. 32)
    Salt
    2 tablespoons lemon juice

Sauté onion in butter until lightly browned. Add meat and sauté 5 minutes longer. Add curry and continue cooking until meat is well browned. Add stock and dash of salt. Cover and simmer until meat is tender, 1½ to 2 hours. Stir in lemon juice. Serves 6. Curries can also be made with fish or shellfish, in which case substitute milk or cream for water or stock.

HOT CHICKEN TAMALES

> 1 3-pound chicken or 3 pounds chicken breasts
>   and thighs (not boneless)
> 2 teaspoons salt
> 12 dried red chili peppers
> 3 tablespoons butter
> 4 cups corn meal
> 2 sliced onions
> 2 sliced tomatoes
> 1 seeded green pepper, cut in strips
> 1 tablespoon flour
> 1 pound corn husks

Dress chicken and wipe with cold, damp cloth. Disjoint if using a whole chicken. Cover with boiling water. Add 1 teaspoon salt. Let simmer until tender, about 1½ hours. Remove the chicken and set aside. Reserve the liquid. Open chili peppers. Discard seeds. Boil them until soft. Drain. Force through a sieve. Melt 1 tablespoon butter in a skillet over medium heat. In it slightly brown onions, tomatoes, and green pepper. Add chili pulp. Pick chicken meat from bones. Cut in little pieces. Add to pan. Mix flour to a smooth paste with a little cold water and stir into contents of pan. When thick, cover. Simmer slowly for 15 minutes over low heat, adding a little of the water in which the chicken was boiled if necessary. Put corn meal in a pan with 2 tablespoons butter, 1 teaspoon salt, and enough boiling water to make a mush-like paste. Beat mixture well with wooden spoon. Add 2½ cups of the liquid in which chicken was boiled. Remove ends from corn husks. Dry insides. Spread thinly with corn meal mixture. Add 1 tablespoon of meat mixture and roll up. Fold ends down. Repeat until all ingredients are used. Stack rolls in a steamer. Pour 4 cups boiling water over them. Cover tightly and steam slowly, for 45 minutes to 1 hour. Serve hot. Beef can be used instead of chicken.

ROAST DUCK

1 roasting duck
½ teaspoon pepper
2 teaspoons salt
3 tablespoons butter
1½ to 2 cups celery and olive stuffing (p. 437)
1 cup basic chicken stock (p. 32)

Preheat oven to 450°F. Wipe duck with cold, damp cloth. Remove any giblets or bones from the cavity. Sprinkle with salt and pepper. Rub with butter. Stuff. Tie and sew securely with wings and legs close to body. Put in roasting pan, breast side up. Cook at 450°F for 15 minutes. Add stock and baste. Reduce heat to 350°F and cook 20 minutes per pound, basting every 5 minutes. Serve with applesauce (p. 190). Other proper stuffings for duck are apple and bacon (p. 436), peanut (p. 440) and onion (p. 431). Cranberry orange sauce (p. 429) or currant jelly make desirable accompaniments for duck. Allow 1 pound per serving.

BRAISED DUCK

1 roasting duck
1 teaspoon salt
½ teaspoon pepper
3 tablespoons butter
4 cups boiling water
1 cup chopped onion
1 cup chopped celery
1 cup chopped carrot
2 cloves
1 bay leaf
2 tablespoons chopped parsley
1 tablespoon flour

Wash and dry duck thoroughly. Sprinkle with salt and pepper. Melt 2 tablespoons butter in a large pan. Put in duck and brown all over at high heat. Add boiling water, onion, celery, carrot, cloves, bay leaf, and parsley. Cover and let simmer over low heat until tender, about 1½ hours. Remove duck. Blend flour and 1 tablespoon melted butter and add to pan liquor. Bring to boil, stirring constantly. Serve duck on hot platter with this gravy or mushroom sauce (p. 425). Allow ¾ pound of duck per serving.

ROAST GOOSE

8–10 pound goose
2 cups celery stuffing (p. 436)
1 ½ teaspoons salt
¼ teaspoon pepper
6 strips bacon
1 cup basic chicken stock (p. 32)

Preheat oven to 450°F. Wash goose thoroughly and dry. Be careful to remove any giblets and bones from the cavity. Stuff. Sprinkle with salt and pepper. Tie and sew securely with wings and legs close to body. Put goose breast up in roasting pan with strips of bacon on top. Bake at 450°F for 15 minutes. Add stock and baste. Reduce heat to 350°F and cook 20 minutes per pound, basting every 15 minutes. Remove bacon during last 30 minutes of cooking. If desired, goose may be rubbed with cut side of an onion or clove of garlic before cooking. Serve with giblet gravy (p. 414) and baked apples (p. 190) or fried apple rings (p. 192). Goose may also be stuffed with mashed potatoes (p. 433), any fruit stuffing, or may be left unstuffed. Allow 1 pound per serving.

ROAST TURKEY

Prepare and cook same as roast chicken (p. 298), using about 10 cups of desired stuffing, and cooking 15 to 20 minutes per pound. Baste every half hour. Allow ¾ pound per serving.

ROAST GROUSE

4 young grouse
Salt
Pepper
3 tablespoons olive oil or melted butter
1 cup basic chicken stock (p. 32)
4 strips bacon (optional)
2 tablespoons flour

Preheat oven to 450°F. Clean grouse, inside and out. Sprinkle with salt and pepper. Brush with oil or fat. Tie wings and legs close to body. Put in roasting pan. Add stock. If desired lay strip of bacon over each bird. Bake at 450°F for 15 minutes, basting frequently with melted butter or pan drippings. Reduce heat and bake 25 minutes more at 350°F. Remove birds. Add flour, mixed to a smooth paste with cold water, to pan drippings. Cook until well blended and thickened. Garnish as desired. Prairie chickens, partridges and pheasants may all be prepared and cooked in the same manner. If desired, birds may be stuffed with poultry stuffing (p. 430) before cooking. Allow 1 grouse per serving.

PHEASANT

To roast pheasant, select hens from 2½ to 3½ pounds. Prepare and cook according to instructions for roast chicken (p. 298), allowing about 1 hour for cooking. Baste frequently. Baked pheasant is prepared by disjointing the dressed and cleaned bird, covering with light cream, and baking, covered, for 30 to 45 minutes at 350°F. To smother pheasant, disjoint and cover with cream as above; then cover and let simmer for 30 to 45 minutes. Braised pheasant is prepared by browning disjointed bird in melted butter after seasoning and rolling in flour and then simmering bird for 30 minutes in covered pan with chopped bacon, carrots, sliced celery, chopped onion, chopped parsley, water or stock, and desired spices and seasonings. One pheasant will provide 4 servings.

ROAST WILD TURKEY

Prepare and cook according to instructions for roast turkey (p. 311), allowing 20 to 25 minutes per pound for roasting.

ROAST WILD DUCK OR GOOSE

1 wild duck or goose
Salt
Pepper
Bread stuffing (p. 430) or an apple
3 tablespoons melted butter or olive oil
3 slices bacon
2 tablespoons flour

Preheat oven to 350°F. Carefully clean, inside and out. Sprinkle inside and out with salt and pepper. Stuff with bread stuffing or place an apple in the cavity. Sew opening and tie legs and wings close to body. Rub body with butter or oil and cook with slices of bacon on breast. Bake in moderate oven (350°F) about 18 minutes per pound, basting often. Serve with gravy made from pan drippings, thickened with a paste of flour and cold water. Season to taste. To make wild duck very rare, cook at 475°F for 15 minutes. Allow 1 pound of duck per serving.

QUAIL

Follow recipes for preparing and cooking grouse (p. 312), cooking quail at same temperatures for about ⅔ as long. Allow 1 quail per serving.

FISH

BROILED FISH

Only small fish, or fish that may be opened out, can be broiled. Put well-dried seasoned fish on hissing hot broiler and cook over or under heat unit until flesh leaves the bone when pierced with a fork. The inside of the fish should always be broiled first and the fish then turned and broiled on the skin side. When the fish is done, it should be carefully loosened from the broiler and slipped onto a hot platter. Allow ⅓ to ½ pound fish per serving.

POACHED FISH

The simplest way to poach fish is to bring 1 cup of water and 1 cup of white wine to a boil in a large skillet. Onions, peppercorns, bay leaves, and other spices may be added if desired. Once the fish has been added, the heat should be reduced to low, and a cover should be placed on the skillet. Cook until the fish leaves the bone, about 10 minutes for every inch of thickness. If the fish is placed in a strainer above the water, it will be steamed, instead of poached. Allow ⅓ to ½ pound fish per serving.

FRIED FISH

Wipe thoroughly with cold, damp cloth. Sprinkle with salt and pepper. Sprinkle with cornmeal. Dip in beaten egg, diluted with a little cold water. Roll in breadcrumbs. Fry in little olive oil or butter until a delicate brown. Allow ⅓ to ½ pound fish per person. To fry fish in batter, mix ½ cup flour, ½ teaspoon salt, ¼ teaspoon pepper, ¼ cup milk, 1 tablespoon lemon juice, 1 tablespoon olive oil and 1 beaten egg. Dip small pieces of fish in this batter and cook in deep hot fat (375°F) for 3 to 5 minutes. Or, dip the fish in batter and sauté in a little fat until well browned on both sides.

FISH BOILED IN PARCHMENT PAPER

2 pounds boneless filets or steaks
2 sheets parchment paper, about 2 square feet
½ teaspoon pepper
2 tablespoons melted butter or cooking oil
2 tablespoons grated onion
2 tablespoon grated carrot
1 tablespoon lemon juice
1 tablespoon parsley, chopped fine
1 tablespoon flour (optional)

Prepare a salt solution using 2 tablespoons salt to 1 cup cold water. Fish that is ⅝" thick should be kept in the salt solution for about 5 minutes. This time may be varied from 5 to 10 minutes, depending upon thickness of flesh and variety of fish. Fill a stockpot ⅔ full of water and start heating. Oil or wet both sides of parchment paper and lay flat. Cut fish to serving size pieces and divide between the 2 papers, arranging the pieces one layer deep on each paper. Mix the pepper with the butter and put 1 teaspoon each of butter, onion, and carrot over each serving of fish. Sprinkle with lemon juice and chopped parsley. Bring edges of paper together and tie. Immerse in boiling water. After water boils, reduce heat, and continue cooking until tender. This will take from 8 minutes for a fish that is less than 1" thick to 15 minutes for a fish that is closer to 2" thick. Remove to a hot platter and pour juices from the parchment packet over the fish, or thicken them with flour for gravy. A tightly covered steamer, lined with oiled or wet parchment paper, may be used in this method of cooking. This fish must be laid in a single layer. Steaming will require more time to cook than boiling. Allow ⅓ to ½ pound fish per serving.

STEAMED FISH

> 1½ pounds fish filets
> Melted butter
> 1 lemon, cut into wedges
> Salt
> Pepper

Cut fish into 4 pieces for serving. Rinse fish thoroughly. Place an oiled steamer in a stockpot or large saucepan and fill with water almost to the level of the steamer. Bring water to a boil. Add the fish and reduce heat to a simmer. Cook until tender, from 5 to 12 minutes, depending on size. When the fish is ready, it will flake when tested with a fork. Serve with melted butter and lemon wedges. Season to taste with salt and pepper. Cream sauce (p. 417) or drawn butter (p. 419) may also be used. Allow ⅓ to ½ pound fish per person.

BAKED FISH

2 whole fish (e.g. red snapper or sea bream)
2 tablespoons flour
2 tablespoons butter, plus more for serving
Salt
Pepper
1 lemon, cut into wedges

Preheat over to 375°F. Rub the prepared (gutted and cleaned) fish with flour and dot with butter. Sprinkle with salt and pepper. Put into a 375°F oven and bake for 10 minutes. Reduce heat to 350°F and cook for another 15 minutes, or until the meat leaves the bone easily. Serve with melted butter and lemon wedges. Allow ⅓ to ½ pound fish per serving.

FISH AND APPLES

2 pounds cod, sole, or perch filets or steaks,
    about ⅝" thick
3 tablespoons butter or fat
2¼ pounds apples
2 tablespoons water
½ teaspoon salt
1 teaspoon sugar
¼ teaspoon black pepper
¼ cup melted butter

Rinse fish thoroughly in cold water. Pat to dry. Slowly heat butter in a deep frying pan. Wash, quarter, and core apples and slice to ¼" thick. Place the apples into the hot fat, adding the water, salt, and sugar. Cover tightly and cook over low heat. Turn apples once and cook until almost tender. Lay the fish, flesh side down, on the apples. Cover and allow fish to steam for 3 to 5 minutes. Remove cover, turn fish, and baste it with a mixture of the pepper and butter. Remove to a greased baking sheet. Cook under the broiler on high heat for 5 minutes, or until well browned. Remove the fish to a hot platter and surround with the apples. Serves 6.

FISH IMPERIAL

2 cups cooked cod or haddock fish flakes
3 tablespoons white wine vinegar
3 eggs, separated
2 cups milk
1 teaspoon salt
¼ teaspoon black pepper
2 tablespoons onion, chopped fine
2 tablespoons parsley, chopped fine

Preheat oven to 325°F. Combine fish flakes and vinegar. Whip the egg whites until stiff and set aside. Beat the egg yolks; add milk, salt, pepper, onion, parsley, and fish flakes. Mix well. Fold in stiffly beaten whites. Pour into greased 8" baking dish. Set in a pan of warm water in a moderate oven and slowly bake about 45 minutes, until an inserted knife will come out clean. Serves 6.

BOILED FISH AND VEGETABLE DINNER

¾ cup uncooked bacon, diced
2 cups water
½ pound turnips, peeled and roughly chopped
½ pound potatoes, peeled and roughly chopped
½ pound onions, peeled and roughly chopped
½ pound carrots, peeled and roughly chopped
1 pound cooked cabbage (p. 220)
1 teaspoon salt
¼ teaspoon pepper
2 pounds filets, steaks, or pan-dressed fish

In a heavy stockpot or Dutch oven, fry the bacon to a golden brown; add 1 cup water and all the vegetables except the cabbage, which is cooked separately. Allow the vegetables to cook for 20 to 25 minutes. Add the salt, pepper, and second cup of water. Lay the fish, flesh side down, across the vegetables, cover with the cooked cabbage, and cook everything about 5 minutes more over low heat. Place the fish in the center of a hot platter, surrounded by the cooked vegetables. The liquid remaining in the stockpot may be served in a side bowl. Allow ⅓ to ½ pound fish per serving.

BAKED FILETS OF BASS, COD, HALIBUT, MACKEREL OR HADDOCK

2 pounds fish filets
3 tablespoons butter, plus more for greasing
Salt
Pepper
Hollandaise sauce (p. 418)

Preheat oven to 400°F. Wipe fish with cold, damp cloth. Cut into 6 small filets. Put in a greased baking pan. Dot with butter. Season to taste with salt and pepper. Cover with greased parchment paper. Bake for 8 to 12 minutes, depending on thickness. Serve with hollandaise sauce. Serves 6.

BAKED BLUEFISH

    3 pounds bluefish, split and boned
    Salt
    Pepper
    Juice of 1 lemon
    ½" slice eggplant
    4 mushrooms
    12 anchovy filets
    1 small onion
    ½ green pepper
    1 teaspoon chopped parsley
    4 black olives
    2 tablespoons butter
    1 tablespoon angostura bitters

Preheat oven to 350°F. Put fish in greased baking dish. Sprinkle with salt, pepper, and lemon juice. Chop eggplant, mushrooms, anchovy filets, onion, green pepper, parsley, and olives. Combine and spread on fish. Cover with buttered brown paper and bake for 20 minutes. Remove to hot platter. Add butter and angostura bitters to dish juice and pour over fish. Serves 6.

PLANKED BLUEFISH

Whole bluefish
3 tablespoons melted butter
Salt
Pepper
Duchess potatoes (p. 249)

Grease well a hardwood fish plank, about 16" by 12". Heat plank in the oven until very hot. Wipe fish with cold, damp cloth. Cut off head and tail. Split down middle. Clean and remove as many bones as possible. Place, skin side down, on plank. Brush with melted butter and sprinkle with salt and pepper. Place under broiler and cook 12 to 20 minutes, depending on size. Rim plank with duchess potatoes, put on with pastry tube. Put in oven and bake at 350°F until potatoes are browned. Arrange hot boiled carrots (p. 222) around fish. Allow ⅓ to ½ pound of fish per person.

SAUTÉED CODFISH

Whole cod
Salt
Pepper
¼ cup cornmeal
2 tablespoons butter or fat

Skin fish and remove backbone. Cut in square pieces. Season to taste with salt and pepper. Roll in cornmeal. Fry in butter or fat over medium-high heat until brown on both sides, about 10 minutes. Drain on paper towels. Serve with tartar sauce (p. 427). Allow ⅓ to ½ pounds of fish per person.

BROILED COD

Split fish down back. Remove backbone and as many bones as possible. Follow recipe for broiled fish (p. 315).

BOILED CODFISH

1 tablespoon butter
2 tablespoons chopped celery
1 chopped onion
1 chopped carrot
1 tablespoon chopped parsley
8 cups water
1 bay leaf
1 tablespoon white wine vinegar
1 teaspoon salt
½ teaspoon pepper
2½ pounds cod
Parsley, for garnish

Melt butter in stockpot over medium heat. Add celery, onion, carrot, and parsley. Sauté for 2 minutes, stirring constantly. Add water, bay leaf, vinegar, salt, and pepper. Bring to boil. Wipe fish with cold, damp cloth. Wrap in cheesecloth. Drop in boiling water. Cover. Reduce heat to low and let simmer for 30 minutes. Remove fish from cloth and serve hot with egg sauce (p. 417), garnished with parsley. Serves 6.

FILET OF FLOUNDER OR SOLE

1½ pounds filets of flounder or sole
Salt
Pepper
¾ cup fine breadcrumbs
1 egg
1 teaspoon water
2 tablespoons butter or fat
1 lemon, cut into wedges
1 tablespoon parsley, finely diced
Tartar sauce (p. 427)

Wipe filets with a cold, camp cloth. Sprinkle with salt and pepper. Dip in crumbs, then in slightly beaten egg diluted with water, and again in crumbs. Cook in a small amount of fat in a frying pan for 8 to 10 minutes over medium heat, or until brown on both sides. Garnish with lemon and parsley and serve with tartar sauce. Serves 4.

FILETS EN CASSEROLE

1 cup breadcrumbs
2 pounds filet of sole
½ cup melted butter
1 tablespoon white wine vinegar
1 tablespoon Worcestershire sauce
1 tablespoon lemon juice
1 teaspoon prepared mustard
1 teaspoon salt
½ teaspoon pepper

Preheat oven to 400°F. Cover bottom of shallow baking dish with breadcrumbs and place filets on the crumbs. Combine other ingredients and pour over fish. Bake for 20 minutes, basting occasionally with sauce. Serves 6.

STUFFED FILET OF FLOUNDER OR SOLE

2 pounds boiled spinach (p. 255)
1 teaspoon salt
½ teaspoon pepper
½ cup white wine
¼ cup breadcrumbs
2 pounds filets of flounder or sole
½ cup finely chopped onion
2 tablespoons finely chopped parsley
1 cup sliced mushrooms
2 medium tomatoes, peeled and quartered
2 tablespoons butter
2 tablespoons flour
¼ cup cream
1 tablespoon lemon juice

Preheat oven to 500°F. Drain and chop spinach. Add salt, pepper, ⅓ cup wine, and breadcrumbs. Place a mound of this dressing on one end of each filet and fold the other end over it. Grease a baking pan with the butter. Place filets in baking pan with onion, parsley, and remaining cooking wine. Arrange mushrooms and quartered tomatoes over the top. Cover with cooking parchment paper and bake for 15 minutes. Remove stuffed filets to a heatproof platter. Thicken gravy remaining in pan with flour, blended with a little cold water. Simmer for 2 or 3 minutes, stirring constantly, until thickened. Remove from heat. Add cream and lemon juice. Pour over filets. Brown in broiler. Serve immediately. Serves 6.

FILET OF SOLE AU GRATIN

1½ pounds filet of sole
2 tablespoons chopped onion
2 tablespoons chopped celery
Salt
Pepper
2 tablespoons water
2 tablespoons lemon juice
2 tablespoons butter
2 tablespoons flour
1 cup milk
½ cup grated Cheddar cheese

Preheat oven to 450°F. Place filets in a shallow baking pan. Sprinkle with onion, celery, salt, and pepper. Add water and lemon juice. Bake for 10 minutes. Melt butter in a saucepan over medium heat. Stir in flour and add milk gradually. Cook, stirring until thickened. Add salt, pepper, and cheese, reserving about 2 tablespoons for top. Heat until cheese is melted. Pour over fish, sprinkle remaining grated cheese over top, and continue baking for another 10 to 15 minutes. Serves 6.

BAKED STUFFED HADDOCK

1 4-pound haddock
Salt
Pepper
2 cups bread stuffing (p. 430)
½ cup white wine
2 tablespoons melted butter

Preheat oven to 350°F. Wipe fish with cold, damp cloth. Cut off and discard head and tail. Split down middle. Clean. Remove backbone and all other bones if possible. Season to taste with salt and pepper. Put stuffing between 2 halves of fish, making a sandwich. Put in baking pan. Add wine. Brush top with butter. Bake for 50 minutes to 1 hour, basting occasionally with melted butter or fat. Allow ⅓ pound fish per person. Any other suitable stuffing may be used.

HALIBUT STEAK

1½ pounds halibut steaks
Salt
Pepper
¼ cup fine cracker crumbs
2 tablespoons butter or fat
1 tablespoon parsley, finely diced
1 lemon, cut into wedges
Hollandaise sauce (p. 418)

Wipe slices of halibut with a cold, damp cloth. Sprinkle with salt and pepper and dust with fine cracker crumbs. Cook in butter in a frying pan over medium heat for 8 to 10 minutes or until brown on both sides. Drain on paper towels. Garnish with parsley and slices of lemon and serve with hollandaise sauce. Allow ⅓ to ½ pound of fish per person.

STUFFED HALIBUT STEAK

1 dozen oysters
2 tablespoons melted butter
1 tablespoon chopped parsley, plus more for garnish
1 cup bread or cracker crumbs
½ teaspoon salt
⅛ teaspoon pepper
2 slices halibut, cut from the middle of fish
1 tablespoon lemon juice
1 lemon, cut into wedges

Preheat oven to 350°F. Drain oysters. Add butter, parsley, crumbs, salt, and pepper. Mix well. Wipe the fish with cold, damp cloth. Place 1 slice on a greased piece of muslin or cheesecloth. Sprinkle with salt, pepper, and lemon juice and spread with the oyster stuffing. Place second slice on top and brush with melted butter. Put in a baking pan with a little water. Bake for 40 to 50 minutes. Baste frequently with melted butter. Remove to hot platter. Garnish with parsley and slices of lemon. Serve with hollandaise sauce (p. 418) or béarnaise sauce (p. 422), if desired. Allow ⅓ to ½ pound of fish per person.

PLANKED HALIBUT

2 pounds halibut steaks
¼ cup olive oil
2 tablespoons diced onion
¼ cup melted butter
¼ teaspoon pepper
Mashed potatoes (p. 244)
1 lemon, thinly sliced
1 tablespoon parsley, finely diced

Put a cold fish plank into a cold oven and gradually pre-heat oven and plank to 450°F. Thoroughly rinse steaks and brush with olive oil. Remove plank from oven, oil it thoroughly and place fish on plank, sprinkle it with onion and return plank to top rack of oven. Cook for 15 to 20 minutes, basting once or twice with dressing made of melted butter and pepper. Remove from the oven; make an ornamental border of mashed potato (p. 244) around the steaks. Return to the oven and cook until potatoes have browned. Garnish with thin slices of lemon and parsley. Allow ⅓ to ½ pound fish per person.

BAKED HALIBUT IN TOMATOES

    2 pounds halibut steak
    2 cups canned crushed tomatoes
    3 tablespoons butter
    3 tablespoons flour
    1 onion, sliced
    ¼ teaspoon rosemary
    1 teaspoon sugar
    ½ teaspoon salt
    ½ teaspoon pepper
    1 tablespoon parsley, finely diced

Preheat oven to 340°F. Wipe the fish. Combine tomatoes, butter, flour, onion, and seasonings in a saucepan. Bring to a boil, and reduce heat, simmering for 5 minutes. Place steaks in a baking dish with half the sauce. Bake for 50 minutes, basting occasionally with sauce in the pan. Serve surrounded with remaining sauce. Garnish with parsley. Serves 6.

BAKED RED SNAPPER

1 5-pound cleaned and boned red snapper
1 teaspoon salt
1 pound boiled shrimp (p. 342)
1 egg
1 cup cream
½ tablespoon anchovy paste
Pepper
Salt
Paprika
1 cup sherry

Preheat oven to 350°F. Wash, drain, and rub fish with salt. Put shrimp through grinder. Beat egg and ½ cup cream together. Mix shrimp and anchovy paste, seasoning with pepper, salt, and paprika. Stir this mixture into the beaten egg and cream, adding sherry and mixing to a smooth paste. Place stuffing inside fish and sew together with twine or hold in place with skewers. Place in a greased baking dish. Pour over the remaining ½ cup cream. Bake until done, about 3 hours. Serves 10.

SALMON CROQUETTES

2 cups canned salmon
3 tablespoons chopped parsley
1 tablespoon lemon juice
1 teaspoon Worcestershire sauce
½ teaspoon salt
¼ teaspoon pepper
1 cup thick white sauce (p. 416)
1 cup breadcrumbs
1 egg
1 teaspoon water
Oil for frying

Drain salmon. Removed skin and bones. Flake. Add parsley, lemon juice, Worcestershire sauce, salt, pepper, and white sauce. Blend well. Chill. Shape into croquettes, roll in breadcrumbs, dip in slightly beaten egg to which water has been added and roll again in crumbs. Fry in deep hot oil (390°F) for 3 to 5 minutes, or until nicely browned. Drain on absorbent paper. Serves 4.

BROILED TROUT

1 lake trout
¼ cup melted butter, plus more for serving
¼ teaspoon pepper
1 lemon, cut into wedges
1 tablespoon parsley, finely diced

Split the trout into 2 filets, removing the backbone. Wash thoroughly, removing all traces of blood or membrane. Rinse thoroughly in cold water. The broiling oven should be preheated about 10 minutes before using. Oil the heated broiler pan. Combine the butter and the pepper. Brush the fish generously with this mixture. Place the trout on the broiler pan, skin side up, about 2" below the heat unit. At the end of 5 minutes the skin should be turning brown. Baste with butter and pepper. Continue cooking until the skin is well browned, then turn the fish with flesh side up and baste again. Cook until the flesh side is well browned. Remove to hot platter, butter the top of the fish, and garnish with lemon slices and parsley. Allow ⅓ to ½ pound fish per person.

STEAMED CLAMS

    8 cups water
    ¼ cup kosher salt (non-iodized)
    1 cup cornmeal
    50 small clams
    ¾ cup water
    ¼ cup melted butter

Soak clams in a mixture of 8 cups water, salt, and cornmeal for 2 hours before cooking. Rinse clams thoroughly. Put ¾ cup water and clams in a saucepan. Cover and steam over medium heat until shells open. Discard clams whose shells don't open. Serve in shells with individual cups of melted butter. The clam liquor may be reserved for cooking. Allow 25 clams per serving.

FRIED CLAMS

    2 cups steamed clams, shelled (above)
    Salt
    Pepper
    2 tablespoons flour
    1 slightly beaten egg
    1 teaspoon cold water
    ½ cup breadcrumbs
    Oil for frying

Pick over clams, removing shell fragments. Dry between towels. Sprinkle with salt, pepper, and flour. Dip in egg, diluted with cold water. Roll in crumbs. Fry in deep, hot oil (375°F) for 4 to 6 minutes. Drain on paper towels. Serves 4.

FRIED CLAMS IN BATTER

2 cups steamed clams, shelled (p. 333)
¼ cup clam liquor (liquid left over from steaming clams)
¼ cup milk
2 beaten eggs
1 teaspoon salt
¼ teaspoon pepper
1 cup flour
½ teaspoon baking powder
Oil for frying

Pick over clams and remove shell fragments. Dry between towels. Mix clam liquor, milk, eggs, salt, and pepper. Mix and sift flour and baking powder and add to first mixture. Beat thoroughly. Dip clams in batter. Fry in deep, hot oil (375°F) for 4 to 6 minutes. Drain on paper towels. Serves 6.

ROASTED CLAMS

8 cups water
¼ cup kosher salt (non-iodized)
1 cup cornmeal
25 large clams or 50 small clams
Salt
Pepper
¼ cup butter

Soak clams in a mixture of water, salt, and cornmeal for 2 hours before cooking. Rinse clams thoroughly. Preheat oven to 350°F. Place clams on a baking sheet. Bake until shells open. Discard clams whose shells don't open. Remove upper shell. Season to taste with salt and pepper. Dot generously with butter. Allow 6 large clams or 12 small clams per serving.

CLAMS NEWBURG

1 tablespoon butter
1 tablespoon flour
1 cup cream
24 steamed clams, removed from their shells (p. 333)
2 beaten egg yolks
½ teaspoon salt
¼ teaspoon cayenne
2 tablespoons Madeira

Melt butter in saucepan over medium heat. Stir in flour and blend. Add cream and clams. Heat, but do not boil. When heated, add egg yolks. Heat clams through. Add salt, cayenne, and wine. Stir. Serve very hot. Serves 6.

BOILED HARD SHELL CRABS

8 cups water
¼ cup vinegar
2 tablespoons salt
1 tablespoon ground red pepper
8 hard shell crabs

Bring water, vinegar, salt, and red pepper to a boil in a stockpot. While this is heating, scrub and rinse the crabs. Boil the crabs over medium-high heat for 5 minutes. Reduce heat to low and simmer 10 minutes longer. Remove the crabs from the water. Pull off the legs and claws. Split these and remove the meat. Break off the segment which folds under the body from the rear. Holding the body of a crab in the left hand, back toward you, pull off the top shell. Discard the digestive tract and rinse in water. Split the crab and remove the hard membrane that covers the body meat with a nut pick or something similar. Allow 1 or 2 crabs per person.

DEVILED CRABS

2½ cups cooked lump crabmeat
1 chopped hard-boiled egg (p. 272)
1 cup milk
1 tablespoon lemon juice
½ tablespoon Worcestershire sauce
½ teaspoon salt
⅛ teaspoon pepper
⅛ teaspoon paprika
3 tablespoons breadcrumbs
1 tablespoon melted butter

Preheat oven to 350°F. Flake crabmeat. Combine with all of the other ingredients, except breadcrumbs and butter. Put in greased individual baking dishes or ramekins. Sprinkle with breadcrumbs. Dot with butter. Bake for 20 minutes, or until well browned. Serves 6.

CRAB CAKES

1 pound cooked lump crabmeat
¼ cup melted butter
½ teaspoon salt
½ teaspoon black pepper
Pinch of cayenne
2 eggs
1 teaspoon water
1 cup fine breadcrumbs
Oil for frying

Mix crabmeat, butter, seasonings, and 1 egg. Mold the crab mixture into small flat cakes, about 3" across. Beat water into the remaining egg and wet the cakes with this mixture, then roll them in the crumbs. Deep fry at about 380° to 400°F in a well oiled frying basket. Serves 6.

CRAB MEAT SOUFFLÉ

¼ cup butter
⅓ cup flour
1⅓ cups milk
1 teaspoon salt
Few grains pepper
4 eggs, separated
1½ cups cooked lump crabmeat

Preheat oven to 350°F. Melt butter in a double boiler. Add flour and mix well. Add milk gradually and cook, stirring constantly, until thickened. Add salt and pepper. Add hot mixture slowly to the well-beaten egg yolks, stirring constantly. Add flaked crabmeat and cool slightly. Stiffly beat the egg whites and gently fold them into the crab mixture, taking care to keep as much volume in the egg whites as possible. Carefully pour into a buttered baking or soufflé dish. Bake for 50 minutes. Serves 6.

CRAB IN WHITE WINE

½ cup white wine
⅛ teaspoon nutmeg
⅛ teaspoon cayenne
½ teaspoon salt
1 pound cooked lump crabmeat
¼ cup milk
¼ cup cream
2 beaten egg yolks

Season wine with nutmeg, cayenne, and salt. Warm in a saucepan over low heat. Add crabmeat. Simmer slowly for 10 minutes, stirring frequently. Add milk and cream. Cook and stir 5 minutes longer. Remove from heat. Add yolks, diluted with a little of the sauce. Heat through. Serves 6.

BOILED LOBSTER

Take the live lobster by the back and plunge it in boiling, salted water, head first. Water should be deep enough to cover. Reduce heat and simmer 35 to 40 minutes. Remove from water and cool. Turn lobster on back and make a cut with a sharp knife from point under head to tail, crack the claws so that the meat may be easily removed. Serve ice cold in the shell with cold hollandaise sauce (p. 418) or mayonnaise (p. 70). Allow 1 lobster per person.

BROILED LIVE LOBSTER

Select small (chicken) lobsters. Place the lobster on its back on a cutting board and kill by cutting down between the body shell and tail segment. Then split from head to tail and remove fat, roe (if present), stomach and the vein that passes through the center of the tail segment. Rinse, brush the flesh with melted butter, season with salt and pepper if desired, and spread out flat on the broiler, flesh side up. Cook slowly for 10 minutes, turn and cook 10 minutes longer. Remove to a hot platter and dress with melted butter to which a little lemon juice has been added. Allow 1 lobster per serving.

STEAMED LOBSTER

Steam live lobsters ½ hour in steamer with rapidly boiling water. Dress according to recipe for boiled lobster (above).

LOBSTER STEW

2 cups milk
1 pound boiled diced lobster meat (p. 338)
1½ tablespoons butter
1½ teaspoons salt

Heat the milk to the boiling point and add lobster meat. Heat thoroughly. Add butter and salt. Stir well. Serves 4.

LOBSTER NEWBURG

2 cups boiled, diced lobster meat (p. 338)
4 tablespoons melted butter
1 tablespoon flour
1 cup cream
2 egg yolks, beaten
¼ teaspoon salt
1 teaspoon lemon juice
Paprika

Heat the lobster in 3 tablespoons melted butter over low heat, taking care that the butter does not brown. In another saucepan, melt the remaining butter over low heat. Add the flour and stir well. Then add the cream. Heat and stir until it the mixture is smooth. When it reaches a boil, remove from the heat, and add the beaten egg yolks. Stir until the mixture thickens. Add the diced lobster, lemon juice, and paprika, but do not heat again or the whole mixture may curdle. Serve with toasted crackers or thin, dry toast. Serves 6.

LOBSTER CASSEROLE

3 ounces broad egg noodles
1 cup boiled lobster (p. 338), flaked and boned
1 cup cream or medium white sauce (p. 416)
2 tablespoons melted butter
Salt
White pepper

Preheat oven to 375°F. Cook noodles in boiling salted water for about 10 minutes. Do not let them become too soft. Drain and mix with remaining ingredients. Turn into greased casserole and bake for 20 minutes, or until thoroughly heated. Serves 6.

STEAMED MUSSELS

2 tablespoons butter
¼ cup onions, minced
¾ cup dry white wine
3 pounds mussels, cleaned and de-bearded
½ cup chopped fresh parsley
Pepper

Scrub mussels, removing string-like beard as best as possible. Melt butter in a stockpot over medium heat. Add onions and sauté for a few minutes, until onions are translucent. Add white wine and cleaned mussels. Bring to a boil over medium heat. Cover and steam mussels for about 5 minutes, until their shells have opened. Discard mussels that do not open. Serve in cooking liquid. Garnish with parsley and pepper. Serves 4.

FRIED OYSTERS

Follow recipe for fried clams (p. 333), using oysters instead of clams.

FRIED OYSTERS IN BATTER

Follow recipe for fried clams in batter (p. 334), using oysters instead of clams.

FRIED SCALLOPS

    4 cups scallops
    Salt
    Pepper
    ¼ cup flour, for dredging
    1 egg
    1 teaspoon cold water
    ¾ cup fine breadcrumbs
    Oil for frying
    8 slices crisp bacon
    Watercress, for garnish

Wash scallops and dry between towels. Sprinkle with salt, pepper, and flour. Dip in slightly beaten egg diluted with cold water and roll in crumbs. Fry in deep hot oil (375°F) for 4 to 6 minutes. Drain on paper towels and garnish with slices of crisp bacon and watercress. Serves 6.

BOILED SHRIMP

2 pounds raw shrimp
1½ tablespoons salt
6 cups water

The edible meat of the shrimp is in the tail. Break off this segment, discarding the remainder of the animal head section as waste. Peel the cover from the meat by breaking the under shell and opening from front to back. Remove the dark vein from the center back of each shrimp and wash the meats in cold water. Bring salt and water to a boil in a stockpot over medium-high heat. Add the shrimp to the boiling water. Cook for 5 to 10 minutes or until shrimp turn pink and are tender. Shrimp may be eaten hot or cold with desired seasonings or may be creamed, used in salads, etc.

FRENCH-FRIED SHRIMP

1½ pounds raw shrimp, peeled and deveined
Juice of 2 lemons
Salt
Pepper
2 beaten eggs
1 cup fine breadcrumbs
Oil for frying

Wash shrimp thoroughly. Place them in a bowl with lemon juice, salt, and pepper and allow to stand for 15 minutes. Dip shrimp into the beaten eggs and then roll in crumbs. Fry in deep, hot oil (390°F) for 3 minutes. Serves 6.

SHRIMP NEWBURG

2 tablespoons butter
1½ tablespoons flour
¾ teaspoon salt
Few grains cayenne
½ cup cream
¼ cup milk
2 cups cooked shrimp (p. 342)
2 egg yolks, beaten
1 tablespoon sherry
Rounds of puff paste (p. 446), for serving
1 tablespoon parsley, finely diced

Melt butter in a skillet over medium heat. Add flour, salt, and cayenne and mix well. Reduce heat to low. Add cream and milk gradually and bring to the boiling point, stirring constantly. Add shrimp. Just before serving, add the beaten egg yolks and sherry. Serve on rounds of puff paste. Garnish with parsley. Serves 6.

SHRIMP CREOLE

1 pound raw shrimp, peeled and deveined
2 tablespoons melted butter
1 cup chopped onions
1 cup chopped green pepper
2 cloves garlic, minced
2 cups canned, crushed tomatoes
⅛ teaspoon paprika
Salt
Pepper

Rinse shrimp thoroughly. Combine butter, onion, green pepper, and garlic in a skillet over low heat. Let this mixture simmer slowly until the pepper is tender, about 10 minutes. Then add tomato and seasonings. Bring to a boil over medium heat. Boil for 5 minutes. Add shrimp to this and boil for 10 minutes longer. Serves 6.

SHRIMP ORLEANS

2 chopped onions
2 tablespoons butter
1 cup boiled shrimp (p. 342)
¼ cup liquid from shrimp
2 tablespoons flour
1 cup sour cream
Salt
Pepper
6 slices buttered toast

Sauté onions in butter to a light brown in a skillet over medium heat. Drain shrimp, reserving ¼ cup liquid. Sprinkle shrimp with flour and add to onions. Cook over low heat for 5 minutes without browning. Add sour cream and simmer slowly 20 minutes. Add shrimp liquid and season to taste with salt and pepper. Heat thoroughly. Serve on buttered toast. Serves 6.

CASSEROLE OF SHRIMP

1 pound spaghetti
1 cup corn, fresh or frozen
2 cups boiled shrimp (p. 342)
6 tablespoons butter
5 tablespoons flour
2 cups milk
½ pound sharp Cheddar cheese
Salt
Pepper

Preheat oven to 400°F. Cook noodles until tender in boiling salted water. Drain and place in a casserole. Arrange corn and shrimp over the noodles. Melt butter in frying pan over medium heat. Add flour and stir until smooth. Add the milk and cook over low heat until the sauce is thick and smooth. Stir constantly. Add cheese, reserving 2 tablespoons. Season with salt and pepper and pour sauce over other ingredients. Mix gently. Sprinkle remaining cheese over the top. Bake for 30 minutes. Frozen peas may be used in place of corn. Serves 10.

FISH CASSEROLE, ITALIAN STYLE

¼ cup butter
1 cup mushrooms, sliced
⅓ cup diced celery
1 medium onion, finely chopped
3 tablespoons quick-cooking tapioca
1¼ teaspoons salt
¼ teaspoon pepper
2 teaspoons sugar
2 cups flaked cooked haddock or cod
3 cups canned crushed tomatoes
Baking powder biscuits (p. 175)

Preheat oven to 425°F. Melt butter in a large skillet over medium heat. Sauté mushrooms, celery, and onion until tender. Combine with tapioca and remaining ingredients (except biscuits) in order given. Turn into a greased casserole and bake for 25 minutes, stirring twice during first 10 minutes of baking. Place unbaked biscuits on top of fish mixture after it has baked 10 minutes; return to oven, and bake 12 to 15 minutes longer, or until biscuits are browned. Serves 8.

MEATS

Finding the best cut of meat for a meal demands both knowledge of the meat, and knowledge of the dish being prepared.

Some cuts of meat, like steak, are so tender that they require little cooking to prepare them for the table. They can be seared, pan fried, or broiled. These cooking methods all involve high heats for a short period of time. The objective is to take advantage of the flavor and the tenderness already in the meat. A steak or a lamb chop needs only minimal dressing—salt, pepper, and melted butter are often good enough.

For a less tender piece of meat, like a leg of lamb, a pork butt, or a chuck roast, longer, slower cooking methods are called for. For these meats, being roasted, simmered, or braised is often the answer. The longer cooking times allow the meat to become tender. Basting the meat in its own juices, or cooking it in wine or stock, are excellent options.

Regardless of the cut or method, the best meat dishes invariably come from the best meat. A truly divine steak is as much a reflection of the way in which the bull was raised as it is a reflection of good cooking methods. If possible, talk to a butcher before selecting a piece of meat. Find out about the animals—where they were raised, what they ate, what their living conditions were like. An animal that was raised on a diet of grains and grasses will usually be more delicious that an animal who ate nothing but grain.

MEAT TEMPERATURES

Beef—rare	140°F
Beef—medium	160°F
Beef—well done	175°F
Veal—well done	170°F
Lamb—medium	170°F
Lamb—well done	182°F
Mutton—medium	170°F
Mutton—well done	182°F
Pork—well done	185°F
Cured ham—well done	163°F

PAN-BROILING—Where a broiler is not available, broiling must be done in a pan. Get pan sizzling hot but use no fat. Sear both sides of meat quickly. Then cook more slowly, using the same time as for broiling. When fat meats are pan-broiled, pour off fat as rapidly as it accumulates to avoid frying.

SAUTÉING—Sautéing is frying in a greased pan or with very little fat. It is usually used to brown meats in preparation for some other form of cooking. (See frying.)

FRYING—Frying is of two types, pan-frying and deep fat frying. In pan-frying the meat is put in a pan with a 1" or 2" layer of melted fat. In deep fat frying the fat is in a stockpot or fryer and the meat is plunged into the hot fat.

PLANKING—The best planks are about 1" thick and of oak or some other hardwood. The same plank should never be used for fish and meats. The plank should be brushed with oil or butter the first few times it is used. After 4 or 5 times this practice will be unnecessary. Planks should never be washed or scrubbed. They should be cleaned by rubbing with a dry cloth or by sandpapering. Planked meats are always pre-cooked, then placed on the plank surrounded by cooked vegetables, and baked for a few minutes to brown the surrounding foods.

POT-ROASTING—The pot-roasting of meats is done by simmering large masses of meat in water in a deep heavy stockpot. Before putting meat in stockpot it must be thoroughly seared on all surfaces. Pot-roasting should be slow and long, and usually vegetables are cooked with the meat, adding them at the proper times so that they will be done when the meat is finished. Always keep the stockpot tightly covered for pot-roasting.

STEWING—Stewing is the method of cooking meat in a small amount of liquid which will later be thickened and used for gravy. Never let a stew boil, as it will toughen and shrivel the meat. For stewing you may use a covered or uncovered pot, saucepan or stockpot.

BOILING—The boiling of meats is done in thin liquid, water, or stock, sufficient to half cover the meat. The water should be boiling when meat is put into it. The stockpot should be tightly covered. The water should be kept just under the boiling point. Seasonings should be added when cooking is half done. The liquid in which meats are boiled should be saved for soup stock.

BRAISING—All meat to be braised must first be sautéed until brown. The meat is then put in a tightly covered saucepan and cooked with vegetables and seasonings. A pot roast or other braised meat dish may be cooked in the oven. This may be convenient when the oven is to be used for cooking other foods at the same time, but if only the meat is to be cooked, it is more fuel efficient to cook on a surface burner. The method is the same in either case.

BEEF

BROILED STEAK

4 steaks, 1" to 1½" thick
Salt
Pepper
Melted butter

Preheat broiler. Wipe meat with cold, damp cloth. Place on slightly greased broiler. Cook at very high heat on 1 side 10 to 12 seconds. Turn and repeat. This sears both sides and holds in juices. Then reduce heat or move broiler farther away from heat and cook more slowly, turning occasionally. A 1½" steak will require from 12 to 30 minutes, depending on preference; a 1" steak, 8 to 20 minutes. When done, sprinkle with salt and pepper and brush top with melted butter. Serve hot. If steak is tough it can be improved by pounding. A tough steak can also be made tender by brushing both sides with a mixture of 1 tablespoon vinegar and 2 tablespoons butter, fat or olive oil, letting stand several hours before cooking. Allow ½ pound of steak per serving. Filet mignon may also be prepared in this fashion. Appropriate steak sauces are mushroom (p. 425), béarnaise (p. 422), and butter sauce (p. 420).

MINUTE STEAK

As its name implies, this is a very thin steak that can be cooked very quickly, figuratively in a "minute." It is prepared and served in the same manner as thicker steak (above), but is cooked for a shorter time.

PAN-BROILED STEAK

4 steaks, 1 to 1½" thick
Butter
Salt
Pepper

Trim excess fat from steak. Wipe with cold, damp cloth. Heat frying pan until it is sizzling hot. Grease pan with removed fat. Put steak in pan, searing it quickly on both sides, turning every few seconds. When evenly seared, reduce heat and cook slowly. Remove fat as it accumulates. A 1" steak will be done rare in about 8 minutes. Well done will require about 12 minutes more. Remove steak to hot platter. Smear with butter. Season with salt and pepper. Garnish as desired. Allow ½ pound of steak per serving.

FRIED STEAK AND ONIONS

3 pounds steak, 1½" thick
1 teaspoon salt
⅛ teaspoon pepper
1 teaspoon flour
¼ cup butter or fat
2 medium-sized onions, sliced

Wipe meat with cold, damp cloth. Sprinkle with salt, pepper, and flour. Melt butter or fat in a deep frying pan over high heat. Put in steak once the fat has melted, and the pan is very hot. Be careful not to splatter oil. Put onions on steak. When well browned on bottom, turn over and brown other side. Serves 6.

PLANKED STEAK

Tender steak, 1½" thick
Duchess (p. 249) or mashed (p. 244) potatoes
Stuffed onions (p. 239)
1 egg yolk
1 tablespoon milk
1 tablespoon butter
Salt
Pepper
Mushroom sauce (p. 425)

Preheat broiler. Wipe meat with cold, damp cloth. Broil on greased broiler over high heat for 12 to 15 minutes, turning frequently. Preheat oven to 400°F. Heat plank, grease with butter, and put steak on it. Arrange potatoes around edge of plank with pastry tube. Place stuffed onions around steak. Dilute beaten egg yolk in milk and brush tops of potatoes and onions. Bake until potatoes are browned, about 8 minutes. Remove from oven and spread butter on steak. Season with salt and pepper. Serve with mushroom sauce. Allow ½ pound of meat per serving.

FRENCH FRIED STEAK

Wipe meat with cold, damp cloth. Cut into 2" squares. Gash each piece on both sides. Fry in hot, deep fat (380° to 390°F) 5 to 7 minutes. Drain on brown paper. Season as desired and serve hot. Allow ½ pound of meat per serving.

ROAST BEEF

Beef for roasting (rump roast or round roast)
Salt, ½ teaspoon per pound
¼ teaspoon pepper
Flour for dredging, plus 2 tablespoons
2 tablespoons cooking oil
2 tablespoons cold water, or red wine.

Preheat oven to 500°F. Wipe beef with cold, damp cloth. Sprinkle with salt, pepper, and flour. Heat the oil over high heat in a deep frying pan. Brown meat on all sides and place in roasting pan with fat side up or with pieces of fat on top. Place in oven, keeping temperature at 500°F for 18 to 20 minutes; then reduce temperature to 300°F and cook, basting occasionally, allowing 16 to 18 minutes per pound for rare meat, 22 to 25 minutes for medium and 30 minutes for well-done. A meat thermometer will show 140°F for rare, 160°F for medium, and 175°F for well done. Allow ½ pound per serving. Skim excess fat off pan drippings. Add 2 tablespoons flour, mixed to a smooth paste with an equal quantity of cold water, for each cup of liquid remaining. Blend well and bring to a boil for gravy. Season to taste with salt and pepper.

POT ROAST

3½ to 4 pound beef shoulder or boneless chuck roast
2 tablespoons cooking oil
1 cup basic beef stock (p. 33) or strained tomatoes
2 tablespoons flour
2 tablespoons cold water
Salt
Pepper

Preheat oven to 250°F. Select a firm piece of beef, either solid or rolled. Almost any inexpensive cut will do, if shoulder or chuck are not available. Wipe meat with cold, damp cloth. Heat oil in frying pan or heavy stockpot and sear meat until uniformly well browned. Move meat to a stockpot, add stock or tomatoes, and cover tightly. Cook for 4 hours, turning often to prevent burning. Make a gravy by adding two tablespoons of flour, mixed in cold water, to some of the liquid from the pot. Stir well and season to taste with salt and pepper. Allow ½ pound of meat per serving.

BEEF STEW WITH DUMPLINGS

3½ pounds beef, either stew meat or chuck
1½ teaspoons salt
¼ teaspoon pepper
3 tablespoons flour
Basic beef stock (p. 33) or canned crushed tomatoes
¾ cup diced carrot
¾ cup turnip
1 diced small onion
4 cups cubed potatoes
Dumplings (p. 165)

Wipe meat with cold, damp cloth; cut in 1½" cubes; sprinkle with salt, pepper, and flour. Melt some of meat fat in frying pan and brown surface of beef cubes thoroughly over high heat. Put meat in stockpot; add drippings from frying pan and enough boiling stock or tomatoes to cover; boil 5 minutes. Reduce heat and let simmer over low heat for 2 hours. Add carrot, turnip, and onion and let simmer ½ hour longer. Add potatoes and cook ½ hour more. Just before serving, add dumplings and allow them to cook through. Remove excess pieces of fat, and skim fat from surface of stew. Adjust seasonings. Serve in deep plates, surrounded with dumplings. Stew can be thickened by adding ¼ cup of flour, mixed with ¼ cup cold water, 5 minutes before removing from heat. Serves 8.

BEEFSTEAK PIE

2 pounds rump, flank, or chuck steak or roasting beef
1 teaspoon salt
⅛ teaspoon pepper
1 medium-sized onion, in ¼" slices
4 cups basic beef stock (p. 33), boiling
Basic pastry dough (p. 445)
2 tablespoons flour
3 tablespoons cold water
1 cup cubed, boiled carrots
2 cups cubed, boiled potatoes
2 tablespoons butter
½ cup celery, chopped fine

Wipe meat with cold, damp cloth; cut in 1½" cubes; sprinkle with salt and pepper. Place meat and onion in pan; cover with boiling stock and let simmer slowly 1 hour. Roll two pieces of pastry out to a ⅛" thickness on a floured board, making both a top and a bottom crust. Preheat oven to 450°F. Line a buttered baking dish with one piece of pastry. Put in layer of meat and onion. Thicken liquid in pan with paste of flour and cold water; pour over meat and onion in baking dish. Add carrots and potatoes, dotted with butter. Add celery. Add another layer of meat and onion. Cover with remaining pastry piece. Bake until brown, about 30 minutes. Serves 6.

SWISS STEAK

1½ pounds steak
⅓ cup flour
½ teaspoon salt
⅛ teaspoon pepper
1 small onion, chopped
2 tablespoons butter or fat
¼ cup chopped green pepper
1 cup stewed tomatoes
1 cup boiling water

Wipe meat with cold, damp cloth. Thoroughly mix flour, salt, and pepper; pound into meat with a potato masher. Cut meat in 2" squares. In a heavy pan, brown steak and onion in butter. Add green pepper, tomatoes, and water. Cover and simmer until meat is tender, about 2 hours. Add more water if needed during cooking. The liquid can be thickened with flour paste for gravy. Serves 4.

HAMBURGER PATTIES

2 eggs
1 pound inexpensive steak, ground, or ground beef
½ cup soft bread crumbs
⅓ cup milk
1 teaspoon salt
½ teaspoon pepper
2 tablespoons chopped onion
1 tablespoon butter
2 tablespoons flour

Beat eggs and mix with meat, bread crumbs, milk, salt, and pepper. Brown onions in butter over medium-high heat in a frying pan; add to meat mixture. Mold into small patties and sprinkle with flour. Fry in small amount of fat, or cook on a grill, turning over until well browned on both sides. Place on hot platter. Serve with buns and other hamburger fixings.

BROILED HAMBURGER STEAK

Prepare meat mixture as for hamburger patties (above). Mold into one flat piece about 1¼" to 1½" thick. Broil at high heat until both sides are seared.

HAMBURGER LOAF

Hamburger patties (p. 358)
3 slices of bacon
2 tablespoons flour
3 tablespoons cold water

Preheat oven to 400°F. Prepare meat mixture as for hamburger patties (p. 358) and form into a loaf. Place in baking pan with slices of bacon laid on top. Bake for 45 minutes, or for 2 hours at 300°F. Serve with gravy made by adding flour paste, mixed in cold water, to fat in pan, cooking until brown, adding boiling water if necessary. Serves 4.

HAMBURGER CASSEROLE

2 tablespoons butter
1 pound ground beef
2 sliced onions
1 cup canned tomato soup
1½ cups canned or fresh corn
1 cup mashed potatoes (p. 244)
1 beaten egg yolk

Preheat oven to 450°F. Melt butter in pan. Sauté meat and onions until brown. Add soup and corn. Mix thoroughly. Put into a greased 9" baking dish. Cover with potatoes. Brush top with egg yolk. Bake in hot oven (450°F) until brown. Serves 4.

MEXICAN TAMALE PIE

1 pound ground beef
1 cup seeded raisins
12 stoned olives, sliced
1 teaspoon salt
½ teaspoon black pepper
½ teaspoon red pepper
6 cups water
1 ½ cups corn meal
1 tablespoon butter

Preheat oven to 350°F. Mix meat, raisins, olives, salt, black pepper, and red pepper. Put in saucepan. Just cover with cold water. Bring to boil over medium heat. Reduce heat to low and let simmer until tender, about 20 minutes. Stir in 1 tablespoon corn meal. In another pan boil 6 cups slightly salted water. Stir in balance of corn meal. Add butter. Boil until mixture resembles mush. Line a greased baking dish with slightly more than half of this batter. Pour in meat mixture. Cover with batter. Bake for 30 minutes. Serve hot or warmed over at another meal. Serves 6.

BEEF HASH

> 2 cups cooked roast beef (p. 353) or corned beef
>   (p. 372), chopped fine
> 3 cups cold boiled potatoes (p. 244), chopped fine
> ½ cup chopped onion
> ½ cup milk
> ¼ teaspoon salt
> ⅛ teaspoon pepper
> Dash of Worcestershire sauce
> 1 tablespoon butter
> 2 tablespoons parsley, finely chopped

Mix thoroughly all ingredients but butter and parsley. Spread evenly in a frying pan greased with the butter and fry slowly over low heat until it is well browned underneath, about 30 to 40 minutes. Turn and fold as an omelet on a hot platter. Garnish with parsley. If desired, chopped parsley, chopped green or red peppers, or diced pimento may be added to mixture; or 1½ cups of chopped cold, boiled beets (p. 217) may be added. Chopped cooked meats, either individually or in combination, can be substituted for beef. Serves 6.

STUFFED FLANK STEAK

1½ pounds flank steak
½ teaspoon salt
⅛ teaspoon pepper
1 tablespoon flour
1½ cups poultry stuffing (p. 430)
1 cup boiling water
2 tablespoons flour
3 tablespoons cold water

Preheat oven to 500°F. Wipe meat with cold, damp cloth. Sprinkle with salt, pepper, and flour. Spread stuffing on meat; form into a roll and fasten with skewers. Place in baking pan, adding 1 cup of boiling water. Sear for 15 minutes in the oven, turning halfway through. Place on hot platter. Thicken with flour paste mixed with cold water for gravy. Season to taste with salt and pepper. Serves 4.

ITALIAN MEAT BALLS

1½ pounds ground beef
4 cups bread crumbs
½ cup raisins, if desired
1 cup grated Parmesan cheese
1 teaspoon salt
½ teaspoon pepper
3 eggs
6 cups beef (p. 33) or chicken stock (p. 32)

Mix thoroughly all ingredients but stock. Mold into small balls. Drop them in boiling stock and cook until well done, 20 to 25 minutes. If desired meatballs may be fried in sizzling hot fat. Serves 6 to 8.

FLANK STEAK WITH TOMATO SAUCE

1½ pounds flank steak
2 tablespoons butter
1 onion, chopped
1 teaspoon salt
¼ teaspoon pepper
Water, to cover
1 cup strained or crushed tomato
2 tablespoons flour
2 tablespoons cold water

Preheat the oven to 350°F. Wipe meat with cold, damp cloth. Melt butter in roasting pan. Add onion and brown lightly. Add meat and brown evenly on both sides. Sprinkle with salt and pepper. Cover with water. Add ½ cup of the tomatoes. Bake for 1½ hours, basting frequently. Add the rest of the tomatoes during last 15 minutes of cooking. Thicken liquid with flour, mixed to a smooth paste with cold water, stirring until thick, and adjusting seasoning. Serve meat on hot platter with this gravy. Serves 4.

STUFFED CABBAGE

1 pound ground beef
½ pound ground pork
1 chopped onion
1 teaspoon salt
¼ teaspoon pepper
1 teaspoon sugar
1 cup raw rice
1 cabbage
1 tablespoon butter
1 cup hot water
1 cup milk or cream

Preheat oven to 350°F. Thoroughly mix beef, pork, onion, salt, pepper, and sugar. Boil rice (p. 128) and add to mixture. Remove and clean several large cabbage leaves. Wilt leaves by scalding in boiling water. Put some of meat and rice mixture in wilted cabbage leaf and roll into balls securely. Repeat until all material is used. Put balls in greased baking pan. Dot cabbage with butter. Add hot water. Bake for 40 minutes. Turn over and bake another 20 minutes. Heat milk or cream and pour over balls. Serves 6.

MEAT CROQUETTES

    1 pound ground pork
    1 pound ground beef
    1 tablespoon chopped celery
    1 tablespoon chopped onion
    1 teaspoon powdered sage
    1 teaspoon salt
    ¼ teaspoon pepper
    1 tablespoon chopped parsley
    1 cup flour
    ¼ cup butter or fat

Mix ground beef and pork thoroughly with celery, onion, sage, salt, pepper, and parsley. Mold into patties, balls or cones. Roll in flour. Melt butter or fat in a large, deep frying pan over medium-high heat. When it is sizzling, put in croquettes. When bottom is well browned, turn and brown evenly all over. Serve hot with white sauce (p. 416). Serves 6.

PINTO BEANS WITH PORK

2½ pounds dried pinto beans
1 pound ground pork
1 medium onion, chopped
1 clove garlic, minced
5 teaspoons olive oil or fat
1 tablespoon flour
1 teaspoon salt
3 bay leaves
½ teaspoon black pepper
1 tablespoon chili powder
1½ cups canned diced tomatoes
1 tablespoon prepared mustard

Wash and soak beans overnight. Drain, cover with hot water and boil gently 25 minutes. Preheat oven to 275°F. Make 5 to 6 small flat patties from part of the meat. Brown the onions, garlic, and meat cakes in the oil. Remove from pan and set aside. Brown the rest of the meat. Add the flour, salt, bay leaves, pepper, chili powder, tomatoes, mustard, onions, and garlic to meat mixture. Combine with beans and pour into well-greased casserole. Add water or tomato juice, if necessary, to cover beans. Place meat cakes on top and bake in slow oven (275°F) 3 hours. Serves 6.

RAGOUT OF BEEF

2 pounds beef
1½ teaspoons salt
¼ teaspoon pepper
½ cup flour, plus 1 tablespoon
2 tablespoons butter or fat
1 cup boiling water or beef stock (p. 33)
1 diced carrot
1 diced onion
1 tablespoon Worcestershire sauce

Wipe meat with cold, damp cloth and cut into small cubes.
Sprinkle with half the salt and pepper and roll in ½ cup flour.
Melt butter in saucepan. Add meat and brown it well. Stir in
1 tablespoon flour. Add boiling water or stock. Bring to boiling point, stirring constantly. Add balance of salt and pepper,
and carrot and onion. Cover tightly and let simmer over low
heat for 1 hour. Add Worcestershire sauce and serve hot.
Serves 6.

BAKED RAGOUT OF BEEF

¼ cup flour
1 teaspoon salt
¼ teaspoon pepper
1 pound beef cut in 1" cubes
2 tablespoons butter
2 sliced onions
1 sliced carrot
2 cups boiled peas or potatoes
1 cup canned crushed tomatoes
1 tablespoon Worcestershire sauce

Preheat oven to 350°F. Mix flour, salt, and pepper. Roll meat in mixture. Melt butter in saucepan. Sauté meat over medium-high heat until it is a light brown. Add onions. Sauté until well browned. Put alternate layers of meat and vegetables in greased baking dish. Add tomatoes, mixed with Worcestershire sauce. Cover and bake for 2 to 3 hours. Serves 6.

BEEF CHILI CON CARNE

2 pounds beef
¼ cup butter
4 medium size onions, sliced
2 cups canned tomatoes
2 cups canned red kidney beans
4 celery stalks, chopped
1 teaspoon salt
1 teaspoon red pepper
1 teaspoon chili powder

Wipe beef with cold, damp cloth. Cut into small cubes. Melt butter in a large pan over medium-high heat. Sauté meat and onions in butter until nicely browned. Put in a large stock pot.

Add tomatoes, beans, celery, salt, and pepper. Simmer 1½ hours over low heat. Add chili powder and simmer 30 minutes more. Serve hot. Serves 6 to 8.

BAKED BEEF CAKE

1 pound round steak
1 cup sifted flour
2 cups milk
1 beaten egg
1 teaspoon salt
¼ teaspoon pepper

Preheat oven to 350°F. Wipe meat with cold, damp cloth. Dice. Make a batter with flour, milk, egg, and half of salt and pepper. Grease a baking dish. Put meat in. Sprinkle with balance of salt and pepper. Pour batter over meat. Bake for 1 hour. Serve hot. Lamb or mutton may be substituted for beef. Serves 4.

BEEF AND TOMATOES

2 pounds steak
3 large onions, sliced
3 cups canned crushed tomatoes
1 teaspoon salt
½ teaspoon pepper

Wipe meat with cold, damp cloth. Cut into 5 pieces. Melt a little beef fat in frying pan over medium heat. Reduce heat and put meat in pan. Arrange onion on top of meat. Add tomatoes, salt and pepper. Cover and simmer at low heat until meat is tender, about 1 hour. Serve on hot platter, using liquid for sauce. Adjust seasonings. Serves 6.

FILET OF BEEF

2 pounds filet of beef
¼ cup melted butter
1 teaspoon salt
¼ teaspoon pepper
3 tablespoons flour

Preheat oven to 450°F. Wipe meat with cold, damp cloth. Remove all ligaments and sinews. Brush meat with butter. Sprinkle with salt, pepper, and 2 tablespoons flour. Put in pan. Bake for 30 minutes. Remove to hot platter. For gravy, thicken liquid with remaining flour, mixed to a smooth paste with cold water, adding boiling water if necessary. Cook until thick, stirring constantly, add season to taste. Mushroom (p. 425) or tomato sauce (p. 424) also go well with this dish. Serves 4.

BOILED BEEF

4 pounds beef (such as chuck or rump)
Cold water or beef stock (p. 33)
2 teaspoons salt
2 carrots, peeled and diced
1 onion, diced
1 stalk celery, diced

Wipe meat with cold, damp cloth. Place in a stock pot. Add cold water to half cover meat. Bring quickly to a boil. Reduce heat and let simmer over low heat until meat is tender, 3 to 4 hours. Add salt, vegetables, and more water, if necessary, when meat is half cooked. To obtain brown stock steak meat should be seared on all sides before simmering, in which case put boiling water in stockpot with beef. For gravy, skim fat off stock and thicken with a little flour, mixed to a smooth paste in cold water. Allow ½ pound per serving.

SOUTHERN GOULASH

2 tablespoons butter
1 pound ground beef
1 finely chopped onion
1 cup beef broth (p. 33) or canned crushed tomatoes
1 teaspoon salt
¼ teaspoon pepper
1 teaspoon Worcestershire sauce

Preheat oven to 325°F. Melt butter in deep oven-safe pan over medium-high heat. Sear beef and onion in it quickly. Add other ingredients. Cover pan and bake for 25 to 30 minutes. Serves 4.

BEEF SAUSAGE MEAT

2 pounds ground beef
1 teaspoon salt
1 teaspoon powdered sage
½ teaspoon black pepper
¼ teaspoon paprika
2 tablespoons chopped parsley
3 cups stale bread crumbs
1 well beaten egg

Mix all ingredients thoroughly. Tie in clean cloth and shape into a log or patty. Drop in stockpot of boiling water and boil 1 hour. Remove cloth when cold and use sausage in thin slices. Serves 6 to 8.

CORNED BEEF

½ pound salt
6 cups water (more as needed)
4 pounds beef brisket
12 cloves
½ cup brown sugar

In a large stock pot, combine the salt, water, and brisket. Allow it to sit for one week in the refrigerator, making sure that the brisket is fully submerged in water. Wipe meat with cold, damp cloth. Put in a stock pot. Cover with cold water. Bring to a boil. Boil 3 to 5 minutes. Skim water. Reduce heat. Let simmer until tender, allowing about 30 minutes per pound. Let cool slightly in liquor. Put on platter. Cover with another dish. Place weight on top to press meat together. To glaze corned beef, finish cooking as above, then transfer to baking pan. Stick in cloves and cover with brown sugar. Add a little water to pan. Bake at 350°F, basting frequently with syrup, until glazed, about 20 to 45 minutes. Allow ½ pound of meat per serving.

NEW ENGLAND BOILED DINNER

Prepare and cook corned beef (above). Add to pot, 40 minutes before meat is done, 1 sliced cabbage, 2 turnips, 6 carrots, and 8 peeled potatoes. To produce corned beef and cabbage, eliminate other vegetables and put cabbage in pot 30 minutes before meat is done.

CORNED BEEF HASH

Follow directions for meat hash (p. 405), using corned beef for meat. Add to hash as desired chopped vegetables such as pimento, green pepper or onion, singly or in any combination.

VEAL CHOPS

   6 veal chops
   Melted butter
   Salt
   Pepper
   ¼ cup flour (for sautéed or breaded chops)
   1 egg, well-beaten (for breaded chops)
   ½ cup bread crumbs (for breaded chops)

Use 1" thick chops. Wipe with cold, damp cloth. Rub all over with butter. Broil in moderate heat (350°F) about 15 minutes, turning when brown on one side. Sprinkle with salt and pepper. Serve hot. If sautéed veal chops are desired, roll in flour, season with salt and pepper, sauté in little fat until brown, cover and cook slowly 20 minutes, turning occasionally. For breaded veal chops dip in flour, then in egg, diluted with water, then in bread crumbs, and follow directions for sautéed veal chops. Chops should be served with hot lemon butter (p. 420), or tomato sauce (p. 424). Allow 1 chop per serving.

BREADED VEAL CUTLETS

2 pounds veal for cutlets cut ½" thick
1 teaspoon salt
⅛ teaspoon pepper
¾ cup dry bread crumbs
1 egg
2 tablespoons cold water
2 tablespoons butter
2 tablespoons flour
1 lemon, sliced

Wipe meat with cold, damp cloth. Cut into 6 pieces. Sprinkle with salt and pepper. Roll in bread crumbs. Dip in egg, well beaten in two tablespoons cold water. Roll again in crumbs. Heat butter in frying pan over medium-high heat and cook cutlets until thoroughly browned on both sides. Remove to hot platter. Thicken remaining liquid with flour, mixed to a paste in cold water, for sauce. Grated Parmesan cheese may be added to the bread crumbs. The seasoned and crumbed cutlets may also be fried in deep, hot fat (380° to 390°F) about 6 to 8 minutes, in which case drain on unglazed paper. Serve with lemon wedges. Serves 6.

VEAL ITALIAN STYLE

2 pounds veal
2 tablespoons olive oil
½ cup sliced, peeled mushrooms
1 teaspoon salt
¼ teaspoon pepper
⅛ teaspoon red pepper
1 tablespoon butter
½ cup water
1 cup boiled spaghetti

Wipe meat with cold, damp cloth. Cut into small cubes. Heat oil in pan. Add veal and sauté until well browned. Cover veal with mushrooms. Sprinkle with seasonings. Dot with butter. Add water. Cover and cook slowly 20 minutes. Add pasta and heat through. Serves 6.

VEAL BIRDS

1½ pounds veal cutlets
1½ cups poultry stuffing (p. 430)
2 tablespoons butter
¼ cup flour

Preheat oven to 375°F. Wipe meat with cold, damp cloth. Trim off fat and cut into 6 pieces of uniform size. Spread each piece with stuffing. Form into a roll and fasten with skewers. Brown the rolls uniformly in melted butter over medium-high heat. Place rolls in baking dish. Thicken remaining liquid with paste of flour and cold water and pour over rolls. Bake for 1 hour. Serves 4 to 6.

VEAL STEW WITH NOODLES

2 pounds breast or neck of veal
¼ cup flour
2 tablespoons butter
1 teaspoon salt
½ teaspoon pepper
Cold water to cover
6 medium onions, roughly chopped
1 cup uncooked wide noodles
1 cup sliced celery
1 tablespoon paprika
1 tablespoon chopped parsley

Wipe meat with cold, damp cloth. Cut into 6 pieces. Roll in flour and brown in melted butter in a large stock pot. Sprinkle with salt and pepper. Cover with cold water. Bring to boiling point. Reduce heat and let simmer for 1½ hours. Add onions, noodles, and celery. Cook 45 minutes longer. Serve on hot platter, garnished with paprika and parsley.

LAMB

ROAST LEG OF LAMB

1 6-pound leg of lamb
1 tablespoon salt
¼ teaspoon pepper
1 tablespoon fresh rosemary, finely diced
¼ cup olive oil
6 cloves garlic, cut into slivers
¼ cup flour
2 cups hot water

Preheat oven to 450°F. Wipe meat with cold, damp cloth. Combine salt, pepper, rosemary, and olive oil; rub on lamb. Pierce the lamb in several places with a sharp knife. Press slivers of garlic into these holes. Place on rack in open roasting pan, fat side up. Roast for 15 minutes; reduce heat to 325°F and cook 30 minutes per pound. If meat thermometer is used it will read 180°F when done. If layer of fat is very thin, place several bacon strips on top and basting will probably be unnecessary. Lamb may also be flavored by: (1) basting with mixture of Worcestershire sauce and tomato juice; (2) covering with buttered pineapple slices for last 45 minutes of cooking; (3) rubbing with chopped mint leaves. For gravy leave two tablespoons of fat in pan; stir in flour and cook until brown; add hot water; bring to boiling point, constantly stirring; cook five minutes more. Serves 8.

TOAST CROWN OF LAMB

Crown of lamb with 12 to 15 ribs
1½ teaspoons salt
½ teaspoon pepper
1 strip of bacon for each rib
Meat trimmings from crown
1 chopped onion

Preheat oven to 450°F. Have butcher prepare crown, reserving meat trimmings. Wipe with cold, damp cloth and sprinkle with 1 teaspoon salt and ⅛ teaspoon pepper. Tie strip of bacon around each rib end to prevent burning. Mix meat trimmings, onion, and balance of salt and pepper. Place in crown. Cook same as roast leg of lamb (p. 377). When lamb is done, replace bacon with paper frills, if desired. In serving, center of crown may be filled with vegetables. Serves 6 to 8.

ROAST STUFFED SHOULDER OF LAMB

1 3-pound shoulder of lamb
2 tablespoons chopped onion
3 tablespoons olive oil
2 cups bread crumbs
1 teaspoon chopped fresh mint leaves
1 tablespoon chopped celery leaves
¼ teaspoon pepper
1 tablespoon salt
2 tablespoons flour

Have shoulder blade removed, leaving pocket for stuffing. Preheat oven to 450°F. Prepare meat as for roast leg of lamb (p. 377). Brown onion in oil. Add bread crumbs, mint leaves, celery leaves, ⅛ teaspoon pepper, and ½ tablespoon salt, mixing thoroughly. Put stuffing in pocket; sew edges. Cook same as roast leg of lamb. Alternate stuffings that may be used are bread (p. 430), onion (p. 431), celery (p. 436), nut (p. 440), rice (p. 435), etc. Serves 8.

BROILED LAMB CHOPS

Whether single or double, from loin, ribs or shoulder, have lamb chops cut in uniform thickness and the membrane removed. Double loin chops may be boned, rolled, and wrapped in sliced bacon. Rib chops are often "Frenched" by trimming the rib ends bare. All lamb chops are best broiled either by direct heat or in a heavy uncovered skillet. To broil by direct heat, lay the chops on a cold greased rack and place under an electric grill or the flame of a gas oven. If a gas oven is used, have the chops 2 or 3" below a moderate flame. Sear them on both sides. Place double rib chops fat side up at first so they will also sear along that edge. After searing, lower the flame and finish the cooking at reduced temperature. Turn the chops occasionally, but do not prick the brown crust. If more convenient, after searing double chops (½" to 2" thick) under the flame, transfer the broiler to a moderately hot oven (375° to 400°F) to finish the cooking. To pan-broil, lay the chops in a heavy, sizzling-hot skillet, sear quickly on both sides, and also turn thick chops on edge so as to brown the fat. Then reduce the heat, turn the chops frequently and finish the cooking at low temperature. Do not add water or cover the skillet. From time to time pour off excess fat so that the chops broil, not fry. If preferred, with very thick chops, after searing, slip a rack under them in the skillet, and finish the cooking in a moderately hot oven (375° to 400°F). Allow 2 thin chops or 1 thick chop per serving.

BREADED LAMB CHOPS

8 lamb chops, ¼" to 1" thick
1 cup flour
2 beaten eggs
2 cups cracker crumbs or bread crumbs
1 teaspoon salt
½ teaspoon pepper
2 tablespoons butter

Wipe chops with cold, damp cloth. Roll in flour. Dip in eggs. Roll in crumbs. Sprinkle with salt and pepper. Melt butter in pan over medium-high heat. Put chops in pan and sauté turning often, 10 to 12 minutes. If desired, the breaded and seasoned chops may be fried in deep, hot fat (380° to 390°F) about 8 minutes. Drain on paper towels. Allow 2 chops per serving.

LAMB CHOPS EN CASSEROLE

8 thin lamb chops
2 tablespoons butter
1 teaspoon salt
½ teaspoon pepper
4 sliced tomatoes
4 cored and peeled apples
4 small onions
4 potatoes, cubed
1 cup canned crushed tomatoes

Preheat oven to 350°F. Wipe meat with cold, damp cloth. Melt butter in frying pan and lightly brown chops on both sides over medium heat. Sprinkle with salt and pepper. Put tomato slices, apples, onions, and potatoes in baking dish. Lay chops on top. Pour in tomatoes. Cover and bake until tender, about 45 minutes. Serves 4.

LAMB EN CASSEROLE

3 cups cold roast lamb, cut in 1" squares (p. 377)
1 tablespoon butter
1 cup broiled carrots diced (p. 222)
1 cup cold boiled potato (p. 244), cut
2 cups brown sauce (p. 418)
8 small boiled onions (p. 237)
½ cup boiled string beans (p. 213)
½ cup boiled peas (p. 240)
1 teaspoon salt
⅛ teaspoon pepper
1 teaspoon Worcestershire sauce

Preheat oven to 400°F. Brown lamb in hot butter in frying pan over medium heat. Put in baking dish. Add carrots, potato balls, brown sauce, onions, string beans, peas, salt, pepper, and Worcestershire sauce. Cover and bake for 20 minutes. Serves 6. The quantities of cooked vegetables can be varied to suit personal preference and the supply on hand.

LAMB STEW

    2 pounds lean lamb
    ½ cup flour, plus 1 tablespoon
    2 tablespoons butter or fat
    ½ cup sliced onion
    4 cups water or stock
    3 cups diced turnip
    1 chopped green pepper
    1 teaspoon salt
    ¼ teaspoon pepper
    Roast potatoes (p. 245)
    1 tablespoon chopped parsley

Wipe meat with cold, damp cloth. Cut into small pieces and roll in ½ cup flour. Melt butter in frying pan over medium heat. Add onion. Cook until yellow. Add meat. When well browned, remove meat and onions and put in a large stock pot. Pour water into frying pan and then into stockpot with browned fat. Cover and let simmer 1 hour. Add turnip, green pepper, salt, and pepper. Cover and cook 20 minutes longer. If desired, thicken stew by adding 1 tablespoon flour, mixed to a smooth paste with 2 tablespoons cold water, cooking 5 minutes longer, stirring constantly. Serve piping hot with roast potatoes (p. 245). Garnish with parsley. Serves 6.

IRISH STEW WITH DUMPLINGS

3 pounds lamb, bones removed
Boiling water or stock
1 onion, sliced
1 cup diced carrot
1 cup diced turnip
3 cups potatoes, in cubes
¼ cup flour
1 teaspoon salt
⅛ teaspoon pepper
Dumplings (p. 165)

Wipe meat with cold, damp cloth; cut into 2" squares. Put in a large stock pot, cover with boiling water, and let simmer 1 ½ hours. Add onion, carrot, and turnip and cook 30 minutes more. Add potatoes and cook another 20 minutes. Thicken with flour mixed to a paste in cold water. Season with salt and pepper. Serve with dumplings. Serves 8.

BRAISED LEG OF LAMB

Leg of lamb, boned, with a pocket for stuffing
Mashed potato stuffing (p. 433)
½ cup butter
1 onion
1 carrot
1 turnip
Bay leaf
Sprig of thyme
Sprig of parsley
1½ teaspoons salt
12 peppercorns
3 cups hot basic chicken stock (p. 32)
¼ cup flour

Preheat oven to 300°F. Wipe meat with cold, damp cloth. Stuff with potato stuffing and sew securely. Place in deep casserole or Dutch oven with ¼ cup butter. Dice the onion, carrot, and turnip and add to pan with bay leaf, thyme, and parsley. Brown meat and vegetables for 5 minutes. Add 3 cups hot stock, salt, and peppercorns, pouring over mutton. Cover tightly and bake for 3 hours, uncovering for the last ½ hour. Remove to hot platter. Brown the balance of butter. Slowly stir in flour. Strain liquid from the pot, and pour into the flour-butter mixture, stirring until thickened. Adjust seasonings. Use this for sauce. Allow ½ pound per serving.

LAMB PIE

2 pounds lamb or mutton
1 teaspoon salt
12 small, tart apples
1 cup sugar
1 teaspoon powdered cloves
1 teaspoon cinnamon
⅛ teaspoon nutmeg
Plain pastry dough (p. 445)

Wipe meat with cold, damp cloth. Sprinkle with salt. Put in stock pot or other heavy-bottomed pan. Cover with boiling water. Cover and simmer over low heat until tender, about 2 ½ hours. Preheat oven to 350°F. Wash apples. Peel, core, and slice. Mix sugar, cloves, cinnamon, and nutmeg. Roll out two pieces of dough to ⅛" thickness on a lightly floured board. Line a greased baking dish with plain pastry. Cut lamb in small pieces. Put layer of lamb in dish. Sprinkle with mixture of seasonings. Add layer of apples. Alternate layers, seasoning each, until all ingredients are used. Add some of the liquid from the pan. Cover with the remaining piece of dough. Bake for 1 hour. Serves 6.

BAKED RICE AND LAMB

2 cups cooked lamb
2 cups meat stock
1 cup canned crushed tomatoes
1 teaspoon salt
½ teaspoon pepper
2 onions, chopped
1 teaspoon whole cumin
4 tablespoons butter
½ cup uncooked rice

Put lamb, stock, tomatoes, salt, pepper, 1 onion, and cumin in pan with 2 tablespoons butter. Heat for 10 minutes over medium heat. Melt remaining butter in frying pan. Add remaining onion and rice. Brown slightly. Add to other mixture. Turn all into a greased baking dish and bake for 40 minutes at 350°F. Serves 6.

PORK AND HAM

ROAST CROWN OF PORK

Crown of pork
1 teaspoon salt per pound
¼ teaspoon pepper
2 tablespoons flour, plus more for gravy

Preheat oven to 475°F. Wipe meat with cold damp cloth. Cut off excess fat. Sprinkle with salt, pepper, and flour. Put in roasting pan, fat side up. Arrange pieces of excess fat around meat. Bake for 15 minutes; baste; reduce heat to 325°F and cook until well done, allowing 40 minutes to the pound. Baste every 15 minutes. A meat thermometer will read 185°F when well done. Serve on platter, surrounded by mashed potatoes (p. 244) and garnished with baked apples (p. 190). Paper frills on the ends of the bones and sprigs of parsley will add to the appearance of the dish. Thicken fat in roasting pan with flour paste, mixed in cold water, for gravy. Allow ½ pound of meat per serving.

ROAST PORK

Prepare and cook same as roast crown of pork (above), allow 30 minutes per pound for large roasts and 45 minutes per pound for small or rolled roasts. When done a meat thermometer will read 185°F.

ROAST SUCKLING PIG

1 suckling pig, 8 to 10 pounds
5 cups onion stuffing (p. 431)
2 teaspoons salt
1 teaspoon pepper
1 cup water
1 small potato
¼ cup butter
Parsley or watercress (for garnish)
1 lemon or apple
2 cranberries
2 tablespoons flour

Select pig from 3 to 6 weeks old. Have it cleaned by butcher. Preheat oven to 350°F. Wash well in warm water, especially the head and throat passages. Wrap cloth around a skewer for this purpose. Wash with cold water and dry. Stuff loosely. Sew securely. Tie legs in toward center. Put pig in kneeling position in roasting pan. Sprinkle with salt and pepper. Add 1 cup water to pan. Prop mouth open with a small potato. Bake for about 3 hours, basting often with melted butter. Serve on platter in a bed of parsley or watercress. Replace potato in mouth with lemon or apple. Put cranberries in eye sockets. Thicken drippings with flour, mixed to a smooth paste in cold water, adding boiling water, if necessary, for gravy. Season to taste. Other proper stuffings are sage and onion (p. 432), bread (p. 430), or mashed potatoes (p. 433). Serves 10 to 12.

CROWN ROAST OF SPARERIBS

2 pounds spareribs
2 cups boiled rice (p. 128)
2 cups bread crumbs
1 minced carrot
1 large minced onion
¼ cup raisins
3 tablespoons butter or fat
½ teaspoon powdered sage
2 teaspoons salt
¼ teaspoon pepper

Preheat oven to 325°F. Have butcher tie spareribs in crown roast shape. Wipe meat with cold, damp cloth. Set upright in baking dish. Mix all other ingredients thoroughly and pack in cavity. Bake for 2 hours. Serve in baking dish. Serves 6.

STUFFED FRESH HAM

6 to 8 pound ham, bone removed
1 teaspoon salt
½ teaspoon pepper
3 cups bread stuffing (p. 430)
3 cups cider

Preheat oven to 475°F. Wipe meat with cold, damp cloth. Sprinkle with salt and pepper. Stuff. Tie securely. Put in roasting pan. Bake for 20 minutes. Pour cider over ham. Reduce heat to 350°F, allowing 30 minutes per pound or until meat thermometer reads (185°F), basting frequently with drippings. Allow ½ pound of meat per serving.

PORK CHOPS, BROILED OR FRIED

6 pork chops, ¾" to 1" thick
1 teaspoon salt
¼ teaspoon pepper
1 tablespoon butter

Wipe chops with cold, damp cloth. Broil at high heat until both sides are seared. Reduce heat or move further from flame and broil 15 to 20 minutes, turning often. Sprinkle with salt and pepper. Dot with butter. To fry pork chops, have pan sizzling and sear chops rapidly on both sides. Reduce heat and cook slowly 20 to 25 minutes, turning often. Season as above. Serves 6.

PORK CHOPS WITH DRESSING

⅛ onion, finely chopped
1½ cups bread crumbs
2 tablespoons pork fat, chopped, or butter
⅛ teaspoon pepper
¾ teaspoon salt
1 egg
6 pork chops
¼ cup hot water

Preheat oven to 350°F. Mix onion, bread crumbs, fat, pepper, salt, and well-beaten egg with ¼ cup hot water. Spread on pork chops. Put chops close together in a pan. Add enough water to cover bottom of pan. Bake for 1 hour, basting every 10 minutes. Serve with applesauce (p. 190), if desired. Serves 4 to 6.

PORK CHOPS WITH CANDIED SWEETS

6 pork chops
6 boiled sweet potatoes
¼ cup brown sugar
1 teaspoon salt
⅛ teaspoon pepper
1 tablespoon flour

Preheat oven to 350°F. Wipe chops with cold, damp cloth. Broil or fry at high heat until well browned on both sides. Lay in greased baking pan. Peel potatoes and cut in half lengthwise. Put in pan with chops. Sprinkle with sugar, salt and pepper. Cover bottom of pan with a little water. Bake for 45 minutes to 1 hour, basting frequently. Thicken liquid from pan with flour, mixed to a smooth paste with cold water, for gravy. Season to taste. Serves 6.

PORK CHOPS EN CASSEROLE

8 small potatoes
2 tablespoons flour
1 teaspoon salt
⅛ teaspoon pepper
2 tablespoons butter or fat
3 cups milk
8 pork chops, ¾" thick

Preheat oven to 325°F. Wash and peel potatoes; slice thin. Place layer of potatoes in greased lasagna dish or Dutch oven. Sprinkle with flour, salt, and pepper and dot with butter or fat. Repeat, until all potatoes are used. Pour in milk. Lay pork chops on top. Bake until potatoes are tender, about 1¼ hours. A slice of orange may be placed on each chop the last 15 minutes of cooking. Serves 4.

SMOTHERED PORK CHOPS

    2 pounds pork chops cut thick
    2 unpeeled lemons, sliced
    1 large sweet onion (such as Vidalia) cut in rings
    1 green pepper cut in rings
    1 teaspoon salt
    2 cups tomato juice
    1 tablespoon butter

Wipe meat with cold, damp cloth. Put chops in large covered skillet or heavy-bottomed sauce pan and cover top of meat with lemon, onion, and pepper. Sprinkle with salt. Pour tomato juice over all and dot with butter. Cover and cook on top of stove over low heat for 1½ hours or until pork is cooked through. Lift on to hot platter, being careful to keep rings in place and serve. Serves 6 to 8.

STUFFED PORK CHOPS

    ½ cup mushrooms, sliced
    2 tablespoons minced onion
    ½ cup boiled rice (p. 128)
    2 tablespoons butter
    1 cup bread crumbs
    1 cup canned crushed tomatoes
    1 teaspoon salt
    ¼ teaspoon pepper
    6 thick pork chops with pockets
    ½ cup water

Preheat oven to 350°F. Brush mushrooms or wipe with a damp cloth to clean. If steams are tender, they may be used. Brown mushrooms, onion, and rice in frying pan with butter. Add bread crumbs, tomato, salt, and pepper. Let simmer 10 minutes over low heat. Let stand until cool. Stuff chops with this mixture and fasten securely with skewers. Brown chops on both sides in frying pan on top of stove, cooking until meat is heated through. Add water. Cover tightly. Bake for 1 to 1¼ hours. Serves 6.

DEVILED PORK TENDERLOIN

2 pork tenderloins
5 tablespoons butter (optional)
2 tablespoons chili sauce
¼ cup boiling water
2 tablespoons tomato paste
1 teaspoon salt
¼ teaspoon paprika
1 teaspoon prepared mustard
1 tablespoon Worcestershire sauce

Preheat oven to 400°F. Wipe meat with cold, damp cloth. Beat hard to flatten. Fry in little butter or bake in greased baking pan, basting often with liquid from pan. Allow 25 to 30 minutes for cooking, depending on thickness of meat. To devil pork tenderloin, baste while cooking, in a sauce made by mixing remaining butter, chili sauce, boiling water, tomato sauce, salt, paprika, mustard, and Worcestershire sauce. Allow ½ pound of meat per serving.

STUFFED PORK TENDERLOIN

2 pork tenderloins
2 cups poultry stuffing (p. 430)
½ teaspoon salt
⅛ teaspoon pepper
2 tablespoons butter

Preheat oven to 350°F. Have each loin split not quite through. Open both flat. Cover one with stuffing and sprinkle with other with salt and pepper. Place together with stuffing, salt, and pepper in center. Sew together. Spread with butter. Bake for about 50 minutes, basting every 15 minutes. Serve on hot platter garnished with fried apple rings (p. 192). Serves 6.

PORK PIE

2 pounds pork
1 teaspoon salt
½ teaspoon pepper
Plain pastry dough (p. 445)
1 pound sausage meat
1 tablespoon parsley
2 tablespoons chopped onion
1 cup stock
2 tablespoons tomato paste

Preheat oven to 350°F. Wipe pork with cold, damp cloth. Sprinkle with salt and pepper. Roll out dough in two pieces to ⅛" thickness on a lightly floured board. Line a baking dish with pastry. Put in layer of sausage meat. Sprinkle with parsley and onion. Put in layer of pork, chopped in small pieces. Alternate layers until all meat is used, sprinkling between each layer with parsley and onion. A layer of sausage should be on top. Pour in stock and tomato paste. Cover with remaining piece of pastry. Cut a 1" opening in center. Bake the pie until crust begins to brown. Then reduce heat and bake at 350°F for 2 hours. It will add to the flavor if pork is soaked for 2 hours in ½ cup sherry or in diluted vinegar before cooking. Serves 6.

PORK WITH RICE

¾ cup butter
1 medium onion, diced
2 cups roast pork, diced
⅛ teaspoon white pepper
1 teaspoon salt
½ teaspoon chili powder
6 cups boiled rice (p. 128)
1 egg
2 tablespoons milk
½ cup diced boiled ham
Tomato slices
Cucumber slices

Melt butter, add onion, sauté until lightly browned over medium heat. Add pork and seasonings and sauté until browned. Add rice and mix well. In another bowl, combine egg and milk, season to taste, and fry over low heat in a skillet to make a thin omelet in narrow strips. Arrange rice and meat mixture on platter, sprinkle with diced ham, and garnish with egg strips and tomato and cucumber slices. Serves 6 to 8.

PORK PATTIES

2 pounds pork, bones removed
1 cup stale bread crumbs
1 teaspoon salt
2 tablespoons chopped onion
½ teaspoon pepper
2 well-beaten eggs
1 tablespoon pork fat or cooking oil

Wipe meat with cold, damp cloth. Chop into very fine pieces. Mix thoroughly with bread crumbs, salt, onion, pepper, and eggs. Form into patties. Melt fat. Fry patties on both sides over high heat or cook on a grill until well done, about 15 minutes. Serve with french fried (p. 244) or creamed (p. 248) potatoes. Serves 6.

BAKED VIRGINIA HAM

1 country ham, with the skin still on
½ cup brown sugar, plus more for apples
2 tablespoons bread crumbs
1 teaspoon prepared mustard
1 tablespoon whole cloves
1 cup water
6 tart apples, cored (optional)

Wash ham thoroughly. Put in deep pot, cover with cold water, and bring to a boil quickly. Reduce heat and let simmer 2½ hours. Remove from pot and take off skin. Preheat oven to 350°F. Mix sugar, crumbs, and mustard and spread over ham. Stick cloves in ham. Put in roasting pan with water and bake until brown, about 30 minutes. A delicious garnish is prepared by coring unpeeled apples, filling openings in each with brown sugar and baking with ham. Allow ½ pound of meat per serving.

BAKED HAM AND SWEET POTATOES

½ fully cooked ham, 5 to 6 pounds
1 cup brown sugar
1 tablespoon bread crumbs
24 cloves
6 sweet potatoes
1 cup crushed pineapple

Preheat oven to 350°F. Wash ham thoroughly. Rub fat side with brown sugar and bread crumbs. Dot with cloves. Peel sweet potatoes. Arrange them around ham. Pour crushed pineapple over ham. Bake for 3 hours. Serves 6.

PLAIN FRIED HAM

Cut a thin slice from the center of a raw ham and gash the fat on the edge in several places. Place in hot frying pan and brown quickly on one side. Turn and brown lightly on other. Cook slowly until tender, about 10 minutes if ¼" thick, 15 minutes if ½" thick, 30 minutes if 1" thick. If desired, apples, cored and sliced with the skin on, may be fried in the ham fat and served. Allow ½ pound of meat per serving.

FRIED HAM AND EGGS

Cook meat, according to recipe for plain fried ham (above), and fry eggs in ham fat. Allow ¼ pound ham and 2 eggs per serving.

BROILED HAM

Broil thin slices of raw ham for about 10 minutes, turning frequently. Serve with fried bananas (p. 194) or pineapple slices, sautéed in little fat until brown on both sides. Allow ½ pound of ham per serving.

COUNTRY STYLE HAM

Slice of raw ham, 1 to 1½" thick
1 onion, chopped
4 carrots, chopped
3 tablespoon seeded raisins
1 cup water
1 tablespoon flour
Juice of 1 orange

Wipe meat with cold, damp cloth. Brown on both sides quickly in saucepan. Add onion, carrots, raisins, and water. Cover and let simmer over low heat for 1½ to 2 hours. Mix flour and orange juice, blending well. Add this mixture to pan. Bring to a boil, stirring constantly. Remove from heat and serve immediately. Allow ½ pound of ham per serving.

BAKED SLICE OF HAM

2 tablespoons brown sugar
2 pounds ham, 1½" thick
1 cup milk
2 tablespoons flour

Preheat oven to 350°F. Melt brown sugar in an oven-safe frying pan. Wipe meat with cold, damp cloth. Put in pan and brown on both sides. Add milk and bake for about 30 minutes. Remove ham to hot platter. Thicken remaining liquid with flour, mixed to a smooth paste with cold water, for gravy. ¼ cup chopped preserved ginger, cooked with the ham, adds a delightful flavor, and pears, cored and halved lengthwise, cooked with the ham are an attractive garnish. Serves 4 to 6.

CREAMED HAM

> 1 slice raw ham, ½" to ¾" thick
> 2 cups thin white sauce (p. 416)
> ¼ teaspoon pepper
> ½ teaspoon dry mustard
> 1 teaspoon sugar
> Milk, as needed

Wipe meat with cold, damp cloth. Brown in frying pan on both sides over medium heat. Drain on a paper towel. Put in saucepan. Add sauce, seasoned with pepper, mustard, and sugar. Cover and simmer 1¼ to 1½ hours, turning occasionally and adding sufficient milk to keep ham covered. Allow ½ pound of meat per serving.

HAM LOAF

3 tablespoons butter
¼ cup brown sugar
2 pounds fully cooked ham, ground
1 cup bread crumbs
¼ teaspoon pepper
2 eggs
½ cup milk
Pineapple slices for garnish (optional)

Preheat oven to 350°F. Melt butter in pan over medium heat. Add sugar and dissolve thoroughly. Mix with ham and other ingredients and form into a loaf. Put in loaf pan. Bake for 1½ hours. Pineapple slices, slightly browned in butter and sugar, and baked under meat make a fine garnish. Serves 6.

FRIED HAM AND RICE

2 tablespoons butter
2 tablespoons chopped onion
1 tablespoon chopped parsley
1 cup chopped cold cooked ham
2 cups boiled rice (p. 128)
1 teaspoon salt
¼ teaspoon pepper
1 egg

Melt butter in pan. Add onion, parsley, and ham. Sauté over medium heat until onions are a light brown. Add rice, salt, and pepper. Mix well. Beat egg and mix into mixture. When heated through, season to taste, and serve on hot platter. Serves 6.

BACON, BROILED OR FRIED

If bacon isn't already sliced, cut in thin slices. To broil, place over dripping pan and sear at high heat, turning to brown both sides. To fry, place in sizzling pan and rapidly sear both sides. If wanted crisp, either broil or fry until all fat is out. Personal preference determines how long to cook. If fried, drain on a paper towel. Allow 2 to 4 slices per serving.

BACON ROLLS

2 cups bread crumbs
½ cup celery, diced
2 teaspoons diced green pepper
1 small onion, finely diced
1 teaspoon salt
½ teaspoon pepper
1 egg
½ cup milk
12 bacon slices

Preheat oven to 400°F. Combine bread crumbs, celery, green pepper, and onion, and season with salt and pepper. Moisten with slightly beaten egg and milk. Place a tablespoon of this dressing on a slice of bacon. Roll the bacon slice around the dressing and fasten the ends with a toothpick. Cook these in the oven until the bacon is crisp and the roll is heated through. Serve while hot. Serves 4 to 6.

FRIED BACON AND APPLES

12 bacon slices
3 firm apples
3 tablespoons sugar

Fry bacon crisp in a skillet over high heat. Remove to hot platter and keep warm. Wash and quarter apples, removing cores and seeds. Put them in hot bacon fat. Cover tightly. Fry over medium-high heat until they are partly soft, turning once. Sprinkle on sugar. Continue frying, uncovered, until well browned. Serve hot, garnished with bacon. Pineapple rings, dipped in flour and browned in bacon fat, are also delicious with bacon. Serves 6.

SAUSAGE MEAT

2 pounds lean pork
1 pound pork fat or fatback
2 tablespoons salt
1 teaspoon black pepper
1 teaspoon powdered sage
1 teaspoon powdered ginger

Grind pork and fat together and mix thoroughly. Add seasonings, mixing well. Keep in cold place at least 24 hours before using.

SAUSAGE PATTIES

Form sausage meat (above) into 3 to 4 inch patties. Pan-broil in hot pan 12 to 15 minutes, pouring off liquid fat. Drain on paper towels. Or bake at 350°F for 30 to 35 minutes. Allow ¼ pound sausage meat per serving.

SAUSAGE TURNOVERS

1 cup sausage meat (p. 402)
1 cup chopped ham
1 cup boiled rice
1 teaspoon Worcestershire sauce
1 egg
Plain pastry (p. 445)

Preheat oven to 400°F. Fry sausage meat slowly for 10 minutes, stirring constantly. Drain off fat. Add ham, rice, and Worcestershire sauce, mixing well. Beat egg thoroughly and add to mixture. Roll pastry to ⅛" in thickness and cut in 4" squares. Place 2 tablespoons of meat mixture in center of each. Moisten edges with water and fold into triangles. Close edges with a fork. Prick the tops and bake for 15 to 20 minutes. Serves 6.

SAUSAGE AND CABBAGE

1½ pounds sausage or sausage meat (p. 402)
4 cups chopped cabbage
1 teaspoon salt
½ teaspoon pepper

Fry sausage in pan about 12 minutes, turning to brown evenly. Drain on paper towels. Reduce fat in pan to 3 tablespoons. Put in cabbage. Sprinkle with salt and pepper. Fry 6 minutes, turning often. Add sausages to pan. Serve hot. Serves 6.

SAUSAGES AND SWEET POTATOES

2 pounds sweet potatoes
½ cup sugar
½ cup brown sugar
2 tablespoons butter
1 teaspoon salt
¼ cup water
1 pound sausage or sausage meat (p. 402)

Preheat oven to 350°F. Boil sweet potatoes for 15 minutes. Peel and cut into strips. Put in greased baking dish. Mix sugar, brown sugar, butter, salt, and water thoroughly and boil in saucepan 3 minutes. Pour syrup over sweet potatoes. Bake for 40 minutes. Put sausages on top and continue baking another 30 minutes. Serves 6.

RABBIT, VENISON, AND OTHER MEATS

MEAT HASH

2 cups chopped cooked corned beef (p. 372) or roast
    beef (p. 353)
2 cups chopped & peeled potato
2 tablespoons butter
¼ cup milk or meat stock
1 teaspoon salt
½ teaspoon pepper
1 chopped onion
1 chopped celery

Meat should be chopped first. Add potato and chop together.
Melt butter in frying pan over medium heat. Spread hash
evenly in pan, moisten with liquid to which seasonings,
onion, and celery have been added, and cook over low heat
for 20 minutes, shaking occasionally to prevent sticking. If
desired, hash may be put in greased pan and baked at 350°F.
Serves 6.

MEAT LOAF

3 pounds chopped cooked meat
2 eggs
1 teaspoon salt
1 teaspoon pepper
1 onion, diced
2 cups bread crumbs
1 cup milk
⅓ cup tomato paste or ketchup
1 teaspoon Worcestershire sauce

Preheat oven to 350°F. Mix all ingredients thoroughly and shape into a loaf. Place in pan and bake for 30 minutes. Serves 6. Roast beef gravy (p. 415) or tomato sauce (p. 424) goes well with this.

MEAT BALLS

2 cups ground beef, turkey, or a combination of ground beef and veal
2 teaspoons chopped chives
1 teaspoon chopped thyme
1 teaspoon chopped marjoram
1 teaspoon chopped parsley
2 tablespoons flour
¼ teaspoon salt
⅛ teaspoon pepper
2 tablespoons butter

Mix thoroughly chopped meat and herbs. Form into balls or patties. Roll in flour, mixed with salt and pepper. Brown well in hot butter over medium heat. Serves 6. Meat balls may also be used in soups or tomato sauce (p. 424)

MEAT PIE

2 onions, thinly sliced
2 cups sliced cooked meat, such as roast beef (p. 353)
    or roast chicken (p. 298)
2 tablespoons flour
1 teaspoon salt
½ teaspoon pepper
2 cups canned or fresh sliced tomatoes
2 cups bread crumbs
1 tablespoon butter

Preheat oven to 350°F. Put alternate layers of onion and meat in greased baking dish until all is used. Sprinkle each layer with flour, salt and pepper. Pour in canned tomatoes or lay fresh tomato slices, peeled, as top layer. Put bread crumbs on top. Dot with butter. Bake until bread crumbs are browned and tomatoes are soft, about 20 to 30 minutes. Serve hot. Serves 6.

SHEPHERD'S PIE

1½ cups hot mashed potatoes (p. 244)
2 cups cold cooked lamb or beef
½ teaspoon salt
½ teaspoon pepper
2 tablespoons diced onion
3 tablespoons leftover gravy
1 egg yolk
2 teaspoons cold water

Preheat oven to 425°F. Grease a baking dish and line bottom with half of the mashed potatoes. Season meat with salt and pepper; add onion; moisten with gravy; place in dish. Cover evenly with remaining mashed potatoes. Spread top with egg yolk, beaten in cold water. Bake until brown and heated through, about 20 minutes. Individual pies may be made in small dishes or custard cups, cooking about 15 minutes. Serves 6.

MEAT STEW

2 cups beef or lamb stew meat, cut in 2" cubes
2 onions, sliced
2 tablespoons butter
1 cup diced carrot
6 medium size potatoes, quartered
Basic beef stock (p. 33), as needed
3 tablespoons flour

Brown meat and onions in melted butter in deep pan. Add carrot and potatoes. Cover with stock. Cover and let simmer until vegetables are almost soft. Thicken by adding flour, mixed into a smooth paste in cold water. Season to taste.

SAUSAGE LOAF

2 pounds pork sausage, or sausage meat (p. 402)
4 cups bread crumbs
1 egg
1 cup sour cream
Paprika

Preheat oven to 350°F. Combine sausage, bread crumbs, slightly beaten egg, and sour cream. Season with paprika. Pack firmly into a loaf pan. Bake until cooked all the way through, about 1½ hours. Serves 6.

STUFFED SAUSAGE ROLL

2 pounds sausage meat (p. 402)
2 cups diced raw apples
2 small onions, diced
2 cups bread crumbs
Salt
Pepper

Preheat oven to 350°F. Pat the sausage on waxed paper into a flat rectangular shape about ½" thick. Mix the apples, onions, and bread crumbs and spread this over the meat. Season with salt and pepper. Roll like a jellyroll, tucking the edges in. Place in a baking dish and bake until cooked through, about 45 minutes. Serves 6.

ROAST VENISON

For roasting, choose leg or saddle. Follow recipes for roasting lamb (p. 377), cooking venison about 12 minutes per pound. Allow ½ pound of meat per serving.

VENISON STEAKS

Cut steaks about ¾" thick. Prepare and cook same as broiled steak (p. 350). If flavor is too strong, venison will be improved by standing for 1 hour in a mixture of olive oil and lemon juice or French dressing (p. 71). Allow ½ pound per serving.

ROAST RABBIT OR HARE

2 to 3 pound cleaned rabbit
Poultry stuffing (p. 430)
¼ cup melted butter
2 tablespoons flour

Preheat oven to 450°F. Use young rabbits, weighing 2 to 3 pounds. When ready to cook, wash thoroughly and dry. Boil heart and liver until tender. Chop fine and mix with poultry stuffing, dampened with water in which giblets were cooked. Stuff rabbit. Sew opening. Tie or fasten legs close to body with skewers. Place on side in roaster. Roast at 450°F for 15 minutes, turning once and basting frequently with melted butter or drippings. Reduce heat and continue cooking at 350°F for 1¼ to 1½ hours, basting every 15 minutes. Make gravy by adding flour, mixed to a smooth paste with cold water, to drippings, blending well. Allow ¾ pound of rabbit per serving.

HASSENPFEFFER

1 2½- to 3-pound cleaned rabbit
2 tablespoons butter
2 tablespoons chopped bacon
2 chopped carrots
1 bay leaf
8 cloves
2 cloves of garlic
1 teaspoon salt
½ teaspoon pepper
1 tablespoon mustard seed
1 chopped onion
½ cup sliced mushrooms
1 cup basic chicken stock (p. 32) or white wine
1 cup cream

Cut meat from bones of rabbit. Melt butter in saucepan. Add bacon, carrots, bay leaf, cloves, garlic, salt, pepper, mustard seed, onion, mushrooms, and rabbit meat. Brown well. Add stock or wine. Cover and simmer over low heat until tender, about 1 hour. Add cream. Mix well and serve hot. Serves 6.

SAUCES
AND
STUFFINGS

SAUCES

Making gravy can be as simple as removing a chicken or turkey from a pan, whisking some flour into the drippings, and seasoning with salt and pepper. The recipes in this chapter build on that basic concept of thickening and seasoning the drippings. The juices and fat that drip from meat or poultry during cooking are almost always delicious. The job of gravy is to highlight that flavor, while turning it into something that can be presented at the table. Gravies are very forgiving, but there are a few things to watch out for. Make sure to whisk the flour with a small amount of liquid before adding it to the drippings. This will prevent the flour from creating lumps in the gravy. Don't add too much flour. It is always easier to add more flour than it is to remove it. Diluting gravy to correct for thickness can dilute the taste as well. Remember that the gravy will thicken as it cools. It doesn't need to become extremely thick during the cooking process.

The other sauces in this chapter are good for both meat and vegetable dishes. Some of them are familiar sauces, like tartar sauce and cocktail sauce. Making these sauces from scratch is quick, easy, and rewarding. The fresh parsley in the tartar sauce and the freshly-squeezed lemon juice in the cocktail sauce elevate both of these above anything you could buy in the store. These sauces are a wonderful way to vary and enliven standard meat and vegetable dishes.

STUFFINGS

The stuffings in this chapter need not be cooked inside a bird or with meat. They can be placed in pan around the roast or can be baked separately in baking pans or molds. If baking the stuffing separately, simply cover with a lid or aluminum foil, and place in the oven at 350°F for 20 to 30 minutes, or until heated through. Chicken stock can be replaced with vegetable stock in any of the recipes to make the stuffing vegetarian.

A good stuffing should be moist without being soggy. The liquid and bread amounts in the recipes are suggestions. The liquid amounts are calculated based on store bought breadcrumbs. If using especially stale bread, more liquid may be needed. If using fresher bread, less liquid may be needed. In any of the recipes, stale or toasted bread may be substituted for bread-crumbs, and vice versa.

SAUCES

GIBLET GRAVY

3 cups water
Chicken or turkey giblets (liver, gizzard, and heart)
4 tablespoons of fat or drippings from cooking poultry
3 tablespoons flour
Salt
Pepper

This gravy should be started about an hour before the poultry is done, in order to have it ready at the same time. Bring water to a boil. Add giblets from chicken, turkey, duck, or other poultry. Reduce heat to a simmer, and cook for 45 minutes, or until giblets are fully cooked. Set aside. Skim 4 tablespoons of fat from the roasting pan in which the bird was cooked. Heat fat in a skillet over medium heat. Add flour and stir until it browns. Add the water in which the giblets were cooked to the browned flour and stir until smooth and thickened. Finely chop the giblets and add to the gravy. Season with salt and pepper to taste. Serve in hot gravy boat with the poultry, reheating if necessary.

ROAST BEEF GRAVY

Drippings from a roast beef (p. 353)
½ cup water or red wine
2 tablespoons flour
Salt
Paprika

Remove roast beef from roasting pan. Bring drippings in pan to a boil over medium heat on the stove. Whisk water and flour together. Add to the drippings, stirring constantly. Season to taste with salt and paprika.

TURKEY GRAVY WITH RED WINE

Drippings from a roast turkey (p. 311)
1½ cups basic chicken stock (p. 32), more as needed
1 cup red wine
6 tablespoons flour
Salt
Pepper

Remove turkey from roasting pan. Pour drippings out, and measure. Skim fat off, if desired. Add enough chicken stock to make 3 cups of liquid. Whisk wine and flour together and add to the drippings. Bring to a boil over medium heat. Reduce heat and simmer until thickened. Season to taste with salt and pepper.

WHITE SAUCE

THIN SAUCE:

   1 tablespoon butter
   1 tablespoon flour
   ½ teaspoon salt
   1 cup milk

THIN TO MEDIUM SAUCE:

   1½ tablespoons butter
   1½ tablespoons flour
   ½ teaspoon salt
   1 cup milk

MEDIUM SAUCE:

   2 tablespoons butter
   2 tablespoons flour
   ½ teaspoon salt
   1 cup milk

THICK SAUCE:

   3 tablespoons butter
   3 tablespoons flour
   ½ teaspoon salt
   1 cup milk

Melt the butter in a saucepan over low heat. Blend thoroughly with the flour and salt, stirring until all lumps are gone. Add the milk and heat slowly, stirring constantly. When the mixture reaches a boil, reduce heat and stir until thickened. If doubling the recipe, use the same method of blending the butter and flour, but add hot milk and finish the cooking in a double boiler to save time and the energy required for stirring.

CREAM SAUCE

Substitute cream for milk in white sauces (p. 416).

CHEESE SAUCE

1 cup grated mild cheese (such as Cheddar or Swiss)
Medium white sauce (p. 416)

Add grated cheese to white sauce or cream sauce after it has thickened. Stir until cheese has melted.

EGG SAUCE

1 hard-boiled egg (p. 272)
2 teaspoons parsley
Medium white sauce (p. 416)

Chop egg and parsley. Add to hot white sauce (p. 416) or cream sauce (above).

BROWN SAUCE

2 tablespoons butter
2 tablespoons onion, diced
2 tablespoons flour
2 cups basic chicken stock (p. 32)
Salt
Pepper

Melt butter. Add onion and brown. Stir in flour, blending well. When brown, add stock. Season to taste with salt and pepper. Cook until it boils and is smooth, stirring constantly. 1 bouillon cube, dissolved in 2 cups water, may be substituted for stock.

BORDELAISE SAUCE

Replace 1 cup stock in brown sauce (above) with 1 cup Bordeaux wine.

HOLLANDAISE SAUCE

½ cup butter
2 egg yolks
½ teaspoon salt
Speck cayenne pepper
1 tablespoon lemon juice

Melt butter in saucepan over low heat. Beat egg yolks in bowl with beater at high speed until thick and lemon colored. Move egg yolks to a blender. Add salt, cayenne, and 3 tablespoons melted butter, one drop at a time while blending on high speed. Then add the remaining butter, alternately with the lemon juice, until all has been added, and the sauce is thickened. Store in refrigerator until ready to use. This sauce melts readily when served on hot vegetables. Serves 6.

DRAWN BUTTER

6 tablespoons butter
3 tablespoons flour
2 cups hot water
Salt
Pepper

Melt 3 tablespoons butter. Add flour and cook, stirring constantly, until smooth. Add hot water. Season to taste with salt and pepper. Bring to boiling point and boil 5 minutes. Add remaining butter.

BROWN BUTTER SAUCE

½ cup butter
3 tablespoons white wine vinegar
1 tablespoon chopped parsley
Salt
Pepper

Heat butter slowly in a skillet until it browns. Add vinegar and parsley. Season to taste with salt and pepper. Chopped onion may be added if desired.

BUTTER SAUCE

½ cup butter, at room temperature
1½ teaspoons lemon juice
⅛ teaspoon salt
⅛ teaspoon pepper
1 teaspoon minced parsley

Cream the butter, gradually working in the lemon juice, salt, and pepper. When well blended, work in the parsley. With a spoon or melon baller, roll into balls about ¾" in diameter. Chill and place 1 butterball at the side of each serving of fish. The butter will melt when put on hot food.

LEMON BUTTER

4 tablespoons butter, melted
1 teaspoon lemon juice
⅛ teaspoon pepper

Blend all together. Serve hot. This is an excellent accompaniment to fish or chicken.

SAUCE PIQUANTE

2 tablespoons butter
2 onions
2 carrots
2 shallots
1 teaspoon fresh thyme, remove from the stems
2 tablespoons parsley, diced
2 cloves of garlic
2 tablespoons flour
1 cup beef stock (p. 33)
½ cup vinegar
Salt
Pepper

Melt butter in a skillet over medium heat. Roughly chop onions, carrots, and shallots. Add vegetables to the butter, cooking until the onions begin to soften. Add thyme, parsley, cloves, and garlic. Let this mixture cook until the carrot is soft and then add flour. Let it cook 5 minutes more and add stock and vinegar, stirring until thickened. Skim and strain through a sieve. Discard the vegetables and herbs. Season to taste with salt and pepper

BÉARNAISE SAUCE

2 tablespoons tarragon vinegar
2 tablespoons red wine or sherry vinegar
1 shallot, finely diced
1 tablespoon chopped tarragon
1 tablespoon chopped parsley
2 egg yolks
½ cup butter, melted and cooled
Salt
Cayenne

Combine vinegars, shallot, and herbs in a small saucepan. Bring to a boil over medium heat, cooking until the liquid is reduced to 1 tablespoon. Strain. Discard the shallot and herbs. Allow the liquid to cool. Add the egg yolks, and beat until the yolks are light yellow and thick, about 5 minutes. Move the egg yolks to a double boiler and add the butter. Cook over hot (but not boiling) water, stirring constantly, until thickened. Add salt and cayenne and cook in a double boiler over hot (but not boiling) water until thickened. Season to taste with salt and cayenne. Serve immediately. This sauce is a classic companion for steak.

BÉCHAMEL SAUCE

1½ cups basic chicken stock (p. 32)
1 slice onion
1 slice carrot
1 bay leaf
Sprig of parsley
6 peppercorns
¼ cup butter
¼ cup flour
1 cup hot milk
½ teaspoon salt
⅛ teaspoon pepper

Cook stock 20 minutes with onion, carrot, bay leaf, parsley, and peppercorns. Strain. Discard the vegetables and herbs. Melt butter. Add flour and gradually add hot stock and milk. Season to taste with salt and pepper. Equal parts of stock and milk may be used.

NEWBURG SAUCE

2 tablespoons butter
1 teaspoon onion, diced
Salt
Red pepper
2 tablespoons sherry vinegar
1 cup cream
3 egg yolks

Gently cook the butter, onion, salt, and pepper for 5 minutes in a skillet over medium heat. Add the vinegar and cook for 3 more minutes. In a separate bowl, add cream to egg yolks and beat well. Combine with the butter mixture and heat gently until the sauce bubbles but does not boil.

TOMATO SAUCE

4 tablespoons olive oil
2 tablespoons onion, chopped
3 cups canned crushed tomatoes
Salt
Pepper
1 tablespoon parsley, finely chopped

Heat olive oil in a skillet over medium-low heat. Add onions and cook until onions have become translucent. Add tomatoes and reduce heat to low. Simmer for 30 minutes, until the mixture has thickened a bit. Season to taste with salt and pepper, and garnish with parsley.

COCKTAIL SAUCE

6 tablespoons tomato paste
2 tablespoons horseradish
4 tablespoons lemon juice
1 teaspoon sugar
Celery salt
Tabasco sauce

Shake ingredients until well mixed, adding celery salt and Tabasco sauce to taste.

HORSERADISH SAUCE

3 tablespoons flour
2 tablespoons butter
1½ cups beef (p. 33) or fish stock (p. 35)
½ teaspoon salt
⅓ cup horseradish
½ teaspoon Worcestershire sauce
Few grains cayenne pepper

Cook flour in butter in a skillet over medium heat. Add stock and salt. Cook until the mixture is smooth and thick. Add remaining ingredients. Serve at once. Tomato juice may be substituted for part of the stock.

MUSHROOM SAUCE

4 tablespoons butter or other fat
2 tablespoons chopped onions
1 cup sliced fresh mushrooms
4 tablespoons flour
Salt
Pepper
2 cups beef stock (p. 33)

Melt butter in a skillet over medium heat. Add onions and mushrooms and brown slightly. Strain. Set onions and mushrooms aside. Add flour to butter. Season to taste with salt and pepper. Mix well. Add stock gradually, stirring constantly. Cook until smooth and thickened. Add onions and mushrooms. Simmer 2 minutes. Serve immediately. This sauce goes well with meat and vegetable dishes.

BARBECUE SAUCE

1 medium onion
2 tablespoons butter
½ cup water
¼ cup lemon juice
1 cup ketchup
3 tablespoons Worcestershire sauce
2 tablespoons cider vinegar
2 tablespoons brown sugar
½ tablespoon prepared mustard
½ cup chopped parsley
Salt
Cayenne pepper

Brown onion in butter over medium heat in a saucepan. Add remaining ingredients, stirring vigorously to combine. Season to taste with salt and cayenne. Reduce heat and simmer for 30 minutes. This makes an excellent marinade for chicken or pork. Simply mix the sauce with raw meat in an airtight container and refrigerate for several hours or overnight before cooking.

MUSTARD SAUCE

1 tablespoon butter
1½ teaspoons flour
1 teaspoon dry mustard
2 tablespoons white wine vinegar
1 tablespoon prepared mustard
1 teaspoon sugar
1 cup hot basic chicken stock (p. 32)
Salt
Pepper

Melt butter in a saucepan over medium heat. Add flour. Cook, stirring until smooth. Add dry mustard, vinegar, prepared mustard, sugar, and stock. Simmer over low heat for 10 minutes, stirring occasionally. Season to taste with salt and pepper.

TARTAR SAUCE

1 cup mayonnaise (p. 70)
1 tablespoon minced pickles
1 tablespoon minced onion
1 tablespoon minced capers
1 tablespoon minced parsley
Salt

Mix ingredients thoroughly and serve cold. Season to taste with salt. This is an excellent accompaniment to fish dishes.

CREOLE SAUCE

¼ cup melted butter
¾ cup minced onion
1 cup minced sweet pepper
3 garlic cloves, minced
2 cups canned crushed tomato
1 teaspoon salt
⅜ teaspoon pepper
⅛ teaspoon paprika

Place the butter, onion, pepper, and garlic in a saucepan. Cook, stirring frequently, over low heat for about 10 minutes or until onion and pepper are tender. Then add tomato and seasoning. Boil for 5 minutes over medium heat. Serve hot.

SWEET PEPPER SAUCE

2 tablespoons butter
1 clove garlic, minced
½ onion, diced
1 tablespoon flour
1 cup boiling water
1 cup chopped sweet peppers
½ teaspoon salt
⅛ teaspoon pepper
½ teaspoon minced parsley

Melt butter in a small saucepan. Add the garlic and onion. Cook over medium-low heat until onions are translucent. Stir in the flour, water, and sweet peppers. Season with salt, pepper, and parsley.

CRANBERRY SAUCE

2 cups water
1 quart fresh or frozen whole cranberries
1¾ cups sugar

Bring water to a boil. Add berries. Cover and cook over medium-low heat until outer skins have burst. Add sugar and let simmer 8 minutes. Pour into mold. Chill. For strained cranberry sauce, cook cranberries as above. Then strain through a sieve, scraping berries to force pulp through. Return strained liquid to stove. Add sugar. Simmer over low heat for 8 minutes. Pour into mold. Chill.

CRANBERRY ORANGE SAUCE

½ teaspoon dry mustard
⅔ cup basic chicken broth (p. 32), plus 2 tablespoons
½ cup strained cranberry sauce (above)
½ cup orange juice
Piece of orange peel
½ tablespoon flour
2 teaspoons butter
Dash of cayenne
Salt

Moisten the mustard with 2 tablespoons chicken broth. Make a smooth paste and add the rest of the broth, moving the mixture to a medium saucepan. Add remaining ingredients. Simmer over low heat for 15 minutes. Cook, stirring constantly, until sauce thickens slightly. Season to taste with salt and cayenne. Remove peel before serving.

STUFFINGS

BREAD STUFFING

¼ cup celery, cut fine
1 small onion, chopped
½ cup melted butter
2 cups breadcrumbs or small cubes of stale bread
Salt
Pepper

Sauté the celery and onion in fat until soft and add to bread-crumbs. Mix well. Season to taste with salt and pepper.

POULTRY STUFFING

1 small onion
3 tablespoons butter or fat
3 cups soft breadcrumbs or cubed stale bread
1 teaspoon salt
⅛ teaspoon pepper
1 teaspoon poultry seasoning

Slice onion and sauté in butter over medium heat until a delicate brown. Add breadcrumbs, salt, pepper, and poultry seasoning. Mix well.

ONION STUFFING

6 tablespoons butter or fat, at room temperature
1½ to 2 cups hot chicken stock (p. 32)
4 cups toasted bread cubes
¼ cup onion, finely chopped
1 tablespoon celery, chopped
1 tablespoon parsley, chopped
1 tablespoon sage
½ teaspoon salt
¼ teaspoon pepper

Melt 4 tablespoons butter in hot stock. Mix with remaining ingredients. Yield: Stuffing for 4 pound chicken.

CRACKER STUFFING

8 cups cracker crumbs
½ pound bacon or salt pork
1 medium onion
3 teaspoons poultry seasoning
1 teaspoon salt
3 to 4 cups hot chicken stock (p. 32), or as needed

Put crackers, bacon, and onion in a food processor and blend until onion and bacon are finely diced, and the mixture has a uniform consistency. Add seasoning and salt. At the same time add enough stock to make it moist and fluffy.

SAGE AND ONION STUFFING

2 medium onions
1½ cups stale breadcrumbs or cubed bread
2 tablespoons butter, melted
1 tablespoon chopped parsley
1 teaspoon powdered sage
Salt
Pepper

Peel onions. Remove to a saucepan and cover with salted water. Bring to a boil over medium-low heat. Cook until tender, about 20 minutes. Drain and chop. Add the rest of ingredients and mix well.

CORNBREAD STUFFING

6 tablespoons butter or fat
⅓ cup chopped onion
⅔ cup chopped celery
3 tablespoons chopped parsley
4 cups cornbread crumbs
¼ teaspoon thyme
¼ teaspoon salt
¼ teaspoon pepper

Melt butter in frying pan over low heat. Add onion, celery, and parsley. Sauté until onions are soft and lightly browned. Remove from heat and mix thoroughly with other ingredients.

MASHED POTATO STUFFING

2 cups mashed potatoes, highly seasoned (p. 244)
2 egg yolks
2 tablespoons melted fat
½ cup chopped boiled onions
¼ teaspoon sage
Salt
Pepper

Mix ingredients in order given. Season to taste.

SWEET POTATO STUFFING

2 cups hot mashed sweet potatoes (p. 259)
1 cup soft breadcrumbs
2 tablespoons chopped onion
2 tablespoons melted butter
Salt
Pepper

Combine sweet potatoes and crumbs. Season with onion and moisten with butter. Season to taste with salt and pepper. 1 cup of sausage meat (p. 402) makes a delicious addition to this stuffing.

OYSTER STUFFING

3 cups soft breadcrumbs
1 teaspoon salt
¼ teaspoon pepper
1 tablespoon diced onion
1 tablespoon chopped parsley
25 oysters
2 tablespoons butter or fat
¼ cup oyster liquid

Mix crumbs, salt, pepper, onions, and parsley. Clean oysters, removing any dirt or particles. Add to the crumbs Reserve ¼ cup of the liquid from the shells; heat in a saucepan over low heat until it almost reaches a boil. Add the butter to the saucepan, stirring until butter melts. Moisten stuffing with this mixture.

CHESTNUT STUFFING

3 cups soft breadcrumbs
1 teaspoon salt
¼ teaspoon pepper
3 tablespoons butter or fat
¼ cup hot milk
2 cups boiled chestnuts (p. 541)

Mix breadcrumbs, salt, and pepper. Moisten with butter, melted in the hot milk. Chop the chestnuts rather fine and add to the breadcrumb mixture. Mix thoroughly.

SPINACH STUFFING

¼ cup butter
1½ cups drained boiled spinach (p. 255)
2 cups soft fine breadcrumbs
2 tablespoons finely diced onion
2 tablespoons lemon juice
Salt
Pepper

Melt the butter. Combine with the rest of the ingredients. Season to taste with salt and pepper.

RICE STUFFING

1½ tablespoons onion, chopped
1 tablespoon olive oil
¾ cup uncooked rice
2 cups chicken stock (p. 32)
1 teaspoon salt
½ teaspoon poultry seasoning

Cook onion in oil until tender. Add rice and cook until the rice is a little golden. Then add soup stock, salt, and poultry seasoning. Cover and bring to a boil. Reduce heat to low and cook for 20 minutes, until rice is tender.

CELERY STUFFING

2 cups toast crumbs
¼ cup butter
1 cup diced celery
1 small onion, minced
½ teaspoon salt
⅛ teaspoon pepper
¼ teaspoon sage
2 to 4 tablespoons basic chicken stock (p. 32)

Toast bread and crumble into small pieces. Melt butter in a skillet over medium heat. Add celery and onion, and cook for a few minutes, until onion begins to soften. Add to crumbs together with seasonings. Add stock and mix thoroughly.

APPLE AND BACON STUFFING

¼ cup diced bacon
½ cup chopped celery
½ cup chopped onion
¼ cup chopped parsley
5 tart apples, diced
½ cup sugar
2 cups fine or dry breadcrumbs

Fry the bacon in a skillet over medium heat until crisp. Remove from the skillet and dice. Cook the celery, onion, and parsley in the bacon fat for a few minutes, until the onions are tender. Remove them, and set aside. Put the apples into the skillet, sprinkle with the sugar, cover, and cook over low heat until tender, about 15 minutes. Remove the lid and continue to cook until the juice evaporates and the pieces of apples are candied. Add the other ingredients to the apples.

RICE AND APRICOT STUFFING

1 small onion, chopped
1 sprig parsley, chopped
1 cup chopped celery and tops
3 tablespoons butter
3 cups boiled rice
½ teaspoon savory seasoning
Salt
¼ pound dried apricots

Fry the onion, parsley, and celery in butter a few minutes. Add rice and other seasonings. Wash and dry the apricots. Then cut them into strips with scissors. Mix with the rice and seasonings.

CELERY AND OLIVE STUFFING

3 cups soft breadcrumbs
1 cup chopped celery
½ cup chopped olives
1 teaspoon salt
¼ teaspoon pepper
⅛ teaspoon paprika
1 tablespoon minced onion
3 tablespoons butter or fat
½ cup hot chicken stock (p. 32)

Mix breadcrumbs, celery, olives, salt, pepper, paprika, and onion. Moisten with butter, melted in hot stock. Mix thoroughly.

LEMON STUFFING

⅓ cup melted butter
1½ cups stale breadcrumbs
2 teaspoons minced parsley
Grated zest of 1 lemon
¾ teaspoon salt
½ teaspoon pepper
2 eggs
Milk

Pour the butter over the crumbs. Add the various seasonings and flavorings stir together well. Beat the eggs and add. Moisten with milk if necessary.

ORANGE STUFFING FOR DUCK

3 cups stale bread cubes, toasted
½ cup hot chicken stock (p. 32)
2 cups diced celery
1 beaten egg
¼ cup melted butter
⅓ cup orange juice
2 teaspoons grated orange zest
¼ teaspoon poultry seasoning
½ teaspoon salt
Dash of pepper

Soften bread cubes in hot stock for 15 minutes. Add remaining ingredients. Combine lightly. Stuff duck.

APRICOT STUFFING

2½ cups fresh apricots.
2 cups soft breadcrumbs
2 cups cracker crumbs
¼ cup melted butter
½ cup basic chicken stock (p. 32)
¼ cup minced celery
½ cup shredded almonds
1½ teaspoons salt
Dash of pepper

Cut apricots in half. Remove the pits and cut into small pieces.
Add the remaining ingredients and stir well.

CRANBERRY STUFFING

1 cup fresh or frozen cranberries, chopped
¼ cup sugar
¼ cup chopped celery
2 tablespoons chopped parsley
4 tablespoons butter
4 cups stale breadcrumbs
½ teaspoon sweet marjoram
1 teaspoon salt

Combine cranberries and sugar. Cook celery and parsley in
butter over low heat until celery is tender. Blend together.

NUT STUFFING FOR POULTRY

1 tablespoon finely chopped onion
2 or 3 sprigs parsley, chopped
½ cup diced celery
3 tablespoons melted butter or fat
2 ½ cups soft breadcrumbs
½ teaspoon salt
½ teaspoon pepper
½ to 1 cup chopped walnuts or pecans

Cook the onion, parsley, and celery in the butter over low heat for 5 minutes, or until the onions are tender. Add the breadcrumbs and seasonings. Stir until well mixed and hot. Add the nuts just before stuffing the fowl.

PEANUT STUFFING

3 cups soft breadcrumbs
¾ cup chopped peanuts
1 tablespoon minced onion
1 teaspoon salt
⅛ teaspoon pepper
1 tablespoon chopped parsley
2 tablespoons butter or fat
½ cup chicken stock (p. 32)

Mix breadcrumbs and peanuts. Add onion, salt, pepper, and parsley. Moisten with butter, melted in hot stock. Mix thoroughly.

PECAN STUFFING FOR TURKEY

1½ cups hot milk
½ cup melted butter
2 cups breadcrumbs
½ cup raisins
½ cup chopped pecans
2 tablespoons onion, chopped
2 eggs, slightly beaten
1 teaspoon sage
½ teaspoon salt
¼ teaspoon black pepper

Pour hot milk and butter over breadcrumbs. Add all of the other ingredients and mix well.

BUTTERNUT STUFFING

4 cups breadcrumbs
1½ teaspoons poultry seasoning
1½ cups butternuts
1 egg, beaten
½ cup cream
4 cups hot mashed potatoes (p. 244)
1 teaspoon salt
½ teaspoon pepper

Mix crumbs with poultry seasoning and nuts. Mix egg with cream and add to potatoes. Add seasonings and beat. Put two mixtures together. Stir to combine.

TOASTED ALMOND STUFFING

1 cup hot milk
½ cup melted butter
2 eggs, slightly beaten
4 cups breadcrumbs
4 cups cracker crumbs
1 tablespoon minced onion
1 cup chopped celery
1 teaspoon poultry seasoning
½ teaspoon salt
½ teaspoon pepper
1½ cups chopped toasted almonds

Pour the hot milk, melted butter, and the 2 eggs over the bread and cracker crumbs. Let stand 10 minutes. Add onions, chopped celery, poultry seasoning, salt, pepper, and chopped almonds.

YORKSHIRE PUDDING

1 cup flour
½ teaspoon salt
1 cup milk
2 eggs, separated
1 tablespoon butter, melted and cooled
Drippings from roast beef (p. 353)

Preheat oven to 400°F. Mix and sift flour and salt. In a separate bowl, beat milk, egg yolks, and butter together. Beat in the flour mixture. Stiffly beat the egg whites and gently fold into the batter. Cover the bottom of an earthenware-baking dish with drippings from roast beef. Pour the batter into the baking dish. Bake for 20 minutes. Baste with drippings from the roast after it is well risen. Cut in squares and serve on platter with the roast.

CROUTONS

Stale bread
Oil for frying
Salt
Pepper

Cut stale bread in thick slices. Remove the crust and cut bread in small cubes. Drop in deep hot oil (375°F) and fry until a delicate brown. Remove with a skimmer and drain on paper towels. Season to taste with salt and pepper. Serve a few croutons in each portion of soup.

CINNAMON ORANGE SLICES

1½ cups sugar
½ cup water
Juice of 1 lemon
2 cinnamon sticks
3 oranges

Make syrup of sugar, water, juice, and cinnamon. Wash oranges and cut in thick slices. Place in hot syrup and boil gently, without covering until rind is clear. Chill in syrup overnight before serving as a meat garnish.

PIES
AND
TARTS

A tender, flaky pie crust is the mark of an excellent baker. The perfect crust doesn't happen by accident. It takes practice and patience. When making a crust, keep the following in mind.

The butter (or fat) and liquid used in the crust should be ice cold. Room temperature butter or water will incorporate into the dough too completely, releasing gluten and producing a tougher crust. The ideal crust will have visible flecks of butter in it. These little leaves of butter are important for creating a flaky crust, once the dough has been put in the oven.

Handling the dough is just as important as the temperature of the ingredients. The dough should be mixed quickly, using as little liquid as possible, in order to create a dough that will just stick together. Cutting the butter in with a knife or pulsing it in a food processor helps to "cut" the ingredients in, rather than "mixing" them. If using a food processor, do not over mix. Pulse judiciously, adding a tiny amount of liquid at a time. As soon as the dough forms a ball, it can be removed to the refrigerator to rest. A perfectly uniform crust is not desirable, but there should not be giant lumps of unmixed flour, either. The goal is a happy medium, with little bits of butter here and there, and a dough that stays together.

The dough must rest for at least an hour before being rolled out. This allows the butter to harden again. Rolling it out immediately would produce a tough crust.

When rolling the dough out, remember to use strong, swift movements, and as little flour as possible. The more the dough is poked and prodded, the more flakiness is sacrificed.

All of the pastry recipes in this chapter call for butter. Lard, vegetable shortening, goose fat, and many other fats can be used in place of butter. Butter produces a richer flavor, while lard and vegetable shortening produce a flakier crust. It is a matter of personal preference.

BASIC PASTRY

> 2 cups flour
> ¾ teaspoon salt
> ⅔ cup butter or lard, cold
> Up to 2 tablespoons ice water or cider vinegar
> (as little as possible)

Mix and sift flour and salt. Cut in the butter with a knife, or pulse in a food processor. Add only water enough to hold the ingredients together. Do not knead. Divide dough in 2 parts and wrap in saran wrap. Chill for at least 1 hour. Thinly roll out on a slightly floured board. Line a pie pan with half the pastry. Pinch pastry with the fingers to make a fancy edge and prick bottom and sides with a fork. Bake at 425°F for 10 to 15 minutes. For a 2 crust pie, line pie pan with pastry, put in a filling, cover with top crust and bake as directed for pies. If a less rich pastry is desired, use only ½ cup butter. Yield: 2 pastry shells. Flaky pastry (p. 446) may be used whenever this is called for.

FLAKY PASTRY

2 cups flour
1 teaspoon salt
⅔ cup butter, cold
Up to 2 tablespoons ice water or cider vinegar

Mix and sift flour and salt. Cut in 2 tablespoons of the butter with a knife, or pulse in a food processor until the butter is in pea-sized pieces. Add enough water to make a stiff dough. Roll out in an oblong piece on a slightly floured board and dot with bits of butter, using ⅓ the remaining quantity. Fold over ends to the center and fold again to make 4 layers. Press ends together and roll out. Dot again with butter, fold and roll. Repeat this process a third time. Chill thoroughly. This pastry may be used whenever a basic pastry (p. 445) is called for.

PUFF PASTE

2 cups flour
1½ teaspoons salt
1 cup butter
Up to 2 tablespoons ice water or cider vinegar

Mix and sift flour and salt. Cut in 2 tablespoons butter with a knife, or pulse in a food processor until the butter is in pea-sized pieces. Add just enough water to bind. Knead 5 minutes, or pulse in a food processor until it forms a ball. Cover. Chill. Roll on slightly floured board to ¼" thickness in rectangular shape with square corners. Slightly soften remaining butter and lay out in a flat circular shape in the center of ½ the dough. Fold other half over it. Press edges tightly together to hold in air. Fold right side over and left side under enclosed butter. Chill. Roll out again in rectangular shape. Fold ends toward center making 3 layers. Chill. Repeat this process 4 times. Chill. Paste should be made at least 24 hours before cooking and should be kept ice cold.

HOT WATER PASTRY

   ½ cup butter
   ¼ cup boiling water
   1½ cups flour
   ¾ teaspoon salt
   ¼ teaspoon baking powder

Cream butter in ¼ cup boiling water. Mix and sift flour, salt, and baking powder. Add dry mixture gradually to butter, blending well. Form into a ball and store in a refrigerator until ready to use. Yield: 1 pastry shell.

FRITTER BATTER

   2 cups sifted flour
   3 teaspoons baking powder
   1 teaspoon salt
   2 tablespoons sugar
   2 eggs, beaten
   1 cup milk
   1 tablespoon butter, melted

Sift the dry ingredients together. Combine the beaten eggs, milk, and melted butter. Add gradually to the dry ingredients, stirring only until the batter is smooth.

TART SHELLS

Preheat oven to 425°F. Roll out puff paste (p. 446) to ⅛" thickness. Fit over inverted pie or muffin tins. Prick with a fork. Bake for 15 to 20 minutes.

APPLE PIE

Basic Pastry (p. 445)
6 cups peeled, cored apples, sliced ¼" thick
⅔ cup sugar
¼ teaspoon nutmeg
⅛ teaspoon salt
¼ teaspoon cinnamon
1 teaspoon lemon juice
2 teaspoons butter

Preheat oven to 425°F. Lightly roll half of the pie crust to ⅛" thickness and about 2½" larger than a 9" pie plate. Fold it in half and fit it into the pie plate. In rolling the pie crust use only enough flour to prevent sticking, handling the dough very lightly and never turning it. Press the pie crust lightly to fit the pie pan and trim even with the edge of the pan, using a knife. Fill the pie shell with the apples. Mix sugar, nutmeg, salt, cinnamon, and lemon juice. Sprinkle over apples and dot with the butter. Moisten the edge of the crust with cold water. Roll the other half of the pie crust to ⅛" thickness and about 1" larger than the diameter of the plate. Fold this in half and make 3 slits, each ½" in length, in the center of the folded side. These will act as vents when the pie bakes. Adjust over the filling, then carefully fold the edge of the upper crust under the lower crust all the way around. Finish by pressing the edges together with a fork dipped in flour. If a glazed surface is desired, brush top of pie with milk, cream or melted butter, or a slightly beaten egg white. Bake for 40 minutes.

ONE-CRUST APPLE PIE, I

4 large tart apples
½ cup sugar
Few grains nutmeg
½ teaspoon cinnamon
1 tablespoon butter
Basic pastry (p. 445)
Whipped cream, sweetened

Preheat oven to 425°F. Wash, peel, and core apples. Cut in thin slices. Put them in the bottom of pie pan and sprinkle with sugar, nutmeg, and cinnamon. Dot with small bits of butter. Roll basic pastry thin and fit over the apples. Trim off edge of the pastry and press with fingers or fork to make a fancy edge. Prick top to allow steam to escape. Bake for 10 minutes. Reduce heat to 325°F and bake 20 minutes. Cool. Turn out upside down on a serving dish. Cover with whipped cream.

ONE-CRUST APPLE PIE, II

4 large tart apples
Basic pastry (p. 445)
1 cup sugar
1 tablespoon butter
¼ teaspoon nutmeg
⅛ teaspoon cinnamon

Preheat oven to 425°F. Wash, peel, and cut apples in quarters. Remove the cores. Roll basic pastry ⅛" thick. Line a pie pan with basic pastry, pinch with fingers to make a fancy edge, and arrange apples in it. Pour the sugar over them and dot with small bits of butter. Sprinkle with nutmeg and cinnamon. Bake for 10 minutes. Reduce heat to 325°F and bake for 20 minutes more.

BERRY PIE

3 cups berries
1 cup sugar
2 tablespoons cornstarch or 4 tablespoons flour
⅛ teaspoon salt
1 tablespoon lemon juice for blueberry pie
Basic pastry (p. 445)
1 tablespoon butter

Preheat oven to 425°F. Mix fruit with combined sugar, corn-starch or flour, salt, and if blueberries, lemon juice. Roll pas-try out to ⅛" thickness. Line pie pan with pastry. Fill with berries and dot with butter. Moisten pastry edge and put top pie crust in place. The upper crust should be cut in several places so that steam can escape. Crimp edge and bake for about 10 minutes, then reduce the oven temperature to 325°F for about 30 minutes to finish baking.

BLUEBERRY PIE

Follow recipe for apple pie (p. 448), using blueberries, flour or quick-cooking tapioca, and the amounts of spice, sugar, salt, lemon juice, and butter given in apple pie recipe. More sugar may be added if fruit is tart. Blackberry, plum, grape, rhubarb or peach pie may be made in the same way.

CHERRY PIE

Basic pastry (p. 445)
2½ cups canned or stewed cherries (p. 196)
Sugar to taste

Preheat oven to 425°F. Roll basic pastry out to ⅛" thickness. Line pie pan with pastry. Drain cherries and place them on top of the pastry. Sprinkle with sugar to taste. Pour over syrup from cherries. Top with layer of pastry. Wet edges of pastry. Press together and trim. Cut the crust in several places so that steam can escape. Bake for 10 minutes. Reduce heat to 325°F and bake 20 minutes longer.

LATTICE CHERRY PIE

Top cherry pie (above) with ⅜" wide strips of basic pastry (p. 445), placed crisscross, instead of with a solid crust. Moisten edge of lower crust and ends of strips and place strip of dough around edge to hold strips in place.

CHESS PIE

Puff paste (p. 446)
⅓ cup butter
½ cup sugar
3 egg yolks, well beaten
½ teaspoon vanilla
Meringue (p. 633)

Preheat oven to 350°F. Roll puff paste out to ¼" thickness on a lightly floured board. Line a pie plate with puff paste. Chill. Cream butter and sugar. Add yolks and vanilla. Turn into pie plate. Bake until very light, about 30 minutes. Top with meringue. Bake again for 12 minutes. Cut in pieces to serve while hot.

CHOCOLATE PIE

Basic pastry (p. 445)
2 ounces dark chocolate
1 cup sugar
2 tablespoons flour
3 well-beaten eggs
½ cup chopped nuts, optional
1 cup cream, whipped

Preheat oven to 375°F. Roll out pastry to ⅛" thickness on a lightly floured board. Line a pie tin with pastry. Pinch edge with fingers to make fancy. Shave chocolate and melt in a double boiler over hot water. Add sugar, flour, and chocolate to eggs. Beat thoroughly. Turn into pie tin. Bake for 20 minutes or until set. Chill. Sprinkle with nuts, if desired. Top with whipped cream. Garnish, if desired with half cherries and whole nuts.

CRANBERRY DREAM PIE

1¾ cups sugar
¾ cup water
4 cups fresh cranberries
2 tablespoons flour
¼ teaspoon salt
3 eggs, separated
1 teaspoon vanilla
2 teaspoons butter
Baked basic pastry shell (p. 445)
3 tablespoons powdered sugar

Preheat oven to 350°F. Cook sugar and water to a syrup, about 170°F. Add cranberries and cook until they stop popping, about 5 minutes. Cool slightly. Mix flour, salt, and egg yolks until smooth. Stir in 3 tablespoons of the juice of the cooked cranberries. Add to berries and simmer several minutes. Add the vanilla and butter. Cool. Roll the pastry out to ⅛" thickness on a slightly floured board. Line a pie tin with the pastry. Pour the cranberry mixture into the pie shell. Cover with meringue made by beating the stiffly beaten egg whites and the powdered sugar together. Bake for 15 minutes.

EGG NOG PIE

1 tablespoon granulated unflavored gelatin
¼ cup cold water
1 cup boiling water
2 eggs, well beaten
¼ teaspoon salt
3 tablespoons powdered sugar
1 cup heavy whipped cream
2 tablespoons whisky or 1 teaspoon vanilla
Baked basic pastry shell (p. 445)
Dash of nutmeg (optional)

Soften gelatin in cold water. Dissolve in boiling water. Chill until slightly thickened. Beat with hand mixer until fluffy. Beat eggs well. Add salt. Beat in sugar. Fold into gelatin. Fold in cream. Add whisky or vanilla. Chill again until thickened. Turn in to baked shell and chill until firm at least 1 hour. Garnish with additional whipped cream and nutmeg if desired.

HUCKLEBERRY PIE

Substitute huckleberries for blueberries in recipe for blueberry pie (p. 450).

JELLY PIE

3 tablespoons flour
1 cup sugar
1 tablespoon melted butter
½ cup jelly of your choice
2 cups warm water
2 beaten eggs
1 baked basic pastry shell (p. 445)

Preheat oven to 350°F. Mix and sift flour and sugar. Add butter. Mix jelly and warm water and add to flour-sugar mixture. Stir mixture into eggs. Turn into baked pastry shell. Bake for 15 minutes.

MOLASSES PIE

1 cup molasses
1 tablespoon flour
1 lemon
Basic pastry (p. 445)

Preheat oven to 425°F. Beat molasses and flour together. Zest and squeeze lemon, and add juice, pulp, and zest to molasses. Line a pie pan with pastry. Turn in mixture. Make a top crust with layer of pastry. Wet edges of pastry with water. Press together and trim. Bake for 10 minutes. Reduce heat and continue baking at 325°F for 20 minutes.

PEACH PIE

8 peaches
⅓ cup water
½ cup sugar, or to taste
Basic pastry (p. 445)
1 tablespoon butter

Preheat oven to 425°F. Peel 8 peaches and slice thin. Simmer in water 10 minutes. Add sugar to taste. Roll pastry out to ⅛" thickness on a lightly floured board. Line a pie pan with pastry and pour the filling into it. Dot with small bits of butter. Moisten edge of pastry, cover with a top crust, and press edges together. Prick top with a fork to allow steam to escape. Bake for 10 minutes. Reduce heat to 350°F and bake 15 to 20 minutes.

PEACH PIE SUPREME

1 package orange-flavored gelatin
1½ cups hot peach juice
2½ cups canned sliced peaches, drained
Baked basic pastry shell (p. 445)

Dissolve gelatin in hot peach juice and water. Add peaches. Chill. When slightly thickened, turn into cold baked pie shell. Chill until firm. Serve with whipped cream, if desired.

PECAN PIE

3 eggs
½ cup sugar
1 cup corn syrup
⅛ teaspoon salt
1 teaspoon vanilla
¼ cup butter, melted
Basic pastry (p. 445)
1 cup pecans

Preheat oven to 350°F. Beat eggs. Add sugar, syrup, salt, vanilla, and butter. Roll pastry out to ⅛" thickness on a lightly floured board. Line pie pan with plain pastry. Put in pecans in a layer. Add mixture. Bake for 50 to 60 minutes. The nuts will rise to top and form a crusted layer.

PUMPKIN PIE

Basic pastry (p. 445)
2 cups canned mashed pumpkin
1 cup milk
3 eggs, separated
½ cup sugar
1¼ teaspoons cinnamon
¼ teaspoon cloves
¼ teaspoon ginger
¼ teaspoon nutmeg
1 teaspoon salt

Preheat oven to 450°F. Roll out pastry to ⅛" thick on a lightly floured board. Line a pie pan with plain pastry and pinch with fingers to make a fancy edge. Mix the pumpkin and milk together. Add the egg yolks. Add the sugar mixed with the cinnamon, cloves, ginger, nutmeg, and salt. Mix well. Stiffly beat the egg whites. Fold them into the pumpkin mixture. Turn into pie pan. Bake for 10 minutes, reduce heat to 375°F, and bake 20 minutes longer or until the filling is firm. Serve with whipped cream, if desired.

RHUBARB PIE

> 3 cups rhubarb
> Basic pastry (p. 445)
> 1 cup sugar
> 2 tablespoons flour
> ⅛ teaspoon salt
> 2 eggs, beaten

Preheat oven to 425°F. Peel rhubarb and cut in ½" pieces before measuring. Roll out pastry to ⅛" thickness on a lightly floured board. Line a pie pan with plain pastry. Mix sugar, flour, salt, and eggs. Add to the rhubarb and turn into pie pan. Moisten edge of pastry with water. Cover with top crust. Press edges together and trim. Gash top to let steam escape. Bake for 10 minutes. Reduce heat and continue baking at 325°F for 30 minutes.

FRESH STRAWBERRY PIE

> 6 cups ripe strawberries
> ¼ cup powdered sugar, more if desired
> Baked basic pastry shell (p. 445)
> Whipped cream

Wash and stem ripe strawberries. Roll them in powdered sugar and fill pastry shell. Top with whipped cream. Chill.

SWEET POTATO PECAN PIE

¼ cup butter, at room temperature
½ cup brown sugar
1 cup mashed boiled sweet potatoes
3 eggs
⅓ cup corn syrup
⅓ cup milk
½ teaspoon salt
1 teaspoon vanilla
1 cup broken pecans
Basic pastry (p. 445)

Preheat oven to 425°F. Cream together the butter and sugar. Add sweet potatoes and slightly beaten eggs. Beat well. Combine with syrup, milk, salt, vanilla, and pecans. Roll pastry out to ⅛" thickness on a lightly floured board. Line pie pan with plain pastry. Turn mixture into pan. Bake for 10 minutes. Reduce heat to 325°F and continue baking 35 to 45 minutes longer. Serve with whipped cream, if desired.

SWEET POTATO PIE

Omit pecans from sweet potato pecan pie (above) and increase amount of mashed sweet potato to 1½ cups.

WASHINGTON PIE

⅓ cup butter, at room temperature
1 cup sugar
2 eggs, well beaten
1¾ cups flour
2 teaspoons baking powder
½ teaspoon salt
½ cup milk
½ teaspoon vanilla
½ cup raspberry jam
2 tablespoons powdered sugar

Preheat oven to 375°F. Cream butter. Add half the sugar gradually. Beat until light. Add remaining sugar to eggs and beat. Combine mixtures. Mix and sift flour, baking powder, and salt and add alternately with milk to first mixture. Beat thoroughly and add vanilla. Bake in buttered 8" layer cake tins for 20 to 30 minutes. Use raspberry jam between layers and sprinkle top with powdered sugar.

BLACKBERRY MERINGUE PIE

⅔ cup sugar, plus 4 tablespoons
2 tablespoons cornstarch
¼ teaspoon salt
¼ teaspoon cinnamon
½ cup water
2 tablespoons lemon juice
1 tablespoon butter
2½ cups canned or stewed blackberries (see stewed
  berries, p. 195)
Baked basic pastry shell (p. 445)
2 egg whites

Preheat oven to 350°F. Combine the ⅔ cup sugar, cornstarch, salt, and cinnamon with water. Cook in a double boiler over medium heat until smooth and thick, stirring constantly. Continue cooking for 10 minutes. Remove from heat and add the lemon juice, butter, and berries. Pour into the pastry shell. Beat the egg whites until stiff. Add the remaining sugar gradually and beat until it will stand in peaks. Spread over pie and bake for about 15 minutes or until the meringue is well browned. Blueberries, raspberries, strawberries, gooseberries or loganberries may be substituted for blackberries.

LEMON MERINGUE PIE

1½ tablespoons butter
½ cup flour
1 cup sugar
¼ teaspoon salt
2 cups water
2 eggs, separated
Juice and zest of 1 lemon
Baked basic pastry shell (p. 445)
2 tablespoons powdered sugar

Preheat oven to 325°F. Melt butter. Add flour, sugar, salt, water, and egg yolks. Mix well. Cook in a double boiler over hot water until thick, stirring constantly. Remove from heat, add lemon juice and zest, and mix well. Pour into the baked pie shell. Cover top with meringue (p. 633) made by beating the powdered sugar into stiffly beaten egg whites. Bake until a delicate brown, about 15 minutes. The filling may also be used for lemon tarts (p. 473).

BANANA FRUIT CHIFFON PIE

1 cup mashed ripe bananas
2 tablespoons lemon juice
½ cup orange juice
¼ teaspoon grated lemon zest
¼ teaspoon grated orange zest
⅓ teaspoon salt
½ cup granulated sugar
3 eggs, separated
1 tablespoon unflavored gelatin
⅓ cup cold water
Baked basic pastry shell (p. 445)

Mix together the bananas, juices, zests, salt, sugar, and egg yolks. Cook in a double boiler until mixture has thickened. Stir in the gelatin which has been soaked for 5 minutes in cold water and stir until dissolved. Cool. Stiffly beat the egg whites. Gently fold in the whites and pour into pie shell. Chill until firm.

CHOCOLATE CHIFFON PIE

¾ cup sugar, divided
4 eggs, separated
⅓ cup milk
2 ounces dark chocolate
½ tablespoon gelatin
1 tablespoon cold water
1 teaspoon vanilla
¼ teaspoon salt
Baked basic pastry shell (p. 445)

Beat 6 tablespoons sugar into egg yolks. Cook in a double boiler, stirring constantly, until thickened. Bring milk to boiling point and shave in chocolate. Blend thoroughly.

Soak gelatin in 1 tablespoon cold water for 5 minutes. Dissolve in milk-chocolate mixture. Add vanilla and salt and pour milk mixture into egg mixture. Mix well and chill. Beat egg whites with remaining sugar until stiff. Fold gently into chilled chocolate mixture. Turn into pastry shell. Chill.

LEMON CHIFFON PIE

½ tablespoon gelatin
2 tablespoons cold water
4 eggs, separated
½ teaspoon salt
1 cup sugar, divided
Juice and zest of 1 lemon
Baked basic pastry shell (p. 445)
1 cup cream, whipped

Soak gelatin in 2 tablespoons cold water 5 minutes. Dissolve in a double boiler over hot water. Mix yolks, salt, ½ cup sugar, lemon juice, and zest in top of double boiler. Cook, stirring constantly, until thick. Add gelatin and cook 1 minute longer. Beat egg whites to peaks with remaining sugar. Gently fold liquid mixture into egg whites. Turn into baked pastry shell. Top with whipped cream. Cool.

LIME CHIFFON PIE

Substitute lime juice and zest for lemon juice and zest in recipe for lemon chiffon pie (above).

ORANGE CHIFFON PIE

Add the juice of 1 orange and 1 tablespoon grated orange zest to recipe for lemon chiffon pie (p. 465), omitting lemon zest and reducing lemon juice to 1 tablespoon.

PUMPKIN CHIFFON PIE

    1 tablespoon unflavored gelatin
    ¼ cup water
    ½ cup milk
    1 cup sugar, divided
    1¼ cups mashed canned pumpkin
    3 eggs, separated
    ½ teaspoon salt
    ½ teaspoon nutmeg
    ½ teaspoon cinnamon
    ½ teaspoon ground ginger
    Baked basic pastry shell, baked according to the
        directions (p. 445)

Soak the gelatin in water for 5 minutes. Combine milk, ½ cup sugar, pumpkin, yolks, and spices and cook over boiling water until thick. Remove from stove and add gelatin. When this begins to set up add stiffly beaten egg whites. Add remaining sugar to egg whites, and gently fold into the pumpkin mixture. Pour into baked pie shell and place in refrigerator.

STRAWBERRY CHIFFON PIE

1½ tablespoons unflavored gelatin
¼ cup cold water
½ cup sugar
1 cup crushed strawberries
⅛ teaspoon salt
1 egg white, stiffly beaten
1 cup cream, whipped
Baked basic pastry shell (p. 445)

Soak gelatin in cold water 5 minutes. Dissolve in a double boiler over hot water. Sprinkle sugar on berries and let stand until sugar dissolves. Add gelatin and salt, mixing well. Chill. When congealing starts, beat until light with a hand mixer. Fold in egg white and whipped cream. Pile into baked shell. Chill.

CREAM PIE

1 tablespoon butter
¼ cup flour
⅔ cup sugar
¼ teaspoon salt
2 cups whole milk
2 eggs, separated
1 teaspoon vanilla
Baked basic pastry shell (p. 445)
2 tablespoons powdered sugar

Preheat oven to 325°F. Melt butter. Add flour, sugar, salt, milk, and egg yolks and cook in a double boiler over hot water until thick, stirring constantly. Add vanilla. Pour into a pie shell. Cover top with a meringue made by beating the powdered sugar into stiffly beaten egg whites. Bake for 15 minutes, or until a delicate brown.

ALMOND CREAM PIE

Add ½ cup chopped almonds and ½ cup chopped walnuts to recipe for cream pie (p. 467).

BANANA CREAM PIE

Make cream pie (p. 467), filling shell with alternate layers of sliced bananas and filling.

BOSTON CREAM PIE

    3 tablespoons sugar
    2 cups milk
    2 tablespoons cornstarch
    1 beaten egg
    1 tablespoon vanilla
    2 Washington pie layer cakes (p. 461)
    1 tablespoon powdered sugar

Dissolve sugar in 1½ cups milk. Combine cornstarch with remaining milk. Combine mixtures. Add egg. Cook slowly, stirring constantly, until thick. Add vanilla. Spread filling between layers of cake. Sprinkle powdered sugar on top.

CHOCOLATE CREAM PIE

2 tablespoons butter
6 tablespoons flour
1½ cups milk
2 ounces dark chocolate, shaved
¾ cup sugar
¼ teaspoon salt
2 eggs, separated
1 teaspoon vanilla
Baked basic pastry shell (p. 445)
2 tablespoons powdered sugar

Preheat oven to 325°F. Melt butter and add flour, milk, chocolate, sugar, and salt. Heat slowly to boiling point, stirring constantly, until thick and smooth. Remove from heat. Add egg yolks and vanilla. Turn into pastry shell. Beat powdered sugar into egg whites until stiff peaks form. Top pie with meringue. Bake until a delicate brown, about 15 minutes. Whipped cream may be substituted for meringue, but it should be added after the pie has cooled. ½ cup chopped pecans may be added to filling just before turning into pastry shell.

COCONUT CREAM PIE

⅓ cup sugar
2 tablespoons cornstarch
¼ teaspoon salt
3 egg yolks
1½ cups scalded milk (brought to a boil and slightly
    cooled)
1 tablespoon butter
½ cup shredded coconut
½ teaspoon vanilla
Baked basic pastry crust (p. 445)

Preheat oven to 325°F. Add sugar, cornstarch, and salt to egg yolks. Add scalded milk, and cook in a double boiler, stirring until thickened. Add the butter, coconut and vanilla. Pour into a pie tin, lined with basic pastry. Bake for 15 minutes, or until the filling has set. The pie may be covered with meringue (p. 633).

VANILLA CREAM PIE

Omit chocolate from recipe for chocolate cream pie (p. 469) and increase vanilla to 2 teaspoons.

CUSTARD PIE

Basic pastry (p. 445)
3 eggs, slightly beaten
¾ cup granulated sugar
½ teaspoon salt
3 cups whole milk
1 teaspoon vanilla

Preheat oven to 450°F. Roll the pie crust to ⅛" thickness and 2" larger than the diameter of the plate. Line a 9" pie plate with the pie crust, fitting it loosely. Fold back the edge of the pie crust all the way round and bring this double fold to an upright position. Flute the double fold of pie crust in the following manner: Place the floured tip or knuckle of the index finger of the right hand against the fold on the inside of the pie crust rim. Pinch gently, then remove the fingers and continue this same fluting motion around the entire rim of the pie. In a separate bowl, combine the eggs, sugar, and salt. Add the milk and vanilla and pour in the pastry shell. Bake for 30 to 40 minutes or until a silver knife inserted in the center comes out clean.

CARAMEL CUSTARD PIE

Melt and brown sugar in frying pan before adding in recipe for custard pie (above).

COCONUT CUSTARD PIE

Add ¼ cup shredded coconut to custard mixture in recipe for custard pie (above).

LEMON CUSTARD PIE

Add the grated zest of 2 lemons to recipe for custard pie (p. 471) and omit vanilla.

FRIED PIES

Follow recipe for basic pastry (p. 445), using only ½ cup butter. Roll out pastry to ⅛" thickness. Cut in large circles, 3½" to 4" across. Put a tablespoon of applesauce (p. 190) in center of pastry. Moisten edges with cold water. Fold over so as to make a semi-circle. Press edges together with tines of a fork. Fry in deep hot fat (375°F) until a delicate brown. Drain on unglazed paper. Sprinkle with powdered sugar and serve warm.

APPLE TARTS

Fill baked tart shells (p. 448) with applesauce (p. 190). Top with whipped cream and sprinkle lightly with cinnamon, nutmeg, chopped nuts or candied ginger.

CHERRY TARTS

> 2½ cups canned red cherries
> 1 cup boiling water
> 1 tablespoon cornstarch
> ½ cup sugar
> 6 tart shells (p. 448)

Drain the juice from the cherries. Combine the cherry juice, boiling water and sugar. Bring to the boiling point and strain. Make a smooth paste of the cornstarch and a little cold water.

Add this to the hot syrup, stirring constantly. Cook, still stirring, over medium heat until the mixture thickens. While hot pour this over the cherries. Let the filling cool before filling the tart shells. Serve with whipped cream, hard sauce (p. 615), or custard sauce (p. 614). Sliced or chopped canned peaches, pineapple, apricots, strawberries, loganberries, raspberries, Royal Anne cherries, blackberries, blueberries or cranberries may be substituted for the red sour pitted cherries in the recipe.

LEMON TARTS

1½ cups sugar, plus 6 tablespoons
½ cup flour
2 tablespoons cornstarch
½ teaspoon salt
2¼ cups boiling water
3 eggs, separated
6 tablespoons lemon juice (2 to 3 lemons)
2 tablespoons grated lemon zest
12 baked tart shells (p. 448)

Combine 1½ cups sugar, flour, cornstarch, and salt. Add boiling water gradually, stirring constantly. Beat egg yolks and pour hot mixture over them, stirring constantly. Cook slowly 5 minutes. Add lemon juice and zest. Mix well. Cool. Pour into tart shells. Cover with meringue made by beating egg whites stiffly with remaining sugar. Yield: 12 tarts.

ORANGE RHUBARB TARTS

2 pounds rhubarb, cut into small pieces
1½ cups sugar
2 oranges, peeled and seeded, membranes removed
1 tablespoon unflavored gelatin
2 tablespoons cold water
12 baked tart shells (p. 448)
Whipped cream

Preheat oven to 350°F. Combine rhubarb with sugar and orange segments cut in small pieces. Put mixture in greased baking dish. Bake for 50 to 60 minutes. Soak gelatin in cold water and then dissolve in a double boiler over hot water. Stir into cooked fruit. Cool. Fill tart shells with chilled mixture and top with whipped cream.

PEACH TARTS

10 ripe peaches
½ cup water
½ cup sugar
Baked basic pastry crust (p. 445)
Whipped cream, sweetened

Remove skins and slice peaches thin. Cook in small amount of water until tender. Drain liquid from peaches. To 1 cup liquid add sugar and cook until thick. Cool. Just before serving put peaches in a baked basic pastry shell and pour the syrup over the peaches. Cover with whipped cream and serve.

PUMPKIN TARTS

Basic pastry (p. 445)
2½ cups mashed canned pumpkin
2 cups brown sugar
4 eggs, slightly beaten
1 cup whole milk
2 tablespoons melted butter
1 tablespoon molasses
1 teaspoon cinnamon
¾ teaspoon ground ginger
½ teaspoon nutmeg
½ teaspoon salt

Preheat oven to 375°F. Roll pastry out to ⅛" thickness on a lightly floured board. Cut dough in circles that are slightly larger than the tart tins. Repeat as necessary to get 6 crusts. Line 6 tart tins with plain pastry. Mix other ingredients and beat well. Pile in tart shells. Bake for 40 minutes. Serve hot or cold. If cold, top with layer of whipped cream. Serves 6.

STRAWBERRY TARTLETS

½ cup sugar
¼ teaspoon salt
2 tablespoons flour
2 eggs, well-beaten
1 cup scalded milk (brought to a boil and slightly
    cooled)
½ teaspoon vanilla
½ cup heavy cream, whipped
Basic pastry (p. 445)
3 cups washed strawberries
¾ cup currant jelly

Preheat oven to 450°F. Combine sugar, salt, flour, and eggs, mixing well. Add milk slowly. Cook slowly over low heat, stirring constantly, until thick. Add vanilla. Fold in cream. Roll pie crust to ⅛" thickness. Cut into rounds with 4 or 5" cookie cutter. Fit these rounds over the bottom of a large muffin pan and trim. Prick the entire surface of each with a fork. Bake for 12 to 15 minutes. Remove from oven. Cool. Lift from pans. Invert on cake rack. Fill shells half full of milk-egg mixture. Put layer of strawberries in tarts. Heat jelly until it melts and put 1 tablespoon over each tart. Yield: 12 tarts.

APPLE TURNOVERS

Basic pastry (p. 445)
4 apples, peeled, cored, and thinly sliced
½ cup sugar
1 teaspoon cinnamon
2 tablespoons butter

Preheat oven to 400°F. Roll out dough into rounds about the size of a large saucer about 6" across. On ½ round arrange thin slices of apple. Sprinkle with sugar and cinnamon. Dot with butter. Moisten the rim of pastry with water. Fold over uncovered half of pastry and press edges together with a fork. Prick top. Bake until apples are tender, about 20 minutes.

CHERRY TURNOVERS

Substitute stoned and sliced cherries for apples in recipe for apple turnovers (above) and omit cinnamon. Serve with cherry sauce (p. 618).

BUTTERSCOTCH STACKS

Basic pastry (p. 445)
3 tablespoons butter
1½ cups brown sugar
¾ cup boiling water
3 egg yolks
1½ cups milk
6 tablespoons flour
⅜ teaspoon salt
Whipped cream

Preheat oven to 400°F. Roll pastry to about ⅛" thickness and cut into 3" rounds with a cookie cutter. Place on a cookie sheet and bake for about 10 minutes. Cool. Melt butter in a small saucepan over low heat, add sugar, allow to brown slightly, then gradually add water. Beat egg yolks. Add 2 tablespoons of milk and the flour, and beat until smooth. Add remainder of milk and salt. Pour this slowly into sugar mixture and cook over medium heat until thick, stirring constantly. Cool and place a spoonful on top of each pastry round. Stack these in threes and top with whipped cream.

PINEAPPLE VANILLA PIE

1 tablespoon cornstarch
¼ teaspoon salt
¼ cup sugar, plus 6 tablespoons
2 cups shredded pineapple
9" baked basic pastry crust (p. 445)
2 cups vanilla ice cream
3 egg whites

Preheat oven to 500°F. Mix together the cornstarch, salt, and ¼ cup sugar. Add the pineapple and cook over medium heat until clear and slightly thickened, stirring constantly, about 5 minutes. Cool and spread over the bottom and sides of the pie shell. Pack the ice cream over the fruit mixture. Put in the freezer while making the meringue. To make meringue, beat the egg whites until stiff. Add the sugar gradually and beat until it stands in peaks. Spread meringue over the top of the pie, making sure there are no air holes. Bake for about 3 or 4 minutes until browned. Serves 8.

ICE CREAM PIES

Follow recipe for pineapple vanilla pie (above), using any desired fruit and ice cream combination. If desired, fruit may be omitted. Individual pies can be made in tart shells.

LEMON ANGEL PIE

4 egg yolks
¾ cup sugar
¼ cup freshly squeezed lemon juice
1 tablespoon butter
2 egg whites
Baked basic pie shell (p. 445)
Lemon meringue (p. 633)

Preheat oven to 325°F. Cream egg yolks and sugar together. Add lemon juice. Cook in double boiler or in pan set in hot water, stirring frequently, until stiffened, about 10 minutes. Add butter. Remove from heat. Meanwhile, beat 2 egg whites until stiff peaks form. Gently fold egg whites into lemon mixture. Pour into pie shell. Top with meringue. Brown for 15 minutes.

ORANGE ANGEL PIE

Substitute orange juice for lemon juice in recipe for lemon angel pie (above).

DESSERTS
AND
CANDIES

DESERTS

Custards, puddings, and candies are at the heart of this chapter. There are two major types of custards: those that are prepared on the stove (such as the soft custard), and those that are baked (such as the baked custard). For each, the key lies in cooking them just until they are done, and no further. For the stovetop custards, the easiest method is to test whether or not the custard will coat a spoon. Though that may sound a bit vague, it means something rather precise. When cooking custard in a double boiler, use a wooden spoon. As soon as the mixture starts to thicken, dip the spoon in the custard and pull it out. Draw a line in the custard with a finger or spoon. If that line stays, and doesn't fill in with custard immediately, the custard is done. To see more of a contrast, try this test as soon as the custard starts cooking. The custard should be runny, and the line should fill in immediately.

For baked custards, there are two ways to check for doneness. Insert a metal knife slightly off center in the custard. If it comes out clean, the custard should be done. Or jiggle the custard pan a bit. If the center (an area no larger than a quarter) is wobbly, but the rest of the custard seems firm, the custard is done. Overcooked custard will have the taste of sweet scrambled eggs. There is a small window in which to remove the custard from heat, because the eggs will thicken when they reach 160°F, and begin to cook when they get to 180°F.

Puddings are much less temperamental than custards. For any bread puddings, the only trick is to make sure that there is enough liquid for the bread. If the bread is especially stale, it may be necessary to add additional milk or butter to ensure that the pudding doesn't dry out. Other than that, puddings are delightfully easy. Just preheat the oven, combine the ingredients, and bake.

CANDIES

Making candy can be broken down into two or three basic steps. The first involves making some sort of sugar syrup. This is usually a combination of sugar or corn syrup and water. This solution is then heated to a very specific temperature. Most candy syrup needs to be cooked to one of following five stages:

Soft Ball	236° to 240°F
Firm Ball	242° to 248°F
Hard Ball	250° to 265°F
Brittle	270° to 290°F
Very Brittle	295° to 310°F

The names correspond to how the sugar mixture would act when dropped in cold water. A mixture at 240°F should form a soft ball in cold water, while a mixture at 295°F should be very brittle. It is possible to test candy in this way without the use of a candy thermometer. However, for beginning candy makers, a thermometer is essential. The temperature can change very quickly, and it isn't always possible to test the syrup in water again and again.

The next stage involves adding some sort of flavoring, such as cream, nuts, or chocolate. This can happen at several different stages of the cooking. Because the steps in a candy recipe can happen quickly, and require an immediate response, it helps to have all of the tools ready and all of the ingredients measured before beginning. Making the sugar syrup may take some practice. If the sugar suddenly becomes brittle, when the recipe called for a firm ball, don't panic. Just try it again, keeping a close eye on the thermometer.

DESSERTS

SOFT CUSTARD (CRÈME ANGLAISE)

2 cups milk
3 slightly beaten eggs
⅓ cup sugar
¼ teaspoon salt
1 teaspoon vanilla, or 1 vanilla bean, scraped

Put 1¾ cups milk in saucepan. Cover and bring to boiling point. Reduce heat. In another bowl, combine eggs, sugar, salt and remaining milk. Add to scalded milk, stirring constantly with a wooden spoon. Cook, stirring constantly, until a coating forms on a spoon. Test this by coating the wooden spoon in custard. Wipe away a swatch of cream—the custard is ready if that spot doesn't immediately fill in. Remove and cool. Add vanilla. Serve in tall glasses with whipped cream and coconut or use as pudding sauce. Yield: 2¼ cups custard.

BAKED CUSTARD

2 eggs
2 tablespoons sugar
Few grains salt
2 cups scalded milk (boiled and slightly cooled)
½ teaspoon vanilla, or 1 vanilla bean, scraped

Preheat oven to 300°F. Beat eggs. Add sugar and salt. Add milk and vanilla or vanilla seeds. Mix well. Pour into custard cups. Set cups in pan of hot water and bake for 25 minutes. Test with a silver knife. When it is done, the custard will not stick to the knife. Graham cracker crumbs browned in a little butter and brown sugar make an excellent topping. Serves 6.

APRICOT CUSTARD

Serve soft custard (p. 483) over halved ripe apricots and top with whipped cream.

CARAMEL CUSTARD

Follow recipe for baked custard (p. 483) but melt sugar to a golden brown over low heat before adding.

COCONUT CUSTARD

Add 1½ tablespoons shredded coconut to baked custard (p. 483) before cooking.

CUSTARD WITH FRUIT

    3 eggs
    3 cups milk
    ¼ teaspoon lemon extract
    ¼ cup sugar
    ¼ teaspoon nutmeg
    1 teaspoon vanilla
    ¼ teaspoon salt

Preheat oven to 350°F. Beat the eggs slightly and combine with the remaining ingredients. Pour into a small soufflé dish (6" wide and 2½" deep). Place in a shallow pan of hot water and bake for about 40 minutes or until an inserted knife blade comes out clean. Chill. Unmold on a platter and surround with fresh fruit. Serves 6 to 8.

MACAROON CUSTARD

Add 1½ cups crumbled macaroons (p. 606) to soft custard (p. 483) just before removing from heat.

PEACH CUSTARD

Add ⅓ cup cream to soft custard (p. 483) when cooking is finished and 2 cups sliced and peeled peaches after cooling. Serve with whipped cream.

BERRY GELATIN

    1 tablespoon unflavored gelatin
    1 cup water, plus 2 tablespoons
    ⅓ cup sugar
    1 cup raspberries, blueberries, or blackberries

Soak gelatin in 2 tablespoons cold water 5 minutes. Add 1 cup boiling water and sugar and stir until dissolved. Cool. Stir fruit lightly into gelatin when congealing starts. Turn into molds. Chill. Serve plain or with cream or whipped cream. Serves 6.

FRUIT MOLD DE LUXE

2 cups cherry juice
½ cup sugar, plus 2 tablespoons
1 package lemon-flavored gelatin
1 cup heavy cream
1 teaspoon vanilla
1 pound pears, peeled and sliced
1 pound apricots, pitted and halved

Heat cherry juice with ½ cup sugar. Add gelatin and stir until dissolved. Pour into a ring mold and chill until firm, about 2 hours. Unmold on large plate. Whip cream, gradually adding remaining sugar and vanilla. Pile in center of ring. Arrange pears and apricots around ring. Cranberry or loganberry juice may be substituted for cherry juice. Peach halves and pineapple chunks may be used instead of pears and apricots. Serves 6.

GRAPE FRAPPE

1½ tablespoons unflavored gelatin
⅓ cup water, plus 3 tablespoons
1 tablespoon lemon juice
1½ cups grape soda
1 cup cream

Soak gelatin in 3 tablespoonfuls of cold water 5 minutes. Add ⅓ cup boiling water. Cool. Add lemon juice and grape soda. When nearly stiffened beat until light and spongy. Add cream, beating into the mixture. Serve very cold in sherbet glasses with spoonful of whipped cream on top. Serves 6.

EASY ORANGE CHARLOTTE

   2 tablespoons unflavored gelatin
   ⅓ cup water
   2 tablespoons lemon juice
   ½ cup sugar
   1 cup orange soda
   1 egg white, beaten stiff
   Ladyfingers (p. 596), macaroons (p. 606),
      or vanilla wafers

Soak gelatin in ⅓ cup cold water and dissolve in a double boiler over boiling water. Stir until dissolved. Add lemon juice and sugar. Cool. Add orange soda. When mixture is nearly firm beat well. Add egg white, folding into mixture. Line a mold or soufflé dish with strips of ladyfingers, macaroons or vanilla wafers, pour in mold and chill. Serves 5.

BAVARIAN CREAM

2½ tablespoons unflavored gelatin
½ cup cold milk
3 egg yolks
½ cup sugar
⅛ teaspoon salt
1½ cups scalded milk (boiled and slightly cooled)
1 teaspoon vanilla, or 1 vanilla bean, scraped
1 cup cream, whipped

Soak gelatin in cold milk 5 minutes. Beat yolks, sugar, and salt together until light. Add scalded milk and mix thoroughly. Cook in double boiler or over hot water, stirring constantly, until mixture coats a wooden spoon. (See the directions for soft custard, p. 483.) Add gelatin. Stir until dissolved. Set in pan of cold water and stir until it begins to thicken. Add vanilla or vanilla beans and fold in whipped cream. Turn into a mold or soufflé dish that has been dipped in cold water. Chill until firm. Serves 6.

CHOCOLATE BAVARIAN CREAM

Add ⅓ cup cocoa mixed with the hot milk to recipe for Bavarian cream (above).

FRESH PEACH BAVARIAN CREAM

Add 1 cup fresh peach pulp, well mashed, to recipe for Bavarian cream (above) and omit vanilla.

STRAWBERRY BAVARIAN CREAM

Substitute 1 cup juice from mashed strawberries for equal amount of milk in Bavarian cream (p. 488).

VANILLA BLANCMANGE

> ½ cup sugar
> 3 tablespoons cornstarch
> 3 tablespoons flour
> ¼ teaspoon salt
> 3 cups scalded milk
> 2 beaten egg yolks
> 1 teaspoon vanilla
> 2 egg whites, stiffly beaten

Mix sugar, cornstarch, flour and salt. Add milk and mix well. Cook in a double boiler until thick, stirring constantly. Cover and cook over low heat for 15 minutes longer. Remove from heat; pour on the yolks and cook 2 minutes longer over gently boiling water, stirring constantly. Add vanilla or vanilla beans. Fold in stiffly beaten egg whites. Pour into a mold or individual molds. Chill. Serve with chocolate sauce (p. 616). Serves 6.

ALMOND PEACH FOOL

1 cup whipping cream
2 tablespoons sugar
¼ teaspoon almond flavoring
½ cup shredded coconut
2½ cups sliced peaches

Whip cream and add sugar and flavoring. Fold in peaches and coconut. Chill. Serves 6.

COEUR DE CRÈME

8 ounces cream cheese
1 cup heavy cream
1 tablespoon powdered sugar
Dash of paprika
Pinch of salt

Blend cream cheese, cream, sugar, paprika, and salt together thoroughly but lightly. Dampen a piece of cheesecloth and spread as smoothly as possible in special heart-shaped basket or mold. Pack cream cheese mixture in this and chill in refrigerator for several hours. Unmold the Coeur and remove cloth. Serve with rich preserves or fresh strawberries, sugar and cream.

PEACH FOOL

6 fresh peaches
2 tablespoons powdered sugar
2 tablespoons peach or apricot preserves
1 cup heavy cream
½ teaspoon almond extract
½ teaspoon vanilla extract

Peel peaches and cut in small pieces. Sprinkle sugar over the peaches. Add preserves and mix with peaches. In another bowl, add almond and vanilla extract to cream and whip. Fold into peaches. Chill. Serves 6.

CHOCOLATE SOUFFLÉ

2 tablespoons butter
3 tablespoons flour
1 cup milk
½ cup sugar
½ teaspoon salt
3 ounces dark chocolate, melted and cooled slightly
3 eggs, separated
1 teaspoon vanilla, or 1 vanilla bean, scraped

Preheat oven to 350°F. Melt butter and blend in flour. Add milk slowly and bring to a boil, stirring constantly. Add sugar and salt. Add chocolate to mixture. Cool. Add egg yolks and beat until light. Add vanilla or vanilla beans. Beat egg whites until stiff. Fold in egg whites gently, deflating as little as possible. Turn onto greased soufflé dish. Set in pan of hot water. Bake for 40 to 45 minutes. Serve immediately with whipped cream if desired. Serves 6.

APRICOT SOUFFLÉ

Substitute ¼ cup apricot jam for dark chocolate in recipe for chocolate soufflé (p. 491), reduce sugar to ¼ cup, and omit vanilla.

CUSTARD SOUFFLÉ

2 tablespoons butter, melted
¼ cup flour
1 cup scalded milk (boiled and slightly cooled)
2 eggs, separated
¼ cup sugar
¼ teaspoon salt

Preheat oven to 350°F. To butter add flour and, gradually, hot milk. Bring to boiling point. Pour this onto egg yolks that have been beaten until thick and lemon-colored and mixed with sugar and salt. Beat together and cool. Beat egg whites until stiff. Gently fold in egg whites. Bake for 40 to 45 minutes and serve immediately.

APPLE SNOW

4 tart apples
Powdered sugar
3 egg whites, stiffly beaten

Peel, quarter, and core apples. Place in double boiler. Cover and steam until soft. Push through a sieve or food mill. Add powdered sugar to taste. Stir apple pulp gradually into egg whites. Pile lightly on serving dish. Serve with soft custard (p. 483). Serves 4.

FRUIT WHIP

> 1 cup mashed fruit pulp (such as peaches, apricots, or
>   raspberries)
> ¼ cup powdered sugar
> 1 egg white
> ½ cup cream, whipped

Put all ingredients in a bowl and beat until stiff, 10 to 15 minutes. Pile in sherbet glasses. Chill. Serve with whipped cream. Serves 6.

APPLESAUCE WHIP

> 6 tablespoons sugar
> 1 tablespoon freshly squeezed lemon juice
> ½ tablespoon vanilla
> ½ tablespoon almond extract
> 3 cups applesauce (p. 190)
> 2 tablespoons cold water
> 2 tablespoons unflavored gelatin
> 2 egg whites

Add sugar, lemon juice, vanilla, and almond extract to applesauce. Soak gelatin in 2 tablespoons cold water 5 minutes. Dissolve in a double boiler over hot water. Stir into applesauce mixture. Stiffly beat egg whites and gently fold into the mixture. Cover and chill. Serve with soft custard (p. 483). Serves 8.

OLD-FASHIONED STEAMED PLUM PUDDING

¼ cup butter, at room temperature
1 cup sugar
3 cups soft bread, cut into small pieces
1 teaspoon baking powder
1 teaspoon salt
¼ teaspoon nutmeg
½ teaspoon cinnamon
¼ teaspoon clove
3 beaten eggs
¾ cup scalded milk (boiled and slightly cooled)
2 tablespoons candied orange peel
2 tablespoons candied lemon peel
1½ cups raisins
¼ cup currants
¼ cup chopped dried figs
½ cup nuts cut in pieces
½ cup grape juice

Cream butter and sugar together. Add bread, baking powder, salt, and spices. Add eggs and mix thoroughly. Add milk. Add orange and lemon peel, raisins, currants, figs, nuts, and grape juice to the first mixture and beat thoroughly. Fill greased pudding mold or coffee can ¾ full. Cover tightly with a lid or waxed paper and aluminum foil. Place pudding container on a rack or other raised surface inside a large stockpot. Bring water to a gentle boil in the stockpot, making sure that the water doesn't actually touch the pudding container. Cover stockpot. Replenish water as necessary. Steam pudding for 5 to 6 hours. Serve with orange (p. 621) or hard sauce (p. 615). For a more traditional flavor, soak the fruits and citrus peels in ⅓ cup cognac the night before.

BREAD PUDDING

1½ cups stale bread or croissants,
  cut into ½" to 1" cubes
3 cups hot milk
2 beaten eggs
⅔ cup sugar
¼ teaspoon salt
1 tablespoon butter
½ teaspoon vanilla
½ teaspoon cinnamon
½ cup apples, peeled and diced
¼ cup raisins
¼ cup walnuts, chopped

Preheat oven to 350°F. Combine bread, milk, eggs, sugar, salt, and butter. Mix well, then add vanilla, cinnamon, apples, raisins, and nuts. Turn into greased 10" baking tin. Bake for 35 to 40 minutes or until firm. Serve with whipped cream or soft custard (p. 483). Serves 6.

BREAD AND BUTTER PUDDING

⅓ cup raisins
5 thin slices stale bread
¼ cup butter, melted
2 eggs
⅔ cup sugar
2 cups milk
½ teaspoon vanilla
½ teaspoon cinnamon

Preheat oven to 375°F. Line bottom of greased baking dish with raisins. Cut bread slices in 3 strips, crosswise. Dip each in melted butter and arrange on top of raisins. Beat remaining ingredients together and pour over bread. Set dish in pan of hot water. Bake for until bread is browned and knife blade comes out clean, about 35 or 40 minutes. Serve plain or with cream. Serves 6.

SPICED BREAD PUDDING

1 cup toasted 1" chunks of bread or croissants
1 cup brown sugar
1 teaspoon baking soda
½ teaspoon ground cloves
½ teaspoon nutmeg
1 teaspoon cinnamon
1 cup buttermilk
1 cup raisins

Preheat oven to 325°F. Combine bread, sugar, baking soda, cloves, nutmeg, and cinnamon. Add buttermilk and raisins. Mix well. Turn into greased pudding dish. Bake for about 1 hour. Serves 4 to 6.

CABINET PUDDING

Follow recipe for bread pudding (p. 495) using sweet rolls, sweet buns, sponge cake (p. 582), or ladyfingers (p. 596) instead of bread. If desired, substitute crushed pineapple for raisins and omit vanilla. Serve with custard sauce (p. 614).

CHERRY BREAD PUDDING

Add 1½ cups stoned and chopped cherries to recipe for bread pudding (p. 495) and increase sugar to 1 cup.

COTTAGE PUDDING

¼ cup butter
¾ cup sugar
2 eggs
2¼ cups flour
3 teaspoons baking soda
½ teaspoon salt
¾ cup milk
1 teaspoon vanilla

Preheat oven to 400°F. Cream butter, sugar, and eggs together. Mix and sift flour, baking soda, and salt. Add alternately with milk to first mixture. Add vanilla. Beat well. Turn onto greased baking pan or muffin tin to a depth of 1" to 1½". Bake for 20 to 25 minutes. Serve with lemon (p. 620) or custard sauce (p. 614). Serves 6.

BAKED CORN PUDDING

¼ cup cornmeal
5 cups milk
¼ cup molasses
½ teaspoon salt
⅛ teaspoon ground ginger
¼ teaspoon cinnamon
1 tablespoon butter
1 pint fresh blueberries (to garnish)

Preheat oven to 275°F. Mix cornmeal with 1 cup milk. Scald
the remaining milk in a double boiler. Add cornmeal,
molasses, salt, ginger, cinnamon, and butter and mix well.
Pour into a greased baking dish and cook for 2 hours. Serve
with blueberries, and whipped cream, if desired. Serves 6.

RICE PUDDING

2 eggs, separated
½ cup sugar
½ teaspoon salt
2¼ cups milk
1 teaspoon vanilla
2 cups steamed rice
Dash nutmeg
Dash cinnamon

Preheat oven to 350°F. Beat egg yolks. Add sugar, salt, milk,
vanilla, and rice. Stiffly beat egg whites and fold into mixture.
Turn into baking dish. Sprinkle with nutmeg and cinnamon.
Bake for 45 minutes. Serves 6.

CREAMY RICE PUDDING

½ cup rice
1¼ cups milk
1 tablespoon unflavored gelatin
3 tablespoons water
1 tablespoon sugar
¼ teaspoon salt
½ teaspoon vanilla, or 1 vanilla bean, scraped
½ cup heavy cream

Bring rice and milk to a boil over medium heat. Reduce heat to a simmer, cover, and cook for 20 minutes, or until rice is fluffy and the milk is absorbed. Soak gelatin in 3 tablespoons cold water 5 minutes. Dissolve over hot water in a double boiler. Add rice, sugar, salt, and vanilla. Mix thoroughly. Cool. Whip cream and fold into mixture. Mold or pile on dessert dishes. Serve cold. Serves 4.

TAPIOCA CREAM

1 cup scalded milk (boiled and slightly cooled)
¼ cup minute tapioca
⅓ cup sugar
¼ teaspoon salt
1 egg, separated
½ teaspoon vanilla

To milk add tapioca and cook in double boiler until it is transparent. Add half the sugar and the salt to milk and half to egg yolk, slightly beaten. Pour hot mixture slowly on egg mixture. Return to double boiler and cook until it thickens, stirring constantly. Add egg white, beaten stiffly. Flavor with vanilla. Serve cold. Serves 4.

TAPIOCA CUSTARD PUDDING

⅓ cup minute tapioca
2 cups scalded milk (boiled and slightly cooled)
2 eggs, slightly beaten
½ cup sugar
1 teaspoon salt
1 tablespoon butter

Preheat oven to 325°F. Add tapioca to milk and cook in double boiler over low heat for 30 minutes. Add the eggs to the sugar and salt. Pour this gradually into the hot mixture. Turn into buttered baking dish. Add butter. Put in pan of hot water. Bake for 30 minutes. 1 cup of almost any fruits or berries may be added. Serves 6.

CHOCOLATE TAPIOCA

1½ cups milk
2 tablespoons minute tapioca
1 egg, separated
3 tablespoons sugar
⅛ teaspoon salt
1 teaspoon vanilla, or 1 vanilla bean, scraped
2 ounces dark chocolate

Scald 1 cup milk in top of double boiler. Add tapioca and cook over low heat for 20 minutes or until tapioca is transparent. Stir frequently. Beat egg yolks. Add sugar and salt. Put tapioca mixture with egg yolks. Put in double boiler and cook until thickened. Remove from heat. Beat egg whites until stiff. Fold egg whites, vanilla, and chocolate blended with ½ cup scalded milk into the tapioca. Serves 4.

COFFEE TAPIOCA

1 egg, separated
1 cup evaporated milk
⅓ cup minute tapioca
⅔ cup sugar
¼ teaspoon salt
1 cup water
2 cups strong coffee
1 teaspoon vanilla

Mix egg yolk with small amount of milk in saucepan. Add remaining milk, tapioca, sugar, salt, water, and coffee. Bring mixture to boil over direct heat, stirring constantly. Remove from heat. Beat egg white until just stiff enough to hold shape. Fold hot tapioca mixture gradually into egg white. Cool. When slightly cool, stir in vanilla flavoring. Chill. Serve in parfait glasses. Serves 8.

PRINCESS PUDDING

1 cup minute tapioca
3½ cups boiling water
½ cup sugar
½ teaspoon salt
1 cup currant or other tart jelly

Cook tapioca in water with sugar and salt until clear and jellied. Add jelly and stir until dissolved. Chill and serve very cold with whipped cream or soft custard (p. 483). Serves 8.

ANGEL PUDDING

5 eggs
½ teaspoon cream of tartar
2 tablespoons sugar
½ cup walnut meats
¾ cup dates, pitted and chopped
2 tablespoons water

Preheat oven to 350°F. Beat eggs until foamy. Add cream of tartar and beat stiff. Add sugar gradually, mixing well. Combine nuts and dates and fold into mixture. Put water in bottom of greased baking pan. Turn in pudding. Bake for 20 minutes. Serve hot with whipped cream or lemon sauce (p. 620). Serves 6.

STEAMED CHOCOLATE PUDDING

1 tablespoon butter
¾ cup sugar
1 egg
1½ cups flour
1½ teaspoons baking powder
½ teaspoon salt
½ cup milk
2 ounces dark chocolate, melted and slightly cooled

Cream butter, sugar, and egg together. Separately mix and sift flour, baking powder, and salt and add alternately with the milk to the first mixture. Beat thoroughly. Add melted chocolate and mix well. Fill greased pudding mold ¾ full. (See old-fashioned steamed plum pudding, p. 494, for steaming directions.) Cover tightly and steam 1 hour. Serve with whipped cream. Serves 4.

CARAMEL PUDDING

1 cup brown sugar
4 cups milk
¼ cup butter
4 eggs, separated
¼ cup cornstarch
1 cup granulated sugar

Preheat oven to 350°F. Bring sugar and milk to boiling point in a saucepan over medium heat, stirring constantly. Add butter. Beat yolks and cornstarch together and add to first mixture. Cook, stirring constantly, until thick. Turn into greased baking pan. Bake until brown. Beat egg whites with sugar and brush on top. Return to oven and brown top. Serves 6.

BUTTERSCOTCH NUT PUDDING

2¼ cups milk
1½ cups brown sugar
3 tablespoons butter
3 egg yolks
6 tablespoons flour
⅛ teaspoon salt
½ cup nuts, chopped
Whipped cream

Preheat oven to 325°F. Bring 1¾ cups milk to a boil over medium heat. Add brown sugar and butter. Remove from heat, stirring until they dissolve. Combine slightly beaten egg yolks with the remaining milk. Mix with flour and salt. Add first milk mixture and nuts. Pour in a greased baking pan. Cover and bake for 45 minutes. Serve with whipped cream. Serves 6.

LEMON SPONGE PUDDING

1 cup sugar
1 tablespoon flour
Pinch of salt
2 eggs, separated
1 cup milk
Zest and juice of 1 lemon
2 tablespoons butter

Preheat oven to 350°F. Sift the sugar, flour, and salt and blend with the egg yolks. Add the milk, lemon juice, and zest, beating thoroughly. Melt butter and add to mixture. Stiffly beat the egg whites and fold them into the mixture. Bake in a baking dish set in a pan of hot water for 45 minutes. Serve cold. Serves 6.

STEAMED CRANBERRY PUDDING

4 tablespoons butter, at room temperature
⅔ cup granulated sugar
2½ cups flour
3 teaspoons baking powder
¼ teaspoon salt
¼ teaspoon nutmeg
2 eggs, beaten
1½ cups fresh or frozen cranberries, diced
1 cup cold water

Cream the butter and sugar. Sift flour, baking powder, salt, and nutmeg together. Combine all of the ingredients. Half fill a greased pudding mold. Cover tightly and steam for 2 hours. (Follow directions for steaming in old-fashioned steamed plum pudding, p. 494.) Serve hot with lemon (p. 620) or any other fruit-flavored sauce. Serves 6.

PEACH CRISP PUDDING

¼ cup butter, at room temperature
½ cup sugar
4 cups bread cubes
2 cups diced peaches and juice
1 tablespoon freshly-squeezed lemon juice

Preheat oven to 375°F. Cream butter and sugar together. Add bread cubes to sugar mixture and blend well. Mix fruit and lemon juice with the bread. Pour into a greased baking pan or individual baking dishes and bake for 35 minutes. Garnish with peaches and whipped cream if desired. Serve hot. Apricots or crushed pineapple may be substituted for peaches. Hot lemon sauce (p. 620) goes well with this. Serves 6.

PEACH CRUMBLE PUDDING

6–8 peaches, peeled and halved
¼ cup brown sugar
½ cup sifted flour
⅛ teaspoon nutmeg
¼ cup butter

Preheat oven to 350°F. Place peaches in greased baking dish. Combine remaining ingredients, working together with fingertips to consistency of fine crumbs. Sprinkle over peaches. Bake for 25 to 30 minutes. Serve warm. Serves 6.

ROLY-POLY PUDDING

2 cups flour
4 teaspoons baking powder
1 teaspoon salt
5 tablespoons butter
½ cup milk
5 tart apples, sliced
½ teaspoon cinnamon
½ teaspoon nutmeg
½ cup sugar

Preheat oven to 350°F. Mix and sift flour, baking powder, and salt. Rub in 3 tablespoons butter with fingertips. Add milk and mix to a soft dough. Turn out on floured board and pat into oblong shape. Spread with remaining 2 tablespoons softened butter. Cover with a layer of thinly sliced apples and sprinkle with cinnamon, nutmeg, and sugar. Roll like a jellyroll. Bake for 30 to 40 minutes. Slice 1" thick and serve hot with lemon sauce (p. 620) or whipped cream.

DELMONICO PUDDING

5 eggs, separated
½ cup sugar
2 tablespoons cornstarch
4 cups milk

Preheat oven to 350°F. Beat egg yolks until they are light. Add 5 tablespoons sugar. Beat again until very light. Mix cornstarch to a smooth paste with a little milk and add to yolks. Bring remaining milk just to boiling point and stir into mixture. Cook, stirring constantly, until thickened. Turn into greased baking dish. Bake until firm, about 30 minutes. Beat egg whites to stiff froth with remaining sugar. Spread on pudding. Return to oven and brown. Serves 6.

CORN FLAKE PUDDING

4 cups corn flakes
4 cups milk
2 eggs, slightly beaten
½ teaspoon salt
¼ cup molasses
¼ cup sugar
¼ teaspoon ground ginger
¼ teaspoon cinnamon
1 teaspoon vanilla
1 tablespoon butter

Preheat oven to 350°F. Stir all except butter together. Turn into greased baking dish. Dot with butter. Place the dish in a pan of water and put in oven. Bake for 45 minutes to 1 hour. Serves 8.

GRATED SWEET POTATO PUDDING

3 cups grated raw sweet potatoes
½ cup sugar
½ cup maple syrup
1 cup milk
1 teaspoon nutmeg
2 tablespoons butter, melted
½ cup chopped nuts
½ teaspoon salt
2 eggs, well beaten

Preheat oven to 375°F. Combine sweet potatoes, sugar, maple syrup, milk, nutmeg, butter, nuts, and salt. Add eggs and pour into buttered shallow baking pan. Bake for 50 to 60 minutes. Serves 6.

KUCHEN PUDDING

1½ cups sifted flour, plus 1½ tablespoons
½ teaspoon salt
2 teaspoons baking powder
½ cup butter, plus 1½ tablespoons
½ cup sugar, plus 4 tablespoons
1 teaspoon vanilla
1 well-beaten egg
¼ cup milk
6 tablespoons apricot jam
12 apricots, halved and pitted
¼ cup water
½ teaspoon cinnamon

Preheat oven to 375°F. Mix and sift flour, salt, and baking powder. Cream ½ cup butter, ½ cup sugar, and vanilla together. Add egg. Combine milk and 2 tablespoons apricot jam and add alternately with the flour to creamed mixture. Pour into a greased baking pan (8" x 8"). Arrange apricot halves on top, pressing into batter. Dot with remaining butter. Boil remaining apricot jam with water, remaining sugar, and cinnamon for 5 minutes over low heat. Pour over pudding. Bake for 45 minutes. Sliced peaches or pineapple chunks may be used in place of apricots.

CHARLOTTES

Line the bottom and sides of a mold with ladyfingers (p. 596). Fill with any desired Bavarian cream (p. 488). When set, unmold on plate. These may be made in large or individual molds.

CHARLOTTE RUSSE

Line small cake molds with ladyfingers (p. 596) or ¼" slices of any kind of cake. Fill center with whipped cream or any desired soft dessert. Serve thoroughly chilled.

APPLE BROWN BETTY

> ½ cup sugar
> ¼ teaspoon cinnamon
> ¼ teaspoon nutmeg
> ¼ teaspoon salt
> 1½ cups bread, cut into 1" cubes
> 3 cups sliced or chopped apples
> ¼ cup apple juice
> Juice and zest of 1 lemon
> 3 tablespoons butter

Preheat oven to 350°F. Mix sugar, spices, and salt. If apples are very tart, use additional sugar—up to 1 cup. Grease a 1½-quart casserole. Put in a third of the bread, then half of the apples. Sprinkle with half of the sugar mixture. Repeat. Mix apple juice, lemon juice, and zest; pour over the casserole. Put on remaining crumbs and dot with butter. Cover and bake in moderate oven for 1¾ hours. Serves 6. Rhubarb, peaches, pineapple, bananas or cherries may be used instead of apples.

APPLESAUCE BROWN BETTY

Substitute 2½ cups applesauce (p. 190) for apples in apple brown betty (above).

APPLE PAN DOWDY

4 cups apples, cored and sliced
1 cup light brown sugar
½ teaspoon cinnamon
⅛ teaspoon clove
⅛ teaspoon nutmeg
4 tablespoons butter
½ cup apple cider
Homemade biscuit dough (p. 158)

Preheat oven to 350°F. Butter a 10" baking dish. Put in sliced apples and spread sugar over apples. Sprinkle the spices over the sugar. Dot top with butter. Add cider and cover with homemade biscuit dough, ¼" thick. Cover with aluminum foil, leaving holes for the steam to escape. Bake for about an hour, or until apples are tender and crust is well browned. Serve with whipped cream. Serves 6.

PEACH COBBLER

2½ cups peeled sliced peaches
2 tablespoons granulated tapioca
¼ cup sugar
¼ teaspoon salt
¼ teaspoon cinnamon
Dash of nutmeg
1 tablespoon butter
Baking powder biscuit dough (p. 175)

Preheat the oven to 400°F. Empty the peaches into a shallow baking dish. Add tapioca and let stand about 10 minutes. Add the sugar, salt, and spices. Mix well. Dot top with butter. Roll biscuit dough to a thickness of ¼". Prick and arrange over the top of the peach mixture. Bake for about 30 minutes, or until well browned. Apricots, blackberries, blueberries, black or red raspberries may be used instead of peaches. Serves 8.

APPLE DELIGHTS

2 cups flour
1½ teaspoons baking powder
½ teaspoon salt
¼ cup butter, cold
1 cup milk
1 egg, beaten
6 tart apples
Brown sugar

Preheat oven to 400°F. Mix and sift flour, baking powder, and salt. Cut in butter with a knife. Add milk and egg and mix well. Drop tablespoons of batter into well-greased muffin pans. Peel apples, cut in half, and take out cores. Put on top of batter, cut side up, and fill the holes with brown sugar. Bake for 25 minutes or until apples are tender. Serve hot with cream or sweetened whipped cream, dusted with cinnamon. Serves 6.

APPLE CROW'S NEST

4 tart apples, cored, peeled, and sliced
4½ tablespoons butter
¾ cup sugar
2½ teaspoons cinnamon
1 cup flour
2 teaspoons baking powder
¼ teaspoon salt
¼ cup milk

Preheat oven to 400°F. Arrange apples in greased pie tin and dot with 1½ tablespoons butter. Sprinkle with 1 tablespoon sugar and 1½ teaspoons cinnamon. Sift flour, baking powder, salt, and ¼ cup sugar together. Cut in remaining butter with a knife or finger tips. Add milk and mix to make a soft dough. Spread over apples. Bake until apples are tender, about 25 minutes. Turn out upside down. Mix remaining sugar (7 tablespoons) and 1 teaspoon cinnamon and sprinkle over apples. Serve hot with whipped cream. Serves 6.

CRANBERRY ROLL

2½ cups flour
4 teaspoons baking powder
1 teaspoon salt
¼ cup sugar, plus 2 tablespoons
2 tablespoons cold butter, plus more for finishing
1 beaten egg
¾ cup milk
2 cups cranberries, fresh or frozen

Preheat oven to 450°F. Mix and sift flour, baking powder, salt, and ¼ cup sugar. Work in butter with finger tips. Add egg and just enough milk, gradually, to make a soft dough. Roll out on floured board to ½" thickness. Spread surface generously with butter. Cover with cranberries. Sprinkle with remaining sugar. Roll as a jelly roll. Put in greased baking pan. Brush top and sides with butter. Bake until it begins to brown, about 15 minutes. Reduce heat to 350°F and bake 45 minutes longer. Slice 1" thick and serve hot with lemon (p. 620) or hard sauce (p. 615). Serves 6.

PEAR BRICKLE

½ cup heavy cream
2 tablespoons sugar
1 teaspoon vanilla
½ cup crushed peanut brittle
1 pound pears, cored, peeled, and sliced
Slice of angel food cake (p. 546)

Whip cream. Add sugar and vanilla. Lightly fold the peanut brittle and pears into the whipped cream mixture. Serve over slices of plain or toasted angel food cake. Garnish with additional peanut brittle. Crushed pineapple, sliced apricots, peaches, or white cherries maybe used instead of pears. Serves 8.

BLUEBERRY SLUMP

4 cups blueberries
3 cups water
2 cups sugar
1½ cups flour
1½ teaspoons baking powder
¼ teaspoon salt
⅓ cup milk

Bring the berries, water, and sugar to a boil over medium heat in a broad saucepan. Remove from heat immediately. Mix the flour, baking powder, and salt together in separate bowl. Add milk and make a soft dough. Pour over the berries. Cover. Cook for 15 minutes or until dough is cooked through on top of stove over medium heat. Turn out on hot platter and serve with ice cream or whipped cream. Serves 6.

PEACH BASKET TURNOVER

2 eggs, separated and beaten
1 cup sugar
1 cup flour
1 teaspoon baking powder
½ teaspoon salt
1 teaspoon vanilla
1 cup brown sugar
2 tablespoons butter
1½ cups peeled, sliced ripe peaches

Preheat oven to 400°F. Beat yolks with sugar until light. Fold in stiffly beaten egg whites. Mix and sift flour, baking powder, and ¼ teaspoon salt. Add to first mixture and mix thoroughly but gently. Add vanilla. Cream brown sugar and butter together. Add peaches and remaining salt and place in shallow, greased baking pan. Pour batter over the peaches. Bake for 45 minutes. Turn out upside down. Serve hot with whipped cream. Serves 6.

UNIVERSAL DESSERT

> 3 cups fresh raspberries
> 2 tablespoons lemon juice
> 2 tablespoons water
> ½ cup sugar
> ½ cup heavy cream
> ½ cup shredded toasted almonds
> Pound cake (p. 578)

Bring 2 cups raspberries, lemon juice, water, and sugar to a boil over medium heat. Remove from heat and set aside. Allow the mixture to cool completely. Whip cream and gently combine with cooked berries, remaining fresh berries, and ¼ cup almonds. Line a shallow dish with thin slices of cake. Spread with half the fruit mixture. Add another layer of cake and remaining fruit. Sprinkle with remaining almonds. Chill several hours. Serve with whipped cream. Strawberries, loganberries or blackberries may be substituted for raspberries. Serves 8.

CREAM CHEESE TORTE

¼ cup butter
25 graham crackers, crumbled
½ pound cream cheese
½ pound cottage cheese
1½ cups sour cream
4 eggs, separated
½ cup sugar
Pinch of salt
1 teaspoon vanilla

Preheat oven to 375°F. Melt butter. Add cracker crumbs, reserving 3 teaspoons. Line a buttered baking dish with crumbs. Blend cream cheese and cottage cheese together. Add sour cream and mix well. Add egg yolks, sugar, salt, and vanilla, and beat thoroughly. Stiffly beat the egg whites and gently fold them into the mixture. Turn into baking dish. Sprinkle reserved crumbs over top. Bake for 35 minutes. Cool before serving. Excellent with fresh berries or other fruit.

VANILLA ICE CREAM

3 cups half-and-half
1 cup heavy cream
8 large egg yolks
1 cup sugar
1 vanilla bean
2 teaspoons vanilla

Bring the half-and-half and cream almost to a boil, stirring frequently to prevent burning. In another bowl, beat egg yolks until light. Add sugar and beat for about a minute more. Add a few tablespoons of the warm cream mixture to the egg yolks, stirring to combine. This will prevent the egg yolks from becoming lumpy. Gently combine the egg yolk mixture and the cream in the saucepan. Slice open the vanilla bean and scrape out the seeds. Add them to the mixture. Cook over low medium-low heat, stirring constantly with a wooden spoon to prevent sticking. The mixture is ready when it thickens enough to coat the back of the spoon. Remove from heat and add the vanilla. Chill for at least an hour, or overnight if possible. Make according to the manufacturer's instructions for ice cream maker.

FRENCH ICE CREAM

2 cups milk
5 egg yolks
Few grains salt
1 cup sugar
2 cups cream
1 tablespoon vanilla

Scald the milk in a double boiler or over hot water. Beat egg yolks, salt, and sugar together until light. Pour the scalded milk on them and stir until well mixed. Return to boiler and cook until the mixture coats the spoon, stirring constantly. Remove from heat. Add cream and stir well. Cool. Add vanilla. Chill for at least 1 hour, or overnight if possible. Make according to the manufacturer's instructions for ice cream maker. Makes 1 quart ice cream.

CHOCOLATE ICE CREAM

2 ounces dark chocolate
⅔ cup sweetened condensed milk
⅔ cup whole milk
1 teaspoon vanilla
⅔ cup whipping cream

Melt chocolate in top of double boiler. Add condensed milk and stir until mixture thickens. Add milk slowly and mix well. Chill thoroughly. Add vanilla. Whip cream slightly and fold into the chilled chocolate mixture. Make according to the manufacturer's instructions for ice cream maker.

STRAWBERRY ICE CREAM

4 egg yolks
1 cup sugar
2 cups cream
2 cups strawberries, finely diced

Beat egg yolks with ½ cup sugar. Add remaining sugar to cream and cook over medium heat, stirring constantly. Bring to boiling point. Stir cream gradually into eggs. Strain to remove any lumps. Cool. Stir in strawberry juice and pulp. Make according to the manufacturer's instructions for ice cream maker.

FROZEN PUDDING

1½ cups orange juice
¼ cup lemon juice
½ cup sugar
2 cups cream
⅓ cup powdered sugar
2 teaspoons vanilla
½ cup raisins
½ cup chopped walnuts

Mix fruit juices. Add sugar and dissolve. Beat cream thick. Add fruit juices, powdered sugar, and vanilla. Stir in raisins, dates, prunes or cherries, and walnuts. Chill. Make according to the manufacturer's instructions for ice cream maker. Yield: 1½ quarts.

APRICOT ICE CREAM

1 cup half-and-half
1 pound dried apricots
1 cup sugar
1 tablespoon candied ginger
Juice of ½ lemon

Scald half-and-half. Cook apricots in enough water to cover. When boiling, add sugar and ginger. Simmer until fruit is plump. Add lemon juice and cool. Fold into half-and-half. Chill. Make according to the manufacturer's instructions for ice cream maker. Serves 6.

BANANA ICE CREAM

Add 3 mashed bananas to vanilla ice cream (p. 516) just before freezing.

BUTTERSCOTCH ICE CREAM

Substitute brown sugar for white sugar in vanilla ice cream (p. 516) and add ½ tablespoon butter during cooking.

CARAMEL ICE CREAM

Make vanilla ice cream (p. 516) but melt and brown sugar in frying pan before adding.

CHOCOLATE MINT ICE CREAM

    1 cup hard peppermint candies
    ¾ cup milk
    3 cups heavy cream
    3 ounces dark chocolate, coarsely grated

Add mints to milk. Melt at low heat, stirring constantly. Remove from heat and cool thoroughly. Whip cream stiff and fold mint mixture into it until well blended. Chill. Stir and fold in grated chocolate. Make according to the manufacturer's instructions for ice cream maker. Serves 6.

HARLEQUIN ICE CREAM

4 cups whipping cream
15 tablespoons powdered sugar, divided into 3 parts
2 ounces dark chocolate, melted
1 cup macaroon crumbs, or other cookie crumbs
1 cup strawberry jam
½ cup crushed almonds

Divide cream in 4 portions and whip. To the first part slowly add 5 tablespoons powdered sugar and the chocolate. Chill. To the second portion of cream add same amount of sugar and macaroon crumbs. Chill. The third layer is made by adding the strawberry jam to another portion of cream, and the fourth layer is composed of the remaining cream, the almonds, and 5 tablespoons of sugar. Chill these as well. Make each mixture separately, according to the manufacturer's instruction. Once frozen, layer the ice creams one on top of the other in a casserole dish.

PEACH ICE CREAM

Follow recipe for vanilla ice cream (p. 516), reducing vanilla content to ½ teaspoon and adding ½ teaspoon almond extract with vanilla and 1½ cups mashed and sweetened peaches when folding in whipped cream.

PEANUT BRITTLE ICE CREAM

Add ½ to ¾ cup crushed peanut brittle to vanilla ice cream (p. 516) when folding in whipped cream.

PEPPERMINT CANDY ICE CREAM

1 cup crushed candy mints
1½ cups hot milk
1½ cups cream
⅛ teaspoon salt

Dissolve the candy in the hot milk over medium heat. Add cream and salt. Chill. Make according to the manufacturer's instructions for ice cream maker. Continue freezing. Serve with hot fudge sauce (p. 616). Serves 6.

PINEAPPLE ICE CREAM

1 egg
½ cup sugar
2 cups evaporated milk
Few grains of salt
1½ cups crushed pineapple
1 teaspoon vanilla
1 cup whipping cream

Beat egg; add sugar, evaporated milk, and salt. Cook in a double boiler over hot water until thick, stirring constantly. Chill. Add pineapple and vanilla. Whip cream and fold in the pineapple mixture. Chill. Make according to the manufacturer's instructions for ice cream maker. Serves 6.

TUTTI-FRUTTI ICE CREAM

3 cups milk
2 slightly beaten eggs
¾ cup sugar
24 macaroons, toasted and powdered
1 cup raisins
1 cup chopped maraschino cherries
2 cups cream, whipped
1 teaspoon vanilla

Put 2½ cups milk in saucepan. Cover and bring to boiling point. Reduce heat. In another bowl, combine eggs, sugar, and remaining milk. Add gradually to scalded milk while stirring. Cook, stirring constantly, until mixture thickens and a coating forms on spoon. Chill. Add macaroons, raisins, cherries, whipped cream, and vanilla. Make according to the manufacturer's instructions for ice cream maker. Yield: 1½ quarts.

ORANGE SHERBET

Add 3 well-beaten egg whites and ⅔ cup heavy cream to orange ice (p. 529) when mixture is chilled but before freezing starts.

LEMON SHERBET

Add 3 well-beaten egg whites and ⅔ cup heavy cream to lemon ice (p. 528) when mixture is chilled but before freezing starts.

PINEAPPLE SHERBET

4 cups water
1½ cups sugar
2 cups shredded pineapple
Juice of 1 lemon
1 egg white

Boil water and sugar together 10 minutes. Drain pineapple and add to the water and sugar mixture along with the lemon juice. Cool. Make according to the manufacturer's instructions for ice cream maker. When partly frozen, fold in stiffly beaten egg white. Continue freezing. If canned pineapple is used, reduce sugar to ¾ cup. Yield: 1 quart sherbet.

LIME SHERBET

2 cups water
2 cups sugar
2 cups freshly squeezed lime juice
3 egg whites, whipped stiff

Bring water and sugar to a boil. Remove from heat. Chill. Add the lime juice. Make according to the manufacturer's instructions for ice cream maker. When partly frozen, at thick mush stage, add egg whites. Serves 8.

LIQUEUR SHERBET

Stir ½ cup claret or sherry into 1 quart lemon ice (p. 528) when frozen to mushy stage.

ITALIAN SORBET

2 cups sugar
2 cups water
1 cup orange juice
½ cup lemon juice
1½ cups orange soda
1½ cups grape soda
1 cup lemon soda

Gently boil sugar and water 20 minutes. Cool. Add fruit juices and then the sodas. Make according to the manufacturer's instructions for ice cream maker. Ginger ale may be substituted for part or all of above beverages. Serves 16.

APRICOT ICE

2 cups fresh apricots, pitted and diced
2 cups hot water
½ cup sugar
1 tablespoon corn syrup
Juice and zest of 1 lemon

Combine all of the ingredients, and stir to dissolve the sugar. Chill. Make according to the manufacturer's instructions for ice cream maker.

BERRY WATER ICE

2½ cups berries, any kind
4 cups water
1 pound sugar
Juice of 2 lemons

Bring berries to a boil in 2 cups water. Add sugar and lemon juice. Stir until dissolved. Let stand in warm place 1 to 2 hours. Rub through a sieve. Add 2 additional cups water. Mix well. Taste and add more sugar if necessary. Chill. Make according to the manufacturer's instructions for ice cream maker.

CRANBERRY ICE

½ cup sugar
1 cup water
2½ cups stewed cranberries (see stewed berries, p. 195)
1 stiffly beaten egg white

Boil sugar in 1 cup water 3 minutes. Add cranberries and boil 5 minutes longer. Rub through a sieve. Cool the strained liquid. Combine mixture with egg white. Chill. Make according to the manufacturer's instructions for ice cream maker. Yield: 1 quart.

PINK FRUIT ICE

3 cups pineapple juice
3 cups orange juice
½ cup lemon juice
2 cups sugar
3 cups strawberry soda or ginger ale

Mix well and chill. Make according to the manufacturer's instructions for ice cream maker. Serves 15.

GRAPE ICE

1½ cups grape soda
Few grains salt
1½ teaspoons lemon juice
1½ to 2 tablespoons sugar

Chill ingredients before combining. Make according to the manufacturer's instructions for ice cream maker. Orange, strawberry or cherry carbonated beverages may be substituted for the grape, depending upon flavor or color desired. Serves 5.

LEMON ICE

2¼ cups sugar
4 cups water
Juice of 4 lemons
Juice of 1 orange
Grated zest of 1 lemon

Dissolve sugar in water and boil 10 minutes. Strain juices and add to syrup. Add zest and mix thoroughly. Chill. Make according to the manufacturer's instructions for ice cream maker. Yield: 1 quart ice.

MINT ICE

1½ cups sugar
¾ cup white corn syrup
1¾ cups water
6 tablespoons lemon juice
½ cup chopped mint
2 cups grapefruit sections and juice

Cook sugar, syrup, and 1 cup water to soft ball stage (238°F). Add lemon juice and remaining water. Cool. Add mint. Cut the grapefruit sections into pieces. Add fruit and juice to cooled syrup. Make according to the manufacturer's instructions for ice cream maker. Yield: 2 quarts.

ORANGE ICE

2 cups sugar
Juice of 6 oranges
Juice of 1 lemon
Grated zest of 1 orange

Make same as lemon ice (p. 528).

ANGEL PARFAIT

¾ cup sugar
¼ cup water
2 egg whites
1½ teaspoons vanilla
2 cups whipped cream

Cook sugar and water, stirring until sugar is dissolved. Continue cooking without stirring until it spins a thread (about 238°F). Beat egg whites until stiff. Add syrup slowly, while continuing to beat. Add flavoring and cream, which as been beaten until thick but not stiff. Freeze quickly without stirring, or chill and make according to the manufacturer's instructions for ice cream maker.

APRICOT FREEZE

2 eggs
½ cup sugar
⅛ teaspoon salt
½ cup milk
2 teaspoons vanilla
Few drops almond extract
½ cup heavy cream, whipped
3½ cups fresh apricots, pitted and diced

Beat the eggs with a hand mixer until very thick, about 5 minutes. Add sugar gradually and continue to beat until thick and smooth. Add salt, milk, and flavorings. Mix well. Chill. Freeze until mushy. Remove and beat with hand mixer. Fold in the whipped cream and the apricots. Make according to the manufacturer's instructions for ice cream maker. Serves 10 to 12.

ORANGE FLUFF

¾ cup sugar
⅔ cup water
Grated zest of 2 oranges
1 cup orange juice
2 cups whipping cream

Cook sugar in water until a little of the mixture dropped in cold water forms a soft ball (238°F). Remove from heat. Add orange zest and orange juice. Mix well and chill. Whip the cream until stiff and add to mixture. Make according to the manufacturer's instructions for ice cream maker. Serves 6 to 8.

ROOT BEER CRÈME

2 cups root beer
2 cups cream
Few grains salt

Chill ingredients before combining. Make according to the manufacturer's instructions for ice cream maker. Sarsaparilla may be used in place of root beer. Serves 8

CHOCOLATE ICE CREAM SODA

3 tablespoons chocolate syrup (p. 532)
1 tablespoon cream
2 tablespoons vanilla ice cream (p. 516)
Soda water

Mix syrup and cream in tall glass. Add ice cream. Fill with soda water. Stir well.

PINEAPPLE CREAM FLOAT

4 cups ginger ale
2 cups pineapple ice cream (p. 522)
6 sprigs mint

Pour ginger ale into 6 tall glasses. Drop several spoonfuls of pineapple ice cream into each glass. Garnish with sprigs of mint. Serve at once. Serves 6.

CHOCOLATE SYRUP

8 ounces dark chocolate
3½ cups sugar
½ teaspoon salt
3 cups boiling water

Melt chocolate in a double boiler over low heat. When chocolate melts, add sugar and salt. Blend well. Add boiling water slowly. Boil until a thin syrup is formed, about 6 minutes. Pour into a jar. Cover and keep cool.

SODA AND ICES

Flavored sodas combine pleasingly with ices or sherbets. Put small servings of ice or sherbet in iced tea glasses. Then pour beverage over them. The following are particularly popular combinations:

- Apricot sherbet with ginger ale, lemon, lime, orange, or raspberry soda.
- Orange sherbet (p. 523) with grape, orange, or "cream" soda.
- Pineapple sherbet (p. 524) with grape soda.
- Pineapple sherbet (p. 524) with lemon, lime, or "cream" soda.
- Lemon sherbet (p. 523) with ginger ale, grape, lime and lemon, lime, pineapple, or raspberry soda.

SNOWBALLS

Roll balls of firmly frozen ice cream in shredded coconut just before serving.

BOMBES

Line a melon mold with any preferred ice cream. Fill center with any desired mousse. Freeze. The center may be filled with almost any pudding, whip, soufflé, custard or cream.

SPUMONI

Line a round-bottom mold with vanilla ice cream (p. 516). Add a layer of chocolate ice cream (p. 518). Fill with mixture of chopped nuts and maraschino cherries, raisins and whipped cream. Freeze solid. Unmold.

ZABAGLIONE

6 egg yolks
⅓ cup sugar
¼ teaspoon grated cinnamon
1 cup Marsala

Beat egg yolks, adding sugar gradually, until firm. Add cinnamon and Marsala slowly, beating in well. Set bowl in a double boiler over simmering water and cook and beat until sugar is dissolved and mixture resembles custard. Serves 8.

CANDIES

CHOCOLATE FUDGE

2 cups sugar
⅔ cup milk
2 tablespoons corn syrup
3 ounces dark chocolate, broken in small pieces
2 tablespoon butter or fat
1 teaspoon vanilla

Put sugar, milk, syrup, and chocolate in a saucepan. Stir until sugar is dissolved. Cook slowly until the temperature reaches 236°F or until the mixture forms a soft ball when a little is dropped into cold water. Remove from heat. Add butter. When cooled to lukewarm, add vanilla. Beat until thick. Pour into shallow, greased pan. Chill. Cut into squares when firm.

PENUCHI

½ cup evaporated milk
2 cups brown sugar
2 tablespoons butter
1 teaspoon vanilla
⅛ teaspoon salt
1 cup broken nuts

Combine milk and sugar. Cook slowly, stirring only until sugar is dissolved, until 236°F is reached, the stage at which a drop of the mixture will form a soft ball when dropped into cold water. Add butter. Cool slightly. Add other ingredients and beat until creamy. Pour into a greased pan. Chill.

KISSES WITH CANDIED CHERRIES

Substitute ½ cup chopped candied cherries for an equal quantity of nuts in recipe for penuchi (p. 534). After beating, drop by teaspoons onto wax paper. Chill.

MOLASSES FUDGE

    1 cup granulated sugar
    1 cup brown sugar
    ½ cup cream
    ¼ cup molasses
    ¼ cup melted butter
    2 ounces dark chocolate, grated
    1½ teaspoons vanilla

Combine sugar, brown sugar, cream, molasses, and butter. Bring to a boil and boil for 2 minutes. Add chocolate. Boil 5 minutes longer, stirring until well blended and, then, only enough to prevent burning. Remove from heat. Add vanilla. Stir until creamy. Turn into buttered pan. Chill.

CHOCOLATE COCONUT FUDGE

After beating chocolate fudge (p. 534), stir in ½ cup shredded coconut.

COCOLATE NUT FUDGE

After beating chocolate fudge (p. 534), stir in 1 cup broken nuts.

BUTTERSCOTCH

¼ cup molasses
2 cups brown sugar
1 tablespoon cider vinegar
½ cup butter, at room temperature

Combine molasses, sugar, and vinegar. Bring to boiling point, stirring only until sugar is dissolved. Boil 2 minutes. Add butter. Cook to 290°F or until syrup becomes brittle when dropped in cold water. Turn into greased, shallow pan. Cool. Before butterscotch completely hardens, cut into small rectangles. Chill.

VANILLA CARAMELS

2 cups sugar
1 cup brown sugar
1 cup light corn syrup
1 cup condensed milk
1½ cups milk
⅓ cup butter, at room temperature
¼ teaspoon salt
1½ teaspoons vanilla

Cook sugars, corn syrup, condensed milk, and milk together in a saucepan, stirring constantly until the sugar is dissolved. Cook slowly over low heat, stirring occasionally to prevent burning, until the temperature is 248°F, or until mixture forms a firm ball when tested in cold water. Remove from heat, add butter, salt, and vanilla and mix well. Pour into a greased pan. When cold remove from pan, cut in cubes and wrap each caramel in waxed paper.

CHOCOLATE CARAMELS

Add 5 ounces melted dark chocolate, cut into small pieces, to recipe for vanilla caramels (p. 536) before cooling.

NUT CARAMELS

Add ⅔ cup broken nuts to recipes for vanilla (p. 536) or chocolate caramels (above) after cooking.

CLUB CARAMELS

Make chocolate (above) and vanilla-nut caramels (above). Pour one batch into chilling pan and top with other.

MOLASSES COCONUT CHEWS

½ cup corn syrup
½ cup molasses
1 tablespoon vinegar
2 tablespoons butter
2 cups shredded coconut

Combine syrup, molasses, vinegar, and butter. Place over low heat and stir until mixture boils. Continue boiling until the mixture reaches 240°F or until a small amount of syrup becomes brittle in cold water. Remove from heat and add coconut. Pour into a greased baking dish. Chill.

NUT BRITTLE

2 cups granulated sugar
¼ teaspoon salt
¼ teaspoon baking soda
1 teaspoon vanilla
2 cups nuts

Heat the sugar gradually in a frying pan. Stir constantly with a wooden spoon until a golden syrup is formed. Remove from the heat immediately, before the sugar darkens more. Quickly stir in the salt, baking soda, and vanilla. Pour the syrup over a layer of nuts in a greased pan. When cold, crack into small pieces.

BLACK WALNUT MOLASSES TAFFY

1½ cups sugar
½ cup molasses
1½ cups water
2 tablespoons cider vinegar
½ teaspoon cream of tartar
4 tablespoons butter
⅛ teaspoon salt
¼ teaspoon baking soda
1 cup black walnuts

Boil the sugar, molasses, water, vinegar, and cream of tartar to the soft-crack stage (270°F). Add the butter, salt, and baking soda and pour into a greased pan. When cool enough to handle, pull until light in color. Add the nuts, and work them into the mass by kneading and pulling. Pull into strips the desired thickness and cut into pieces about 1" long with scissors. If desired, wrap pieces in wax paper.

LOLLIPOPS

2 cups sugar
⅛ teaspoon cream of tartar
⅔ cup water
Any desired flavoring (such as peppermint, strawberry,
    or grape)
Coloring, if desired

Combine sugar and cream of tartar with water. Stir until sugar
is dissolved. Boil until a temperature of 290°F is reached or
until a drop of mixture will become hard when dropped into
cold water. Remove from heat. Add flavoring and coloring.
Pour into greased pans or molds. When partly cooled, insert
wooden sticks. Chill.

CHOCOLATE COCONUT KISSES

1 tablespoon sifted flour
1½ cups sifted powdered sugar
3 egg whites
1 teaspoon vanilla
1 7-ounce bar semi-sweet chocolate, cut in pieces
½ cup shredded coconut

Sift flour and sugar. Beat egg whites until they stand in peaks.
Gradually sprinkle sugar and flour mixture over egg whites,
beating constantly. Add vanilla, chocolate, and coconut. Drop
by teaspoonfuls on greased cookie sheet and bake at (450°F)
10 minutes. Yield: 4 dozen kisses.

CHOCOLATE MARSHMALLOWS

4 ounces milk chocolate
32 marshmallows
½ cup grated coconut

Place chocolate in a double boiler and heat slowly until chocolate is melted. Quickly dip marshmallows into chocolate, roll at once in coconut, and place on buttered plate. Chill.

SPICED NUTS

2 cups powdered sugar
½ cup cornstarch
2 teaspoons salt
1 teaspoon nutmeg
1 teaspoon cinnamon
2 teaspoons ginger
1 tablespoon ground cloves
1 egg white
2 tablespoons cold water
1¾ cups nut kernels

Preheat oven to 250°F. Sift together the sugar and other dry ingredients. Divide into two portions. Beat the egg white slightly and add the cold water. Put the nuts in a wire strainer and dip into the egg mixture until each nut is well coated. Drain. Roll the nuts in a part of the spice mixture. Spread some of the spice mixture ¼" thick in a shallow pan and place the nuts on this, separating each one. Cover with the rest of the spice mixture and bake for 3 hours. Remove from the oven and sift. Save the spice mixture to use again.

POPCORN BALLS

1¼ cups sugar
1¼ cups brown sugar
½ cup light corn syrup
⅔ cup water
1 tablespoon butter or fat
14 cups popped corn
1¼ teaspoons salt

Put sugar, brown sugar, syrup, and water in a saucepan, stirring until sugar is dissolved. Add butter and continue cooking, without stirring, until the temperature reaches 240°F, or until mixture forms a soft ball when tested in cold water. Put popped corn in a large bowl and sprinkle with salt. Pour the hot syrup over it and mix thoroughly with a wooden spoon. When it has cooled slightly, shape in small balls, and wrap in wax paper.

BOILED CHESTNUTS

Blanch. Cover with boiling, salted water. Cover pan and simmer until tender, from 10 to 15 minutes. Drain. Mash to a paste or grind. Season to taste with butter, salt, and pepper.

COCONUT CHERRY DIVINTY

2 cups sugar
⅔ cup water
½ cup light corn syrup
2 egg whites, stiffly beaten
1 teaspoon vanilla
Dash of salt
½ can moist, sweetened coconut, toasted and crumbled
¾ cup candied cherries, thinly sliced

Bring ½ cup sugar and ⅓ cup water to a boil and boil until a small amount of syrup forms a slightly firm ball in cold water (240°F). While this mixture is boiling, bring remaining sugar and water and the corn syrup to a boil in another pan. Boil until a small amount of syrup forms a hard ball in cold water (252°F). Remove first syrup (240°F) from heat and cool slightly. Pour slowly over egg whites, beating constantly until mixture loses it gloss, about 1½ minutes. Then add second syrup (252°F) slowly, beating as before. Fold in vanilla, salt, coconut, and cherries, and turn immediately into greased pan, 8" x 8". Cool until firm. Cut in pieces, 1½" x 1". Roll in additional toasted coconut, if desired. Makes 42 pieces. Broken pecans, chopped dates, or raisins may be substituted for candied cherries in this recipe.

CAKES, COOKIES,
AND
FROSTINGS

CAKES

Cakes come in two major types: foam and buttered. Foam cakes, such as angel food cake and sponge cake, contain no butter or shortening. They get all of their volume from stiffly beaten egg whites. As a result, they have a light, spongy texture. The egg whites for these cakes should be beaten just until stiff. Overbeaten egg whites will become grainy and lose some of their volume, resulting in a heavier cake. Care should be taken to fold in the egg whites with the rest of the batter as gently as possible, so as to maximize their effect. Mixing the egg whites in by hand, rather than with a mixer, will provide the best results.

Most cakes are buttered. They contain a combination of eggs, flour, and butter or shortening. The recipes in this book all call for butter. Shortening may be substituted in any of the recipes. Butter provides a richer taste, but shortening can sometimes provide a superior texture. Using butter or shortening is a matter of personal preference.

Most buttered cakes use a creaming method. For the creaming method, all of the ingredients for the cake should be at room temperature. (If using cold butter just microwave it for a few seconds, making sure the butter is softened, but not hot.) The butter and sugar are creamed together, and the eggs are added one at a time, and beaten until they are fully incorporated. This butter-sugar-egg mixture should be beaten thoroughly. This not only makes a uniform mixture, but also incorporates air into the batter. The flour should be sifted with the other dry ingredients, and then added to the butter mixture. This should be done as swiftly as possible. The batter should only be beaten until the flour is incorporated. Mixing beyond that point can result in a tougher cake.

Whether making a foam cake or a buttered cake, the oven should be preheated to the correct temperature and the cake pans should be ready and waiting. Once the batter is ready, it should go in the oven as quickly as possible. Try not to disturb the cake for the first 15 or 20 minutes of baking. Opening and closing the door too many times can cause the cake to fall. The easiest way to test a cake for doneness is to stick a knife or toothpick into the cake. If it comes out clean, the cake is done. Cakes should be allowed to cool for a few minutes after they have been removed from the oven. They should then be moved to a cooling rack. Doing this too soon can result in a broken cake. The cake should be completely cooled before it is frosted.

COOKIES

Many of the rules for cake-making apply to cookie-making as well. Most cookies use a creaming method, for instance. Having the oven preheated, and all of the ingredients measured and at room temperature, will make for excellent cookies. Using a silicone mat (or silpat) in cooking-making can also make a big difference. Silicone mats can be put directly in top of a normal cookie sheet. They prevent the cookies from sticking, and help them to cook more evenly. Use the middle oven racks when baking cookies. The upper and lower racks may produce burnt or undercooked cookies. If forced to use these racks, be careful to rotate the cookies during baking.

FROSTINGS

Frosting a cake makes it more beautiful and more delicious. Frosting or icing can be applied in one coat or two. If only using one coat, make sure both the cake and the frosting are at room temperature. Use the thickest and most even layer for the bottom, if making a layer cake. This will provide a better foundation for the cake. The frosting should be easy to spread. If it is too thick, dilute with a drop or two of milk. Using a knife or an offset spatula, glide the frosting over the cake's surface. Try not to touch the surface of the cake with the spatula, as that can result in crumbs getting in the frosting. Fill the layers and frost the top of the cake before worrying about the sides.

Applying the frosting in two layers uses a "crumb coat." A crumb coat is a thin layer of frosting that is applied first. It does not need to be neat. It should be applied evenly, and as thinly as possible, using a knife or an offset spatula. The frosting should then be allowed to set, either by sitting for 40 minutes at room temperature, or by being refrigerated for 10 minutes. The second coat can then be applied. The advantage of the crumb coat is that it makes it easier to get a smooth, crumb-free surface on the cake. It looks better, and is easier to decorate.

CAKES

BASIC CAKE

   3 cups sifted flour
   4 teaspoons baking powder
   ½ teaspoon salt
   ¼ cup butter, at room temperature
   1 cup sugar
   1 beaten egg
   1 cup milk
   1 teaspoon vanilla

Preheat oven to 350°F. Sift flour, baking powder, and salt. Combine butter and sugar and beat until fluffy. Add the egg, beating until incorporated. Beat in milk and vanilla. Combine 2 mixtures and stir until smooth. Pour into a greased and floured 10" cake pan. Bake for 25 minutes. If formed into cupcakes, bake for 20 minutes. Test for doneness by inserting a toothpick. When the toothpick comes out clean, the cake is done. Allow the cake to cool for at least 15 minutes before removing from the pan.

ANGEL FOOD CAKE

   1 cup sifted flour
   1 to 1¼ cups sugar
   8 egg whites
   ½ teaspoon salt
   ¾ teaspoon cream of tartar
   1 teaspoon vanilla

Preheat the oven to 325°F. Sift the flour and half the sugar together several times. Beat the egg whites with the salt until frothy. Add the cream of tartar and beat until the whites start to peak. Gently fold in the other half of the sugar. Then fold in the flour-sugar mixture gradually and gently, and when the whole is partly blended add the vanilla. Only a gentle folding motion should be used in mixing, for stirring releases the air depended on for leavening. A tube pan is best for baking angel food. Bake for about an hour. After baking, invert the cake and remove from the pan when almost cold.

CHERRY ANGEL FOOD CAKE

⅓ cup maraschino cherries, sliced or chopped
¼ teaspoon salt
1 teaspoon cream of tartar
¼ teaspoon almond flavoring
¾ teaspoon vanilla
8 egg white
1¼ cups granulated sugar
1 cup sifted cake flour

Preheat oven to 325°F. Drain cherries thoroughly. Add salt, cream of tartar, almond flavoring, and vanilla to egg whites. Beat until foamy but not stiff. Beat in sugar, 2 tablespoons at a time. Sift flour and fold into mixture. Pour a layer in the bottom of an ungreased tube pan. Sprinkle in ½ cherries. Add remainder of batter. Top with remaining cherries. Bake for 50 minutes. Remove pan. Invert and allow to hang until cake cools and pulls away from sides of pan.

CHOCOLATE ANGEL FOOD CAKE

Substitute ¼ cup cocoa for an equal quantity of flour in recipe for angel food cake (p. 546). Sift cocoa with flour.

LEMON ANGEL FOOD CAKE

Substitute the grated zest of ½ lemon for vanilla in angel food cake (p. 546).

MOCK ANGEL FOOD CAKE

> 1 cup milk
> 1 cup flour
> 1 cup sugar
> 3 teaspoons baking powder
> 2 egg whites, beaten stiff
> 1 teaspoon vanilla

Preheat oven to 300°F. Heat milk almost to boiling point. Mix and sift flour, sugar, and baking powder. Pour milk gradually into dry mixture, blending well. Fold in egg whites. Add vanilla. Pour into ungreased tube pan and bake for 45 minutes. Cool.

APPLE UPSIDE-DOWN CAKE

¼ cup butter, at room temperature
½ cup sugar
1 egg
1 teaspoon vanilla
1½ cups sifted flour
2 teaspoons baking powder
¼ teaspoon salt
2 to 4 firm-fleshed apples, such as Granny Smith
½ cup milk
2 teaspoons cinnamon mixed with ¼ cup sugar
Hard sauce (p. 615) or whipped cream

Preheat oven to 425°F. Cream the butter and sugar together. Beat in the egg and vanilla. Sift the dry ingredients together and alternately add it and the milk to the first mixture. Spread a thick coating of butter on the bottom and sides of a 10" x 10" glass baking dish or a very heavy pan. Peel, quarter and slice the apples thin. Spread in an overlapping layer on the bottom of the baking dish and sprinkle with the cinnamon and sugar. Pour the cake mixture over the apples. The batter is rather thick and may need to be smoothed on top with a knife. Bake for 45 minutes. Loosen the sides of the cake, turn it carefully upside down and the top will be covered with a neat layer of transparent apples. Serve hot with hard sauce or whipped cream.

PINEAPPLE UPSIDE-DOWN CAKE

Substitute canned or fresh pineapple slices for apple in apple upside down cake (above) and omit cinnamon.

APPLESAUCE CAKE

½ cup butter, at room temperature
1½ cups brown sugar
1 egg
1 teaspoon baking soda
1 cup thick applesauce (p. 190)
1 teaspoon salt
1 teaspoon cinnamon
½ teaspoon ground clove
1½ to 2 cups flour
1 cup raisins (optional)

Preheat oven to 350°. Cream butter, sugar, and egg together. Dissolve baking soda in applesauce and add to the egg mixture. Sift salt, cinnamon, and clove with part of the flour and add to the first mixture. Add enough more flour to make a fairly stiff batter. Add raisins, if desired. Pour into a greased loaf pan and bake for 50 to 60 minutes until a toothpick inserted into the cake comes out clean.

CHOCOLATE RIBBON CAKE

3 cups sifted cake flour
3 teaspoons baking powder
½ teaspoon salt
⅔ cup butter, at room temperature, plus 2 tablespoons
1½ cups sugar
2 eggs, plus 2 egg yolks
1 cup milk
1 teaspoon vanilla
4 ounces dark chocolate, melted and cooled
2 tablespoons sugar
¼ cup buttermilk
½ teaspoon baking soda

Preheat oven to 375°F. Sift flour once, measure, add baking powder and salt, and sift again. Cream butter thoroughly. Add sugar gradually, and cream together until light and fluffy. Add eggs and beat well. Add flour mixture, alternately with milk, beating until smooth. Add vanilla. Combine remaining ingredients in another bowl. Cool slightly. Turn a generous ⅓ batter into greased 9" layer pan. Add chocolate mixture to remaining batter; turn into 2 greased 9" layer pans. Bake for 30 minutes or until a toothpick inserted in the cake comes out clean. Frost with chocolate icing (p. 630), arranging the light layer between the dark ones.

BIRTHDAY CAKE

½ cup butter
1½ cups sugar
3 eggs
2¼ cups flour
1 teaspoon salt
3 teaspoons baking powder
⅔ cup milk
1 teaspoon almond extract

Preheat oven to 350°F. Cream butter, sugar, and eggs together. Mix and sift flour, salt, and baking powder. Alternately add the flour mixture and the milk to the first mixture. Add almond extract and beat thoroughly. Pour into a greased tube pan. Bake for 50 to 60 minutes or until a toothpick inserted in the cake comes out clean. Cover and decorate with ornamental icing (p. 627) and sprinkles.

MARASCHINO CHERRY CAKE

4½ cups cake flour
4½ teaspoons baking powder
1 teaspoon salt
¾ cup butter, at room temperature
2¼ cups sugar
1¾ cups milk
2 egg yolks
1½ teaspoons vanilla extract
½ teaspoon almond extract
5 egg whites
¼ cup maraschino cherries

Preheat oven to 375°F. Sift flour once. Measure and sift with baking powder and salt. Cream butter. Continue creaming, gradually adding 1½ cups sugar and 3 tablespoons of milk. Add egg yolks and flavorings to remaining milk. Add sifted dry ingredients alternately with the milk mixture to the creamed butter and sugar. Beat egg whites until stiff, but not dry. Add remaining sugar and beat until sugar is dissolved. Fold into cake mixture. Pour batter into 3 greased 9" layer pans. Sprinkle ¼ cup finely cut pieces of maraschino cherries over the batter. Bake for 25 minutes or until a toothpick inserted in the cake comes out clean. Frost with seven-minute icing (p. 626).

CHOCOLATE REFRIGERATOR LAYER CAKE

    2 8" yellow cake layers (p. 557)
    4 ounces dark chocolate, melted and slightly cooled
    1 cup heavy cream

Split each layer in half, making 4 layers in all. Melt chocolate over a double boiler and set aside to cool. Whip the cream until it begins to thicken. Add the melted chocolate all at once, and continue to beat until the mixture is smooth, thick and well blended. Spread between the cake layers and top with the remainder. Chill in the refrigerator for 24 hours. Then cut as a cake and serve. Serves 8 to 10.

CRUMB CAKE

½ cup butter, chilled
1½ cups brown sugar
2½ cups sifted flour, divided
2½ teaspoons baking powder
1 teaspoon cinnamon
1 teaspoon salt
1 beaten egg
¾ cup milk

Preheat oven to 375°F. Mix butter, sugar, and 2 cups flour to a fine crumb. Reserve ¾ cup of this crumb. Sift remaining flour, baking powder, cinnamon, and salt. Combine with remaining crumb mixture. Add egg and milk and mix well. Pour into an 8" square pan that has been lined with parchment paper. Sprinkle reserved crumbs on top. Bake for 35 to 40 minutes, or until a toothpick inserted in the center comes out clean.

DATE CAKE

4 eggs, separated
1½ cups brown sugar
⅔ cup butter, at room temperature
3¼ cups flour
5 teaspoons baking powder
1 teaspoon salt
1 teaspoon cinnamon
½ teaspoon nutmeg, ground
¾ cup milk
1½ cups chopped dates

Preheat oven to 350°F. Separate eggs. Cream yolks, brown sugar, and butter. Mix and sift flour, baking powder, salt, cinnamon, and nutmeg. Add dry mixture to first mixture alternately with milk. Beat egg whites well, until they form peaks. Stir into mixture. Add dates, mixing well. Turn into a greased loaf pan. Bake for 50 to 60 minutes. Cool and frost as desired.

DEVIL'S FOOD CAKE

½ cup butter, at room temperature
1½ cups granulated sugar
2 eggs, separated
½ cup cocoa
1½ cups buttermilk, divided
2 cups sifted cake flour
1½ teaspoons baking soda
¼ teaspoon salt
1 teaspoon vanilla

Preheat oven to 375°F. Cream the butter. Add the sugar a little at a time, creaming after each addition until the mixture is light and fluffy. Add the egg yolks and blend thoroughly. Add enough buttermilk to the cocoa to make a smooth paste. Then add an additional amount to make 1 cupful of the cocoa mixture. Add to the creamed mixture. Sift together the flour, baking soda, and salt and add alternately with the sour milk and vanilla to the chocolate mixture. Mix thoroughly. Stiffly beat the egg whites and fold gently into the batter. Turn into 2 greased and lightly floured 9" layer cake pans. Bake for 30 to 40 minutes or until a toothpick inserted in the center comes out clean. Frost with caramel icing (p. 629) or any desired frosting.

FOUNDATION CAKE

½ cup butter, at room temperature
½ teaspoon vanilla
1½ cups sugar
2 eggs, separated
3 cups sifted flour
4 teaspoons baking powder
½ teaspoon salt
1 cup milk

Preheat oven to 350°F. Cream butter, vanilla, and sugar together until light and fluffy. Continue creaming while adding yolks slowly. Sift flour, baking powder, and salt and add alternately with milk to creamed mixture. Beat the egg whites until stiff. Fold in beaten egg whites. Turn into 2 lightly greased 9" cake pans. Bake for 25 minutes, or until a toothpick inserted in the center comes out clean.

RICH CAKE

1 cup butter, at room temperature
½ teaspoon vanilla
2 cups sugar
4 eggs, separated
3 cups sifted flour
4 teaspoons baking powder
½ teaspoon salt
1 cup milk

Mix and bake same as foundation cake (p. 556).

CHOCOLATE CAKE

Add 2 ounces melted, dark chocolate just before egg whites are folded into foundation cake (p. 556), reduce butter to ⅜ cup and reduce flour to 2⅞ cups.

WHITE CAKE

Use 4 to 6 egg whites and omit egg yolks in recipe for foundation cake (p. 556).

YELLOW CAKE

Use 4 to 6 eggs yolks and omit egg whites in recipe for foundation cake (p. 556).

FOUR-EGG CAKE

4 eggs, separated
¾ cup butter, at room temperature
1½ cups sugar
3 cups flour
3 teaspoons baking powder
1 teaspoon salt
¾ cup milk
2 teaspoons vanilla

Preheat oven to 400°F. Separate eggs. Cream yolks, butter, and sugar together. Mix and sift flour, baking powder, and salt. Add this mixture alternately with milk to egg mixture. Beat egg whites stiff. Add vanilla. Fold gently into dough. Turn into greased cupcake pans or into 3 greased layer cake pans. Bake cupcakes for 20 minutes; layer cakes for 25 minutes. Spread layers and top of cake with seven-minute icing (p. 626), to which has been added ½ cup chopped nuts, ¼ cup chopped candied cherries and ½ cup chopped raisins, if desired.

NUT CAKE

Preheat oven to 350°F. Follow recipe for four-egg cake (above). Add 1 cup walnuts or other preferred nuts, cut in pieces and mixed with a little of the flour. Bake in a greased loaf pan for 60 to 80 minutes, or until a toothpick inserted in the center comes out clean.

FRUIT CAKE

2 cups butter, at room temperature
2 cups light brown sugar
7 eggs, separated
2 tablespoon milk
2 tablespoons apple juice
1 pound walnuts, chopped
2 pounds currants
2 pounds raisins, finely chopped
½ pound date meats, finely chopped
½ pound citron, thinly sliced and cut into short strips
4 cups flour
2 teaspoons mace
2 teaspoons cinnamon
2 teaspoons baking powder
Few grains salt

Preheat oven to 350°F. Cream butter. Gradually add sugar and beat for 5 minutes. Beat egg yolks until light and lemon-colored and whites until stiff and dry. Add these to the butter and sugar mixture, folding egg whites in gently. Add milk, juice, chopped nuts, and fruits, which have been rolled in flour. Lastly, add well-sifted dry ingredients. Beat mixture thoroughly and place in deep, round cake pans lined with parchment paper. Bake for 80 to 90 minutes, or until a toothpick inserted in the center comes out clean.

FUDGE CAKE

½ cup butter, at room temperature.
1¼ cups brown sugar
1 teaspoon vanilla
2 eggs
3 ounces melted dark chocolate, cooled
2 cups sifted flour
1½ teaspoons baking powder
½ teaspoon baking soda
1 cup milk

Preheat oven to 350°F. Cream butter and brown sugar together. Add vanilla. Add eggs, one at a time, beating thoroughly after each addition. Beat in chocolate gradually. Sift flour, baking powder, and baking soda until smooth. Fold the dry ingredients alternately with the milk into the chocolate mixture. Turn into 2 greased 9" cake pans. Bake for 25 minutes, or until a toothpick inserted in the center comes out clean.

GINGERBREAD

2 cups sifted cake flour
2 teaspoons baking powder
¼ teaspoon baking soda
2 teaspoons ground ginger
1 teaspoon cinnamon
½ teaspoon salt
⅓ cup butter, at room temperature
½ cup sugar
1 egg, well beaten
⅔ cup molasses
¾ cup sour milk or buttermilk

Preheat oven to 350°F. Sift flour, baking powder, soda, spices, and salt. Cream butter thoroughly, add sugar gradually, and cream together until light and fluffy. Add egg and molasses; then flour, alternately with milk. Beat after each addition until smooth. Pour into a greased loaf pan. Bake for 75 minutes, or until a toothpick inserted in the center comes out clean. Serve with whipped cream.

GINGERBREAD SHORTCAKE

    2 cups flour
    1 teaspoon baking powder
    1 teaspoon baking soda
    1 teaspoon ground ginger
    2 teaspoons cinnamon
    1 cup molasses
    ⅓ cup butter, at room temperature
    ½ cup buttermilk
    1 egg
    1 cup heavy cream, whipped

Preheat oven to 375°F. Sift together the dry ingredients. Heat the molasses and butter almost to boiling. Add the buttermilk and egg to the dry ingredients and stir quickly into the hot molasses mixture. Bake for 20 to 25 minutes in 2 greased 8" layer pans. Cool and cover with whipped cream to serve.

GOLDEN PINEAPPLE CAKE

4½ cups cake flour
4 teaspoons baking powder
1½ teaspoons salt
1 cup butter, at room temperature
2⅔ cups sugar
1½ cups canned unsweetened pineapple juice
4 eggs, separated
1½ teaspoons vanilla

Preheat oven to 375°F. Sift flour. Measure and sift again with the baking powder and salt. Cream butter with 2 cups sugar and 2 tablespoons pineapple juice until light and fluffy. Add unbeaten egg yolks and beat well. Alternately add the sifted dry ingredients and the pineapple juice to the egg mixture. Add vanilla. Mix until smooth. Beat the egg whites until stiff but not dry, and fold into the batter. Add remaining sugar and beat until it just disappears. Bake in 3 greased 8" cake pans for 25 to 30 minutes or until a toothpick inserted in the center comes out clean. Spread golden pineapple icing (p. 631) between layers and on top and sides of cake.

GOLD CAKE

½ cup butter, at room temperature
1 cup sugar
8 egg yolks
1½ cups flour
4 teaspoons baking powder
1 teaspoon salt
½ cup milk
1 teaspoon vanilla

Preheat oven to 400°F. Cream butter and sugar together. Add egg yolks and beat until smooth. Mix and sift flour, baking powder, and salt and add alternately with the milk to the first mixture. Add vanilla and beat thoroughly. Bake in 2 greased 9" layer cake pans for 20 minutes, or until a toothpick inserted in the center comes out clean. When cool, put layers together and ice top and sides with honey icing (p. 632).

GUMDROP CAKE

½ cup butter, at room temperature
1 cup sugar
2 eggs, beaten
2¼ cups flour
¼ teaspoon salt
2 teaspoons baking powder
1 pound gumdrops, black ones removed, chopped fine
¾ cup raisins
1 teaspoon vanilla
¾ cup milk

Preheat oven to 300°F. Cream butter, while adding sugar and beaten eggs. Sift flour, salt, and baking powder together over chopped candy and raisins. Dredge well. Add vanilla to milk. Then add flour mixture and milk alternately to first mixture. Stir well to combine. Bake in a large greased loaf tin for 90 minutes, or until a toothpick inserted in the center comes out clean.

HONEY CAKE

1 cup honey
1 cup sugar
½ cup butter, melted and cooled
2 slightly beaten eggs
2 cups flour
1 teaspoon baking powder
1 teaspoon caraway seeds

Preheat oven to 375°F. Cream honey, sugar, butter, and eggs. Mix and sift flour, baking powder and seeds. Combine mixtures and mix until smooth. Turn into a greased baking pan and bake for 30 to 40 minutes, or until a toothpick inserted in the center comes out clean.

JELLY ROLL

CAKE:

2 eggs
⅞ cup sugar
Grated zest of 1 lemon
1 cup flour
1½ teaspoons baking powder
¼ teaspoon salt
3 tablespoons milk

FILLING:

Jelly
Powdered sugar

Preheat oven to 350°F. Beat eggs. Add sugar and beat well. Add lemon zest. Sift flour with baking powder and salt and add, alternately with milk, to first mixture. Pour into a shallow pan, about 14" x 10", lined with waxed paper or parchment paper. Bake for 15 to 20 minutes. Turn out on damp cloth. Spread with jelly and roll up. Wrap in wax paper and cool. Sprinkle with powdered sugar just before serving.

CHOCOLATE ROLL

CAKE:
- 4 eggs, separated
- ½ cup sugar
- 4 tablespoons cold water
- 4 tablespoons cocoa
- 1 cup flour
- 1 teaspoon baking powder
- ½ teaspoon salt

FILLING:
- 1 cup cream
- ½ teaspoon vanilla
- 2 tablespoons powdered sugar

Preheat oven to 400°F. Beat egg whites until stiff. Add sugar gradually, beating constantly. Beat in egg yolks and water. Mix and sift cocoa, flour, baking powder, and salt and fold into the first mixture. Line a long shallow pan with greased paper or parchment paper. Pour the batter into the pan. Bake for 15 to 20 minutes. Turn out on a damp cloth and cool slightly. Beat cream stiff with vanilla and powdered sugar and spread on cake. Roll like a jelly roll (p. 564). Sprinkle with powdered sugar.

FRUIT ROLL

CAKE:
>   ¾ cup cake flour
>   1 teaspoon baking powder
>   4 eggs
>   ¼ teaspoon salt
>   ¾ cup sugar
>   Juice ½ lemon
>   1 teaspoon grated lemon zest

FILLING:
>   ⅓ cup sugar
>   3 tablespoons cornstarch
>   ¼ teaspoon salt
>   Dash nutmeg
>   Dash cinnamon
>   1 cup water
>   2½ cups canned or stewed raspberries (see stewed
>   berries, p. 195)
>   Juice of ½ lemon
>   Powdered sugar
>   1 tablespoon butter

Preheat oven to 400°F. Sift the flour. Measure and sift again with baking powder. Put the eggs and salt in a bowl. Set the bowl in a larger bowl of simmering water and beat until eggs are thick and lemon colored. Remove bowl from water and add the sugar, a tablespoon at a time, beating after each addition. Add lemon juice and zest and fold in the dry ingredients. Grease a shallow 10" x 14" pan. Pour the batter in the pan and bake for 15 minutes. Meanwhile, to make the fruit filling: mix together the sugar, cornstarch, salt, nutmeg, and cinnamon. Bring water to boil in a medium saucepan. Stir in the dry ingredients and cook until thick and clear, about 5 minutes. Place over a double boiler and continue to cook for 10 minutes. Remove from heat and stir in the raspberries, lemon juice, and butter. Turn from the pan onto a cloth covered with powdered sugar. Quickly spread with the fruit mixture and roll. Wrap in the cloth and cool on a rack. Slice and serve with whipped cream.

JIFFY CAKE WITH SELF ICING

4 tablespoons butter, at room temperature
1 cup sugar
1 egg
½ cup milk
⅓ teaspoon salt
1½ cups sift flour
1½ teaspoons baking powder
1 teaspoon vanilla
½ cup grated sweet chocolate
½ cup chopped almonds

Preheat oven to 350°F. Combine butter, sugar, egg, milk, salt, flour, baking powder, and vanilla. Beat with a hand mixer until light and smooth. Pour into a greased deep 10" cake pan. Mix chocolate and almonds and spread evenly over cake. Bake for 35 to 40 minutes, or until a toothpick inserted in the center comes out clean.

LAYER CAKE

⅓ cup butter, at room temperature
¾ cup sugar
2 eggs
1½ cups flour
3 teaspoons baking powder
½ teaspoon salt
½ cup milk
1 teaspoon vanilla

Preheat oven to 400°F. Cream butter, sugar, and eggs together. Mix and sift flour, baking powder and salt and add alternately with the milk to the first mixture. Add vanilla and beat thoroughly. Bake in 2 greased 9" layer cake pans for 20 to 25 minutes. Cool. Put layers together with any cream filling, chocolate (p. 622) or coconut (p. 623), for example. Ice top with powdered sugar icing (p. 626).

CHOCOLATE LAYER CAKE

Use fudge icing (p. 631) between layers and on top and sides of baked layer cake (p. 568).

STRAWBERRY LAYER CAKE

Spread strawberry jam between layers of baked layer cake (p. 568) and sprinkle top with powdered sugar.

CHOCOLATE CHIP LAYER CAKE

2¼ cups sifted cake flour
2¼ teaspoons baking powder
½ teaspoon salt
½ cup butter, at room temperature
1 cup sugar
3 egg whites, unbeaten
¾ cup milk
1½ teaspoons vanilla
1 8-ounce package semi-sweet chocolate chips

Preheat oven to 375°F. Sift flour, baking powder, and salt together. Cream butter thoroughly, add sugar gradually, and cream together until light and fluffy. Add egg whites, one at a time, beating thoroughly after each. Add flour, alternately with milk, a small amount at a time, beating after each addition until smooth. Add vanilla. Grease 2 8" pans, lined with waxed paper, and grease again. Pour about ⅛ of batter into each pan. Sprinkle ⅛ of the chocolate chips over each lot. Repeat, ending with chocolate. Bake for 30 minutes, or until a toothpick inserted in the center comes out clean. Frost with your favorite frosting, decorate with shredded chocolate. To make cupcakes, add chocolate chips to cake batter with vanilla. Bake in greased cupcake pans for 20 minutes, or until done.

MARBLE CAKE

¾ cup butter, at room temperature
2 cups sugar
1 ½ cups milk
4 egg whites
3¼ cups flour
½ teaspoon salt
3 teaspoons baking powder
3 teaspoons vanilla
2 ounces dark chocolate
¼ teaspoon baking soda

Preheat oven to 350°. Cream butter, sugar, and 2 tablespoons milk until light and fluffy. Beat unbeaten egg whites one at a time into mixture. Sift flour with salt and baking powder. Add sifted dry ingredients alternately with remaining liquid to cream mixture. Add vanilla. Melt chocolate slowly over a double boiler and combine with baking soda. Divide batter into 2 equal parts. Add chocolate mixture to one part. Drop batter by spoonfuls into a greased and floured 10" cake pan, alternating the white and chocolate batter until all is used. Bake for 50 minutes, or until a toothpick inserted in the center comes out clean.

MILE-A-MINUTE CAKE

1¾ cups flour
2 teaspoons baking powder
1 teaspoon salt
½ teaspoon cinnamon
½ teaspoon nutmeg
⅓ cup butter, at room temperature
1⅓ cups brown sugar
2 eggs
½ cup milk
½ pound dates, pitted and chopped
½ cup nuts, chopped

Preheat oven to 350°F. Sift the flour. Measure and sift again with the baking powder, salt, and spices. Combine all ingredients in the order given, adding the pitted, chopped dates and chopped nuts last. Beat all together just until blended. Bake in a greased 9" square pan for 50 to 60 minutes. Ice with peanut butter icing (p. 632).

QUICK RAISIN COFFEE CAKE

2 cups flour
4 teaspoons baking powder
½ teaspoon salt
¼ cup sugar, plus 3 tablespoons
⅓ cup butter, cold
2 eggs
½ cup milk
1 cup raisin
¼ cup cream
1 teaspoon cinnamon

Preheat oven to 375°F. Sift flour with baking powder, salt, and ¼ cup sugar. Cut in the butter. Beat 1 egg. Add milk and stir into the dry ingredients, mixing only enough to moisten them. Put into a greased 8" pan. Spread the raisins over the dough. Beat the remaining egg and mix with cream. Pour over raisins. Sprinkle with the sugar and cinnamon, mixed. Bake for 1 hour, or until a toothpick inserted in the center comes out clean. Serve hot as a dessert with whipped cream or sauce of choice.

MOLASSES CAKE

½ cup butter, at room temperature
½ cup sugar
3 eggs, separated
¾ teaspoon baking soda
⅔ cup molasses
2¼ cups flour
1 teaspoon cinnamon
¼ teaspoon clove
¼ teaspoon mace
1 teaspoon salt
½ cup milk
½ cup raisins

Preheat oven to 350°F. Cream butter, sugar, and egg yolks. Add baking soda, mixed with the molasses. Mix and sift flour, cinnamon, clove, mace, and salt, and add alternately with the milk to the first mixture. Beat egg whites and fold into the batter. Stir in the raisins. Pour into a greased loaf pan and bake for 50 to 60 minutes, or until a toothpick inserted in the center comes out clean.

MOTHER'S TEA CAKES

⅓ cup butter, at room temperature
1 cup sugar
½ teaspoon salt
2 eggs
1½ cups flour
1 teaspoon baking powder
½ cup milk
½ teaspoon vanilla
Powdered sugar (for serving)

Preheat oven to 400°F. Cream butter, sugar, salt, and eggs together. Beat until light and soft. Mix and sift flour and baking powder and add to the first mixture alternately with the milk. Add vanilla. Beat thoroughly and pour into well-greased shallow baking pan. Bake for 30 minutes, or until a toothpick inserted in the center comes out clean. When partly cool, dust with powdered sugar, cut in squares, and serve while warm.

NUN'S CAKE

1 cup butter, at room temperature
1½ cups sugar
5 eggs, separated
3 cups sifted cake flour
2½ teaspoons baking powder
1 teaspoon salt
¼ teaspoon mace
¾ cup milk
1 teaspoon vanilla

Preheat oven to 350°F. Cream the butter, add sugar gradually and continue creaming. Add egg yolks and 2 egg whites gradually, beating constantly, until light and fluffy. Sift flour, baking powder, salt, and mace together. Add to egg mixture, alternately with milk. Add vanilla. Bake in a greased 10" cake pan for 1 hour, or until a toothpick inserted in the center comes out clean.

QUICK ORANGE CAKE

½ cup melted butter
1 cup sugar, plus 3 tablespoons
2 eggs
¾ cup orange juice
2 cups flour
4 teaspoons baking powder
¼ teaspoon salt
Zest of 2 oranges

Preheat oven to 350°F. Add hot butter to 1 cup sugar. Add well-beaten eggs and orange juice. Add sifted dry ingredients and beat well. Pour into a greased pan. Grate orange zest and mix with 3 tablespoons sugar. Sprinkle on cake. Bake for 50 minutes, or until a toothpick inserted in the center comes out clean.

SUNNY ORANGE CAKE

3 cups flour
4 teaspoons baking powder
1 teaspoon salt
1⅔ cups sugar
½ cup butter, at room temperature
3 eggs
1 cup milk
1 teaspoon vanilla
¼ cup orange juice

Preheat oven to 375°F. Sift flour. Sift one more time with baking powder, salt, and sugar. Soften butter, but do not melt, and add to dry mixture. Combine other ingredients and add slowly to first mixture. Beat 1 minute. Bake in 2 greased 9" layer cake pans for 25 to 30 minutes, or until a toothpick inserted in the center comes out clean. Ice with boiled egg yolk icing (p. 628).

PEACH CAKE

½ cup butter, at room temperature
1 cup sugar
2 eggs
2 cups flour
2 teaspoons baking powder
¼ teaspoon salt
½ cup milk
1 cup diced fresh peaches

Preheat oven to 375°F. Cream butter and sugar. Add eggs, one at a time, beating well. Sift flour with baking powder and salt. Add alternately with milk to first mixture. Add peaches and mix. Bake in a greased 9" square pan for 30 to 35 minutes. Serve warm with lemon sauce (p. 620) or top with sweetened whipped cream.

PEPPERMINT CANDY LAYER CAKE

2⅔ cups flour
3 teaspoons baking powder
1 teaspoon salt
½ cup butter, at room temperature
1½ cups sugar
1¼ cups milk
1 egg yolk
3 egg whites
1 teaspoon vanilla
½ cup finely ground peppermint stick candy
½ cup coarsely ground peppermint stick candy

Preheat oven to 375°F. Sift flour with baking powder and salt. Cream butter. Continue creaming, gradually adding ⅘ cup of sugar and 3 tablespoons milk. Add 1 egg yolk and vanilla to remaining milk. Add sifted dry ingredients alternately with milk to creamed mixture. Beat egg whites stiff but not dry. Beat in remaining sugar. Fold into cake batter. Pour into 2 greased 9" layer pans with wax paper or parchment paper in bottom. Sprinkle with the finely ground peppermint candy. Bake for 25 minutes, or until a toothpick inserted in the center comes out clean. Ice with seven-minute icing (p. 626), colored pink. Sprinkle coarsely ground peppermint candy over top and sides of cake.

POUND CAKE

1 cup butter, at room temperature
1½ cups sugar
5 eggs
2 cups flour
1 ½ teaspoons salt
⅛ teaspoon mace (optional)
1 teaspoon vanilla

Preheat oven to 350°F. Cream butter and sugar together. Add eggs, one at a time, beating well after the addition of each egg. Add the flour, salt, and mace. Add vanilla and beat thoroughly. Bake in a greased loaf pan for 60 to 80 minutes, or until a toothpick inserted in the center comes out clean.

BRIDE CAKE

Substitute 8 egg whites for 5 eggs in recipe for pound cake (above).

COCONUT POUND CAKE

Add ⅔ cup shredded coconut to recipe for pound cake (above).

FRUIT POUND CAKE

Add ½ cup seedless raisins, ⅓ cup chopped preserved cherries, ¼ cup grated orange peel, ¼ cup grated lemon peel, and ¼ cup chopped nuts to recipe for pound cake (above). Place halved almonds on top of cake before baking.

LEMON POUND CAKE

Add ¼ cup grated lemon zest to recipe for pound cake (p. 578).

VANILLA POUND CAKE

Increase vanilla to 2 teaspoons in recipe for pound cake (p. 578).

PUMPKIN CAKE

½ cup butter, at room temperature
1 cup brown sugar
½ cup granulated sugar
1 egg or 2 egg yolks
¾ cups mashed or canned pumpkin
2 cups flour
¼ teaspoon baking soda
3 teaspoons baking powder
1 teaspoon salt
1 teaspoon cinnamon
⅔ cup chopped nuts (optional)
⅓ cup sour milk or buttermilk

Preheat oven to 350°F. Cream butter and sugars together. Add egg and pumpkin. Sift flour, baking soda, baking powder, salt, and cinnamon together. Add nuts and dry mixture alternately with sour milk to creamed mixture. Mix well. Turn into 2 greased 8" layer pans with oiled paper or parchment paper in the bottom. Bake for 25 minutes, or until a toothpick inserted in the center comes out clean. Cool. Put together with spiced whipped cream (p. 634) between layers.

QUICK CAKE

1 cup sugar
1½ cups flour
2 teaspoons baking powder
½ teaspoon salt
¼ cup melted butter, cooled
2 eggs
Milk (not skim)
1 teaspoon vanilla

Preheat oven to 400°F. Mix sugar, flour, baking powder, and salt and sift. Put butter in measuring cup, add eggs, and fill cup with milk to the 1 cup mark. Add liquid to the sifted flour mixture. Add vanilla and beat thoroughly. Bake in 2 greased 8" layer cake pans for 15 to 20 minutes, or until a toothpick inserted in the center comes out clean. Cool. Put layers together and ice top with quick icing (p. 625). This cake may also be baked in greased muffin pans.

SNOW CAKE

¼ cup butter, at room temperature
1 cup sugar
1 ⅔ cups flour
½ teaspoon baking powder
½ cup milk
1 teaspoon vanilla
¼ teaspoon almond extract
2 beaten egg whites

Preheat oven to 350°F. Cream butter and sugar together. Mix and sift flour and baking powder and add alternately with milk to creamed mixture. Add vanilla and almond extract. Fold in egg whites. Turn into a greased 9" cake pan.

Bake for 30 to 40 minutes, or until a toothpick inserted in the center comes out clean.

OLD FASHIONED SPICE CAKE

2 cups flour
2 teaspoons baking powder
1 teaspoon cinnamon
1 teaspoon salt
¼ teaspoon nutmeg
¼ teaspoon cloves
¼ teaspoon allspice
½ cup raisins
1 cup sugar
½ cup butter, at room temperature
1 cup milk
1 egg

Preheat oven to 350°F. Sift flour. Measure and sift together with other dry ingredients. Add raisins. Cream sugar and butter with 2 tablespoons milk. Add egg and mix well. Add sifted dry ingredients alternately with remaining milk. Bake 30 to 40 minutes in a greased loaf pan, or until a toothpick inserted in the center comes out clean. Serve with whipped cream.

PLAIN SPONGE CAKE

1 cup sifted flour
4 or 5 eggs, separated
1 cup sugar
2 tablespoons lemon juice
1 teaspoon lemon zest, grated
½ teaspoon salt
Powdered sugar (optional)

Preheat oven to 350°F. Sift the flour. Beat the egg yolks until thick and lemon-colored. Gradually add half the sugar, beating thoroughly, and then the lemon juice and zest. Beat until thick. Beat the egg whites and salt until they start to peak but will still flow. Fold in the rest of the sugar, then the yolk mixture. Fold in the flour gently. Pour the batter as soon as it is mixed into an ungreased baking pan. For a large or medium-sized loaf a tube pan is best, because the center opening allows the mixture to heat evenly. Powdered sugar sifted over the top makes a more desirable crust. The oven should be ready for the cake as soon as it is mixed and in the pan. The cake should be baked for 50 to 60 minutes. After baking, invert the cake to cool, but remove from the pan before it is entirely cold.

SUNSHINE CAKE

1 cup sifted flour
6 whites and 3 yolks of eggs
1 to 1¼ cups sugar
¾ teaspoon cream of tartar
1 teaspoon vanilla or almond extract
½ teaspoon salt

Mix and bake as directed for plain sponge cake (above).

SWEDISH TEA CAKES

½ cup butter, at room temperature
¼ cup brown sugar
1 egg, separated
1 cup sifted flour
½ cup chopped walnuts
Raspberry or strawberry jam

Preheat oven to 300°F. Cream butter and blend in sugar. Add egg yolk, then flour. Roll dough into small balls 1" in diameter. Dip in egg white, then roll in chopped nuts. Place on greased cookie sheet and press centers down with finger. Bake 5 minutes in a slow oven (300°F). Remove and press down centers again, being careful not to burn yourself. Bake 15 minutes longer. Cool slightly. Fill centers with jam. Yield: 12 cakes.

TWO-EGG CAKE

½ cup butter, at room temperature
1 cup granulated sugar
2 eggs, separated
1¾ cups sifted cake flour
2 teaspoons baking powder
½ teaspoon salt
½ cup milk
½ teaspoon vanilla

Preheat oven to 350°F. Cream butter for 1 minute at high speed. Add sugar gradually, beating swiftly. Add eggs, unbeaten, one at a time, and beat well. Sift flour, baking powder, and salt. Alternately add sifted dry ingredients with the milk to which the vanilla has been added. Beat well. Pour batter into a loaf pan, well greased and lightly floured or lined with waxed paper or parchment paper. Cut through the batter to break any large air bubbles. Or, if preferred, turn into 2 greased 8" layer cake pans or into 2 dozen greased cupcake pans. For a loaf cake, bake for 50 to 60 minutes. A layer cake is baked for 25 to 30 minutes and cupcakes for 20 to 30 minutes. To check for doneness, insert a toothpick into the center. It will come out clean when the cake is ready. After removing from oven, loosen edges, invert on rack, removing pan and turning right side up. Cool. Frost with fudge icing (p. 631) or any desired icing.

OLD-FASHIONED WEDDING CAKE

1 cup butter, at room temperature
1¾ cups brown sugar
6 eggs
½ cup molasses
1 cup white grape juice
2 cups flour
1½ tablespoons cinnamon
1 tablespoon mace
½ tablespoon ginger
½ tablespoon clove
1 cup raisins
1 cup currants
1 cup lemon and orange peel, chopped
1 cup citron, chopped

Preheat oven to 225°F. Cream butter and sugar together. Add the eggs, molasses, and grape juice and mix well. Mix and sift flour, cinnamon, mace, ginger, and clove. Add enough of the sifted flour mixture to the fruit to keep it from sticking together. Add remaining flour and fruit to the first mixture and beat thoroughly. Line bottom of a large round pan with greased paper or parchment paper and grease sides of pan. Pour mixture into it and bake for 3 to 4 hours or until a toothpick inserted in the center comes out clean. A small pan of water in the oven helps to keep the cake from burning during the long cooking. Ice and decorate with ornamental icing (p. 627).

DANISH APPLE CAKE

½ pound almond macaroons (p. 606)
3 cups toast crumbs
3 tablespoons butter
2½ cups applesauce (p. 190)
1 cup heavy cream, whipped

Crumble the macaroons. Mix macaroons and toast crumbs. Sauté them lightly in the butter. Pack in layers in a mold alternately with applesauce. Allow to harden in the refrigerator. Serve with whipped cream. Peach butter, apricot butter, crushed pineapple, raspberries, loganberries, cherries or practically any fruit may be substituted for the applesauce if the fruit is cooked to a sauce consistency.

BASIC CUPCAKES

½ cup butter, at room temperature
1 cup sugar
3 eggs
1¾ cups flour
2 teaspoons baking powder
½ teaspoon salt
½ cup milk
1 teaspoon vanilla

Preheat oven to 375°F. Cream butter, sugar, and eggs together until light and fluffy. Sift flour, baking powder, and salt and add alternately with milk to creamed mixture. Add vanilla. Beat thoroughly. Turn into greased cupcake pans. Bake for 15 to 20 minutes, or until a toothpick inserted in the center comes out clean. Yield: 18 cupcakes.

SOUR CREAM CUPCAKES

1 tablespoon butter, at room temperature
1 cup sugar
2 eggs
½ teaspoon baking soda
½ cup sour cream
1½ cups flour
1½ teaspoon salt
½ teaspoon cream of tartar
⅛ teaspoon mace

Preheat oven to 400°F. Cream butter, sugar, and eggs together until light and fluffy. Dissolve baking soda in sour cream. Sift flour, salt, cream of tartar, and mace together and add alternately with cream to first mixture. Beat thoroughly. Bake in greased cupcake pans for 15 to 20 minutes. Yield: 18 cupcakes.

FROZEN CUPCAKES

1 cup heavy cream
¼ cup sugar
1½ cups crumbled sponge cake (p. 582) crumbs
2½ tablespoons chopped nuts
½ teaspoon vanilla
3 tablespoons chopped maraschino cherries,
    plus more for garnishing
1 tablespoon maraschino cherry juice
½ teaspoon salt

Whip the cream stiff and then fold in the rest of the ingredients, lightly but thoroughly. Fill tiny cups with the mixture and place in freezer. Chill for 2 to 3 hours, until solid. Garnish with maraschino cherries. Serves 4.

FILLED CUPCAKES

Make basic cupcakes (p. 586). Cool. Cut in halves, crosswise. Remove a bit of cake. Fill with whipped cream. Return to original shape and ice with boiled frosting (p. 625) or creamy chocolate frosting (p. 630).

FILLED CHOCOLATE CAKES

Mix batter for devil's food cake (p. 555). Bake in greased cupcake pans at 375°F for 15 to 20 minutes. While hot remove a small square from top of each cake and insert marshmallow. Ice with boiled frosting (p. 625).

PETITS FOURS

Bake a sponge (p. 582) or pound cake (p. 578) in a shallow pan so that the finished cake is not more than 1" high. When cool, slice in 1" strips. Then cut into various fancy shapes, half moons, circles, triangles, etc. Cut each small cake in half, crosswise. Remove a portion of insides and fill with whipped cream, custard (p. 483), or any desired filling. Put together again and dip in any desired icing or icings. Where a large number are prepared it adds to the beauty of the table to color the tiny cakes in various brilliant colors. Garnish tops with nuts, candied fruits, maraschino cherries, etc., with an eye to beauty as well as taste. Various designs can also be made on tops of cakes with various-colored frostings. Place each cake in a paper cup.

CREAM PUFFS

½ cup butter, at room temperature
1 cup boiling water or milk
1 cup flour
4 eggs
1 teaspoon salt

Preheat oven to 450°F. Add butter to milk and bring to a boil. Add flour all at once and stir vigorously until ball forms in center of pan. Cool slightly. Add unbeaten eggs, one at a time, beating after adding each egg and salt. Mixture should be very stiff. Shape on oiled cookie sheet by dropping from spoon or using pastry bag and tube. Bake for fifteen minutes at 450°F. Reduce temperature to 350°F and continue baking for 30 minutes or until done. If in doubt, remove one from oven to test. The puffs should be hollow and dry. Cool. Fill with cream filling (p. 622), ice cream or whipped cream. Makes 2 dozen small puffs.

CHOCOLATE CREAM PUFFS

Fill baked cream puffs with chocolate cream filling (p. 622) and frost with chocolate icing (p. 630).

ÉCLAIRS

Prepare as for cream puffs (p. 589). Press dough through pastry bag and tube onto greased shallow pan in strips 4" long and 1" wide. Bake same as cream puffs and fill as desired. Ice with any desired frosting.

CHOCOLATE ÉCLAIRS

Fill baked éclairs (above) with chocolate cream filling (p. 622), and frost with chocolate icing (p. 630).

COOKIES AND BROWNIES

DATE BARS

    1 cup walnuts, chopped
    1 cup pitted dates, chopped
    1 cup powdered sugar
    2 beaten eggs
    1 tablespoon lemon juice
    ¼ cup flour
    1 tablespoon melted butter
    ½ teaspoon salt
    Powdered sugar, for serving

Preheat oven to 350°F. Combine nuts, dates, sugar, and eggs. Mix well. Add other ingredients and mix thoroughly. Turn, ¼" thick, into greased, shallow pan. Bake for 20 to 25 minutes. While hot, cut into strips or bars and roll in powdered sugar.

SCOTCH FANS

    1 cup butter, at room temperature
    ¾ cup brown sugar
    2¼ cups flour, plus more for rolling out the dough
    1 teaspoon salt
    1 egg yolk

Preheat oven to 350°F. Cream butter and sugar together. Add flour and salt and knead until ingredients hold together. Roll out on slightly floured board to ¼" thickness. Cut in circles with large fluted cooking cutter, then cut each circle in 3 fan-shaped pieces. Brush with egg yolk diluted with 1 tablespoon water. Bake for 15 to 20 minutes. Yield: 36 fans.

APRICOT SQUARES

½ cup butter, plus 6 teaspoons, at room temperature
1 cup sugar
2 eggs
1 cup flour
1 teaspoon baking powder
9 ripe apricots
3 teaspoons butter
6 teaspoons brandy
1 teaspoon grated orange zest

Preheat oven to 350°F. Cream ½ cup butter and half the sugar. Add eggs and beat until very light. Sift flour with baking powder and stir into creamed mixture. Pour into a buttered and floured square cake pan. Press apricot halves, pitted but not peeled, into the batter, skin side down. Place in each half ⅓ teaspoon of butter and an equal amount of brandy. Sprinkle over all the remaining sugar and orange zest mixed. Bake for 30 minutes and cut into nine squares.

BLUEBERRY SQUARES

2 cups flour
4 teaspoons baking powder
¼ teaspoon salt
5 tablespoons butter, melted and cooled
⅔ cup milk
1½ cups blueberries
½ cup granulated sugar
½ teaspoon cinnamon

Preheat oven to 375°F. Mix flour, baking powder, and salt. Add butter and milk. Mix lightly and pour at once into a buttered shallow pan. Press down until soft dough is about ⅔" thick. Mix blueberries with sugar and cinnamon. Quickly spread this mixture on the dough. Bake for 12 minutes. Cut in squares and serve fresh with butter.

BUTTERSCOTCH SQUARES

¼ cup butter, at room temperature
1½ cups brown sugar, divided
2 eggs
1½ cups flour
½ teaspoon salt
⅓ cup heavy cream
½ cup chopped walnuts

Preheat oven to 350°F. Cream butter. Add ¾ cup sugar and cream thoroughly. Add 1 egg and beat well. Mix the flour and salt and add to the first mixture alternately with the cream. Spread ⅛" thick on cookie sheets. Brush with the remaining egg, and sprinkle with remaining sugar mixed with the nuts. Bake for 15 to 20 minutes. Cut into 2" squares while still hot.

CHOCOLATE ROBINS

½ cup flour
½ teaspoon salt
¼ cup butter, at room temperature
2 ounces dark chocolate, melted
2 eggs
1 cup sugar
½ cup chopped nuts
1 teaspoon vanilla

Preheat oven to 350°F. Sift flour once. Add salt and sift again. Place butter in mixing bowl and cream until soft. Add warm melted chocolate and stir until thoroughly blended. In a separate bowl, beat the whole eggs until very light and fluffy. Add sugar, a small amount at a time, beating after each addition. Add egg mixture to chocolate mixture and fold in flour, nuts, and vanilla. Bake in a shallow oiled cookie pan for 25 to 30 minutes. Cool and cut into squares.

BROWNIES

1 cup sugar
1½ tablespoons cocoa
¼ cup butter, melted
1 egg
½ cup flour
1 teaspoon vanilla
½ cup chopped nuts, optional

Preheat oven to 350°F. Cream sugar, cocoa, and butter together and add other ingredients, mixing well. Spread dough in shallow, greased and floured pan. Bake for 30 minutes. Cut into pieces while warm.

BANGOR BROWNIES

1 cup flour
1 teaspoon baking powder
Dash salt
¼ cup melted butter
⅓ cup molasses
1 egg
2 ounces dark chocolate, melted
1 cup nuts, chopped

Sift flour, baking powder, and salt together. Mix other ingredients in the order given and beat thoroughly. Combine the two mixtures. Spread the mixture evenly in a 9" cake pan that has been lined with oiled paper or parchment paper. Bake about 15 minutes. Remove the paper from the cake as soon as it is taken from the oven and cut into small squares or strips with a sharp knife.

BROWN SUGAR BROWNIES

1 cup flour
2 teaspoons baking powder
1 teaspoon salt
⅝ cup butter (10 tablespoons)
2 cups brown sugar
2 eggs
2 teaspoons vanilla
1 cup chopped nuts

Preheat oven to 450°F. Sift flour. Sift again with baking powder, and salt. Melt butter. Beat in sugar, eggs, vanilla, and sifted dry ingredients mixed with the nuts. Spread thinly in a well greased and floured 10" x 15" pan. Bake for 30 minutes. Cool and cut.

LADYFINGERS

½ cup sifted cake flour
⅛ teaspoon salt
⅔ cup powdered sugar, divided
3 eggs, separated
½ teaspoon vanilla

Preheat oven to 350°F. Mix flour, salt, and ⅓ cup sugar and sift together. Beat egg whites until stiff and gradually beat in remaining sugar. Fold in vanilla and well-beaten egg yolks beaten until thick and very light colored. Carefully fold in the flour-sugar mixture, sprinkling about 3 tablespoons at a time over surface. Press through pastry tube on a cookie sheet or silpat, making strips 4" x ¾", or bake in ladyfinger pans. Dust with additional powdered sugar and bake for 10 to 12 minutes. Batter may be dropped from teaspoon to make rounds if desired. Yield: 24 ladyfingers.

FIG NEWTONS

½ cup butter, at room temperature
1½ cups sugar
1 well-beaten egg
½ cup milk
1 teaspoon vanilla
½ teaspoon salt
3 cups flour
3 teaspoons baking powder
1 cup dried figs, chopped
1 cup water

Preheat oven to 400°F. Cream butter and 1 cup sugar. Add egg and beat until light. Mix milk and vanilla. Sift salt, flour, and baking powder together and add alternately with milk to creamed mixture. Blend well. Roll out ⅛" thick on slightly floured board in a rectangle. Put figs in saucepan with remaining sugar and 1 cup boiling water. Boil 5 minutes. Cool. Spread cooked mixture over ½ of the dough. Cover with uncovered half of dough. Cut in oblong pieces. Bake for 12 to 15 minutes.

HERMITS

    1 cup butter, at room temperature
    1½ cups sugar
    3 eggs
    3 cups flour
    1½ teaspoons salt
    ½ teaspoon baking soda
    1 teaspoon allspice
    1 teaspoon cinnamon
    1 teaspoon clove
    1 teaspoon nutmeg
    1½ cups raisins
    ½ cup chopped nuts

Preheat oven to 350°F. Cream butter, sugar, and eggs together until light and fluffy. Sift flour, salt, baking soda, allspice, cinnamon, clove, and nutmeg together and add to creamed mixture. Add raisins and nuts and mix well. Drop by teaspoons on greased baking sheet. Bake for 15 to 20 minutes. Yield: 70 cookies.

BROWN SUGAR COOKIES

7 cups sifted flour
1 tablespoon baking soda
1 tablespoon cream of tartar
4 cups brown sugar
1 cup melted butter
4 eggs

Mix ingredients well and form into logs that are 1½" thick. Wrap in saran wrap and let stand in refrigerator for at least 1 hour. Slice and bake at 400°F for 8 to 10 minutes, or until lightly browned. Yield: 100 cookies.

BUTTERSCOTCH COOKIES

¾ cup butter, at room temperature
¾ cup brown sugar
1 teaspoon vanilla
4 cups sifted flour
1 teaspoon baking powder
¼ teaspoon baking soda
½ teaspoon salt
2 well-beaten eggs

Cream butter and sugar together. Add vanilla. Sift flour, baking powder, baking soda, and salt together and add alternately with eggs to creamed mixture, beating well after each addition. Shape into rolls 3" thick and 6" long. Wrap each in waxed paper or saran wrap and chill for several hours or overnight. Cut in slices and bake at 375°F for 8 minutes. Yield: 36 cookies.

CHOCOLATE NUT COOKIES

½ cup butter, at room temperature
1 cup brown sugar
1 egg
2 ounces dark chocolate, melted
1½ cups flour
¼ teaspoon salt
½ teaspoon baking soda
1 teaspoon baking powder
½ cup milk
1 teaspoon vanilla
1 cup chopped walnuts

Preheat oven to 400°F. Cream butter, sugar, and egg. Add melted chocolate. Sift together flour, salt, baking soda, and baking powder. Add the sifted dry ingredients alternately with the milk and the vanilla and the nuts last. Drop on cookie sheet. Bake for 15 to 20 minutes. Yield: 24 cookies.

CHOCOLATE WALNUT COOKIES

½ cup butter, at room temperature
1 cup sugar
1 egg
1 teaspoon vanilla
2 ½ cups flour
1 teaspoon baking powder
½ teaspoon cinnamon
2 tablespoons milk
2 ounces melted dark chocolate
½ cup chopped walnuts

Cream butter, sugar, and slightly beaten egg. Add vanilla. Add dry ingredients, which have been sifted together, alternately with milk. Add chocolate and nuts. Form into roll. Wrap in waxed paper or saran wrap. Chill. Slice thinly. Bake at 350°F for about 10 minutes. Yield: 40 cookies.

CORN FLAKE COOKIES

1 cup butter, at room temperature
1½ cups sugar
2 well-beaten eggs
¼ cup milk
1 cup raisins
2 cups flour, plus more for rolling out
2 teaspoons baking soda
2 cups corn flakes

Preheat oven to 350°F. Cream butter and sugar. Add eggs and beat until light. Add milk and raisins. Sift flour with baking soda and add, blending well. Add corn flakes. Roll ¼" thick on slightly floured board. Cut with a cookie cutter. Place on baking sheet and bake for 12 to 15 minutes. Yield: 48 cookies.

COCONUT ORANGE JUMBLES

¾ cup butter, at room temperature
1¼ cups sugar
2 eggs
1 cup shredded coconut
2½ cups sifted flour
¼ teaspoon salt
½ teaspoon baking soda
¾ cup orange juice
3 tablespoons grated orange peel

Preheat oven to 425°F. Cream butter and sugar together. Beat in eggs. Beat in coconut. Sift flour, salt, and baking soda together and add alternately with orange juice to creamed mixture. Beat until smooth. Drop by teaspoons on ungreased baking sheet. Sprinkle with additional coconut and orange peel. Bake for 10 to 12 minutes. Yield: 48 cookies.

DROP COOKIES

¾ cup butter, at room temperature
3 teaspoons vanilla
1½ cups sugar
2 eggs
4 cups sifted flour
4 teaspoons baking powder
½ teaspoon salt
¾ cup milk

Preheat oven to 400°F. Cream butter, vanilla, and sugar together until light and fluffy. Continue creaming while adding well-beaten eggs. Sift flour, baking powder, and salt together and add alternately with milk to creamed mixture. Drop small portions of mixture on greased baking sheet and bake for 12 to 15 minutes. Yield: 72 cookies.

CRISP COOKIES

1 cup butter, at room temperature
2 teaspoons vanilla
2 cups sugar
2 eggs
4 cups sifted flour
4 teaspoons baking powder
½ teaspoon salt
¼ cup milk

Mix ingredients as for drop cookies (p. 601). Form dough into a roll 3" thick and 6" long. Wrap in wax paper or saran wrap and chill. Cut off thin slices and bake at 375°F for 10 to 12 minutes. Yield: 72 cookies.

ROLLED COOKIES

Make dough as for crisp cookies (above). Roll on lightly floured board to ¼" thickness. Cut into any desired shape and bake on greased baking sheet at 375°F for 10 to 12 minutes. Yield: 72 cookies.

GINGERSNAPS

1 cup sugar
1 cup molasses
1 cup butter, at room temperature
1 egg
1 teaspoon cinnamon
2 teaspoons ground ginger
2 teaspoons baking soda
1 tablespoon cider vinegar
1 teaspoon vanilla
2½ cups flour, more if needed

Preheat oven to 325°F. Combine sugar, molasses, butter, egg, cinnamon, ginger, and soda. Mix well. Add vinegar, vanilla, and enough flour to make a stiff dough. Roll very thin. Cut with cookie cutter. Bake for 10 to 12 minutes. Yield: 48 gingersnaps.

GINGER COOKIES

½ cup butter, at room temperature
½ cup molasses
½ cup sugar
½ teaspoon nutmeg
½ teaspoon cinnamon
½ teaspoon ground ginger
1 beaten egg
½ cup chopped walnuts
2½ cups flour
½ teaspoon baking powder
⅔ teaspoon salt

Cream butter, molasses, sugar, nutmeg, cinnamon, and ginger together in a medium saucepan. Mix well and bring slowly to boiling point. Cool. Add egg and nuts, combining well. Sift flour, baking powder, and salt together and add to first mixture. Mix thoroughly. Shape into a roll about 2½" thick. Roll in wax paper or saran wrap and chill for at least 1 hour. Slice and bake at 375°F for 12 minutes. Yield: 48 cookies.

HAZELNUT COOKIES

4 ounces milk chocolate
¼ pound finely chopped hazelnuts
¼ pound finely chopped almonds
⅔ cup powdered sugar
2 egg whites
¼ teaspoon cinnamon
Few grains ground clove
2 tablespoons butter, melted

Melt chocolate in a double boiler. Add chopped nuts and sugar and mix well. Add stiffly beaten egg whites, spices, and butter. Mix well. Shape into a roll about 2½" thick. Chill. Roll out thin, a small quantity at a time, on slightly floured board. Cut with cookie cutter. Placed on greased pans and bake at 325°F for 12 to 15 minutes. Yield: 4 dozen cookies

OATMEAL LACE WAFERS

2 tablespoons butter, at room temperature
1 cup sugar
2 eggs
½ teaspoon salt
½ teaspoon nutmeg
2½ cups rolled oats
2½ teaspoons baking powder
1 teaspoon vanilla
¼ teaspoon almond extract

Preheat oven to 350°F. Cream butter, sugar, and eggs together until light and fluffy. Combine salt, nutmeg, rolled oats and baking powder and add to creamed mixture. Mix thoroughly. Add vanilla and almond extract. Drop by teaspoons on greased baking pan. Bake for 12 to 15 minutes. Yield: 60 cookies.

ALMOND MACAROONS

3 egg whites
1 cup sugar
½ pound finely ground almonds
½ teaspoon almond extract
1 tablespoon melted butter

Preheat oven to 275°F. Beat egg whites. Add sugar gradually, beating constantly. Add almonds, flavoring, and butter. Mix well. Drop by teaspoons on a greased cookie sheet. Bake for 30 to 40 minutes. Yield: 48 macaroons.

CORN FLAKE MACAROONS

2 egg whites
½ cup granulated sugar
½ cup brown sugar
1 tablespoon flour
2 cups corn flakes
½ cup walnuts, finely chopped
1 cup shredded coconut
1 teaspoon vanilla

Preheat oven to 350°F. Beat egg whites until very stiff. Add sugars, flour, and other ingredients. Mix well and drop by teaspoonfuls on buttered cookie sheet. Bake for 20 minutes. Yield: 60 macaroons.

MOLASSES CRISPS

¼ cup butter
½ cup sugar
¾ cup molasses
1 cup flour
¾ teaspoon salt

Preheat oven to 350°F. Melt butter. Add sugar and molasses and bring to boiling point. Cool slightly. Add flour and salt. Drop by teaspoons on greased baking sheet. Bake for 12 to 15 minutes. Yield: 36 cookies.

OATMEAL COOKIES

1½ cups rolled oats
½ cup brown sugar
¾ cup flour
1 teaspoon salt
½ teaspoon baking soda
½ teaspoon cinnamon
¼ cup milk
½ cup melted butter

Combine oats, sugar, flour, salt, baking soda, and cinnamon. Add milk and melted butter. Mix well. Roll into a ball and wrap in waxed paper or saran wrap. Chill for at least an hour. Roll out ¼" thick on slightly floured board. Cut into circles and place on baking sheet. Bake at 350°F for 12 to 15 minutes. Yield: 60 cookies.

OATMEAL JELLY COOKIES

Make a slight depression in center of oatmeal cookies (p. 607) before baking and fill with currant jelly or jam.

PEANUT DROP COOKIES

2 cups brown sugar
1 cup butter, at room temperature
½ teaspoon salt
2 eggs
1 teaspoon vanilla
2 cups flour
½ teaspoon baking soda
1 teaspoon baking powder
1 cup corn flakes
2 cups rolled oats
1½ cups peanuts with skins left on

Preheat oven to 400°F. Cream the sugar with the butter and salt. Add the eggs and vanilla and beat until creamy. Sift the flour, baking soda, and baking powder together and add to first mixture. Add other ingredients. Drop by small spoonfuls on cookie sheet and bake for 12 to 15 minutes. Yield: 72 cookies.

PEANUT BUTTER COOKIES

2 cups sifted flour
1½ teaspoons baking powder
½ teaspoon salt
2 tablespoons butter, at room temperature
½ cup peanut butter
1 cup sugar
1 egg
1 teaspoon vanilla
⅓ cup milk
½ cup peanuts, chopped

Sift flour, baking powder, and salt together. Cream butter and peanut butter together. Beat in other ingredients (except chopped peanuts) one at a time. Stir in flour mixture, blending well. Roll into a ball and cover with waxed paper or saran wrap. Chill for at least 1 hour. Roll out to ¼" thickness on slightly floured board. Cut with cookie cutter. Place on ungreased baking sheet. Sprinkle with peanuts. Bake at 350°F for 12 to 15 minutes. Yield: 50 cookies.

MOLASSES NUT COOKIES

1 cup butter
1 cup sugar
1 tablespoon molasses
¾ cup chopped nuts
2¾ cups sifted flour
1 teaspoon baking soda

Cream butter. Blend in sugar and molasses. Add nuts, then sifted dry ingredients. Form dough into 2½" thick rolls and chill thoroughly. Cut into thin slices. Bake on greased cookie sheet at 350°F about 12 to 15 minutes. Yield: 60 cookies.

PECAN WAFERS

½ cup butter, at room temperature
1 cup brown sugar
2 eggs
4 tablespoons flour
½ cup chopped pecans
½ teaspoon salt
½ teaspoon maple syrup

Preheat oven to 300°F. Cream butter and sugar. Add eggs, one at a time, beating well after each is added. Stir in flour and blend well. Add nuts, salt, and syrup. Drop by teaspoons, 5" apart, on greased baking sheet. Spread out very thin with spoon. Bake for 10 to 12 minutes. If desired, these may be turned around finger to form rolls while warm. Yield: 36 wafers.

SUGAR COOKIES

⅔ cup butter, at room temperature
1¼ cups sugar, plus more for sprinkling
2 eggs
3 cups flour
1 ½ teaspoons salt
2 teaspoons baking powder
Grated zest of 1 lemon
1 tablespoon freshly squeezed lemon juice

Cream butter, sugar and eggs together until light and foamy. Sift flour, salt, and baking powder together and add to first mixture. Add lemon zest and juice. Mix until smooth. Roll into a ball, and wrap in waxed paper or saran wrap. Chill for at least an hour. Roll to ¼" thickness, on slightly floured board. Cut with cookie cutter. Sprinkle with sugar and bake at 350°F for 12 to 15 minutes. Yield: 60 cookies.

ALMOND COOKIES

Substitute 1 teaspoon vanilla for lemon zest and juice in recipe for sugar cookies (p. 610). After cookies have been cut, brush with egg and dip in chopped almonds. Cook same as sugar cookies.

CHOCOLATE COOKIES

Add ½ cup cocoa, mixed with 3 tablespoons hot coffee, to recipe for sugar cookies (p. 610) when eggs are added and substitute 1 teaspoon vanilla for lemon juice and zest.

COCONUT COOKIES

Add 1 cup shredded coconut to recipe for sugar cookies (p. 610).

FIG COOKIES

Add ⅔ cup chopped dried figs to recipe for sugar cookies (p. 610) and substitute brown sugar for granulated sugar and 1 teaspoon vanilla for lemon zest and juice.

HALLOWEEN COOKIES

Cut sugar cookies (p. 610) into half moons, witches, elves, pumpkins, etc. Ice cookies with orange icing (p. 632) and decorate with tiny black candies.

LIME COOKIES

Substitute lime zest and juice for lemon zest and juice in recipe for sugar cookies (p. 610).

MAPLE SUGAR COOKIES

Substitute ¾ cup maple sugar for an equal amount of granulated sugar and eliminate lemon zest and juice in recipe for sugar cookies (p. 610).

NUT COOKIES

Prepare recipe for sugar cookies (p. 610). Before baking, brush cookies with egg white and sprinkle with chopped nuts and sugar.

SAND TARTS

Substitute 1 teaspoon vanilla for lemon juice and zest in recipe for sugar cookies (p. 610). Cut into diamonds or squares, brush with white of egg, sprinkle with sugar and cinnamon, and place an almond in the center of each cookie.

SPICE COOKIES

Sift ⅛ teaspoon clove, ¼ teaspoon nutmeg, and ½ teaspoon cinnamon with flour in recipe for sugar cookies (p. 610) and substitute 1 teaspoon vanilla for lemon juice and zest.

FILLED COOKIES

Roll out sugar cookie dough (p. 610) ⅛" thick. Cut into circles. Put 1 teaspoon jam in center of ½ the circles. Top with other circles, pressing edges firmly together. Bake same as sugar cookies. Another good filling is made by combining 1 cup chopped raisins, figs or dates with 1 cup sugar and ¼ cup water and boiling until fruit is tender.

CHOCOLATE CHIP COOKIES

½ cups butter, at room temperature
¼ cup brown sugar
½ cup white sugar
1 well-beaten egg
1 cup flour
½ teaspoon salt
½ teaspoon baking soda
1 8-ounce package semi-sweet chocolate chips
½ cup chopped nuts (optional)
1 teaspoon vanilla

Preheat oven to 375°F. Cream butter. Add sugars gradually while creaming until light and fluffy. Add egg and mix well. Sift flour once. Measure. Sift again with salt and soda. Combine mixtures thoroughly. Add chocolate chips, nuts, and vanilla. Drop from teaspoon on baking sheet. Bake for 10 to 12 minutes. Yield: 50 cookies.

FILLINGS AND FROSTINGS

CREAM SAUCE

   1 cup sugar
   3 egg yolks, plus 1 egg white
   1 cup cream
   1 teaspoon vanilla

Combine all ingredients except vanilla and beat until very light. Heat in a double boiler over hot water, beating until foamy. Remove from heat. Add vanilla. Stir well.

CUSTARD SAUCE

   1 cup whole milk
   2 beaten egg yolks
   2 tablespoons sugar
   $\frac{1}{8}$ teaspoon salt
   $\frac{1}{4}$ teaspoon vanilla

Scald milk in a double boiler over hot water. Beat yolks, sugar, and salt together in a separate bowl and pour milk over them. Cook in a double boiler over hot water, stirring constantly, until mixture coats the spoon. Chill. Add vanilla.

FOAMY SAUCE

 ¼ cup sugar
 2 tablespoons flour
 ½ teaspoon salt
 1 cup whole milk
 1 egg yolk, plus 2 egg whites
 2 tablespoons sherry
 Few grains nutmeg

Mix sugar, flour, and salt together. Add milk and beaten egg yolk and cook in a double boiler over hot water until thick. Add sherry and nutmeg. Stiffly beat the egg whites, and gently fold them into the mixture.

HARD SAUCE

 1 cup powdered sugar
 ½ teaspoon vanilla
 ½ cup butter, at room temperature
 ⅛ teaspoon salt

Combine ingredients and cream well. Press into mold or 8" baking dish. When firm unmold and serve.

CHOCOLATE SAUCE

1¼ cups whole milk
2 ounces unsweetened chocolate
½ tablespoon butter or other fat
1 cup powdered sugar
1 teaspoon vanilla
⅛ teaspoon salt

Cook milk, chocolate, and butter over a low heat and stir until chocolate melts and the mixture thickens. Add sugar and cook until it thickens again, stirring constantly. Add vanilla and salt. Mix well.

HOT FUDGE SAUCE

1 ounce dark or milk chocolate
2 tablespoons butter
1½ cups sugar
1⁄16 teaspoon salt
⅓ cup hot strong coffee
⅓ cup thin cream or half-and-half
1 teaspoon vanilla

Bring water in bottom of double boiler to a boil. Reduce heat to a simmer. Melt chocolate in top of double boiler. Add butter, sugar, salt, and hot coffee. Heat until all sugar crystals are dissolved. Cook about 10 minutes. Remove from heat, add cream and vanilla. Beat well and serve hot.

CHOCOLATE CARAMEL SAUCE

2 ounces dark chocolate
2 cups light brown sugar
2 tablespoons butter
½ cup whole milk
1 teaspoon vanilla

Butter the inside of a saucepan. Melt chocolate in a double boiler over hot water. Add brown sugar and mix well. Add butter and milk. Cook until the mixture forms a soft ball in cold water (about 236°F), then take from heat and flavor with vanilla.

CARAMEL NUT SAUCE

Add ½ cup chopped nuts to recipe for chocolate caramel sauce (above) after cooking.

CREAMY CHOCOLATE SAUCE

1 ounce dark chocolate
1 cup sugar
1 cup water
Few grains salt
½ to ¾ cup light cream
1 teaspoon vanilla
cinnamon if desired

Cut chocolate into small pieces. Add sugar, 1 cup water, and salt and let boil for 5 minutes. Remove from heat, cool and add cream, vanilla, and cinnamon, if desired.

CHERRY SAUCE

1 tablespoon cornstarch
1 tablespoon cold water
2 cups canned cherries and juice
1 teaspoon lemon juice

Mix cornstarch with cold water, bringing it to a pouring consistency. Add cherries and juice. Cook, stirring constantly. When thickened and smooth, put pan in a double boiler over hot water and cook 5 to 10 minutes. Add lemon juice just before serving.

HOT CHERRY GLAZE

2 tablespoons cornstarch
½ cup sugar
¼ teaspoon salt
1½ cups hot cherry juice
2 tablespoons lemon juice
¼ teaspoon almond extract

Mix cornstarch, sugar, and salt. Pour the hot fruit juice over the dry ingredients, stirring constantly. Cook over medium heat until thick and clear. Remove from heat and add the lemon juice and almond extract.

CHOCOLATE MINT SAUCE

2 cups sugar
Dash of salt
2 ounces dark chocolate
¾ cup whole milk
1 tablespoon butter
¼ cup crushed peppermint candy

Combine sugar, salt, chocolate, milk, and butter and cook over low heat, stirring until sugar is dissolved and chocolate melted. Boil, covered, 2 minutes; then boil, uncovered, until a small amount forms a very soft ball when dropped into cold water (236°F). Remove from heat. Add crushed mints and beat slightly. Serve hot or warm. If it seems too thick, dilute with a small amount of cream. Yield: 2 cups sauce.

COCOA SAUCE

½ cup cocoa powder
1 cup water
1 cup sugar
¼ teaspoon salt
1 tablespoon butter
1 teaspoon vanilla

Cook cocoa and water together over medium until it is smooth and thick. Add sugar and salt and cook a few minutes longer. Add butter and vanilla.

LEMON SAUCE

1 tablespoon cornstarch
½ cup sugar
1 teaspoon grated lemon zest
2 tablespoons lemon juice
2 tablespoons butter
nutmeg
salt

Combine cornstarch, sugar, zest, and lemon juice. Bring to a boil over medium heat. Boil for 5 minutes. Remove from heat. Add butter. Season to taste with nutmeg and salt. Serves 4.

LEMON HARD SAUCE

⅓ cup butter, at room temperature
2¼ cups powdered sugar
3 tablespoons lemon juice
1 egg white

Cream the butter and powdered sugar with the lemon juice. Beat the egg white until stiff peaks form. Gently fold into the lemon mixture.

ORANGE SAUCE

1 tablespoon cornstarch
½ cup sugar
1 teaspoon grated orange zest
1 cup orange juice
1 tablespoon lemon juice
2 tablespoons butter

Mix cornstarch, sugar, zest, and orange juice in a medium saucepan. Boil 5 minutes. Remove from heat. Add lemon juice and butter. Serve hot.

ORANGE PINEAPPLE SAUCE

½ cup pineapple juice
⅔ cup sugar
Zest and juice of 1 orange
3 egg yolks, well beaten
1 cup cream, whipped

Bring pineapple juice, sugar, and juice and zest of orange to boiling point and add to yolks. Cook in double boiler over medium heat until thick. Cool and add cream.

RUM SAUCE

    1 egg yolk
    2 tablespoons rum
    2 tablespoons confectioner's sugar
    1 egg white, stiffly beaten
    ½ cup cream, whipped
    Grated zest 1 lemon

Beat the egg yolk with the rum and sugar. Gently fold in the stiffly beaten egg white, whipped cream, and the grated lemon zest.

CREAM FILLING

    ⅓ cup flour
    ⅔ cup sugar
    ¼ teaspoon salt
    2 cups milk
    2 tablespoons butter
    3 egg yolks, beaten
    ½ tablespoon vanilla

Mix flour, sugar, and salt. Bring milk to a boil and remove from heat. Add slowly to dry mixture, stirring while adding. Cook over hot water, stirring until thick, about 15 minutes. Add butter. Pour mixture over egg yolks, stirring constantly. Cool. Add vanilla.

CHOCOLATE CREAM FILLING

Melt 2 ounces dark chocolate in milk in recipe for cream filling (above) and increase amount of sugar to 1 cup.

COCONUT CREAM FILLING

Add 1 cup shredded coconut to recipe for cream filling (p. 622).

FRUIT FILLING

¾ cup chopped dried figs
½ cup chopped dates
¼ cup chopped raisins
½ cup sugar
½ cup boiling water
3 tablespoons lemon juice

Mix figs, dates, and raisins. Add sugar, water, and lemon juice and cook in a double boiler over hot water until thick, about 10 minutes. Spread while hot between layers of cake.

MARSHMALLOW CREAM FILLING

¾ cup sugar
⅓ cup corn syrup
¼ cup water
16 large marshmallows, cut in quarters
2 egg whites, stiffly beaten

Cook sugar, corn syrup, and water together in a saucepan until it spins a long thread (240°F) when dropped from a metal spoon. Remove from heat and immediately add the marshmallows. Beat until thoroughly blended. Pour the hot syrup over the egg whites and continue betting until mixture is smooth.

PINEAPPLE FILLING

½ cup sugar
¼ cup flour
⅛ teaspoon salt
1 egg, beaten
1 cup pineapple, cut in pieces
¾ cup pineapple juice
1 tablespoon butter

Mix sugar, flour, and salt. Add egg, pineapple, and juice. Cook in a double boiler over boiling water until thick, stirring constantly. Add butter and mix well. Cool.

FONDANT

2½ cups sugar
⅛ teaspoon cream of tartar
1 cup water

Combine ingredients. Heat to the boiling point, stirring until sugar is dissolved. Continue boiling, brushing syrup from sides of pan until the temperature reaches 238°F or until a small amount of syrup dropped into cold water will form a soft ball. Remove to shallow dish. When lukewarm, beat or stir vigorously until white and creamy. Add any desired flavoring. Cool. When ready to use for icing, warm slightly over hot water.

QUICK ICING

1 cup sugar
¼ cup water
1 egg white
½ teaspoon vanilla

Put sugar, water, and egg white in saucepan and cook in a double boiler over boiling water. Beat constantly until frosting is the proper consistency to spread. Add vanilla.

BOILED ICING

1¾ cups sugar
½ cup water
2 egg whites
1 teaspoon vanilla

Cook sugar and water together, stirring until the sugar is dissolved. Boil, without stirring to 238°F or until the syrup forms a soft ball when tested in cold water. Pour over the stiffly beaten egg whites and beat constantly until the mixture holds its shape. When cool, add vanilla. Food coloring may be added, if desired.

BROWN SUGAR ICING

Substitute brown sugar for white sugar in boiled icing (above) and cook until 240°F is reached.

POWDERED SUGAR ICING

1½ tablespoons butter
1½ cups powdered sugar
3 tablespoons cream
⅛ teaspoon salt
1 teaspoon vanilla

Cream butter and continue creaming while slowly adding sugar. Add cream, salt, and vanilla and mix smooth. Add food coloring as desired.

SEVEN-MINUTE ICING

2¼ cups sugar
3 egg whites
7½ tablespoons water
3 egg whites
1½ tablespoons white corn syrup
1½ teaspoons vanilla

Combine all ingredients, except vanilla, in top of double boiler and mix well. Cook over boiling water for 3 minutes. Remove from heat but leave over hot water and beat with hand mixer for 7 minutes, or until it reaches spreading consistency. Add vanilla and blend well. Add food coloring as desired.

REFRIGERATOR ICING

2 cups sugar
⅓ cup light corn syrup
⅓ cup water
2 egg whites
1 teaspoon vanilla

Cook sugar, corn syrup, and water together, stirring until sugar is dissolved. Boil, without stirring, until it forms a rather firm ball when dropped in cold water, about 240°F. Pour over stiffly beaten egg whites, beating constantly. Continue to beat until mixture holds its shape. Add vanilla. Store in a covered jar in the refrigerator. If it becomes too hard, add a few drops of hot water before using.

ORNAMENTAL ICING

1 egg white
2¾ cups powdered sugar
½ teaspoon lemon juice

Beat egg with 1 cup sugar until stiff. Add lemon juice and beat in. Add remaining sugar, a small amount at a time, beating after each addition. Cool. Any desired coloring may be beat into this icing.

BOILED EGG YOLK ICING

2 cups sugar
1 teaspoon vinegar
½ cup hot water
2 tablespoons butter
2 egg yolks, well beaten
1 teaspoon baking powder
1 teaspoon orange juice
1 teaspoon lemon juice
1 teaspoon grated orange zest

Combine sugar, vinegar, and water. Bring to boiling point, stirring constantly. Cover and cook without stirring until syrup spins a thread 10 to 12" long, or reaches 240°F. Add butter. Pour the syrup over egg yolks in a fine stream, beating vigorously. Add other ingredients. Beat with a stand mixer or hand mixer until mixture is creamy. Cool and store in refrigerator.

BOILED CORN SYRUP ICING

2½ cups sugar
½ cup corn syrup
¼ teaspoon salt
½ cup water
2 egg whites, well beaten
1 teaspoon vanilla

Cook sugar, syrup, salt, and water together to the firm ball stage (240°F). Pour over egg whites slowly, beating vigorously. Add vanilla. Continue beating until icing stands in peaks. Cool and keep in refrigerator.

BROWN BUTTER ICING

½ cup butter, at room temperature
¼ cup light cream
2 cups powdered sugar, more as needed
1 teaspoon vanilla
½ cup nuts (optional)

Brown the butter in a saucepan, being careful not to burn it. After it is melted, add the cream and enough powdered sugar to make the right consistency to spread. Add the vanilla and nuts, if desired.

CARAMEL ICING

2 cups brown sugar
1 cup granulated sugar
1 cup sour cream or milk
1 tablespoon butter
1 teaspoon vanilla
¼ cup cream, or as needed

Combine the sugars and sour cream in a large saucepan and cook over low heat until the sugars are dissolved. Cook until a little of the mixture dropped in cold water forms a soft ball (about 238°F). Remove from heat, add butter and vanilla, and cool to 145°F or until the outside of the saucepan feels warm (but not hot) to the touch. Beat until quite stiff, then add enough cream while beating to make of a spreading consistency. Frosts and fills a two-layer cake, 8" in diameter.

CHOCOLATE ICING

Add 3 ounces melted dark chocolate to recipe for boiled corn syrup icing (p. 628) after all the syrup has been added.

CREAMY CHOCOLATE ICING

4 ounces dark chocolate, grated
1½ cups milk
1½ cups powdered sugar
1 teaspoon vanilla
1 tablespoon butter
Salt

Cook chocolate, milk, and sugar together, stirring constantly until sugar is dissolved. Then stir only enough to prevent burning. Cook to the soft ball stage (240°F). Add vanilla, butter, and a few grains salt. Beat to proper spreading consistency.

COCONUT ICING

Add ½ cup shredded coconut to recipe for seven-minute icing (p. 626) after cooking is finished and sprinkle more coconut on cake after icing is put on.

FUDGE ICING

2 ounces dark chocolate
1 cup milk
2 cups granulated sugar
⅛ teaspoon salt
2 tablespoons white corn syrup
2 tablespoons butter
1 teaspoon vanilla

Add chocolate to milk. Cook slowly while stirring until smooth and blended. Add sugar, salt, and corn syrup. Cook until sugar is dissolved and mixture boils. Continue cooking until mixture forms a very soft ball when a little is dropped in cold water (240°F). Add butter and vanilla. Cool to lukewarm. Beat until thick enough to spread. Makes enough to frost a loaf cake about 8" x 8" x 2".

GOLDEN PINEAPPLE ICING

¼ cup butter, at room temperature
¼ teaspoon salt
2 egg yolks
6 cups sifted powdered sugar
¼ cup canned crushed pineapple
¼ cup pineapple juice

Cream butter and salt with egg yolks. Add sugar and well-drained pineapple. Add pineapple juice gradually to make proper consistency.

HONEY ICING

Beat ½ cup honey into boiled icing (p. 625) after it has been beaten with egg whites.

ORANGE ICING

1 teaspoon light corn syrup
⅞ cup sugar
¼ teaspoon grated orange zest
1 egg white
3 tablespoons orange juice
Few grains salt
½ teaspoon lemon juice

Beat together in top part of double boiler all ingredients except lemon juice. Place over rapidly boiling water and beat constantly with a hand mixer for 6 to 7 minutes, until stiff enough to stand in peaks. Remove from heat. Add lemon juice. Continue beating until right consistency to spread.

PEANUT BUTTER ICING

2 cups powdered sugar
3 tablespoons peanut butter
1 teaspoon cinnamon
1 teaspoon nutmeg
4–6 tablespoons milk

Combine the sugar, peanut butter, cinnamon, and nutmeg. Add the milk slowly while beating with a hand mixer until the right consistency is reached.

LEMON SEVEN-MINUTE ICING

Substitute 3 tablespoons lemon juice for an equal amount of water in seven-minute icing (p. 626) and add ¼ teaspoon grated lemon zest.

MERINGUE

    3 egg whites
    ¼ teaspoon salt
    ¼ teaspoon vanilla
    1 teaspoon lemon juice
    6 tablespoons sugar

Beat egg whites until foamy. Add salt, vanilla, and lemon juice. Continue beating until egg whites form a thick foam. Add sugar, a tablespoon at a time, beating after each addition. After last addition of sugar, beat until mixture forms soft peaks and sugar is dissolved.

LEMON MERINGUE

    2 egg whites
    4 tablespoons sugar
    1 teaspoon lemon juice

Beat egg whites until frothy. Continue beating while adding sugar gradually until egg holds its shape in soft peaks. Fold in lemon juice.

SPICED WHIPPED CREAM

1 cup heavy cream
3 tablespoons powdered sugar
1 teaspoon cinnamon
1 teaspoon ginger

Whip cream until stiff and add sugar and spices.

GLOSSARY

Baking
This is cooking in an oven. For best results the temperature of the oven should be regulated exactly as specified in all recipes for baked food.

Barbecuing
The roasting of meats or other foods on a revolving spit before an open flame or glowing coals.

Basting
To pour fat, pan drippings, or other liquid over roasting, baking, or broiling foods either to prevent burning or to flavor.

Beating
Beating can be done manually or with any of several hand-operated or electrical devices. Its purpose is to trap air within the food. In general, the motion of food undergoing a beating should be from underneath to the top. Beating should always be vigorously done so that the entire contents are kept constantly in motion.

Blanching
This is plunging into boiling water to either remove a skin or to whiten.

Boiling
This consists of heating water or other liquid until it bubbles rapidly. These bubbles rise to the surface of the liquid and leave it in the form of steam. A liquid, if the steam is permit-

ted to escape freely, can never be heated to a higher temperature than its boiling point. At sea level water boils at 212° F. or 100° C. The temperatures at which water will boil at higher altitudes are shown in the following table:

Altitude feet	Temperature of boiling water	
	° F.	° C.
1,025	210	99
2,063	208	98
3,115	206	97
4,169	204	95
5,225	202	94
6,304	200	93
7,381	198	92
8,481	196	91
9,031	195	90

The recipes in this book are all based on sea-level conditions. To boil food at 5,000 feet will require a slightly longer time than is stipulated in this book.

Braising
Braising in a method of slow-cooking meats or vegetables in a small amount of liquid, often in a pot with a tight fitting lid. This is an especially useful method for tougher cuts of meat.

Creaming
This is the softening of fat by means of pressure and beating at room temperature. Sugar or other ingredients are often added to the fat during the process of creaming.

Cutting In
This is a method for combining flour and shortening. They are combined in small, crumbly particles by blending them with the fingertips, two knives, or a pastry mixer.

Deep-Fat Frying

This consists of cooking food by immersing it in deep, hot fat or oil. Food cooked by this method should always be placed on a paper towel as soon as it is taken from the fat so that as much fat as possible may be absorbed. If possible, the exact temperature of the fat should be determined by a thermometer.

Dredging

This is the sprinkling of flour or some other dry, pulverized or granulated ingredient. It is often used before frying or roasting a meat or vegetable.

Drippings

The fat and juices that drop into the pan from roasting meats.

Folding In

This is the process of mixing foods without releasing the air bubbles, which may have been beaten or cooked into any of the ingredients. Folding in is done by lifting a part of the liquid from the very bottom of the bowl through the rest of the mixture to the top. This is continued until the foods are thoroughly blended. This method is commonly used with egg whites.

Kneading

This is the stretching and contraction of dough with the hands as more flour is worked into the mixture. Sometimes kneading is done only to smooth the texture of the dough. It can be done by hand or in a **Stand Mixer**.

Measurements

All measurements in this book are level. Follow them exactly. This is a table of equivalent measures:

3 teaspoons = 1 tablespoon
16 tablespoons = 1 cup
2 cups = 1 pint
2 pints = 1 quart
4 quarts = 1 gallon

Oven Broiling

This consists of cooking foods in the oven of a gas or electric range. The food is placed in the broiler pan and cooked close to the heat.

Pan Broiling

This method calls for the cooking of food on a hot pan or griddle with only enough fat to prevent burning. Any excess fat that accumulates should be poured off at once or the food will fry instead of broil.

Pan Frying

This is frying in a hot pan in a small amount of fat. It differs from pan broiling in that the fat is allowed to accumulate. It differs from sautéing in that the food is not stirred frequently but is simply turned to cook both sides or, as in the case of fried eggs, the food may be cooked on one side only.

Poaching

To poach, foods are dropped into simmering water or other liquid and cooked for a short time. Poaching is used most commonly only for eggs and fish.

Pressure Cooking

To cook by pressure it is necessary to have a pressure cooker manufactured for this purpose. The food is cooked in trapped steam at pressures ranging up to 30 pounds per square inch with temperatures running up to 275° F. For most pressure cooking the pressure is kept from 10 to 15 pounds and temperature at 240° F. to 250° F.

Roasting

Modern cooking stoves have eliminated the difference between baking and roasting. In early times roasting consisted of cooking before an open fire. Today there is no technical distinction between baking and roasting but the latter term is often applied to meats and some vegetables dishes.

Roux

A smooth mixture of flour and fat used to thicken gravies, sauces and soups.

Sautéing

This is frying using a little fat in a hot pan. The food is stirred frequently so that the hot grease reaches all sides.

Scalding

This is to heat a liquid briefly to a point just below boiling or to briefly heat a solid food in liquid at the scalding point.

Searing

This is the very rapid cooking of the exterior of a food at high heat. It is usually done to seal in juices in foods to be cooked at lower temperatures for an extended period.

Shortening

This important ingredient in all kinds of batters, pastries and doughs is synonymous with fat. It includes butter, all of the trademarked vegetable fats, margarine, lard, oil or drippings. In most recipes any a specific type of shortening is suggested, but it is a matter of personal preference.

Silicone Mat (Silpat)

This is a mat, usually about the size of a cookie sheet, which is made of silicone. It can go in the oven directly on top of a cookie or baking sheet. It is heat resistant, and helps foods baked on it to cook more evenly. Foods baked on it can be easily removed as well. It is primarily used for cookies and candies, though it could be used for other things as well.

Simmering

This is heating water or other liquid to a temperature above 175° F. but under the boiling point. Bubbles rise infrequently to the surface during simmering.

Stand Mixer

A type of electric mixer in which the bowl is attached to a stand. The beater or hook is attached to the stand as well. It operates with a switch, and does not need to be attended to or held while mixing or beating. It can mix, beat, and knead doughs, batters, and other mixtures.

Steaming

Food is steamed when it is cooked in a bath of steam from boiling water. Often a steamer, made of bamboo or metal, sits in the water and hold the food so that it steams rather than boils.

Stewing

Stewing consists of either simmering or boiling food in a small amount of water or liquid.

Stirring

Always stir with a circular motion. It is done either to make certain that heat reaches every part of the food or to thoroughly mix or dissolve ingredients.

Whipping

Same as **Beating**.

INDEX

Egg Dishes, 271–294

Fruit, 187–206

Sandwiches, 101–116